Frankenstein in Theory

Frankenstein in Theory

A Critical Anatomy

Edited by
Orrin N. C. Wang

BLOOMSBURY ACADEMIC
NEW YORK • LONDON • OXFORD • NEW DELHI • SYDNEY

BLOOMSBURY ACADEMIC
Bloomsbury Publishing Inc
1385 Broadway, New York, NY 10018, USA
50 Bedford Square, London, WC1B 3DP, UK

BLOOMSBURY, BLOOMSBURY ACADEMIC and the Diana logo
are trademarks of Bloomsbury Publishing Plc

First published in the United States of America 2021

Cover design by Namkwan Cho
Cover image © Giulio Gonella / Getty Images

Library of Congress Cataloging-in-Publication Data
Names: Wang, Orrin N. C., 1957- editor.
Title: Frankenstein in theory : a critical anatomy / edited by Orrin N.C. Wang.
Description: New York : Bloomsbury Academic, 2021. | Includes bibliographical references
and index. | Summary: "A collection of essays on Frankenstein written by distinguished and
younger scholars of Romantic studies, utilizing ambitious critical theories in literary and
cultural studies"– Provided by publisher.
Identifiers: LCCN 2020028001 (print) | LCCN 2020028002 (ebook) |
ISBN 9781501360794 (hardback) | ISBN 9781501372209 (paperback) |
ISBN 9781501360800 (epub) | ISBN 9781501360817 (pdf)
Subjects: LCSH: Shelley, Mary Wollstonecraft, 1797-1851. Frankenstein. | Horror tales,
English–History and criticism–Theory, etc. | Frankenstein, Victor (Fictitious character)
Classification: LCC PR5397.F73 F725 2021 (print) | LCC PR5397.F73 (ebook) | DDC 823/.7–dc23
LC record available at https://lccn.loc.gov/2020028001
LC ebook record available at https://lccn.loc.gov/2020028002

ISBN: HB: 978-1-5013-6079-4
          ePDF: 978-1-5013-6081-7
          eBook: 978-1-5013-6080-0

Typeset by Integra Software Services Pvt. Ltd.

To find out more about our authors and books visit www.bloomsbury.com
and sign up for our newsletters.

Contents

Figures

Acknowledgments

This collection began with a one-day symposium celebrating the bicentennial publication of the 1818 edition of Mary Shelley's novel. My thanks to the University of Maryland's Division of Research, the College of Arts and Humanities, the English Department's Center for Literary and Comparative Studies, and the Center's Director, Edlie Wong, for making the event happen. Thanks also to Chris Washington for his advice and support of this publication from its inception, as well to the book proposal's anonymous readers for their helpful suggestions. A final thanks to Haaris Naqvi and the Bloomsbury team for taking care of things so well on their end. An earlier version of Andrew Burkett's essay was originally published in *Studies in Romanticism* 51, no. 4 (2012): 579–605. Adriana Craciun and the Trustees of Boston University have kindly granted the permissions to reprint this essay. Samuel Otter's essay reprints, with some revision, a short extract from his earlier piece, "Reading *Moby-Dick*," which was published in *The New Cambridge Companion to Herman Melville*, ed. Robert S. Levine (New York: Cambridge University Press, 2014), 68–84; the reproduced material appears on 78–9. © Cambridge University Press, 2014. Reprinted with permission.

Introduction: *Frankenstein* in Theory

Orrin N. C. Wang

In her famous 1831 account of the ghost-story writing contest that inspired her 1818 novel, Mary Shelley relates how

> The noble author [Byron] began a tale, a fragment of which he printed at the end of his poem of Mazeppa. Shelley, more apt to embody ideas and sentiments in the radiance of brilliant imagery and in the music of the most melodious verse that adorns our language than to invent the machinery of a story, commenced one founded on the experiences of his early life. Poor Polidori had some terrible idea about a skull-headed lady who was so punished for peeping through a keyhole—what to see I forget; something very shocking and wrong of course; but when she was reduced to a worse condition than the renowned Tom of Conventry, he did not know what to do with her and was obliged to dispatch her to the tomb of the Capulets, the only place for which she was fitted. The illustrious poets also, annoyed by the platitude of prose, speedily relinquished their uncongenial task.[1]

There is much to be said about this remarkable passage, not least how "poor" Polidori's contribution anticipates through the figures of the old lady and peeping Tom the way that optics work in the novel, how the Creature surreptitiously spies on the De Laceys to learn language and domestic affect; and how in its motely references to Lady Godiva and Shakespeare his tale models the fabricated, never quite proportionate creation that Victor puts together. Polidori's piece is also implicitly contrasted with the creative attempts of the "noble author" Byron and Mary's husband, Percy, and it is with this distinction that I especially want to linger. Percy's disposition to "embody ideas and sentiments in the radiance of brilliant imagery and in the music of the most melodious verse" especially associates Poliodori's abject attempt with what the passage pejoratively calls "the machinery of story," itself not only a generic put down of prose by verse, but again a pointed anticipation of how Victor's own attempted techné never quite measures up—indeed, turns murderous instead. Two distinctive uses of language and thought—Percy's and Polidori's—organize Mary's account of the contest, with her own novel, her "hideous creation," quietly but noticeably aligned with the latter: *Frankenstein; or, the Modern Prometheus* as "the machinery of a story" about a creature that Frankenstein literally makes up, and as a creation apparently more like the generic expectations of Polidori's tale than the ambitious visions that characterize the two poets' accomplishments.

This dynamic leads directly to the passage's concluding sentence, extraordinary and unsurprising at once. Unsurprising, given how much the 1831 Introduction consistently undercuts Mary's talent and responsibility for her own novel. Extraordinary, given how that observation is upended by a simple rethinking of the sentence's tone, if we put a quiet tartness and irony in place of the sincerity organizing the hierarchical assumptions realized by the two "illustrious poets" "speedily relinquish[ing]" their "uncongenial task." A hierarchy remains, but now one that doesn't so readily complicate feminist estimations of Mary Shelley that have to confront an Introduction where she seemingly downgrades her literary practice by implicitly comparing it to the dismissive actions of the two male Romantic poets.[2] Rather, their gendered "annoyance" doesn't have the last word (something literally true, in fact) but instead generates a new set of questions—why exactly do they find this contest "uncongenial"? What limitation on their part does that reveal? What might the "platitude of prose" inspired by a ghost story contest do as well or even better than Romantic poetry itself?

Like Mary's description of her husband's work and the High Romanticism associated with it, that poetry has been understood to engage with another horizon of intellectual activity altogether, "ideas and sentiments" not readily contained by simple narrative or formulaic exposition, the "platitudes of prose." Instead, the thought of such writing, dizzying, difficult, abstract, and ambitious all at once, demands a new understanding and use of language, described in the ghost story passage as Percy's adornment of the linguistic with "the radiance of brilliant imagery and ... the music of the most melodious verse." I want to suggest, however, that these formal properties attempting to articulate such adventurous thought can retrospectively be read as a code for something else. That is, such language today could just as easily also apply to the discourse of *theory* that has in many ways shaped academic practice in the humanities for the last fifty years, since the late 1960s and early 1970s—when, not at all coincidentally, readings of Romantic poetry in such collections as Harold Bloom's 1970 *Romanticism and Consciousness* became synonymous with this new, dynamic brew of literary criticism and philosophy.[3]

I'll return to the connection between Romanticism and theory momentarily, but first want to spell out the meanings of the parable about theory, Mary Shelley, and *Frankenstein* that I see her ghost story anecdote staging for us. With the passage's last lines read sincerely, theory becomes the provenance of a serious, male intellectual enterprise that the limited uses of prose (in a novel written famously written by a "young girl," no less) can neither participate in, be the topic of, nor express.[4] This was actually the fate of *Frankenstein*, which up until the end of the 1960s garnered little attention from literary criticism, what in cultural and literary studies can be considered the most immediate ancestor or elder sibling of critical theory as the latter comes to be recognized in the 1970s and onward.[5] As William Christie puts it, echoing a version of what a sincere reading of Mary's account of the ghost story contest might imply, "By saying badly what the canonical male Romantic poets were saying well, *Frankenstein* was thought to function at once to justify their canonization and to illuminate the otherwise difficult, self-reflexive enterprise of Romanticism."[6] Until the 1970s, Mary's novel was considered at best an ancillary demonstration of what the meta-critical character of Romantic poetics already theorized.

Its last sentence read ironically, however, the ghost story passage becomes something else: the failure of Percy and Byron to see in the "platitudes of prose" an intellectual potentiality akin to or surpassing their own demanding, High Romantic, ideation, where Mary's novel becomes as much a cynosure for theory as her husband's poetic works, such as his compulsively read "The Triumph of Life."[7] An ironic reading of the ghost story passage suggests the Introduction's own awareness of how much a prose piece inspired by that contest could attain the same theoretical heights as Percy's last, incomplete poem, where training theory upon such works exposes how much they are already works of theory, theory *avant la lettre*. Exploring the path opened up by this second reading is the spur for this present collection, Frankenstein *in Theory: A Critical Anatomy*, a collection put together shortly after the bicentennial publication of the 1818 edition of Mary's work.

In doing so, Frankenstein *in Theory* follows not only Mary's novel but also an impressive archive of past critical writings, by figures such as Barbara Johnson and Jerrold E. Hogle, which see in *Frankenstein* the same demand for intense theoretical reflection that motivates this present collection. Taking off in the 1980s, these other works arguably limn the rhizomatic growth of theory in literary and cultural studies throughout the decades, with both Fred Botting's *Making Monstrous:* Frankenstein, *Criticism, Theory* and his edited collection of readings of the novel summarizing what the expanse of critical theory looked like in the 1990s.[8] One practical merit of Frankenstein *in Theory*, then, is the way it speaks to how much contemporary theory has been inflected by a host of new discourses—cog-sci studies, the new materialisms, race studies, trans studies, affect studies, and media studies, for example. At the same time, Frankenstein *in Theory* has not attempted to be an exhaustive survey of the contemporary theoretical landscape, a point to which I will return to later in the Introduction. More immediately, I want to circle back to my earlier point that the link between *Frankenstein* and theory punctuates, how much Romanticism and theory have also been entangled together.

Much has been written attempting to explain this overarching connection.[9] Three reference points for such a discussion especially speak to the writings collected in the present book. First is the way that British Romanticism has long been associated with the contemporaneous workings of German idealist philosophy, with works from both archives overlapping in their interrogation of perception, phenomenal knowing, subject and object, and ideal and material existence—in a word, the volatile interface between mind and body. This duality very much informs the operations of Mary's novel, to which the subtitle to this collection, *A Critical Anatomy*, alludes. Indeed, the very proposition of the body in *Frankenstein*, rather than simply asserting one side of this dyad, arguably encodes the volatility of this binary as an ongoing problematic theorized by the text even as it invites more theorizations of this question. It is thus perhaps not surprising that a notable number of the theoretical readings of *Frankenstein* have been either feminist or psychoanalytic in nature.[10] Continuing to heed the call of thinking the relationship of mind and body in Shelley's work is exactly what a number of the authors in the present book (Sha, Washington, Faflak, and Otto) do from a number of different theoretical positions and through a range of cultural and literary texts and disciplinary debates.

Second, as many know, the knot between mind and body or subject and object was cut in an altogether new way by the linguistic turn of deconstruction, whose radical provocations in the North American academy in the 1970s so shaped the critical habitus that it became for a time—and for some still is—synonymous with the term "theory." Generated largely by a linguistic rereading of the question of mind and body in British and German Romantic texts, deconstruction is one reason why Romanticism and theory seem intuitively to inhabit the same critical space. Another group of thinkers showcased in this book (Clark, Guyer, Khalip, and Terada) write within the wake of this particular theoretical disposition. These thinkers, however, do not uniformly signal their contemporary affiliation with deconstruction through a linguistic approach, as sensitive to the novel's language they and the other contributors to this book all are. Rather, they demonstrate this connection by confronting the negative as an incalculable and non-subsumable component of the topos they identify in Shelley's novel, including those of voicing the last word, race and anthropogenesis, the non-event of no regret, and the held-together. In doing so, they not only reflect an intellectual disposition that speaks to the latest ways deconstruction still informs critical thought; they also affirm how much *Frankenstein* can be, among many things, part of that particular theoretical enterprise.[11]

Third, I have elsewhere suggested that Romanticism and theory are braided together because both are discourses of a *fantastic modernity*, a reflexive sense of a modernity that is at once the specular and necessary backdrop to our social, philosophic, and cultural activities.[12] Another set of writers in Frankenstein *in Theory* (Burkett, Goss, Hofkosh, Lee, Matthew, Soni) implicitly take up this proposition through a number of intellectual discourses and a variety of topics, including new media, social justice, technologies of genre and representation, and utopian thought. In their contributions one can see something also very much active in other writings in this collection, a meditation on how resolutely and vertiginously *Frankenstein* is temporally part of our present, now matter how friable or fragmentary that condition might be—how in theorizing Mary's novel we see how much it theorizes us, now.

Readers delving into Frankenstein *in Theory* will soon notice, however, the degree to which many of its writings share themes and traits associated with each of these initial groupings. As such, this exercise can be understood as a useful though preliminary heuristic to help people begin to navigate the way these writings play off of one another and build upon the energies generated by any serious consideration of the assemblage of relations that theory, Romanticism, and *Frankenstein* incite. The essays gathered here are too conceptually rich, unpredictable, and nimble to be uniformly bound by one intellectually category or another. It is thus now appropriate to emphasize what this collection is *not*: a schematic rendering of literary analyses that employ readings of Mary's novel to show what different schools of theory are or are not. As helpful as such renderings can be, the intellectual ambitions of this collection did not allow this one approach to circumscribe its writings.[13] Many of the chapters do engage with a particular theoretical discourse or thinker in a sustained, explicit manner, while others wear their theory more lightly on their sleeves, though in a manner equally effective in dramatizing how intensely Mary's novel operates as an intellectual and theoretical provocation. Likewise, while one truism still operating in literary studies poses theory as the antagonistic other of historical thinking, some of the essays find their theoretical intervention in an explicitly historicist method. It is my belief that in all these cases students both attracted to and challenged by the promises of that elusive term "theory" will have a more deft sense of its wagers by experiencing the encounter between *Frankenstein* and theory cathected in these pages. Indeed, I assume that people attracted to the proposition of this collection will know enough about theory to understand the limited nature of any one working definition of that term in literary and cultural studies, including those I have referenced, even as they recognize how much theory has spurred on critical thought in the humanities. Regardless, the hope is that they will never quite read Mary's novel the same way as before opening this book.

I have thus eschewed organizing the essays into sections along these initial groupings, although these and other through lines of thought, some between two chapters and some among several more, will hopefully be seen shaping the order of what follows. Readers on their own might recognize how essays resonate with other themes often associated with *Frankenstein*, such as the predicament of monsters and Others, the scandal of technology and science, the wager of radical politics, and the question of the (non-) human, for example. This predicament is not something I simply acknowledge, but actively welcome. Diffident as Mary's novel and the essays collected here often are about Victor's obsession with life, the encounter between *Frankenstein* and theory is ineluctably generative in ways that readers of this collection should join in discovering.

We thus begin with an end of sorts. David L. Clark's "Last Words: Voice, Gesture, and the Remains of *Frankenstein*" focuses on the conclusion of Mary's novel, noting the way that the odd staging of Frankenstein and the creature's last meeting and the impersonal voice narrating the book's last sentences highlight together how, in a work obsessed with the power of voice, the reader never witnesses its two protagonists speaking to one another in real time. Bringing together Derrida, Blanchot, and Mladen Dolar, Clark conjures out of *Frankenstein* the status of voice as already its own remains, an acousmatic phenomenon defined by its illegible yet irrepressible soundings, one that survives the novel's anthropocentrism and the call for redeemable, productive life. For Clark, what remains is a subtle gesture of the creature's hand over Frankenstein's corpse, life left as it is, a world without "us." Sonia Hofkosh's "When Jane Met Mary; or, *Frankenstein*'s Romantic Comedy" also involves a missed encounter, so tantalizing in the asymptotic nature of its what-if proposition, a biographical friendship between Mary Shelley and Jane Austen. For Hofkosh, thinking through this counterfactual means not only reflecting upon the writing styles and generic modes of writing each author made famous, such as free indirect discourse and metalepsis, but also specifically how much *Frankenstein* formally, affectively, and conceptually can be considered a romantic comedy. Read through Derrida's thoughts on the law of genre and Stanley Cavell's philosophic musings on the screwball comedy, Hofkosh's counter-intuitive proposal illuminates the nuanced affective charge of Mary's novel as a generic enterprise that can never quite catch up with itself, a predicament that haunts both literary genre as a concept and romantic comedy as a generic proposition.

We then move onto a group of writings explicitly concerned with the fault lines between mind and body in *Frankenstein*. Richard C. Sha's essay plays off the ongoing debate among cognitive scientists over the idea of embodied cognition, the degree to which mind itself might be seen as an extension or set of effects of the body. In his "*Frankenstein*'s Embodied Imagination; Or, the Limits of Embodied Cognition," Sha sees Mary Shelley acknowledging cognition's embodiment while remaining skeptical of the ethical promises current proponents of this view advance. While many today believe embodied cognition positively makes thought relational, social, and environmentally connected, the eponymous figure in *Frankenstein* presents a more complicated, less promising model of this condition: if Victor's imagination is synonymous with his nervous body, he also models thought as a form of solipsism and egoism. For Sha, Mary Shelley provides cognitive scientists with a critique of embodied cognition they would do well to consider. In contrast to Sha's disciplinary intervention, Chris Washington's new materialist "Non-Binary *Frankenstein*" orients its focus on the body in Shelley's novel through a sustained engagement with transgender and trans theory. In doing so, Washington sees *Frankenstein* eschewing not only the mind-body binary but binary thought itself, staging a non-binary rendition of gender whose implications are not only social but also ontological and epistemological. Deploying Jack Halberstam and other trans theorists, Washington argues for a body in *Frankenstein* that exploits the non-binary in order to resist returning to a knowledge of monstrosity based on the hypostatized conflict between human and nonhuman being.

As previously noted, with its particular investments in mind and body, psychoanalysis has had its own storied, critically hermeneutic relationship with Shelley's work. Joel Faflak's "What's Love Got to Do with It? *Frankenstein* and Monstrous Psychoanalysis" allegorizes the endpoint of that theoretical narrative, where the ontological underpinnings of psychoanalytic categories of the psyche are upended in Shelley's first novel. For Faflak, *Frankenstein* constructs the psychoanalytic subject as a monstrous entity, where Victor's creation dramatizes how psychoanalysis exposes its own subject as the opposite of the human, and its and society's collusion in the fantasy of their own humanity. What remains is psychoanalysis on the other side of its own human death. Samuel Otter's "The 'very creature he creates'": *Frankenstein* in the Making of *Moby-Dick*" focuses on a traversal of a very different kind, a Transatlantic crossing that like Hofkosh's essay links Mary Shelley to another nineteenth-century author Herman Melville. Through close readings of both *Frankenstein* and *Moby-Dick* and the front-piece of the third edition to Shelley's novel, Otter's genealogical argument shows how these two authors bring together a similar set concerns about identity, gender, and epistemology that coalesce around the radically defining nature of masculine obsession in both Victor and Ahab. In both characters, we see a hyper-mental affect that *avant la lettre* resists new materialist appeals to physical existence, dissolving the somatic references of each, transforming both into something akin to pure ideation.

Recording the action of both body and mind is a fundamental way we understand what narrative is. In Yoon Sun Lee's "Finitude, Frames, and the Plot of *Frankenstein*," however, the narrative plot of Shelley's novel is best understood as an encounter with its complex framing structure, one that enacts the epistemic shift asserted in Foucault's *Order of Things*. In the classical episteme, frames support and express knowledge's totalizing character as representation. In contrast, the modern episteme asserts the frame as a sign of finitude, a situation that gestures toward the limits of what can and cannot be seen, conditioning both what is and what we know. Instead of dwelling on any one character's plot, Lee suggests that the plot of *Frankenstein* as a single action dramatizes this Foucaultian break in the framing of knowledge and the position of the viewer.

Foucault's *Order of Things* ends with a meditation on the passing of man, and, like Faflak and Washington's different explorations of posthuman meaning in *Frankenstein*, Rei Terada focuses on the rendering of the anthropos in Shelley's work. Also sharing Lee's interest in the novel's use of frames, Terada's "Blackness and Anthropogenesis in *Frankenstein*" retools these terms in order to consider the relation of Blackness to Black people as an open theoretical question in *Frankenstein*. Noting the necessarily speculative nature of Blackness implicit in past historicist treatments of race in *Frankenstein*, Terada engagement with the novel through Black studies discovers another dynamic, where the humanistic dependence on errant Blackness is oriented around an eschatology that subsumes racial slavery into a mystic anthropogenesis.

Terada's intervention speaks to how *Frankenstein* theorizes its relevance for contemporary culture and society, something that the following chapters also explicitly take up. Andrew Burkett's "Mediating Monstrosity: Media, Information, and Mary Shelley's *Frankenstein*" does so by exploring the interface between *Frankenstein* and the digital humanities, with the novel becoming the object of study for a number of DH projects even as its own material, formal, and scientific moment maps out the theoretical landscape of information technology, mediation, and communication that we now call new media. Invoking thinkers like Deleuze, Kittler, and Katherine Hayles, Burkett argues for a vision of Mary's novel reflexively informed by its existence as a mediatized event. Patricia A. Matthew's "'a daemon whom I had myself created': Race, *Frankenstein*, and Monstering" also focuses on contemporary media, but from the angle of race and Blackness. Keying off of the same historicist archive on abolition and slavery that Terada invokes, Matthew sees the De Laceys episode modeling a form of monstering immediately recognizable in the fate of Michael Brown at the hands of the Ferguson police and then mainstream news outlets. For Matthew, the creature's encounter with Felix and Safie dramatizes the convergence between epistemological violence and physical threat perpetuated on the lived experience of Black men in the United States to this day. By connecting Shelley's novel to the predicament of Black men in contemporary America, Matthew theorizes a historicism that is defiantly presentist in its critical aims and procedures. A similar topical urgency characterizes how gender both forms and deforms justice in Erin M. Goss's "The Smiles That One Is Owed: Justice, Justine, and Sympathy for a Wretch." If for Derrida justice is a call to the impossible, for Goss Shelley novel witnesses the unavoidable failure of an androcentric, heternormative justice that cannot separate itself from the punishment of a woman like

Justine for not providing the creature with the affection he believes he deserves. Justine not only names the abstract idea of justice; she also embodies a womankind beset by an entitled masculine violence that is the very sign and outcome of the semiotic fissure that "Justine" signifies.

Vivasvan Soni's "The Utopias of *Frankenstein*" addresses the question of a relevant modernity in Shelley's work from yet another angle, how her work envisions a practice of utopia that in our own political episteme is still incomplete. For Soni, *Frankenstein* is a thought experiment that considers a number of utopian and anti-utopian propositions, including Victor's creation of a new being as the dark side to Hannah Arendt's notion of "natality," a freedom without ends. His chapter sees Shelley eschewing all these various responses to the question of utopia save one, modeled counter-intuitively on Victor's memories of his upbringing in Geneva. There, Shelley theorizes a "utopian realism" that not only problematizes prior readings of *Frankenstein* as a counter-revolutionary work, but also stresses the necessary role of art and narrative in political philosophy's attempt to realize what it argues.

In reading *Frankenstein* as a response to the question of utopia, Soni confronts the political character of an exorbitance often associated with Romanticism. Jacques Khalip's "Is That All There Is? No Regrets (after 1818)" takes a different tack, working in the vein of recent studies contemplating a Romanticism associated not with the hyperbolic but the recessive.[14] Considering the seemingly wayward proposition that *Frankenstein* is a text in which little, or nothing, happens, Khalip mines the affective logic that sees regret as the spur for existential and epistemological crisis. Playing also off Cavell's famous riposte to Kant ("thanks for nothing") as well as key moments in Austen's *Persuasion*, Khalip then moves on to Keats's "La Belle Dame Sans Merci" as an exploration of what it means to think without regret, where irrecoverability might be welcomed for its nothingness.

Contrasting with but also complementing Khalip's study is the concluding essay in this collection, Sara Guyer's "*Frankenstein* in Practice (as Theory)." Taking as its conceptual and material horizon our contemporary moment of failed politics and a global pandemic, Guyer's essay explores through Shelley's novel the affective, figural, and existential logistics emanating from the call to hold ourselves together in a moment of crisis. For Guyer *Frankenstein* clarifies the different meanings associated with that trope—from the creature's literal assemblage of body parts; to Victor's feverish attempt to hold himself together through a disaster of his own making; to the novel's active participation in what we now call Romanticism, the archetypal proposal of a literary, philosophic, and aesthetic movement held together by more than simply the boundaries of an historical period. As the humanities themselves continue to look for new ways to legitimate the holding together of their own aspirations, Guyer's essay suggests how much one response might be found in the deconstructive aporia that simultaneously thinks holding apart and holding together together—the inescapable way that for Victor, his creature, and for us the figure of holding together is crucial precisely because it asserts figure *as* a holding together.

I end this Introduction with two final observations. One is to reiterate my earlier point that Frankenstein in *Theory* is neither a schematic nor comprehensive survey of all the critical theories deployed in literary and critical studies today. As rich and expansive as the writings in this collection are, it could have easily grown to include chapters explicitly organized around ideological criticism, object-oriented ontology, race and environmental studies, Agamben inflected post-humanism, the anthropocene, and disability studies, to name a few of the other approaches that would have energized and been energized by their encounter with Mary's novel. Rather than seeing this as an unavoidable or even unforgiving lack, I would simply suggest this non-closure to be a sign of the capacious, indeed unbound nature of Mary's creation, and an indication of what might opportunistically follow: more thought, more theoretical *poiesis*, on *Frankenstein* and her other literary works.

Finally, as Sara Guyer's contribution explicitly records, this collection was submitted to Bloomsbury Academic at the start of the summer of 2020, during the COVID-19 global pandemic. Shortly thereafter, the United States and the rest of the globe have witnessed numerous civil insurgencies following George Floyd's violent death at the hands of members of the Minneapolis police force. I write these words with the immediate and distant future ramifications of these two ongoing events by no means clear. For a book about the ongoing relevance of *Frankenstein* as a text that, like theory, stages the difficult, often aporetic contours of our present life and non-life, it would be remiss of me not to mark the historical moment accompanying this book's entrance into the world. And, insofar as our world is the same one examined by the authors of this book *and* Mary Shelley's *Frankenstein*, I do not discourage anyone from searching how our current state of affairs permeates these intellectual explorations that were largely written before the summer of 2020. If in some small way its chapters provide people with a set of vocabularies, tropes, and ideas to clarify the now we continue to inhabit, that would not be something to underestimate. That that possibility is synonymous with the call to read, and reread, Mary's novel in both its 1818 and 1831 renditions goes without saying, even as each essay here says that very thing.[15]

Notes

1 Mary Shelley, "Introduction (1831)," in *Frankenstein; or, the Modern Prometheus*, ed. D. L. Macdonald and Kathleen Scherf (Peterborough, ON: Broadview Press, 2003), 362–3.

2 For an overview of such responses to Shelley's Introduction, see James O'Rourke, "The 1831 Introduction and Revisions to *Frankenstein*, Mary Shelley Dictates Her Legacy," *Studies in Romanticism* 38, no. 3 (Fall 1999): 365–6.

3 Harold Bloom (ed.), *Romanticism and Consciousness: Essays in Criticism* (New York: W. W. Norton, 1970). For one overview of the key works making up the relation of Romanticism to the theory boom of the 1970s, see Orrin N. C. Wang, "Romanticism and Theory: The 1970s" (August 2016), *Romantic Circles Reviews and Receptions*. https://romantic-circles.org/reviews-blog/romanticism-and-theory-1970s-orrin-nc-wang. Accessed May 4, 2020.

4 Shelley, *Frankenstein*, 360.

5 William Christie, "The Critical Metamorphoses of Mary Shelley's *Frankenstein*,"

Sydney Studies in English 25 (1999): 47–9. The arrival in literary studies of
Frankenstein as a legitimate object of critical study can be seen in a collection like
George Levine and U. C. Knoepflmacher (eds.), *The Endurance of* Frankenstein:
Essays on Mary Shelley's Novel (Berkeley: University of California Press, 1979).

6   Ibid., 48.

7   This very comparison structures Barbara Johnson's anecdote about coming up with a
counter-publication to the thought experiment in Harold Bloom et al., *Deconstruction
and Criticism* (New York: Continuum, 1979) where Bloom, Jacques Derrida,
Geoffrey Hartman, J. Hillis Miller, and Paul de Man were each invited to read Percy's
"Triumph": "At the time of the publication of … *Deconstruction and Criticism*, several
of us—Shoshana Felman, Gayatri Spivak, Margaret Ferguson, and I—discussed the
possibility of writing a companion volume inscribing female deconstructive protest
and affirmation centering not on Percy Bysshe Shelley's 'The Triumph of Life' (as
the existing volume was originally slated to do) but on Mary Shelley's *Frankenstein*"
(Barbara Johnson, *A Life with Mary Shelley* [Stanford: Stanford University Press,
2014], 28).

8   Fred Botting, *Making Monstrous:* Frankenstein, *Criticism, Theory* (Manchester:
Manchester University Press, 1991); and Fred Botting (ed.), Frankenstein, *Mary
Shelley: Contemporary Critical Essays* (New York: Palgrave Macmillan, 1995). For an
overview of the literary critical approaches to *Frankenstein* by the end of the 1970s,
see Levine and Knoepflmacher. More recently, see the "Theories and Forms" section
of Andrew Smith (ed.), *The Cambridge Companion to* Frankenstein (Cambridge:
Cambridge University Press): 101–74. See especially George Haggerty, "What Is
Queer about *Frankenstein*," in Smith, 116–27; Timothy Morton, "*Frankenstein* and
Ecocriticism," in Smith, 143–57; and Andy Mousley, "The Posthuman," in Smith,
158–69. Likewise, see the critical essays section of Virginia Brackett (ed.), *Critical
Insights: Mary Shelley* (Ipswich, MA: Salem Press, 2016). For a consideration of the
afterlife of *Frankenstein* in world literature and artistic and popular culture, see Carol
Margaret Davison and Marie Mulvey-Roberts (eds.), *Global Frankenstein* (New York:
Palgrave Macmillan, 2018). For a by no means complete list of other past theoretical
engagements with *Frankenstein*, see notes 10 and 11; many of these works as well as
other studies of *Frankenstein* are referenced in the following essays of this collection.

9   For one account, see Orrin N. C. Wang, *Fantastic Modernity: Dialectical Readings in
Romanticism and Theory* (Baltimore: Johns Hopkins University Press, 1996), 1–11.
Consider also Paul Hamilton's stress on the trait of reflexivity that Christie also
sees characterizing Romantic writing, an impulse that especially in its philosophic
forms, whether self-abnegating or not, speaks to a fundamental coordinate in critical
theory to this day; see his *Metaromanticism: Aesthetics, Literature, Theory* (Chicago:
University of Chicago Press, 2003).

10   See, for example, Julie Carlson, *England's First Family of Writers: Mary Wollstonecraft,
William Godwin, Mary Shelley* (Baltimore: Johns Hopkins University Press, 2006);
Sandra Gilbert and Susan Gubar, *The Madwoman in the Attic: The Woman Writer
and the Nineteenth-Century Imagination* (New Haven: Yale University Press, 1979);
Elizabeth Fay, *A Feminist Introduction to Romanticism* (Oxford: Basil Blackwell, 1998);
Mary Jacobus, *Reading Women: Essays in Feminist Criticism* (New York: Columbia
University Press, 1986); Margaret Homans, *Bearing the Word: Language and Female
Experience in Nineteenth-Century Women's Writing* (Chicago: University of Chicago
Press, 1986); Mary Poovey, *The Proper Lady and the Woman Writer: Ideology as*

Style in the Works of Mary Wollstonecraft, Mary Shelley, and Jane Austen (Chicago: University of Chicago Press, 1984); Ann K. Mellor, "Possessing Nature: The Female in *Frankenstein*," in *Romanticism and Feminism*, ed. Anne K. Mellor (Bloomington: Indiana University Press, 1988) 220–32; Frann Michel, "Lesbian Panic and Mary Shelley's *Frankenstein*," *GLQ* 2 (January 1995): 237–52; and Ellen Moers, "Female Gothic," in Levine and Knoepflmacher, 77–87. For readings especially deploying a psychoanalytic strategy, see Jerrold E. Hogle's "An Introduction" in *Frankenstein's Dream* (June 2003), ed. Jerrold E. Hogle, in the *Romantic Circles Praxis Series*. https:// romanticcircles.org/praxis/frankenstein/index.html. Accessed May 20, 2020; see also Anne Williams, "'Mummy possest': Sadism and Sensibility in Shelley's *Frankenstein*," in Hogel, *Frankenstein's Dream*; and John Rieder, "Patriarchal Fantasy and the Fecal Child in Mary Shelley's *Frankenstein* and Its Adaptions," in Hogel, *Frankenstein's Dream*. Accessed May 4, 2020. See also Peter Brooks, "What Is a Monster? (According to *Frankenstein*)," in Botting, Frankenstein, 81–106; David Collings, "The Monster and the Maternal Thing," in Frankenstein: *Case Studies in Contemporary Criticism*, 3rd ed., ed. Joanna M. Smith (Boston, MA: Bedford/St. Martin's, 2016), 323–39; and Hogle's influential mixture of Kristevan abjection and Baudrillard's simulacrum in his "*Frankenstein* as Neo-Gothic: From the Ghost of the Counterfeit to the Monster of Abjection," in *Romanticism, History, and the Possibilities of Genre: Re-forming Literature, 1789–1837*, ed. Tilottama Rajan and Julia Wright (Cambridge: Cambridge University Press, 1998), 176–210. Among a number of these studies from this first theoretical wave of feminist and psychoanalytic readings of *Frankenstein*, the figure of the maternal is especially prevalent, so much so that one could say that this trope along with questions of monstrosity and technology was a dominant reference point for theorizing Shelley's novel into the millennium.

11 Deconstructive encounters with *Frankenstein* would include Barbara Johnson's landmark "My Monster/My Self," *Diacritics* 12, no. 2 (Summer 1982): 2–10. See also Barbara Claire Freeman, "*Frankenstein* with Kant: A Theory of Monstrosity or the Monstrosity of Theory," in Botting, Frankenstein, 191–205; Sara Guyer, "Testimony and Trope in *Frankenstein*," *Studies in Romanticism* 45, no. 1 (Spring 2006): 77–115; Marc Redfield, "*Frankenstein's* Cinematic Dream," in Hogel, *Frankenstein's Dream*; and Gayatri Spivak, "Three Woman's Texts and a Critique of Imperialism," *Critical Inquiry* 12, no. 1 (Autumn, 1985): 243–61. As Johnson's feminist and Spivak's post-colonialist provocations especially show, such studies already bear the excess of thought beyond any one simple theoretical categorization. Post-millennial engagements with *Frankenstein* from an array of methodological and theoretical perspectives would include David Collings, *Monstrous Society: Reciprocity, Discipline, and the Political Uncanny at the End of Early Modern England* (Bucknell: Bucknell University Press, 2009); Siobhan Carroll, "Crusades against Frost: *Frankenstein*, Polar Ice, and Climate Change in 1818," in Smith, Frankenstein: *Case Studies*, 502–29; Robert Mitchell, "Population Aesthetics in Romantic and Post-Romantic Literature," in *Constellations of a Contemporary Romanticism*, ed. Jacques Khalip and Forrest Pyle (New York: Fordham University Press, 2016), 267–89; Allan Lloyd Smith, "'The Thing in Darkness': Racial Discourse in Mary Shelley's *Frankenstein*," in Smith, Frankenstein: *Case Studies*, 547–69; Paul Youngquist, *Monstrosities: Bodies and British Romanticism* (Minneapolis: University of Minnesota Press, 2003); and Nancy Yousef, "The Monster in a Dark Room: *Frankenstein*, Feminism, and Philosophy," *MLQ* 63 (2002), 197–226.

12 Wang, *Fantastic*, 2–3.
13 Two examples of this approach would be Smith, Frankenstein: *Case Studies*; and
    Broadview Press's electronic Frankenstein: *Online Theory and Criticism*.
14 See, for example, Anne-Lise François, *Open Secrets: The Literature of Uncounted
    Experience* (Stanford: Stanford University Press, 2008); Jacques Khalip, *Last Things:
    Disastrous Form from Kant to Hujar* (New York: Fordham University Press, 2018);
    and Anahid Nersessian, *Utopia, Limited: Romanticism and Adjustment* (Cambridge,
    MA: Harvard University Press, 2015).
15 For a sense of uniformity and in light of the recent bicentennial anniversary of the
    novel's first publication, the authors on the whole have used versions of the 1818
    edition, though as in my introduction the 1831 edition has been called upon at times
    to advance particular moments of analysis.

1

Last Words: Voice, Gesture, and the Remains of *Frankenstein*

David L. Clark

The end begins with a voice.—A voice and nothing more.[1]

Victor Frankenstein is dead. The strident, self-exculpating, and melodramatic voice that dominates the novel is in fact the voice of one who is already dead. "And where does he now exist?" (167), Walton asks.[2] Where indeed? The creature is also gone, although his demise remains promised and presumed rather than witnessed and remembered. His voice and Frankenstein's are voices without places and without bodies except in the mediated form of the memories that Robert Walton commits to letters to his sister. For all we know, Walton too has passed away, leaving behind a written reliquary that speaks autonomously for him, and for those whose lives and deaths he recalls, whether he is dead or alive. That the novel's narrative is utterly careless of whether Walton tracks the creature into the "darkness and distance," or, leaving the creature to kill himself, he returns to England and reunites with his beloved sister, is the most definitive sign that his words live on without being, strictly speaking, alive or answerable to life. *Frankenstein* helps us imagine two forms of possible closure but refuses both. Toward the end of the novel, prior to the point that Walton abandons writing letters that are addressed and dated, he confesses to Margaret Seville that he "cannot forbear recording" his story, even though he knows that "these papers may never reach you" (213). But by the conclusion of that tale, when Walton gazes blankly out at "the wasteland" (221) into which the creature has flung himself, nothing of that pathos or regret remains to haunt his compulsion to write. The novel's last two sentences, which are barely enough to close the frame around the creature's *apologia pro vita sua*, feel dispossessed and affectless, so that the narrative doesn't end as much as cease functioning. This indifference both to the fate of the writer of the letters and of the letters themselves is telling in a novel that is a story principally *about* life, which is to say about the discovery of the origins of life, the invention and administration of what Foucault would call "a technology of power centered on life,"[3] not to say the sovereign determination of life monstrously unworthy of life. We could say that *Frankenstein* is the tale of the paroxysm of the biopolitical, its plot a macabre story of two creatures, one human, the other not, each of whom license "life-affirming killing."[4] But whatever stake that Walton has in telling the story of the "communication" of life (to recall Shelley's remarks in her 1831 Introduction [351]), as a set of remains *Frankenstein* is "a living-dead machine," as Jacques Derrida says, "sur-viving, the body of a thing buried in a library, in cellars, urns, drowned in the world-wide waves of the Web, etc., but a dead thing that resuscitates each time a breath of living reading, each time the breath of the other or the other breath, ... makes it live again by animating it."[5] Derrida has Daniel Dafoe's *Robinson Crusoe* in mind but the philosopher's gothic rhetoric makes *Frankenstein* seem more eerily apposite. Indeed, read through Shelley's novel, Derrida's remarks from *The Beast and the Sovereign* come across as oddly–ironically?–reliant on figures of vitality ("a breath of living reading," "making live") when figures more compellingly at odds with the primacy of the organic ("a living-dead machine") seem truer to the radical, Benjaminian impetus of his concept of survival as *survivance*.[6] In any case, *Frankenstein* makes Frankenstein's of us all, if not by making life out of assembled lifeless remains, as the natural philosopher is said to do, then, with each reading of the narrative, quickening what is "neither life nor death pure and simple."[7] The novel is, in other words, not only Walton's epistolary recollections of the lives and deaths of Frankenstein and his creature but a figure for and a theory of that which *survives* Walton, beyond his life and beyond life—a world without us, without those who say that they are human and alive.

Survival and the living-on or *survivance* of words—last words in particular, and the lastness of words, spoken and unspoken—is the question that will preoccupy me here. It is a question to which Shelley certainly returns.[8] In 1826 Shelley possesses the authorial confidence both to sign her name to *The Last Man* and to inhabit her own story as its frame narrator; but that shift should not obscure how, in 1818, Shelley's nominal anonymity rhymes with the ways that she puts a certain impersonality to work in her novel: the detachment of writer from novel reproduces the complex fission of voice and body, gesture and meaning, world and human, within the narrative, as we shall see. The letters making up Shelley's first novel are addressed to one woman (rather than anticipatorily received, as in *The Last Man*, by two, Mary Shelley and the Cumaean Sibyl) but that implied audience only serves to throw into relief that they are not marked, finally, as retrieved by anyone. Notwithstanding the fact that they share initials, Margaret Seville is no "Mary Shelley," since, unlike in *The Last Man*, she is barred from inhabiting a framing space of her own. She is a ghostly premonition of the auto-fictional role that Shelley herself will assume in the later novel, but her virtual and voiceless presence within the narrative, far from being meliorative because locating the novel in the web of human things, only underlines the text's complicated refusal of refuge in the social. To be sure, the elemental addressee of the letters remains "the big Other, the Symbolic Order itself, which receives [them] ... the moment the sender externalizes his message," as Žižek says,[9] but that reading does little to mitigate the narrative effect of the novel's blunt indifference to whether Walton's recollections are ever taken up by the fictional world in which they are set. The last thing that Walton exclaims to his sister, before ceding the narrative to Frankenstein's monologue, is that he looks forward to picking up the "manuscript" "in some future day!" (63), identifying himself not as author but as reader of the words that he writes, as if he were principally a character in his own text. Of that happy hereafter, brother and sister together taking "the greatest pleasure" (63) in reading the story, we hear nothing further. Walton opens the frame of the novel with this hopeful scene of domestic aesthetic bliss but does not dare or care to close it unequivocally. The point is that nothing definitive *becomes* of the letters or, for that matter, of Walton or his sister. Their fate remains unknown; for his part, Walton eventually abandons anything resembling a salutation or a valediction, and he concludes his last letter with unexpectedly becalmed and wide-eyed sentences that are much closer to a "blank opening unto futurity" (to recall a phrase from Tres Pyle)[10] than anything approaching a good-bye, much less finale. After having said farewell no less than three times, the creature's lamentations and recriminations conclude, offering Walton a chance to speak up once more. But rather than excoriating his reviled guest or expressing satisfaction in seeing him off to die, the narrative yields to quite another kind of speech, as if the novel had, at the very last moment, found a voice and omnisciently taken over for Walton. Walton's unhoused gaze and voice float away from the ship, turned as they are impassively toward the "darkness and distance" (221), while his vessel and body head toward home in England. In that strange depersonalizing moment of *Gelassenheit*, absent the drama and melodrama of the preceding pages, we approach "the experience without poetry," as Rei Terada says, "that Keats was able to know at the end of his life."[11] The ending leaves the letters simply *there*, suspended in an inoperative space, not so much *en route* as in-between, neither having arrived nor not arrived, "borne"—metaphorically, if not literally—"away by the waves, and lost in darkness and distance" (221), to recall the novel's spacy final words. The point is that Shelley asks us to read the letters as unread, which is to say, without knowing if they were either sent or received and without knowing if the addressor lives or dies. *Frankenstein*'s detachment from itself, the way in which it stalls its own uptake, or rather invites readers to take it up *as* stalled (a phenomenon that I elsewhere call "scarcity"),[12] makes it function like a *Rückenfigur*, a compositional strategy common to certain canonical Romantic paintings whose organizing human figure is facing away, directing the gaze of the viewer, as if wanting to share the visual field, while also isolated and aloof from her. But this is a strange quarantine, for without any confirmation of the fate of the letters, we become the default recipients, anonymously transformed into addressees like inquisitive but accidental readers of a post-card that is endlessly passing through the mails without ever arriving at its destination. In this way, the novel is both encrypted and transparent, undeliverable and deliverable, an assemblage of words and voices that obey the skewed logic of the supplement. At the moment we take up the letters, and only then, we become their fitting recipient, but we take them up not knowing whether anyone else in the novel's world has.

Once Frankenstein's death ensures that he can say nothing else, Walton hears the creature speak and indeed, after a telling moment of confusion, unable to determine at first if what he hears is a voice, and unable to locate that voice in a body, speak eloquently, passionately. Letting Frankenstein's voice die is what makes the creature's reported voice live. The creature appears to grasp that he is living under the aegis of that implacable biopolitical calculus: "He is dead who called me into being" (216), he declares, standing before Frankenstein's corpse, meaning not only that the one who gave him life is now gone but also that his creator's demise hails him into a new, hitherto unheard of existence, one that flickers into life before quickly being subsumed by the plot that requires him to die because he is deemed and deems himself to be abhorrent, unworthy of life. A certain narrative logic in the novel makes it impossible to imagine Frankenstein and the creature speaking together in Walton's presence or, for that matter, in anyone's presence: within earshot of the captain, their voices must follow each other not only in time (first Frankenstein's last words to Walton, then, and only then, the creature's words) but also in space (first Frankenstein speaks in Walton's cabin, and then, once dead, the creature is "permitted" to speak in the same space, in the company of his creator's corpse but not of his creator). At any point in the novel do we ever hear of Frankenstein and the creature in a conversation that is heard by a third? No; their conversations are theirs and theirs alone. Frankenstein can fearfully *imagine* such a colloquy taking place, as when, for a hallucinatory moment, he fears that Mr. Kirwin, the local magistrate, is about to usher the creature into his Irish jail-cell, where, presumably, he would get an earful about Frankenstein's offences (185–6). But that is precisely not what happens. In a novel that brims with improbabilities, it is telling that this is the scene that feels so preposterous. The absurdity of that feared encounter only serves to underline the novel's refusal to have conversations between Frankenstein and the creature take place in the presence of any auditor—except, of course, the reader, who, strictly speaking, doesn't over-hear the two men either except via the figurative translation of writing into speech. Shared spoken words are the pact that irrevocably joins the creature and Frankenstein together, while safely quarantining them from the rest of the novel's world.

On deck, at midnight, after the death of Frankenstein, Walton hears sounds that will resolve into the voice of the creature. Never before in the narrative have we heard the creature say anything that hadn't first been remembered, reported, and reworded by his creator. We pass from one vocal imaginary to another in the novel's narrative. Shelley sharpens the nowness of this break in the text by narrowing the delay between the events that are unfolding and Walton's record of them. "I am interrupted," he writes, moving suddenly into the present tense, disturbing the narrative with a disturbance, namely the noises coming from the direction of Frankenstein's corpse.

> What do these sounds portend? It is midnight; the breeze blows fairly, and the watch on deck scarcely stir. Again there is a sound as of a human voice, but hoarser; it comes from the cabin where the remains of Frankenstein still lie. I must arise, and examine. Good night, my sister. (217)

Hailed by sounds that bear the likeness of a human voice, Walton bids Margaret farewell for the last time in the novel. Social graces like opening and closing salutations will subsequently evaporate as the creature's speech, new to Walton and new to us, surges into the foreground and impairs his correspondence with Margaret, separating him from his relationship to her in decisive ways from which he neither recovers nor shows any interest in recovering. When he writes, "Good night, my sister," he is also saying goodbye to goodbyes. He continues to write, of course, but most of his remaining remarks, culminating in the strange last two sentences of the novel, feel less and less addressed, as if the monstrous intrusion of "a sound as of a human voice" disrupts his own voice, impeding it from continuing to sound sociably human.

At first, if only for a moment, Walton does not hear a voice or a semblance of a voice but "sounds" emanating from "the cabin where the remains of Frankenstein still lie," not *phōnē* or *logos* but *psophos*, something closer to the barking and braying of animals, those soulless creatures who, Aristotle claimed, and Descartes reiterated, vocalize without intent or imagination.[13] Still, these noises emanating from the vicinity of Frankenstein's corpse are not heard as mere animal bellowing (I am here reproducing the assinanities of an abiding philosophical tradition for which non-human animals reflexively cry in pain but do not possess a voice or express ideas[14]) but vocalizations on the very threshold of intentionality and meaningfulness. These sounds "portend," as Walton says, and what they foretell, what they give voice to, is the becoming-voice of a voice; in the first instance, they do not mean something but instead bear the promise, the sound, of meaningfulness. That is what makes them "a *sound* as of a human voice." These sounds do not only augur a particular event or signal a warning about, for example, the presence of the creature on Walton's ship, of whose voice, initially "suffocated" but then full-throated, Walton will indeed hear plenty in a moment; they also perform portentousness—that is, they refer, mark, substitute, repeat, and temporalize the capacity to refer, to mark, to substitute, to repeat, and to temporalize, as if spoken language speaks first of itself, allegorizing itself, and thus beginning in sound where it has already begun. Auspicious sounds are irreducible to noises; they perhaps resemble "the voice ... like a stream" heard in Wordsworth's "Resolution and Independence"; even and especially if the boundaries between distinct words disappear ("nor word from word could I divide"), the speaker in Wordsworth's poem still hears what Simon Jarvis calls "the intonation contour" or "the leech-gatherer's prosody," that is, the sound that a voice *as* voice makes, even if the individual words or, for that matter, the particular language being spoken, is indiscernible—the sound, for example, that a sea-captain might hear through a cabin door without being able to pick out words and yet know that those sounds are neither the wind in the rigging nor the creaking of a wooden ship but a voice.[15] And if certain sounds portend a voice then a voice remembers sounds, for what but the most idealized of voices, an unearthly and disembodied speech purged of all material resonances, "the voice of conscience," for example, is truly without sound, without a certain "hoarseness" that remembers the prehistory of speech in noisy animality or at least what is imagined to be animality?

Now the difference between sounds said to be without sense and an emerging voice, as between nature and culture, tenuous as that distinction is, repeats a similarly unstable difference *within* the voice that Walton discerns; for when he hears "a sound as of a human voice," he hears two voices, stereophonically, as it were. On the one hand, he hears the likeness of a human voice, and, on the other hand, a human voice against which a likeness can be heard *as* a likeness, as a distorted, noisier, and hoarser echo of the former. In this scene, the animalistic likeness is what is substantial and effective. It interrupts and hails Walton, it moves him to seek out its source—while the original or human voice is wholly spectral, not so much unheard as unspoken, all the better to be unassailable. That pure voice is impossible to locate because experienced as everywhere there are, were, or could be beings who call themselves human. Where the human is, so too the voice (the capacity to speak, to respond, to mean, to portend), each ideality confirming the other. Against the hoarseness of its likeness, that human voice is presumably sonorous and clear, and especially clear about the human; the human voice would—if it were to be heard—demonstrate, exemplify, sound, and sound out, first and foremost, the general singular and the givenness of the human. Such is the enduring power of the metonymic relationship between the human and the voice, not unlike the relationship conjoining the human and the hand, a question to which we will turn in a moment. Under these conditions, replete with many unarticulated presuppositions that we cannot explore here, one could say that, according to a certain anthropocentric law, "the human voice" is a pleonasm, except of course Walton tells us that he hears sounds that are also a voice, even if they aren't altogether human—not entirely a nonhuman voice, and not *not* a voice either. Through the figure of the voice, Walton narrows the distance between the human and its likeness without actually saying that they are the same thing. In Walton's ears the voice endures a kind of fission, but the difference is not so defined that the creature's sounds cannot be called a "voice," and indeed, a "voice" whose sounds "portend." In other words, before Walton sees the creature face to face and attaches the disembodied sounds to a body that he then denounces as life unworthy of life, he divides the sound of a human voice from its likeness without making its humanity completely inaccessible. After seeing the creature in the flesh and hearing the words come out of his mouth such subtleties and instabilities are erased. What exactly then is the sound *of* rather than *as of* a human voice? The sliver of a conjunction is all that stands between the two kinds of spoken language, as much a passageway as a dividing line. Would a human voice be thinkable if not for hearing it differentially *through* the other? Now, the human voice isn't in all rigor Walton's particular voice either. He would nevertheless claim unequivocally to be speaking *in* a human voice, and perhaps never more vehemently and anxiously than when matched against the voice of the creature; but the human voice is rather, in general, the abstraction of the sound and shape of all voices that attest to being human when spoken. But if there is a general singular human voice, isn't Walton's voice too not "a sound as of a human voice," which is to say an iteration, mediation, and likeness of the dreamed-of original? Has anyone in all rigor ever heard or spoken in "a human voice" and nothing more, even and especially when saying something like "I am human, you are not" or "I am speaking to you *as* a human being and I am telling you that you, sir, are not human," which are the normative syntagms that are at the core of Frankenstein's vengeful narrative and that Walton reproduces so thoughtlessly, as if having lost his voice to his eloquent and garrulous guest? Yet all that one could do vis-à-vis the human voice is *claim* to be speaking on its behalf or in its name in the form of a surrogate or semblance, sounding as of a voice that you have never actually heard, not as such, nor, it should be added, would necessarily want to hear, for fear that perfection would extinguish what it perfects.[16] A human voice and nothing more might well come in the form of what Marc Redfield describes as "a fully intended, absolutely transparent speech act—as unmediated and instantaneous as Robespierrean justice."[17] The difference between a human voice and the likeness of a human voice reproduces a difference within the human voice, making it originarily a likeness of itself: here "voice" stands as a figure for the way in which the human appears *to* itself and *for* itself, that is, *monstrates*, stands out, shows, or portends. In other words, the "human voice" is the figure for the human's marking of itself *as* human, and thus its re-marking. Walton listens for and insists upon the difference between his voice and the voice that he claims and needs to claim is the spectral double of a human voice, when his own voice is itself its own other.

To Walton's ears, ominous noises quickly become a vocal likeness, the source of which he traces to the creature, whose first audible words, addressed to Frankenstein's remains ("That is also my victim!" [218]), come in the form of a pained exclamation that also "seemed suffocated." Perhaps what makes this voice so touching, at least at first, is that the creature is choked with feeling—not at all the stone-cold sociopath that Frankenstein had made him out to be. What inhibits the creature's voice is *his* voice; choking is what at that moment singularizes his speech, brings him sharply into a new audibility after all of Frankenstein's editing, monitoring, and translating efforts. It is telling that the first indication that we get of the inimitable timbre of the creature's voice is that it is stifled or at least seems so. The creature struggles to speak while the corpse that he addresses cannot respond at all: "he may not answer me," he says (217). Seeing the creature beside himself in rage, grief, and guilt, and hearing his strangled voice, at once emphatic and choked, Walton is struck dumb ("the words died away on my lips" [218]), as if bearing witness to the sounds of the creature's throttled words momentarily robs him of own speech, leaving his words stillborn—this, moments before the creature describes himself as an "abortion." It is a remarkable aural scene, populated by three figures who are, respectively, either dumb, unresponsive, or muted. Walton's speechlessness symptomatizes two seemingly antithetical things. First, his inability to say the words that are on his lips expresses his sympathetic identification with the creature, his dead words mirroring the creature's muffled cries. Second, feeling "a mixture of curiosity and compassion" for the creature Walton discovers that he suddenly possesses the strength to deny "the dying request of my friend, in destroying my enemy" (217). Walton manages briefly to break free of Frankenstein's spell, but quieting the man's otherwise commanding voice leaves him unable to say anything. He feels pity for the creature but possesses no language with which to speak of it except as an hysterical loss of speech. Muteness is the price Walton pays for refusing in particular to be ventriloquized by Frankenstein's Socratic notion of justice, which calls for an uncompromising division between friends for which one feels compassion and enemies for which one should only feel violent contempt. But that ethos, inculcated in Walton while listening to Frankenstein's long narrative, proves to be irresistible, the sign of which is that Walton recovers the power of speech at the instant that he dismisses the creature's "wild and incoherent self-reproaches" (218) as hypocritical and exculpatory rather than pitiable and interesting. His own voice recovered, Walton immediately denounces the creature for failing to listen "to the voice of conscience" (218), as if he were now in a position to eschew British moral philosophy for German, the tug of sympathetic feelings for the power to judge the creature from the inviolable position of "the bearer of moral injunctions and commands, the imperative inner voice, inescapable and compelling in its immediacy and overwhelming presence, a voice one cannot silence or deny," as Dolar notes.[18] Walton speaks up when he speaks for that voice and gives himself over to it. He gives voice to a voice that is as soundless as it is impregnable. One wonders if the appeal to this unearthly law offers Walton an escape from the complexities of the human, all too human voices with which he has been encumbered. As Werner Hamacher notes in a discussion of "the voice of conscience" in Kant's *Metaphysics of Morals,* "What man as a rational being cannot avoid hearing and perceiving, what thus marks an absolute limit to his powers and faculties—and defines him by this inability—is a 'fearsome voice:' a non-human voice, not his own voice, not the autonomous voice of himself but the voice of something 'other (than man as such).'"[19] *"Other than man as such:"* for a moment, Kant's phrasing makes the moral law sound alien, even monstrous. But that other voice offers or seems to offer Walton a panoptic vantage point from which to discern the differences between human voices and their rebarbative imposters. "Seems" is the operative word, since his appeal to an inhuman arbiter only entangles him all the more in the human world, for the "voice of conscience" that he evokes is only a screen for Frankenstein's designs on him, including his mendacious claim that murdering the creature would not be for "selfish and vicious motives" but instead "induced by reason and virtue" (216). Walton never speaks more slavishly for Frankenstein than at this moment, when the natural philosopher is sublimated into an avatar of the moral law.

A loop threaded through the figure of hearing voices has been closed: we have moved *from* Walton following a disembodied voice that comes from the direction of Frankenstein's remains *to* Walton castigating the creature for failing to follow a disembodied voice that, it turns out, also comes from the direction of Frankenstein's remains. Whose voice is that? To answer that question, Walton must return to the cabin where Frankenstein's corpse lies and, by doing so, attach those sounds and that inhuman voice to a body. Whose body? Walton presumably knows that the creature is nearby but at this point he has no reason to assume that he is already onboard, much less holding a fraught vigil over his creator's corpse. Could the "sounds" be emanating from "the remains of Frankenstein"? How ghastly. Acousmatic voices, voices heard off-stage whose origins are indeterminate, as Michel Chion points out, "naturally" remind us of "the voice of the dead."[20] What Walton hears, as he quickly discovers, is of course the creature, but the novel momentarily indulges in the haunting possibility that the sounds could be coming from a corpse. That a dead body might make "a sound as of a human voice, but hoarser" isn't necessarily any more outlandish than the idea of a creature composed of the body parts of human and nonhuman animals learning French but ending up, of all things, speaking English. You almost feel sorry for Walton who at this instant faces the grim possibility, however fleeting, that Frankenstein, dead though he is, has not yet finished talking. And he isn't alone. One of the last things that the creature will subsequently tell Walton, before lighting out for the "darkness and distance," is that he pictures Frankenstein surviving his own death, continuing "to think and feel," as he says, "in some mode unknown to me" (221).

If a corpse could talk, would we understand it? So much depends on the enigmatic space of separation marked by Walton's "as of," which brings to mind the "deconstructive ferment" and force of virtualization that Derrida observes at work in Kant's *als ob* ("as if").[21] The "as of" in "as of a human voice" opens a zone of difference, doubles, analogies, and the uncertainty of the same-not-same. Walton listens to the disembodied voice emanating from the room where Frankenstein's remains lie the way that Descartes looks at the humanoid figures outside of his window, unsure, based on his perceptions, if he observes men or "automatic machines" clothed as men, human beings or their simulacra.[22] The comparison to Descartes is hardly fortuitous, for he was a philosopher who was entranced by automata from a young age, and whose name and reputation were, by the eighteenth century, trolled by a story—undoubtedly dreamt up by those who were disgusted by his "materialism" and the barrenness of his philosophical system, offences for which Frankenstein could also be held accountable—about his fondness for a "talking" doll that he had manufactured to take the place of his beloved, deceased daughter, Francine. Where he went, the doll followed, bourne in a small coffin, of all things. One night on a ship bound for Sweden, so the story goes, superstitious sailors overheard the sound of a human voice coming from the philosopher's cabin, where he was supposedly alone, and, upon investigating its source, discovered the android. Fearful of its uncanny powers, the sailors cast it overboard. In some versions of the tale, the loss of Descartes's mechanical surrogate spelled the end of his reason for living.[23] Is the midnight scene in *Frankenstein* an anamorphic reproduction of this philosophical fable about a philosopher who was, by the turn of the nineteenth century, often denounced in terms that might well be applied to Frankenstein, that is, "a cold scientist for whom a lifeless mechanism was … as good as a real person"?[24] Is this uncanny scene at the end of Shelley's novel a *dream* of that already fantastical story about Descartes? It brims with many Frankenstinian syntagms, including: overhearing a disembodied, inhuman voice coming from the bowels of a ship; the repulsion and violence with which the source of that voice is met; the automata eventually lost to the "distance and darkness" of the polar seas; the fathering of a "child" without a mother; the manufacture of a being in a place of death; the intensely affective bonds joining creator and created; their intertwined fates, culminating in their mutual destruction, neither able to survive in the world without the other; and finally, and perhaps most evocatively, the ill-fittedness of the voice to the source-body. One wonders if what flashes up here at the conclusion of Shelley's novel is the uniquely unsettling threat of hearing the sounds of a recorded or mechanically produced voice, the haunting words of the one who is absent, dead, or otherwise spoken-for by speech? We could say that there is something pre-phonographic about this scene, except by Shelley's day, and indeed before she was born, there were already devices capable of imitating human voices, including a contraption built by Wolfgang von Kempelen, an Austrian court official, whose *Sprech-Maschine* wowed audiences in St. Petersburg by saying phrases in French, Italian, and Latin.[25] The apocryphal story told about Descartes's talking doll may well have been impossible to tell if it hadn't been for the invention of just this sort of gadget. What is revealing is that in 1780 auditors experienced this recital as if they were characters in or readers of a gothic novel, the equivalent of someone today witnessing something remarkable and breathlessly telling others that "it was like being in a movie:" "We looked at each other in silence and consternation," one attendee recalls, "and we all had goose-flesh produced by horror in the first moments."[26] The stagy fervor of this response suggests something significant is at stake. The source of the frisson and recoil in hearing "a sound as of a human voice"— the pleasure taken in the repugnance—is not that an ingenious device, through some triumph of technology, encroaches upon a realm where it shouldn't properly be but, quite to the contrary, that the human voice is so readily susceptible to thoughtless, repeatable, machinic reproduction that it must itself already be machinic. The *Sprech-Maschine* demonstrates exactly what its name suggests, the techne or gadgetry of spoken language. The head-shaking surprise of the eighteenth-century listeners comes not principally from encountering a lifelike machine but from hearing, as if for the first time, the machinic life of one's own voice, now no longer unproblematically one's own. Hence the muteness of the auditors who stand before the machine ("We looked at each other in silence"), struck dumb by the dumbness of their own spoken words. The device splits voice from speaker, and in such an obvious and irrevocable way as to suggest that they were never substantially joined in the first place. Not only is speaking shown to be composed of so many discreetly reproducible sounds, different for each language (it seems important for von Kempelen's automaton to be multilingual, the better to make the arbitrariness of the signifier audible), but also the words that are formed by those sounds can mean something in the complete absence of an intelligence for which they would be meaningful. In other words, the words and phrases coming out of the mouth of the *Sprech-Maschine* signify without being significant, just as they sound out words and phrases without a speaker. The automaton threatens to destabilize the difference between "man" and "machine" (which materialists like La Mettrie had renounced, on the supposed authority of Descartes), but as Kant grasps in *The Metaphysics of Morals* this danger is not contingent and external but a possibility structured into human experience. As Kant argues, human beings not only treat each other as things; they too often reduce *themselves* to things, and not just any kind of thing, but "a speaking machine" each and every time they tell a lie.[27] What haunts Kant's work, and perhaps accounts for his elaborate exploration of the question of lying, not to mention his absolutizing prohibitions regarding telling a lie, is the prospect of never knowing with certainty whether one was listening to a human being speak or a lifelike machine, a voice or "a sound as of a human voice." What makes turning one's ear to "the sound as of a human" voice so irresistible and disturbing is that it makes palpable the workings of an automatism that menaces all language that clamors to be heard, namely the separability of words from understanding, volition, or agency, and thus the chance that machines, corpses, or monsters can speak.

Tracking down the sounds that he has heard, Walton enters the cabin and sees the creature standing before Frankenstein's corpse. At first, neither Walton nor the creature acknowledges each other. The three figures momentarily form a curiously static tableau. But because he is as yet unobserved, Walton is afforded a uniquely intimate perspective on the creature: "As he hung over the coffin," Walton recollects, "his face was concealed by long locks of ragged hair; but one vast hand was extended, in colour and apparent texture like that of a mummy" (217). Walton gives us to see the creature not only in the throes of grief, loss, and self-excoriation, all familiarly human affects, but, more important, in an initial, brief, and wholly unguarded moment, a glimpse of how he looks and sounds in close quarters when he believes that he is completely alone. At no other point in the novel's narrative are we afforded this perspective, which is equivalent to looking in on the conduct of a newly discovered life form, behaving in ways that are part of its *Umwelt*, not meant for human eyes or ears—a moment when the creature is allowed his finitude and self-separation, where he may be what he is.[28] A perspectival reversal takes place: with Walton, we peer at the creature's alien singularity as the creature once did the De Lacey's. It can be no accident that this unusual point of view—unusual because we glimpse, with Walton, the lineaments of a world without us—is possible because Frankenstein is removed from the equation, as if only his radical absence makes it possible for us to look with Walton into the private arena of the creature's life and to see him, as it were, being him, in all his otherness. Under Walton's momentarily unmet gaze, the creature is alone with his thoughts, words, and feelings. That his face is obscured gives visual expression to that isolation; the creature is visible to Walton, but what he sees is not for Walton—or anyone—to see. Under these unprecedentedly esoteric conditions in the novel, the small gesture that the creature makes extending his "one vast hand" takes on an unexpected weightiness. Fleeting as it is, the hand should mean nothing, yet it feels like it could mean anything.

The body language directly recalls a slightly earlier moment in the narrative, when Frankenstein offers Walton his out-stretched hand "before his eyes closed forever" (216). Hands joining hands of course affirms the value of human connectedness even in the midst of great adversity and especially when Frankenstein is calling for solidarity against an inhuman threat. Frankenstein's hands grasp Walton's in a gesture of greeting and reciprocity that claims, right up until the man's last moment, that he and Walton remain alive together, *vivre ensemble*. We might compare this intimate *parle* between men to Frankenstein's reluctance to provide a hand-written letter to Elizabeth, notwithstanding her express wish that he do so. In the absence of face-to-face contact, Elizabeth longs for the prosthetic extension of Frankenstein in the form of his holograph, but as we know, another artificial device has captured his arduous attention and ferociously blocks her access to him. Frankenstein never clasps hands with the creature the way he and Walton do in their final moments together. And yet hands do figure complexly in their tortured relationship. Their hands *do* things, including horrid things. The creature is of course Frankenstein's handiwork; it is by his skilled hands that the creature is given hands, hands that were presumably once someone else's hands, then no longer, and then made again into hands once they are made part of the larger assemblage that is his body. (Are they in fact "his" hands? They are the hands that he has but how he has them is singular. As David Collings argues, the creature bears "a relation to his body that no *human being* ever endured."[29]) Frankenstein's hands are the same hands that brutally unmake the creature's mate, thereby setting the plot of their conjoined lives on its perilous and fatal course. Frankenstein assures Walton that even after his death his hands will guide the captain's hands as he assassinates the creature. For their part, the creature's hands are murderously destructive, leaving their trace on the bruised bodies of his victims. Hands *speak* and, like all speech acts, suffer infelicities and misunderstandings. When the creature appears to Frankenstein in his bedroom in Ingolstadt, it is the creature's hands, not his voice, that most capture his attention. "He might have spoken, but I did not hear," Frankenstein recalls; "one hand was stretched out, seemingly to detain me, but I escaped, and rushed down stairs" (84). The natural philosopher acknowledges that the creature may have been trying to communicate with him but represses that knowledge by muting his voice, just as he admits to not knowing with complete certainty if the creature's outstretched hand constituted a threat; it "*seemingly*" seeks "to detain" him, meaning that that single hand might have been extended for quite other reasons. One wonders if the real threat here is that the creature already has language before he learns *a* language, namely French, and that his yearning to address Frankenstein is the outward expression of an inner necessity that Werner Hamacher describes as a "longing for language ... that exceeds every given language."[30] The creature is not some inarticulate life-form but already part of a symbolic order, driven to address his creator using the sounds and gestures to hand. But Frankenstein is as blind to those characteristics of the creature as he is deaf. Subsequently barred the opportunity to converse with Frankenstein, the creature communicates with him through the murders that he commits. Like speech, the killings seek and elicit a response. That dreadful colloquy is, as it were, the engine of the narrative of the communication that Walton has with this sister; the latter sputters out when the former comes to an end. With Frankenstein's death, the creature announces that he will die by his own hand.

Hovering in the background of the creature's hovering hand are many other eery hands: the nightmarish vision of the enormous armored hand that Walpole said inspired *The Castle of Otranto*, for example, or Macbeth's indelibly stained hands, toward which the handle of the dagger-apparition is inexorably drawn.[31] (The complexly macabre deixis of John Keats's "This living hand" is still two years in the future.) And yet even amid the supernatural and gothic trappings of the scene in *Frankenstein* (the midnight hour, the corpse in the coffin, the mysterious sounds), the creature's "extended" hand seems inert, a posture that approaches a propositionless monstration or showing-forth. "Extended" how and for what reason? The gesture is at once purposive and unclear, prodigious and an act whose intention is occluded. Given its size, color, and unusual, mummified texture, it is a hand that is hard to miss, even if it is not meant to be seen by either Walton or, of course, Frankenstein. The hand is literally suspended, but so too is its meaning, as if calling for a kind of deceleration of thought as the novel ends. Walton subsequently tells us that he overhears the creature "utter exclamations of grief and sorrow" (217), but that vocal commotion, which he hears *after* observing the bestilled hand, only serves to throw into relief the blankness and silence of the creature's frozen attitude. Words that Walton only hears as hypocritical howlings are prefaced by an unobtrusive gesture that all but escapes his attention, as if the creature were speaking in two tongues, one for Walton's world and the other for a world that lets the creature be.[32] We recall that he had once longingly imagined such a locale, far from Europe (157); perhaps this gesture, along with his vegan practice, is all that remains of that dream. Already "extended," the hand threatens to float free from the creature's body, as if it possessed a significance irreducible to his body, otherwise convulsed with distress. It exclaims nothing. A kind of blazoning takes place, the disarticulation of the creature's form into an obscured face, ragged hair, grieving cries, and a hovering mitt.

Questions proliferate. Has Walton interrupted the creature *en route* to doing something with his hand? Is this a farewell? A greeting? A blessing? A gesture of remorse? A blow? These possibilities wash up against the mutism and inactivity of the gesture. What does seem clear is that the outstretched hand doesn't constitute a threat, although it is hard not to interpret it as such given the way in which Walton shrinks in fear and revulsion from what he observes of the creature. As at so many other points in the novel, Shelley is testing us, confirming that we remain vigilantly wary of the novel's untrustworthy narrators. Instead, for a moment, she asks that we let the creature's gesture stand, asks us to refuse to know in advance what a body, what a hand, can do. Primed by Frankenstein, Walton perceives only menace in the creature's appearance and reacts by menacing him in return. He is, after all, responsible for what Tres Pyle calls "British Romanticism's most famous threat—'*I'll be with you on your wedding night.*'"[33] But this is not like that. There is nothing declarative much less overtly hostile in the hand. If it could be said to say anything it might be something more neutrally descriptive, an address to no-one, "I'm with 'the remains of Frankenstein'"— which is, oddly enough, what the natural philosopher feared the creature would one day say, but in the form of gleeful satisfaction rather than the quiet, private gesture that Walton here observes, unobserved. What then is it that we see? It is the detachment of the gesture, its queer indifference to everything that the novel encourages us to see in it, that is remarkable. The hand is extended—extended and nothing more. Is it possible to think that just-enoughness? To borrow a phrase from Maurice Blanchot, it is "the immobility of its position that repudiates all depth."[34] What does this hand, neither taken nor given, seemingly advancing and withdrawing at the same motion, portend? No one is present to grasp the hand, certainly not in the manly way that Walton accepts the dying hand of Frankenstein; nor, it should be emphasized, is anyone present to detect it being offered—or rather, "extended," since the creature does not and cannot volunteer his hand in anticipation of it being received but instead, as it were, cantilevers or projects it without support at the outer end. A starred fragment from Maurice Blanchot's *Le pas au-delà* helps illuminate the suspended fixedness of this moment in *Frankenstein*: "♦ A hand that extends itself, that refuses itself, that we cannot take hold of in any way."[35] There is much to say about this prickly shard of writing, but what bears emphasizing here is the way in which Blanchot's language captures the nature of a relation without relation, a relation that immediately and irrevocably cancels itself. A hand is outstretched, yet refuses to be grasped, and, more radically, refuses the very idea of grasping and clasping, of reciprocality or mutuality, of giving or taking—a hand that takes away and gives away both giving and taking. Is that the all but inexpressible nature of the creature's gesture? Without expectation of a return, without even the "without," that is, *sans* the sense that something is missing or negated, it is a gesture that refuses or interrupts even the gestural, as if the creature's hand, separate from the creature, were capable of bidding *adieu* to the world of Frankenstein and *adieu* to the very idea of *adieu*.

Walton talks to or at the hand in telling ways. Characterizing his concluding meeting with the creature as "this final and wonderful catastrophe," he confirms that he wants what he sees and records for posterity to look theatrical, that is, to appear as a story shaped for and given to human sight. "Great God!," he exclaims, "what a scene has taken place!" (217) Walton makes the cabin where the remains of Frankenstein lie into a kind of studio, an *atelier* where the creature must play out the final, thrilling act of his performance as the monster. He is certainly dressed for the part, his suspended hand appearing "in colour and apparent texture like that of a mummy" (217). As a thing composed of dead, desiccated, or embalmed flesh (such are some of the meanings of "mummy" available to Shelley), the creature is pictured as disappearing, fated for sacrificial death because in some sense already deceased. Walton reacts angrily to the creature's presence and words, but his staging of the scene reminds us that he also marvels and wants others to marvel at the capacity of this insurgent, dark-skinned body to endure mortal pain, and yet speak eloquently and even stoically of that agony. But at the heart of this scene and scenography, the arrested hand stands out, visible but not meant to be seen. Is that why Walton falls momentarily blind, as well as mute? "I shut my eyes involuntarily," he writes, "and endeavoured to recollect what were my duties with regard to his destroyer" (217). Not looking returns him to his senses, giving him an opportunity to listen to "the voice of conscience"—or at least its likeness—again. Walton claims that it is the monster's "horrible" and "loathsome" face that robs him of his sight. Yet that face, he has just told us, is obscured, "concealed by long locks of ragged hair." If not the face, then, perhaps there is something in the creature's extended hand that is unbearable to observe. Walton's closed eyes return the gesture to itself, letting it be unseen, as if his body were automatically negating his desire to compel the creature to yield to his human, all too human gaze. But like a camera shutter, the same reflex also preserves the imprint of this particular image on his mind—"as if that look must be the last," we might say, recalling a verse from "The Triumph of Life" whose strange power Jacques Khalip has parsed so well.[36] The fact is that Walton sees a hand doing something that is not for his eyes to see; he sees *that*. What better way to capture this folding together of blindness and sight than for his eyes to close, thereby seeing but not seeing in the form of a hungry glare? Closing his eyes, he at once shrinks from and tarries with the creature's moment of sheer self-sufficiency. Whatever takes place over Frankenstein's coffin arrests itself and in doing so looks away from and suspends itself from the august philosophical tradition which identifies the hand with the human. Hegel argues that human beings manifest themselves *as* human and as thinking beings not only in spoken language, but also in the use of hands:

> Next to the organ of speech, it is the hand that most of all by which a man manifests and actualizes himself. It is the living artificer of his fortune. We may say of the hand that it *is* what a man *does*, for in it, as the active organ of his self-fulfilment,

he is present as the animating soul; and since he is primarily his own fate, his hand will thus express this in-itself.[37]

The creature's inhuman hand, neither reaching out nor taking in, not a blow or a blessing, suspends this otherwise ancient, powerful and mutually reinforcing identification of handedness and humanity. Walton can only see that unhandedness as a monstrous abomination, as part of a larger picture of disgust, both fascinating and scenic, on the one hand, and repulsive and worthy of the death penalty, on the other. But in reacting this way he only reiterates the ferocious biopolitical regime that is at work in *Frankenstein*, in which the human must be sifted from the less than or other than human to remain human, and where, by analogy, the hand that does absolutely nothing can only be a dead or undead limb, a waste and a wasting away. That is the ultimate import of the enigmatic fragment from Blanchot about the hand that is also the site of its declination. Before Walton arrives on the scene to make a scene, before the creature once more embraces the role of the proud, wronged, and scrimshawed monster, and for the moment that Walton sees what he was not meant to see, the creature's hand is unshared and unexpressed. Radically inoperative, it abstains from productivity. Doing and saying nothing, it is soulless but in a manner otherwise than a privation. Like the creature's voice, the hand is a likeness, "as of a human," but a likeness that isn't immediately and solely an impoverished reflection of the *anthropos*. It is extended to the side of the vast, imperious, and unforgiving world of the creatures who call themselves human. Peter Brooks argues that "the symbolic order of language seems to offer the monster his only escape from the order of visual, specular, and imaginary relations, in which he is demonstrably the monster."[38] But the creature's hand points without pointing, as if eschewing even that minimal concession to signification, to a different get-away, an escape not only from the regime of sight but also from the regime of "man," including and especially the symbolic order with which self-manifestation of the human is so closely identified. It says "no" to Hegel & Co. If the creature's gesture does not reject the symbolic order as much as stalls it, that is because it belongs to that order but in mode of the refusal of its anthropocentrism. What remains to be read in the creature's gesture remains to be read, the fleeting afterimage and echo of a world without us.

The end begins with a voice.—A voice and nothing more.

James A. Heffernan notes that filmed versions of Shelley's novel focus on what the creature looks like, whereas "a faithful [cinematic] re-creation of the novel's central narrative … would never show the monster at all—would only give us the sound of his voice over shots of what he perceives."[39] But in what language would that voice be? In the novel's last pages, the creature speaks to Walton in the same language— English—that Frankenstein had only minutes before been using with Walton, even though this is not a language that he has learned or could have learned. Shelley after all makes a point of having the creature tell us that he has one language, namely French: "I … understand that language only (147)," he says to the blind Parisian, De Lacey, for whom, at that moment, he is only a disembodied voice. And yet when, with Frankenstein's death, he speaks through Walton in his "own" voice, he has perfect

English, indeed, seemingly unaccented English, unlike Frankenstein. It is as if the creature had absorbed the language once he boarded Walton's ship, breathing in some form of novel virus hovering in the arctic air. Of all the improbabilities that enliven this novel, which include the creature's innate moral imagination, not to mention his rapid acquisition of the French language, his capacity to speak English is perhaps the most fantastical. But the truth is that we do not hear the creature speak at all. Instead, what we are given to read and hear is an unexplained and inexplicable *dubbing* of his voice. For reasons that I can't explore here, this dubbing is at once seamless, naturalized, and all but unnoticeable *and* unexpected, wildly imposed, even bizarre. At no point in the novel is the *survivance* of language more legible than at this moment, when the creature endures the superimposition of his last words. Whence comes this translation? Who or what is speaking when the creature speaks? Of this depersonalizing experience of the foreign, the novel says nothing.[40] Like lip-synching in cinema, the substitution of an "alien" voice is disorienting not so much because the spoken words are ill-fitted to the speaker (even though they most certainly are) but because this translation brings out the acousmatic uncanniness of all voices, whose origins in the body are impossible to fathom. The instant that they are spoken, whether aloud nor not, those words have survived the life with which they are so intimately associated. "The source of the voice," Dolar argues, "can never be seen, it stems from an undisclosed and structurally concealed interior, it cannot possibly match what we can see."[41] "I see a voice," Bottom announces to comical effect in *A Midsummer Night's Dream*, when everyone knows he can do no such thing.[42] The source of the voice, like the seat of life, recedes even as it is approached, leaving us to fathom an assignable non-place, both necessary and impossible to discern. When it comes to novels, authors stitch voices to bodies and characters that are then required to be the expressive origins of those voices. Words demand a speaker to say and think them. That way there can never be the vocal or gestural equivalent of "thoughts without a thinker," that is, words and signs circulating in a narrative that survive life, at once wild, undomesticated, and monstrous.[43]

Notes

1   I here recall Mladen Dolar's rendering of Plutarch's remarks in *Apophthegmata Laconica*, a collection of sayings of the Spartans: "A man plucked a nightingale and, finding but little to eat, said: 'You are just a voice and nothing more.'" See Mladen Donar, *A Voice and Nothing More* (Cambridge, MA: MIT Press, 2006), 3; and Plutarch, *Plutarch's Moralia*, trans. Frank Cole Babbitt (Cambridge, MA: 1949), 3:398–9.

2   All references to Shelley's text in this chapter are to the following edition: *Frankenstein, or, The Modern Prometheus*, ed. D. L. Macdonald and Kathleen Scherf (Peterborough, Ontario: Broadview Press, 2012). Page references to this edition are cited parenthetically in the text.

3   Michel Foucault, *History of Sexuality: Volume 1: An Introduction*, trans. Robert Hurley (New York: Pantheon, 1978), 144.

4   I borrow this phrase from Nick Mansfield, "Derrida, Democracy and Violence," *Studies in Social Justice* 5, no. 2 (2011): 240.

5   Jacques Derrida, *The Beast and the Sovereign, Volume II*, trans. Geoffrey Bennington (Chicago, IL: University of Chicago Press, 2011), 131.

6   As Derrida argues, "Survivance in a sense of survival that is neither life nor death pure and simple, a sense that is not thinkable on the basis of the opposition between life and death, a survival that is not, in spite of the apparent grammar of the formation of the word (*überleben* or *fortleben*, living on or to survive, survival), [that is not] *above* life, like something sovereign (*superanus*) can be above everything, a survival that is not more alive, nor indeed less alive, or more or less dead than death, a survivance that lends itself to neither comparative nor superlative, a survivance or a surviving (but I prefer the middle voice 'survivance' to the active voice of the active infinite 'to survive'…)." See *The Beast and the Sovereign*, 130–1.

7   Derrida, *The Beast and the Sovereign*, 130.

8   Throughout this essay, my understanding of Romantic "lastness" has been immeasurably enriched by Jacques Khalip's brilliant exploration of the concept (which has the force of refusing conceptuality) in *Last Things: Disastrous Form from Kant to Hujar* (New York: Fordham University Press, 2018).

9   Slavoj Žižek, "Why Does a Letter Always Arrive at Its Destination?" *The Symptom* 16 (2011). https://www.lacan.com/symptom16/why.html.

10 Forest Pyle, *Art's Undoing: In the Wake of a Radical Aestheticism* (New York: Fordham University Press, 2014), 47.

11 Rei Terada, "Looking at the Stars Forever," *Studies in Romanticism* (Summer 2011), 301.

12 See David L. Clark, "Goya's Scarcity," in *Constellations of a Contemporary Romanticism*, ed. Jacques Khalip and Forest Pyle (New York: Fordham University Press, 2016), 86–121.

13 Aristotle's remarks about animal sounds and human voices are principally to be found in *De Anima*, Book II, 420b5-10. See *The Complete Works of Aristotle*, ed. Jonathan Barnes (Princeton University Press, 1984), 420b5-10, 204–5.

14 "Assinanities" is a neologism coined by Derrida: "[T]his agreement concerning philosophical sense and common sense that allows one to speak blithely of the Animals in the general singular is perhaps one of the greatest and most symptomatic *assinanities* of those who call themselves humans." See *The Animal That Therefore I Am*, trans. Marie-Louise Mallet (New York: Fordham University Press, 2008), 41.

15 William Wordsworth, "Resolution and Independence," in *The Collected Poems of William Wordsworth* (Hertfordshire: Wordsworth Editions, 1994), 228; and Simon Jarvis, "Thinking in Verse," in *The Cambridge Companion to British Romantic Poetry*, ed. James Chandler and Maureen N. McLane (Cambridge, MA: Cambridge University Press, 2008), 112.

16 "Perfection extinguishes what it perfects" is a phrase that I happily borrow from my late friend and mentor, Balachandra Rajan, *Form of the Unfinished: English Poetics from Spenser to Pound* (Princeton, IA: Princeton University Press, 1985), 129.

17 Marc Redfield, *The Rhetoric of Terror: Reflections on 9/11 and the War on Terror* (New York: Fordham University Press, 2009), 93.

18 Dolar, *A Voice and Nothing More*, 85.

19 Werner Hamacher, *Premises: Essays on Philosophy from Kant to Celan* (Cambridge,

MA: Harvard University Press, 1997), 103. Hamacher cites Immanuel Kant, *Metaphysics of Morals*, in *Practical Philosophy*, 560.

20 Michel Chion, *The Voice in Cinema*, trans. Claudia Gorbman (New York: Columbia University Press, 1999), 46.

21 Jacques Derrida, "The Future of the Profession or the University without Condition (Thanks to the 'Humanities' What Could Take Place Tomorrow)," in *Jacques Derrida and the Humanities: A Critical Reader*, ed. Tom Cohen (Cambridge: Cambridge University Press, 2001), 31–4.

22 Descartes, *Meditations on First Philosophy*, in *Philosophical Works*, vol. 1, trans. and ed. by E. S. Haldane and G. R. T. Ross (New York: Dover Publications, 1955), 155.

23 For an overview of this fable about Descartes, see Minsoo Kang, "The Mechanical Daughter of René Descartes: The Origin and History of an Intellectual Fable," *Modern Intellectual History* 14, no. 3 (November 2017): 633–60.

24 Susan Bordo, "Introduction," in *Feminist Interpretations of René Descartes*, ed. Susan Bordo (University Park, Pennsylvania: University of Pennsylvania Press, 1999), 4.

25 See Alice Reininger, *Wolfgang von Kempelen: A Biography*, trans. Peter Waugh (New York: Columbia University Press, 2011).

26 Cited and translated by Dolar, *A Voice and Nothing More*, 7.

27 Immanuel Kant, *Metaphysics of Morals*, in *Practical Philosophy*, 553.

28 My phrasing here owes a great deal to a talk by John Paul Ricco, "Isolation, Loneliness, Solitude: The COVID-19 Pandemic Has Brought Us Too Close Together," Centre for Ethics, University of Toronto, May 29, 2020.

29 David Collings, *Monstrous Society: Reciprocity, Discipline, and the Political Uncanny at the End of Early Modern England* (Lewisburg: Bucknell University Press, 2009), 199. Emphasis mine.

30 Werner Hamacher, *Ninety-Five Theses on Philology*, trans. Catharine Diehl (New York: Fordham University Press, 2015), 22.

31 For a discussion of the armored hand, see Frederick S. Frank, "Introduction," in *The Castle of Otranto and The Mysterious Mother* (Peterborough: Broadview Press, 2003), 13–15. For *Macbeth*, see Act 2, Scene 1, l. 33–4. In *The Complete Works*, ed. Alfred Harbage (Baltimore: Penguin Books, 1969), 1116.

32 Bonnie Konig argues that Antigone speaks in an analogously multi-channeled way. "Words that Kreon hears as mere self-indulgent lamentation," Honig points out, are also "seeking, soliciting, constituting publics elsewhere." See Bonnie Honig, *Antigone, Interrupted* (Cambridge, MA: Cambridge University Press, 2013), 90.

33 Pyle, *Art's Undoing*, 83.

34 Maurice Blanchot, *The Step Not Beyond*, trans. Lycette Nelson (Albany: SUNY Press, 1992), 75.

35 Ibid., 106.

36 Khalip, *Last Things*, 74–102.

37 G. W. F. Hegel, *Phenomenology of Spirit*, trans. A. V. Miller (Oxford: Oxford University Press, 1977), 189.

38 Peter Brooks, "What Is a Monster? (According to Frankenstein)," in *Frankenstein/Mary Shelley*, ed. Fred Botting (New York: St. Martin's Press, 1995), 101.

39 James A. Heffernan, "Looking at the Monster: *Frankenstein* and Film," *Critical Inquiry* 24 (1997), 147.

40 An analogous silence about translation shrouds the language of the conversation

between the poet and the remains of Rousseau in Percy Shelley's "The Triumph of Life." As Khalip asks, "what language do the poet and Rousseau speak in this strangely asocial meeting?" See Jacques Khalip, *Anonymous Life: Romanticism and Dispossession* (Stanford: Stanford University Press, 2009), 184.

41 Dolar, *A Voice and Nothing More*, 60.

42 William Shakespeare, *A Midsummer Night's Dream*, in Act V, Scene 1, l. 190. In *The Complete Works*, ed. Alfred Harbage (Baltimore: Penguin Books, 1969), 171.

43 "Thoughts without a thinker" is Bion's evocative phrase: "If a thought without a thinker comes along, it may be a 'stray thought,' or it could be a thought with the owner's name and address upon it, or it could be a 'wild thought.' The problem, should such a thought come along, is what to do with it. Of course, if it is wild, you might try to domesticate it… What I am concerned with at the moment is the wild thoughts that turn up and for which there is no possibility to trace immediately any kind of ownership, or even any sort of way of being aware of the genealogy of that particular thought." See Wilfrid Bion, *The Complete Works*, ed. Chris Mawson (London: Routledge, 2014), May 28, 1977, vol. X, 175.

2

When Jane Met Mary; or, *Frankenstein*'s Romantic Comedy

Sonia Hofkosh

What is sport to one, is death to another.

William Hazlitt, "On Wit and Humor"[1]

I begin this discussion of Mary Shelley's most widely read novel by citing a less well-known text which, like *Frankenstein*, was penned by a precocious teenager, though unlike *Frankenstein*, it is usually considered juvenilia, immature work, not yet what it promises to become. In the opening letter to her "dear freind" [*sic*] Charlotte in "Lesley Castle: An Unfinished Novel in Letters," Margaret Lesley laments:

> that two such tender Hearts, so closely linked together by the ties of simpathy [*sic*] and Freindship [*sic*], should be so widely removed from each other, is vastly moving. I live in Perthshire. You in Sussex. We might meet in London, were my Father disposed to carry me there, and your Mother to be there at the same time. We might meet at Bath, at Tunbridge, or anywhere else indeed, could we but be at the same place together.[2]

In the essay that follows, I will not be presenting any newly discovered evidence that Jane Austen, the adolescent author of "Lesley Castle," and Mary Shelley were "closely linked together by ties of simpathy and freindship" or that they knew each other at all or even knew *of* each other or of each other's writing; nor do I hope to convince you that *Frankenstein; or, the Modern Prometheus* must be cataloged as a romantic comedy, at least not in the prescriptive or regulative terms that the genre of romantic comedy—or any genre, understood as a "fixed form" or an "institution"—might be taken to encode and enforce.[3] The title of my essay alludes to Rob Reiner's 1989 Hollywood romantic comedy *When Harry Met Sally* (book by Nora Ephron), which has been characterized as "a benchmark in the reaffirmation of romance."[4] Even if you haven't seen it, you might know this film for the scene in which Meg Ryan's Sally fakes an orgasm during lunch in Katz's Delicatessen, in response to which a woman at the next table deadpans, "I'll have what she's having" when the waiter arrives to take her order.[5] Such an allusion may strike you as not quite kosher, somewhat inappropriate or a bit shocking, perhaps as out of place in an essay on *Frankenstein* as faking an orgasm during lunch at a deli; implying an intimate relationship between Austen and Shelley, the reference to Reiner's film is meant to be provocative, a conjecture or hypothetical that posits what we might think of as an impossible possibility, that is, a possibility simultaneously imagined and foreclosed, and thus something like Margaret's speculation in "Lesley Castle" that she and her dear friend Charlotte might meet anywhere if only they could be in the same place at the same time.

There is not a shred of historical evidence—no mention in a letter, no private journal entry, no eye witness account—that Jane Austen and Mary Shelley were ever introduced. Their life circumstances were "so widely removed from each other" that it seems unlikely their paths would have crossed—Austen, a clergyman's spinster daughter, was residing rather uneventfully with her mother and sister in a cottage in a small country village when the teenaged Mary Godwin fled her father's house in London to embark on an amorous adventure with an atheist (and married) poet. Could two so differently situated individuals indeed have met anywhere? Could they have met in London or at Bath? When Austen visited London for extended periods in 1813 and 1814 to ready her novels for the press, Mary Godwin was in Scotland, having departed in early June 1813 around the time Austen arrived for the summer and returning at the end of March 1814 just as Austen concluded her visit that year. During 1815, Austen stayed with her brother Henry at #23 Hans Place in Knightsbridge from early October to mid-December. Mary and Percy had moved into #41 Hans Place in January of that year and then to #1 Hans Place, where they stayed until early March, but by the time Austen was in the vicinity, they had relocated to Bishopsgate near Windsor Great Park, some twenty-five miles away. However one might measure such a distance—"the far and the near must be relative, and depend on many varying circumstances," as Elizabeth Bennett observes about the proximity of married women to their friends and family—when Mary removes to Bishopsgate, she and Jane miss living as near neighbors on the same garden square by a matter of months. Similarly, they might have met at Bath, where Austen lived from 1800 to 1809, were it not for the fact that by the time Shelley was there working on her first novel in the fall of 1816, Austen was ailing in Hampshire and soon to abandon writing her last. Although they most likely strolled the same streets at Bath or could well have sat upon the same bench in the garden at Hans Place ("quite a Love," according to Austen), they were in fact never together in the same place at the same time.

Despite my title, then, Jane and Mary never actually met. Moreover, Austen could not have read the published text of *Frankenstein* (she dies in July 1817) and not a single one of her novels shows up in the careful record Shelley kept of her own copious reading, though that list includes more than a few contemporary novels that Austen also read, such as works by Francis Burney, Maria Edgeworth, and Ann Radcliffe, among others. Yet Austen's last published novels and Shelley's first one might well have occupied the same shelf in a bookseller's shop or circulating library when they appeared in London as new releases within a few weeks of one another. The four-volume set of *Northanger Abbey* and *Persuasion* "by the Author of *Pride and Prejudice, Mansfield Park*, &c.," was advertised in *The Morning Chronicle* on December 17, 1817;

1750 copies were issued shortly thereafter by John Murray, dated 1818. *Frankenstein; or the Modern Prometheus* had been rejected by Murray; it was announced in *The Literary Panorama and National Register* in early December 1817 and appeared anonymously in three volumes in a run of 500 copies from Lackington & Co. on January 1, 1818. Here I take the simultaneous circulation of their novels as permission to explore some of the ways that Austen and Shelley could be supposed to meet, if not in fact, then in fiction, virtually or by proxy. Although their paths did not actually cross, they could be said to meet at different times and in various places in writing. One obvious place they meet virtually in the current time is in recent mashups such as *Frankenstein Darcy* (2016) by Cass Grix—with its Regency Romance tagline, "Neither of them realize how dangerous falling in love can be"—and *Pride and Prometheus* (2018) by John Kessel, who sutures Shelley's storyline together with a sequel to Austen's most popular novel in which the still unmarried Mary Bennet falls in love with Victor and helps him animate a female creature made from the corpse of her sister Kitty. Or we could take a broader look at the mashup series initiated by Seth Graham-Smith's *Pride and Prejudice and Zombies* (2009), which splices "scenes of bone-crunching zombie mayhem"[6] directly into the "beauty and perfection" of Austen's prose.[7] Perhaps less obviously, we could consider some of the ways Jane and Mary also meet in writing in their own time and even in their own writing, in the novels that I want to suggest are themselves already mashups of a sort.

But first, let us consider for a few moments what might have happened if Jane and Mary could but have been together in the same place at the same time. Perhaps, as when Harry met Sally, they would not have liked each other very much, at least not at first. One possessed a rather lively wit from girlhood and her irony could at times be surprisingly cruel in spite of her uncanny ability to discern the thoughts and feelings of others. The second tended to be more reticent, "averse to bringing [herself] forward in print" or asserting her views in conversation; she preferred to be "a devout but nearly silent listener,"[8] although she, too, had a vivid imagination and turned to writing as a very young girl. One declared "3 or 4 Families in a Country Village the very thing to work on," devising marriage plot after marriage plot with microscopic attention to the experience of an ordinary young woman in the everyday world of the English gentry, by her own account a miniaturist working "with so fine a brush" on a "little bit (two inches wide) of Ivory."[9] Making rather less dainty strokes on a more capacious canvas stretching over centuries both past and future and across national boundaries into foreign territory, the other depicted extreme emotions and events—transgressive passions, desolating loss, political intrigue and war, the extinction of the human race. What would two writers whose subjects and styles were "so widely removed from each other" talk about if they had met? Perhaps they would talk about the weather, that first and last resort of conversation among those who have nothing else in common? They might have done so had they met in late 1816, for the weather was remarkable enough during that "wet, ungenial" summer, when Jane, revising the final chapters of *Persuasion* at Chawton Cottage, confesses with uncharacteristic gloom that she "begin[s] to think it will never be fine again," while Mary and her companions "amused" themselves at the Villa Diodati reading ghost stories by a blazing fire, and she begins to think of writing a story of her own.[10] Or, perhaps, instead of the weather, they would talk about books, discovering that they had both read *The Mysteries of Udolpho* with great interest, for example, and their shared pleasure as readers would start to bridge the distance between them as writers, forging at least a tenuous intimacy not so unlike the one Catherine Morland and Isabella Thorpe establish through reading Radcliffe in *Northanger Abbey*. Or maybe they would discuss recent poetry, as Anne Elliot and Captain Benwick do in *Persuasion*, "trying to ascertain whether *Marmion* or *The Lady of the Lake* were to be preferred, and how ranked *The Giaour* and *The Bride of Abydos*."[11] If their conversation did turn to Byron, or eventually to Percy Shelley, would Jane be horrified or only pretend to be, by the scandalous details that Mary could have told her? Would Austen be horrified or only pretend to be by Shelley's own scandalous life? Whether really horrified or only faking it, would Austen appear "rather formidable" to the novice writer, "stiff" and "taciturn," as Mary Russell Mitford described her, like "a poker of whom every one is afraid," and would Shelley thus find the clergyman's spinster daughter "terrific indeed"[12]—as terrifying, perhaps, as the "hideous progeny" she had conceived in a dream during that cold and rainy summer?

I conjure these counterfactual speculations in order to ponder what linking Austen and Shelley together as an unlikely or mismatched couple could reveal or bring out in each writer—for example, the gloom that shades the edges of Austen's conventional romance plot or the investment in a form of normative realism embedded within Shelley's fantasy fiction. Putting Austen and Shelley together side by side may exaggerate their distinctive features, as if in a kind of funhouse mirror. And yet that mirror also reflects some of the characteristics that they could be seen to share. To see those commonalities and begin to discern what is important about seeing them, I propose to read *Frankenstein; or the Modern Prometheus* through questions that the odd coupling of Austen and Shelley raises about genre, form, and style. In particular, I want to think about how *Frankenstein* deploys some of the strategies or produces some of the effects of Austen's signature brand of romantic comedy, including the unsettling effects of shifting narrative voice and of metalepsis, the destabilizing crossing of narrative boundaries, shifts and crossings that create the conditions for reading otherwise that is sometimes called irony. I want specifically to suggest that considering the apparently impossible possibility of an intimacy between Austen and Shelley highlights a tendency in *Frankenstein*, as well as in Shelley's later writing, toward something resembling romantic comedy, a version of the marriage plot that (not so unlike Austen's) may be cast in shadow or queerly construed, but which nonetheless functions as an insistent shaping (or unshaping) force within Shelley's work.

If in *Frankenstein* the conventional marriage plot remains for the most part an unfulfilled desire, a propensity or disposition rather than a foregone conclusion, the potential for romantic comedy in Shelley's story has been more fully realized in some of its many reincarnations, especially those created for the stage and screen. Beginning with Richard Brinsley Peake's melody drama *Presumption; or, the Fate of Frankenstein*, which "much amused" Mary Shelley when she saw it upon her return from Italy in 1823, through James Whale's classic 1931 film, to Mel Brooks' 1974 burlesque homage to Whale in *Young Frankenstein* and Tim Burton's 2012 animated

Frankenweenie, rated PG, about a lonely boy who brings his beloved dog, Sparky, back to life, these remediations incorporate song and dance routines, farcical characters, or happy endings into their versions of *Frankenstein*; and such remediations may well be responding to an aspect of Shelley's narrative at once compelling ("vastly moving") and only incompletely enacted within it. Let me appeal to Susan Sontag to help me make this point. In her effort to identify the qualities of a Camp aesthetic, Sontag states that "to say things are Camp is not to argue they are simply that. A full analysis of Art Nouveau, for instance, would scarcely equate it with Camp. But such an analysis cannot ignore what in Art Nouveau allows it to be experienced as Camp."[13] Likewise, I would suggest, to say *Frankenstein* is or even that it tends toward romantic comedy, is not to argue that the novel is simply that or to equate it with a genre that is also apparently antithetical to it; but it is to say that we cannot ignore what in Shelley's text allows it to be experienced—read and reimagined—as romantic comedy, specifically as that genre is both repeatedly elaborated and self-consciously ironized in Jane Austen's novels. When Elsa Lancaster, playing Mary Shelley in the opening frames of James Whale's 1935 *The Bride of Frankenstein*, declares her tale "something stronger than a pretty little love story," she invokes at the very moment that she disavows the more or less latent structures of romantic comedy refracted in her tale of terror.[14]

Austen's novels explicitly raise the question of genre. For example, *Northanger Abbey* at once parodies Gothic conventions and defends novels as a "species of composition" "in which the greatest powers of the mind are displayed."[15] In addition, when Catherine Morland admits her preference for reading fiction over "real, solemn history," she nonetheless acknowledges that history, too, "must be invention" (79), thus simultaneously distinguishing and confusing genres; Eleanor Tilney does this as well when she mistakes Catherine's remark that "something very shocking indeed will soon come out in London" (81) for news of an impending riot rather than the publication of a new gothic romance. The question of genre is also raised in *Persuasion*, where Anne Elliot expresses the hope that the mournful Captain Benwick "did not always read only poetry," which is "seldom safely enjoyed by those who enjoyed it completely"; she ventures "to recommend a larger allowance of prose in his daily study" (85), despite occupying "her [own] mind as much as possible" (72) by repeating autumnal verses to herself during an emotionally difficult walk to Winthrop.

Shelley similarly addresses the problem of genre in *Frankenstein*.[16] Not unlike Catherine Morland, for example, the creature reads literature as if it were "true history" (98), that is, as if Plutarch's *Lives*, *The Sorrows of Young Werther*, and Milton's epic poem could all be taken as accounts of events that have actually taken place or as factual representations of things as they are. Victor makes a similar category error when he regards the work of Cornelius Agrippa as reputable science rather than as "sad trash" (22), as his father dismissively calls it, or as the "nonsense" (28) M. Krempe authoritatively pronounces it to be. Moreover, the consequences of thus misreading or mixing up genres are shown to be quite profound in Shelley's novel. The blurring of distinctions between categories or systems of language in his reading practice prompts the creature's own painful identity crisis: "Who was I? What was I? Whence did I come? What was my destination?" (97). Furthermore, how the nameless creature is identified in the text is also a significant concern—he is variously called "animal," "insect," or "object" (54, 72, 53), among other names, and alternately designated "master" and "slave" (131, 176). How he is labeled in the order of things or of social relations and what values or powers attach to him with those labels surely matters, and not only to him; it matters (or should) to us, the readers, whose understanding of the novel crucially depends on whether or how we identify with some aspect of this shifting "shape" (53)—his alienation, say, or his rage. Although Victor designs him to be beautiful, the being he animates does not quite fit even into its own body, its skin an insufficient envelop that "scarcely covered the work of muscles and arteries beneath" (37). As bare life, an amorphous "mass that moved and talked" (113), the creature cannot be acknowledged as fully human and yet neither can he be dismissed as not human; at once sui generis, an anomalous lifeform, and "a filthy type" (99) of who or what we presume ourselves to be, the creature represents a challenge to the coherence or fixity of categories, including the category of the human.

Such categorical indeterminacy or disorder also characterizes the body of *Frankenstein*, the novel, as more than one reviewer opined upon its publication: "We are in doubt to what class we shall refer writings of this extravagant character."[17] Since its earliest appearance, readers have been keen to sort Shelley's narrative into one class or another; *The British Critic* finds that "it is formed on the Godwinian manner" and the reviewer for *The Monthly* observes that it is "in the taste of the German novelists," while in *Blackwood's Magazine* Walter Scott (who had also reviewed Austen's *Emma*) determines that it belongs to a "more philosophical" subdivision of "the class of marvelous romances."[18] More recent readers have located it within the Gothic tradition, or distinguished it further as Neo-Gothic or female Gothic;[19] it has been labeled horror fiction and proto-science fiction, and also considered a kind of autobiography.[20] It includes features or facets of multiple genres: the epistolary form; melodrama and the sentimental mode; tales of exploration and discovery; the bildungsroman; ballad and lyric poetry.[21] Like the body Victor Frankenstein pieces together out of diverse materials from "the dissecting room and the slaughter-house" (35), Shelley's text does not conform to a single anatomy. In her study of Shelley, originally published in 1951, Muriel Spark points to this genetic and generic hybridity. She argues that *Frankenstein* "was the first of a new and hybrid fictional species," and isolates the "two forces" that Shelley so powerfully fuses (mostly unconsciously, according to Spark, in that "she was not yet well acquainted with her own mind") as "the supernatural and harrowing" (absorbed from Coleridge) and "scientific empiricism" (absorbed from Godwin).[22] Recognizing that there are opposing currents in play in Shelley's text, Spark nevertheless appeals to taxonomic discriminations in order to explain it, situating the "work in the category of the 'horror' novel as distinct from that of 'terror'—the former comprehending disgust and dismay ... and the latter, merely panic and alarm" (159).

Rather than luring us to distinguish ever more finely among categories by analyzing the double strands of *Frankenstein*'s DNA, the genetic and generic hybridity to which Spark points could suggest instead that Shelley's text exemplifies the impossibility of *not* mixing genres that in Jacques Derrida's formulation enacts the very law of genre. For Derrida, a generic designation, such as "the novel," "gathers together the corpus, and at the same time, in the same blinking of an eye, keeps it from closing, from identifying itself with itself."[23] It is worth noting the resonance in this formulation of the scene in which Victor animates the body he has gathered together from disparate parts:

> I collected the instruments of life around me, that I might infuse a spark of being into the lifeless thing that lay at my feet. It was already one in the morning; the rain pattered dismally against the panes, and my candle was nearly burnt out, when, by the glimmer of the half-extinguished light, I saw the dull yellow eye of the creature open; it breathed hard, and a convulsive motion agitated its limbs. (I, iv)

In the very instant "the dull yellow eye" opens, what has been merely a "lifeless thing" becomes a breathing, moving "creature." In the same blinking of that eye, the consummation toward which Victor has labored so long and with such "ardour" is regarded with "horror and disgust": "How can I describe my emotions at this catastrophe, or how delineate the wretch whom with such infinite pains and care I had endeavored to form?" (37). The catastrophe of fulfilled desire is rendered here as a crisis of description or delineation, that is, as the impossibility of determining genre. Not unlike the counterfactual posited in my title, "When Jane Met Mary," what Derrida calls "this axiom of non-closure or non-fulfillment" (65) invites us to query the complex admixture of genres, including romantic comedy, incorporated into *Frankenstein*'s monstrous corpus.

Given the miscellany or mosaic of genres ascribed to Shelley's text since its publication, perhaps adding romantic comedy into the mix doesn't work against type quite as much as may at first appear. In a much-cited essay on "Gothic Laughter," Victor Sage traces the relationship between farce and horror, and Avril Horner and Sue Zlosnik see comedy as "intrinsic" to Gothic writing, which, they assert, has been a hybrid mode "since its inception."[24] The philosopher Noël Carroll examines the "intimate relation of affinity between horror and humor";[25] he cites Alfred Hitchcock on the "very fine line between getting someone to laugh and getting someone to scream" (145). Moreover, Stanley Cavell has argued that in *North by Northwest* (1959), Hitchcock weaves "the themes of the murder thriller together with the themes of romance," proposing that the film "derives from the genre [he calls the comedy of remarriage], or rather from whatever it is that that genre is derived."[26] In *The Pursuits of Happiness: The Hollywood Comedy of Remarriage*, Cavell specifies Shakespearean romance, especially *The Winter's Tale*, as well as Ibsen's even darker *A Doll's House*, as among the sources from which the comedy of remarriage (and thus also Hitchcock's murder thriller) derives. The genre emerges, then, as if out of the shadows, though only into what could be regarded as the "glimmer of [a] half-extinguished light," a dim light, indeed, because such comedies "harbor a vision which they know cannot fully be domesticated" and which therefore require, as Cavell puts it, "a new creation of the human."[27] The subset of romantic comedies Cavell designates comedies of remarriage thus typically proceed from "an unending quarrel" in that they recognize "marriage has its disappointment ... [a]nd the disappointment seeks revenge, a revenge, as it were, for having made one discover one's incompleteness, one's transcience, one's homelessness" (31). In her guidebook *Romantic Comedy*, Claire Mortimer similarly explains:

> The narrative often hinges around the central couple, who initially are antagonistic towards each other, but who come to recognize their inescapable compatibility in the face of great adversity and, often, mutual loathing … One half of the couple may prove themselves to be crippled by need and incompleteness.[28]

If you do not immediately hear a partial abstract of *Frankenstein* resonating in such descriptions of romantic comedy—"a new creation of the human," "unending quarrel," "mutual loathing," "disappointment," "revenge," "need and incompleteness"—I hope such language will at least begin to persuade you that romantic comedy is itself a more complex genre than its formulaic happy endings are usually taken to instantiate, happy endings that may themselves, as in Austen's novels, betray more than a hint of disappointment if not outright "horror and disgust" at their own wished-for fulfillment.

Romantic comedy "can often be found in the most unexpected places," film historian Celestino Deleyto declares in *The Secret Life of Romantic Comedy*,[29] hidden, for instance, in Hitchcock's murder thrillers and dramas of suspense. In pursuing romantic comedy to its hiding places in *Frankenstein*, places where Jane and Mary may meet (if in secret) and find they have something to talk about (if in furtive whispers), I am not exactly looking for comic elements such as those Philip Stevick has detected by considering the novel in retrospect or as the secondary elaboration of a dream. In "Frankenstein and Comedy," Stevick maintains that "at some distance from the experience of reading,"[30] Victor's abandonment of the newly animated creature plays "closer to low comedy" than tragedy—he comes across as "bumbling" and "inept" (225); even the desperation of the abandoned creature, who seeks sanctuary in a low hovel where he devotedly peers through a tiny chink at the mundane lives of the cottagers, takes on a "faint ridiculousness when it is remembered" (232). There is more to be said about the discrepancy between action and affect in Stevick's examples, and more broadly about how incongruity as a modality of comedy inflects character or action in Shelley's novel.[31] But tracing the latent structures of romantic comedy in *Frankenstein* also means recognizing that the "pretty little love story" is itself a conflicted or vexed genre, that is, a genre that entails conflict and vexation as fundamental to its catalogue of effects. According to Deleyto, the marriage plot lurks in dark and shadowy places. We might say in addition that darkness and shadow lurk in the marriage plot.

In their introduction to *Comedy: An Issue*, Lauren Berlant and Sianne Ngai assert that comedy bears the weight of modernity's most pressing concerns, among them "the problem of figuring out distinctions between things, including people, whose relation is mutually disruptive of definition."[32] According to Berlant and Ngai, comedy is the genre in which genre as a principle of distinction or a drawing of definitional boundaries is most subject to contestation: "the funny is always tripping over the not funny, sometimes appearing identical to it" (234). Arguing further in her own contribution to the volume that "whatever else structures it, the comic is motivated by the pressure of humorlessness," Berlant proposes that comedy is as much conditioned by its generic and affective opposites as it is opposed to them.[33] Humor that includes humorlessness within its operative logic is dramatized in "a balding man's anxiety to be taken in as a successful arrangement of ill-fitting parts" (313), which is to say, as an "arrangement of personhood we call identity" (314). Although his "hair was of a lustrous black, and flowing" (37), the creature in *Frankenstein*, like the bald man, anxiously hopes to be taken in as a person (by the cottagers, by "society," 102) despite the "failed aesthetic or personhood project" (Berlant, 311) he so conspicuously embodies. Insofar as comedy can be understood as itself a mixed mode that is as such necessarily always negotiating "the relation between comic and tortured life" (311), romantic comedy may be hiding in plain sight in *Frankenstein* precisely where it appears to be most vehemently denied or disrupted.

If comedy as a conflicted genre can be seen to figure in *Frankenstein* as an oppositional potential instantiated by the creature's "arrangement of ill-fitting parts,"[34] so can romantic comedy be seen to structure the novel even, or especially, by virtue of the threat it contains, a threat explicitly articulated in the creature's promise to Victor, "I shall be with you on your wedding night" (131). Repeated again and again as Victor contemplates his marriage to the woman he loves with "horror and dismay" (117), that threat bespeaks the compelling force of the marriage plot in the novel. Indeed, once you start to look, the marriage plot is everywhere in *Frankenstein*. It is found in miniature forms, such as in the tale Walton tells of the shipmaster who generously enables the marriage of his mistress "according to her inclinations" (10), and in more elaborate detail in the romance of Felix and Safie. It compels the narrative most pressingly in the creature's desire for a mate. As if he were "a single man in possession of a good fortune," the creature's "want of a wife" is framed in imperative terms, as a demand that "must" be both felt and fulfilled,[35] although, it is important to notice, he admits that the happiness it will produce is necessarily limited and imperfect—"I demand a creature of another sex, but as hideous as myself: the gratification is small, but it is all that I can receive, and it shall content me ... Our lives will not be happy, but they will be harmless, and free from the misery I now feel" (112).

Such a declaration may represent a particularly dark version of romantic comedy's normative drive to a happy ending. Yet even Austen's most "light & bright & sparkling"[36] novel acknowledges the limits or imperfection of the marriages it plots and the compromises necessary to create the couplings upon which romantic comedy by definition insists: think of the relationship between Mr. and Mrs. Bennett (an "endless quarrel"), or Charlotte encouraging Mr. Collins to be out in the garden as much as possible, or the patched up nuptials of Lydia and Wickham. Examining the dark inflections in Austen's writing—the painful deferrals; the humiliations and injuries suffered; the narratorial evasions that call the claims to "perfect felicity" at the end into question (185)—is an undertaking for another essay, the unfinished companion to this one. Here I can only glance at those shadowy places in passing to urge the point that *Frankenstein*'s romantic comedy manifests in difficulties or distortions that do not constitute an aberration so much as an inherent feature of Austen's marriage plot. *Frankenstein* is not so unlike an Austen novel in imagining many possible couples only to frustrate or foreclose that coupling: the creature and his half-finished mate, and

Victor and Elizabeth, of course; but also the creature and Victor, a co-dependency that leads Victor's fiancée to wonder if he may "love another" (147) and his father repeatedly to ask if he has "some other attachment" (150); as well as Victor and Walton, who finds his new friend "so attractive and amiable" that he "begins to love"(14) him soon he appears on his ship and finds his "affection ... increases every day" (15).

A strong undercurrent or, it may be more apt to say, a strong countercurrent in the novel's trajectory, these and other possible couplings and uncouplings are among the elements of romantic comedy Frankenstein deploys in its tale of terror. In the pages that remain, I want to connect Shelley's fantasy fiction with Austen's brand of romantic comedy by briefly considering some of the novel's formal features as they are reflected or refracted through Austen's narrative strategy, specifically, as I have said, her use of free indirect discourse and metalepsis, the crossing of narrative boundaries between the virtual worlds her novels construct and the actual ones in which they are read, between the tale and the technologies of its telling. Reading Frankenstein in intimate relation to Austen's romantic comedy discloses a text at once more familiar—more like normative realism, more like real life—and yet stranger, "more horrid from [that] very resemblance" (99).

This is not to assert that Shelley's narrators employ free indirect discourse in Frankenstein, but instead to propose that insofar as Austen's signature style is, as D. A. Miller has put it, "given over to broaching an impossible identification,"[37] we might see something like its effects operating in the very generic (de)formations of Shelley's narrative. Regarding his own "deformity" reflected in a transparent pool, the creature confesses, "I started back, unable to believe that it was indeed I who was reflected in the mirror"(85); and when he learns to read, including the story of his own creation, he is puzzled to find himself "similar, yet at the same time strangely unlike the beings concerning whom I read" (97). Performing such "impossible identification" across their narratives, the multiple voices we hear in Shelley's novel sound unlike, yet at the same time strangely similar to the voice of Austen's nameless narrator. Understood in Miller's account as a non-person, invisibly presiding over the events of the novel from outside of its reality effects, or, conversely, in William Galperin's view, fallible rather than omniscient, and thus all too human, Austen's human/nonhuman narrator slips in and out of what we could call "specific embodiment,"[38] in and out of individual character(s) or personhood or identity, a slippage that thus simultaneously affords opportunities for identification and dis-identification. Austen's narrator, like Shelley's novel, speaks in multiple voices, or perhaps we could say through multiple bodies; like a mimic or a ventriloquist, free indirect discourse operates through a dynamics at once of intimacy and estrangement.

As has been widely remarked, Frankenstein is presented as three distinct narratives; each first-person narrator speaks in his own voice and tells his own part of the story. And yet the parts of the story are not as neatly packaged as the images of Chinese boxes or Russian nesting dolls often enlisted to describe it would imply. Rather than a series of separate containers fashioned to fit neatly one inside the other, the multiple narrations of Frankenstein unfold more messily, with more slippage and border crossing among them than is often noted—between the function of a character as a narrator of one story and a character in another or between characters as tellers and as listeners of one another's stories. In such slippages and crossings, the novel's structure, like the question of its genre, remains open and unfulfilled. For example, the three narrators encroach on one another's stories. As Mary Favret has remarked, the novel is punctuated by such interruptions: Victor "intrudes" on Walton's account of his own adventure in his letters to his sister, and the monster likewise "invades" Victor's narrative.[39] Repeatedly, as well, the narrators interrupt their own tales to speak directly to their audience or to comment on the experience of telling of the tale, thereby shifting from their status as narrator of one story to their role as a character in another, as, for instance, when Victor exclaims to Walton, "I see by your eagerness, and the wonder and hope which your eyes express, my friend, that you expect to be informed of the secret with which I am acquainted" (33) or "I must pause here; for it requires all my fortitude to recall the memory of the frightful events which I am about to relate, in proper detail, to my recollection" (136). The creature also disrupts the progress of his tale to provide commentary on it, for example, when he proclaims, "I now hasten to the more moving part of my story" (86), a part of his story, it is worth noting, that is not quite only his own, but also Safie's, a story with a (mostly) happy ending that is however foreclosed to him. He calls attention to the medium of this ("vastly") moving story when he offers to give Victor copies of Safie's letters, as later he presents the journal in which Victor had recorded the history of his own creation; "You, doubtless, recollect these papers. Here they are" (99), he declares, handing Victor the journal in a gesture by which he moves from being the teller of a story to being a figure in a story Victor tells.

Another way Shelley's narrators create the mobility effects of free indirect discourse is by speaking in one another's voices, as or through each other, reiterating the same or similar phrases—"I bitterly feel the want of a friend" (8); "I desired love and fellowship" (177); "I was a wretch, and none ever conceived of the misery that I then endured" (64); "I was a poor, helpless, miserable wretch" (75); "I ardently desired the acquisition of knowledge" (27); "This was indeed a godlike science, and I ardently desired to become acquainted with it" (83). Can you identify who is speaking? We might say that such reiteration is "given over to broaching an impossible identification," not unlike the accomplished mimicry or ventriloquism that is Austen's free indirect style. Reading Shelley through Austen's narrative technique highlights what may be the novel's central question—does replication constitute or break the law of genre, including the genre of the human? Reading Shelley through Austen also discloses a possible answer to that question—rather than defining or delimiting *Frankenstein*'s form, its structure of repetition, like the axiom of genre, "keeps it from closing, from identifying itself with itself."

This essay will end, then, as it began, with a letter penned by a precocious teenager, itself performing something very close to mimicry or ventriloquism.

I dare say you wish to be indulged in a little gossip … The pretty Miss Mansfield has already received the congratulatory visits on her approaching marriage with a young Englishman, John Melbourne, Esq. Her ugly sister, Manon, married M. Duvillard, the rich banker, last autumn. Your favorite schoolfellow, Louis Manoir, has suffered several misfortunes since the departure of Clerval from Geneva. But he has already recovered his spirits, and is reported to be on the point of marrying a very lively pretty Frenchwoman, Madame Tavernier. She is a widow, and much older than Manoir; but she is very much admired, and a favourite with everybody. (45)

This letter is signed by Elizabeth, the woman Victor is bound to marry; but you only have to change how you pronounce a few of the names to hear in it the familiar voice of romantic comedy, including Austen's characteristic double-edged irony that is at once funny and a little bit cruel. Finding Austen's romantic comedy embedded in *Frankenstein* suggests at the very least that we should read the novel as by definition open or unfulfilled, not only in that it takes the form of letters that "may never reach" (169) their intended reader, but also in that it mobilizes even as it resists the impossible possibility of a happy ending.

Notes

1   William Hazlitt, "On Wit and Humor," in *Lectures on the English Comic Writers* (London: Taylor and Hessey, 1819).

2   Jane Austen, "Lesley Castle: An Unfinished Novel in Letters," in *Catherine and Other Writings*, ed. Margaret Anne Doody and Douglas Murray (Oxford: Oxford University Press, 1993), 107–33; 109.

3   See Fredric Jameson's critique of such an understanding in "Magical Narratives: Romance as Genre," *New Literary History* 7, no. 1 (Fall 1975): 135–63. Jameson's exposition of "generic distinction" as, instead, "an instrument of exploration" "not unlike an X-ray technique designed to project a model of the layered or marbled structure of the text" (152), suggests one logic for bringing romantic comedy to bear in reading *Frankenstein*.

4   Leger Grindon, *The Hollywood Romantic Comedy: Conventions, History, Controversies* (Chichester: Wiley-Blackwell, 2011), 168.

5   Rob Reiner, *When Harry Met Sally*, Columbia Pictures, 1989.

6   Cass Grix, *Frankenstein Darcy* (Beverly: Farr Giroux, 2016); John Kessel, *Pride and Prometheus* (New York: Saga Press, 2018); Jane Austen and Seth Grahame-Smith, *Pride and Prejudice and Zombies* (Philadelphia: Quirk Books, 2009).

7   D. A. Miller, *Jane Austen, or the Secret of Style* (Princeton: Princeton University Press, 2005), 23.

8   Mary Shelley, "Introduction" (1831) to *Frankenstein; or, the Modern Prometheus*, ed. Susan Wolfson (New York: Pearson Education, 2007), 186–91. All references to Shelley's novel in this chapter will be to this edition and are noted by page number in the body of the essay.

9   *Jane Austen's Letters*, ed. Deirdre Le Fay, 4th ed. (Oxford: Oxford University Press, 2011), 287; 337.

10 Austen, "Introduction" (1831), 187; *Jane Austen's Letters* (July 9, 1816), 316; "Preface" (1818), 3–5.

11 Jane Austen, *Persuasion* (Oxford: Oxford University Press, 2004), 84.

12 *The Life of Mary Russell Mitford Related in a Selection from Her Letters to Her Friends,* ed. A. G. K. L'Estrange. 3 vols. (London: Printed by Richard Bentley), vol. 1, 305–7. [April 3, 1815].

13 Susan Sontag, "Notes on Camp," *Partisan Review* 31, no. 4 (1964): 515–30; 520.

14 James Whale, *The Bride of Frankenstein,* Universal Pictures, 1935. The movie ends with Henry (Victor) and Elizabeth embracing ("Darling, darling") while the laboratory burns in the background, destroying the creature and his reluctant bride. The invented character of Dr. Pretorius provides additional comic elements, including a parodic romance enacted in miniature by the creatures he grows, "like nature does, from seed," when a king repeatedly escapes from his own glass enclosure in a desperate attempt to join the queen in hers.

15 Jane Austen, *Northanger Abbey, Lady Susan, The Watsons, Sanditon* (Oxford: Oxford University Press, 2003), 23–4. Quotations from *Northanger Abbey* refer to this edition and are noted by page number in the body of the essay.

16 While the difficulty of determining genre pertains to most if not all of Shelley's writing, starting with the hybrid *History of a Six-Weeks Tour through a Part of France, Switzerland, Germany, and Holland; with Letters Descriptive of a Sail Round the Lake of Geneva and of the Glaciers of Chamouni* (1817) through the later fiction, variously read autobiographically or as conventional sentimental romance, *Frankenstein* highlights the stakes of this difficulty thematically as well as formally.

17 *The British Critic* (April 1818) in Shelley, *Frankenstein,* ed. Susan J. Wolfson, 386–9.

18 See the early reviews included in the "Reviews and Reactions" section of Shelley, *Frankenstein,* ed. Susan J. Wolfson, 372–401.

19 Jerrold Hogel, "Frankenstein as Neo-Gothic: From the Ghost of the Counterfeit to the Monster of Abjection," in *Romanticism, History and the Possibilities of Genre: Re-forming Literature 1798–1837,* ed. Tilottama Rajan and Julia M. Wright (Cambridge, MA: Cambridge University Press, 1998), 176–210; Ellen Moers, "Female Gothic," in *Literary Women: The Great Writers* (New York: Doubleday, 1976), 90–8.

20 James B. Twitchell, "*Frankenstein* and the Anatomy of Horror," *The Georgia Review,* 37, no. 1 (Spring 1983): 41–78; Brian Aldiss, "The Origins of the Species: Mary Shelley," in *Billion Year Spree: The True History of Science Fiction* (Garden City, NY: Doubleday, 1973), 7–39; for (auto)biographical among other nuanced insights into Shelley's novel, see Anne K. Mellor, *Mary Shelley: Her Life, Her Fiction, Her Monsters* (New York: Methuen, 1988) and Barbara Johnson, *A Life with Mary Shelley* (Stanford: Stanford University Press, 2014).

21 For treatments of these various facets of Shelley's novel, see, for example, Mary A. Favret, *Romantic Correspondence: Women, Politics and the Fiction of Letters* (Cambridge: Cambridge University Press, 1993); James Chandler, *An Archeology of Sympathy: The Sentimental Mode in Literature and Cinema* (Chicago & London: University of Chicago Press, 2013); Jessica Richard, "'A Paradise of My Own Creation': Frankenstein and the Improbable Romance of Polar Exploration," *Nineteenth-Century Contexts* 25, no. 4 (2003): 295–314: 71–84; Shun-liang Chao, "Education as Pharmakon in Mary Shelley's *Frankenstein,*" *The Explicator* 68, no. 4 (2010): 223–6; Mary A. Favret, "Telling Tales about Genre: Poetry in the Romantic Novel," *Studies in the Novel* 26, no. 2 (1994): 153–72.

22 Muriel Spark, *Mary Shelley: A Biography* (New York: New American Library, 1987), 153.

23 Jacques Derrida, "The Law of Genre," trans. Avital Ronell, *Critical Inquiry* 7, no. 1 (Autumn 1980): 55–81; 65.

24 Victor Sage, "Gothic Laughter: Farce and Horror in Five Texts," in *Gothick: Origins and Innovations*, ed. Allan Lloyd Smith and Victor Sage (Amsterdam & Atlanta, GA: Brill/Rodopi, 1994), 190–203; Avril Horner and Sue Zlosnik, *Gothic and the Comic Turn* (Hundsmills & New York: Palgrave, 2005), 3.

25 Noël Carroll, "Horror and Humor," *The Journal of Aesthetics and Art Criticism* 57, no. 2 (Spring 1999): 145–60; 146. See also Wes D. Gehring, *Hitchcock and Humor: Modes of Comedy in Twelve Defining Films* (McFarland, 2019).

26 Stanley Cavell, "North by Northwest," *Critical Inquiry* 7, no. 4 (Summer 1981): 761–76; 762-3.

27 Stanley Cavell, *The Pursuits of Happiness: The Hollywood Comedy of Remarriage* (Cambridge: Harvard University Press, 1984), 18; 16.

28 Claire Mortimer, *Romantic Comedy* (London and New York: Routledge, 2010), 4–6.

29 Celestino Deleyto, *The Secret Life of Romantic Comedy* (Manchester and New York: Manchester University Press, 2009).

30 Philip Stevick, "*Frankenstein* and Comedy," in *The Endurance of Frankenstein*, ed. George Levine and U. C. Knoepflmacher (Berkeley: University of California, 1979); 221–39; 226.

31 The incongruity theory of comedy, which Hazlitt addresses in the essay from which my epigraph is drawn, is usually traced to Francis Hutcheson, *Reflections upon Laughter, and Remarks upon "The Fable of the Bees"* (Glasgow: R Urie, 1750). For an overview of 18th C theories of comedy and some current applications, see the special issue of *Eighteenth-Century Fiction* on "The Senses of Humour/Les Sens de l'humour," ed. Eugenia Zuroski Jenkins and Patrick Coleman, especially their "Introduction: The Senses of Humour/Les Sens de l'humour," *Eighteenth-Century Fiction* 26, 4 (Summer 2014): 505–14; also see the survey of recent scholarship on 18th C humor Eugenia Zuroski provides in "British Laughter and Humor in the Long 18th C," *Literature Compass* (John Wiley & Sons), April 26, 2019.

32 Lauren Berlant and Sianne Ngai, "Comedy Has Issues," *Critical Inquiry* 43, no. 2 (Winter 2017): 233–49; 233.

33 Lauren Berlant, "Humorlessness (Three Monologues and a Hairpiece)," *Critical Inquiry* 43, no. 2 (Winter 2017): 305–40; 308.

34 "Humorless comedy locates the comic in its proliferation of complications, threats, potential, constraints, and consequences that are never definitively ordered" (Berlant, "Humorlessness," 313).

35 Jane Austen, *Pride and Prejudice* (Oxford: Oxford University Press, 1990), 1.

36 *Jane Austen's Letters*, 112.

37 Miller, *Jane Austen*, 60.

38 I borrow this phrase from Donna Haraway, "Situated Knowledges: The Science Question in Feminism and the Privilege of Partial Perspective," *Feminist Studies* 14, no. 3 (Autumn 1988): 575–99.

39 Favret, *Romantic Correspondence*, 178–9. See also Marshall Brown on the "open-ended novel's exploding frames" as the expression of "the unsettling nature of childhood" in "*Frankenstein*: A Child's Tale," *Novel: A Forum on Fiction* 36, no. 2 (Spring 2003): 145–75; 147; 167.

Frankenstein's Embodied Imagination: Or, the Limits of Embodied Cognition

Richard C. Sha

Within cognitive studies, there has recently been an explosion of interest in "embodied cognition." A recent literature review notes 15,000 books and articles on the subject since 2000.¹ Loosely defined, "embodied cognition" understands thinking to be informed by the body, to be situated in the environment, and in its most radical form, to occur without internal representation.² Some believe that internal representation would take too much time, and thus would impede Darwinian survival. "Embodied cognition" further stipulates that perception is coupled to action largely through sensorimotor system, and thus to talk about these activities as separable reinforces false Cartesian binaries. Hence cognition becomes a social, relational, and environmental act, instead of something which occurs in the minds of autonomous thinkers. Embodied cognition gains influence because of models of the dorsal system visual pathway which "extend from the primary visual cortex into secondary areas in the occipital and parietal lobe [of the brain] and uses depth and motion information to represent the location of the object in space, enabling bodily movements to be directed to the object."³ Here, perception enables action (is enaction), rather than implying a mind separable from the world. All this relationality is intensified by affective accounts of embodiment and of cognition, in which affect shapes interest and investment.

Embodied cognitive approaches to Romanticism challenge the degree to which transcendence of the body and of the material and social world becomes the exception and not the rule: if cognition is systematically embedded within the body and its environment, then there are clear limits to transcendence, the individual subject, and any autonomy, and any idealism—here understood as a kind of utopian thought—cannot afford to forgo contact with the world. In this view, embodied cognition grounds an embodied imagination. Mary Shelley recognizes the extent to which the body can block this relationality, and thus her version of the embodied imagination poses a challenge to embodied cognition. She also worries about the costs of this ground because it can strengthen the given at the expense of creativity, idealism, and concepts. While *Frankenstein* has been read as a critique of idealism, I highlight how the body is the unacknowledged source of this idealism, thus undermining both embodied cognition's account of cognition and its failure adequately to address the benefits of idealism and abstraction.

Embodied cognition promises to heal the Cartesian divide between thinking and things, but how? I will show how Shelley through a concept of embodied imagination challenges not only how literary theorists have understood embodiment, but also whether embodied cognition ultimately has the resources to defeat Cartesian and other kinds of idealism. Although "embodied cognition" tries to resolve the differences between phenomenal consciousness and its neural substrate, it often merely moves or temporarily sutures the gap.[4] That the two poles of embodied cognition, body and cognition, are dynamic alone provides a serious challenge. Catherine Malabou argues: "the space and the cut that separate the neuronal from the mental ... are comparable not to synaptic gaps, ... but rather to theoretical fissures that, in order to be minimized, require that scientific explanation be relayed by interpretation."[5] In the process, I explain why the Romantic period also considered cognition to be embodied, while remaining skeptical of the alleged differences it makes. Embodiment is about a promise of a kind of mechanism that delivers the limits to idealism rather than an instantiation of the mechanism that is embodiment. Embodiment in this account is structured by a metonymy in time and space that localizes a mechanism that must strain to deliver unity in part due to the difference in scales between any particular example of the body and the larger theoretical generalization it can only gesture toward. For instance, is all cognition based on perception and is all perception for the purpose of action? Rather than being a clear antidote to idealism, embodied cognition engages in idealism when it selects examples that support its ethical commitments and/or assumes a unified brain/body/environment system or network that cannot be broken or ignored or considered separately.

Embodied Cognition and Its Challenges

Embodied cognitive science understands the mind to be on the same footing as the world, and as a result classifies behaviors as cognitive acts which enhance feedback loops between mind and world,[6] making "causality and constitution not independent."[7] As such it "challenges ... the standard science of cognition, especially ... cognitive neuroscience."[8] The empirical data for cognition thereby expand to their "external" signs even as the problem of how to access the mental diminishes, although the problems of collapsing behavior and mental states and of identifying the mechanisms for cognition never quite go away. Is constitution necessarily causal, or are constitution and causality different ways of perceiving? Within cognitive studies in particular, the turn to embodiment declares a turn away from Cartesianism insofar as these approaches insist on the formative role of the body and of emotion in producing cognition. *Res cogitans* (Descartes's thinking things) are built upon *res extensa* (things which extend in space), and there is, despite Descartes, only one kind of thing. Varela and Thompson argue in *The Embodied Mind* that human experience itself is "consensual and intersubjective," neither the abstract reflection typically invoked in Western especially Cartesian philosophy, nor the heavily symbolic cognition of artificial intelligence.[9] Embodied models are "connectionist models [which] generally trade localized, symbolic processing for distributed operations (ones that extend over an entire network of components)."[10] Philosopher Andy Clark submits, "work on embodied cognition ... calls into question the idea that there is a sequential flow of processing whose stages neatly correspond to perceiving, thinking, and acting ... Sensing, thinking, and acting conspire, overlap, and start to merge together as whole perceptual-motor systems engage the world."[11] Philosopher Alva Noë writes, quoting Susan Hurley, "the skull is not a 'magical membrane;' why not take seriously the possibility that the causal processes that matter for consciousness are themselves boundary crossing, and, therefore, world involving."[12]

With these instances, we see why "embodied cognition" compels: its "boundary crossing" ability gives it the charge of transgression, and what is being transgressed is really a Cartesian or cognitive sciences version of cognition, one that relies upon distinct modules, and machine-like processing. Modules are replaced by extended networks, even as the functional distinctiveness of any module is challenged by the collapse of perception, thinking, and action. Much "embodied cognition" thus claims to throw off the shackles of artificial intelligence in favor of a version of embodiment that delivers connectionism and worldliness. For our purposes, what is being set up is a philosophical debate about the scale of cognition, and whether it is localized, abstract, and symbolic; or embodied, distributed, and connective. Of course, the desire to throw off machine models of cognition is not new. Alison Muri charts the Enlightenment discourse of the man-machine and shows how mechanism has long been at the root of apocalyptic fears and utopian hopes. The body, in embodied cognition, therefore, is neither a neutral body, nor a stable one. It is a body oriented against imaginative abstraction, sometimes against machines, but nonetheless offers unity with the mind and environment (a different idealism) as perception shades into action and becomes sociality and worldliness.[13] However, does not the very possibility of idealism itself challenge the degree to which cognition must be based upon perception and perception on enaction?

All this is to say that the body as a subset of nature can only offer a vexed essence for the mind and its thoughts. This is why Judith Butler talks about the "citation" of the body and the performativity which surrounds it. This is also why embodied cognition acknowledges that the coupling of body to environment is "dynamic" without taking seriously enough that the coupling may be about choice, not embodiment. To what extent is a commitment to the body about a commitment to what it is that the body explains or does for us or constitutes? As we will see, it is the capacity of embodied cognition to revise our assumptions about cognition and Romanticism—how Romanticism thinks and behaves—that are at issue. As Lorraine Daston has recently observed, arguments that rely upon nature as a foundation are doomed to fail in part because there are so many versions of nature to cite.[14] With regard to embodied cognition, there are so many locales, networks, and features to draw upon, not to mention emergent phenomena between levels, that particular versions of embodiment resist generalization. In fact, much embodied cognition relies upon a body inextricable from the environmental system, and in this way, system screens the selection of bodily and cognitive examples. Within emergence, as Colin Jager notes, is the problem of what exactly physical reduction can tell us if the interaction between levels produces something surprising.[15] To return briefly to the example of dorsal stream visual activity, the fact is that both the dorsal and ventral visual streams are capable of interaction, which means that whether perception is about action, and whether idealism is defeated, is less clear: the ventral stream is about pattern information, and is also connected to the attention network. If we limit our network to the dorsal stream, action and perception blend, but if we take a wider aperture and include the interaction between streams, the evidence is murkier. Shaun Gallagher defends embodied cognition (EC), but admits "although a good deal of the attuning process remains non-conscious, the intentional interests of the subject, in part, help to define that attunement."[16] If the constitution is causal, how can these intentional interests be accounted for?

There are good reasons to look back and to see Romanticism as an especially robust moment within the history of EC. George Rousseau, Alan Richardson, Mark Bruhn, John Savarese, and Lisa Ann Robertson have documented many of them.[17] Rousseau in *Nervous Acts* shows how deeply a culture of the nerves shapes the Enlightenment to Romanticism.[18] Richardson develops the physiological and embodied implications of Romantic brain science, and argues that Romanticism saw the beginning of what we now call cognitive science.[19] His cognitive turn, however, is bound up with his desire to move Romanticism away from German idealism.[20] Savarese highlights Wordsworth's "networked accounts of mental life,"[21] and in *Romanticism's Other Minds*, takes what has been understood as evidence of cultural difference and shrewdly repurposes it as developing social accounts of cognition.[22] Robertson argues that Romantic embodied cognition helps writers forge an aesthetics that avoids "pernicious Cartesianism" by refusing to separate mind from body and objects from subjects.[23] While all this work has helpfully complicated our understanding of Romantic thought, I urge caution against simply assuming that embodiment delivers a different Romanticism, be that social, scientific, ecological, environmental, or materialist. The embodied brain/body through the imagination is also capable of abstraction. More importantly, there are signal uses for such abstraction, as when Shelley contemplates justice (60), human rights (118), duties (77),[24] and learning or considers the uses of form.

Even Kant, that most idealistic of philosophers, did not reject things, especially when he warned us that we can never get to things in and of themselves. Kant submits, "inasmuch as the understanding warns sensibility not to claim to deal with things in themselves but solely with appearances, it does think an object in itself. But the understanding thinks it only as transcendental object. This object is the cause of appearance (hence it is not itself appearance)."[25] Our knowledge about objects is based upon our sensory experience of them, and that sensory experience was central to how human beings necessarily produce what they take to be knowledge. When Kant concedes that objects cause experience, he reminds us that "transcendental" is not a doing away with experience but rather captures the abstract conditions necessary for human experience. Kant aside, Jager worries about how brain-based accounts of consciousness and cognition have literary payoffs,[26] and here I simply note that the cash out of embodied cognition within literary criticism is often expressed in ethical rather than strictly literary terms, raising the specter of how the cognitive acquires specific ethical consequences, and whether it has the power to do so.

My opening up of the relation of embodiment to ethics underscores that embodiment is about the problem of reference, rather than a solution to Cartesian dualism. Although the body seems to speak for itself, the fact that the body within embodied cognition is against certain kinds of abstraction means that even here reference is neither simple nor direct, especially since embodiment via generalization has become an abstraction. In *Body and Story*, Richard Terdiman traces the larger theoretical conflict between bodily materiality and language, and he points us toward the difficulties of reference that this conflict tries to manage within Diderot's Enlightenment and today's Postmodernism.[27] Although bodies promise to simplify reference especially because they are such a powerful source of our most primal metaphors (Brooks), bodies are never quite self-explanatory.[28] Embodied cognition, I suggest, suffers from the same problem. Which version or locale or level of the "body" is being cited? And which theories—even physiological and scientific ones—of the "body" and of "cognition" help us operationalize them into functions, much less mechanisms? Even neural networks have synapses that may or may not be crossed by neurotransmitters. Lisa Feldman Barrett speaks of brain complexity, and by this she implies "that the wiring diagram of a brain is not a set of instructions for a single kind of mind with universal mental organs."[29] Malabou describes how "synapses can see their efficacy reinforced or weakened as a function of experience."[30] Within biology, epigenetics makes clear that the surround of the gene matters as to whether the gene will be turned on or off: genes are contextually informed.

We see this theoretical conflict in literary criticism, too, and prominently in Peter Brooks's *Body Work*. Brooks attends to the body as a site of inscription by desire, and he reads monstrosity as an excess of psychoanalytic meaning. He posits the body as a limit, the limit beyond which culture can do no work, and the limit where language itself becomes impotent. Brooks insists the body provides a "fall from language, a return to an infantile pre-symbolic space in which primal drives reassert their force."[31] But why should the body function as a limit if it, *pace* Papoulias and Callard, embodies dynamic change?[32] For Brooks, the body demands its own psychoanalysis, a primal return to a prelinguistic and symbolic space, one that encourages the scaffolding of language onto the body. Leo Bersani explains psychoanalysis this way: it is about the drive to make sense of sensation itself.[33] The aporia of the body becomes the impossible ground for knowledge in much the same way that Hume thought the excessive nature of sensation could never amount to empirical evidence for a self. Bersani thereby arrests Foucault's critique of psychoanalysis as a disciplinary will to power by showing Freud's awareness of the gaps within his foundational concept of the drive, gaps intensified by the fact that they paradoxically embody the drive. Those gaps refuse to foundationalize either knowledge or power because they are about absence. Hence the body is only as useful as its ability to call into being its very opposite—it is a foundation for anti-foundationalism—and in this way the oscillation of the body into its psychoanalytic other and resistance to that other is what paradoxically grants it theoretical interest.

Fittingly, Brooks offers a reading of *Frankenstein* where language provides a temporary escape from the monster's visual body, a kind of cultural compensation for his "deficient nature" or "lack of relation."[34]

Today, Constantina Papoulias and Felicity Callard connect this problem of reference to foundationalism. They wryly note that the citation of biology and neuroscience within the humanities is precisely an anti-foundational gesture: the body in question is one livened by affect, and thus the body becomes an "open system" and creative space.[35] I add that the body's capacity to surprise makes it matter: this too, too solid flesh not only melts into plasticity in the face of challenges, but also facilitates creativity. Thus, they show how this antifoundational biology is made persuasive through a language of verification and of experimental method. That such verificationalism is applied to a vitalist biology threatens to make such claims incoherent, a form of having one's cake and eating it, too, as vitalism often assumes a principle of life that cannot be reduced to physical entities. More damningly, Papoulias and Callard show the selectivity of scientific citation of the creative vital body: they argue that proponents of affect simply ignore arguments detailing the intransigence of emotional conditioning.[36] In short, the body once again functions as a foundation against anti-foundationalism.

When proponents of embodied cognition declare victory over Cartesianism as if it were a victory over idealism and abstraction, they are being overly optimistic at best. The real question here is what does the embodiedness mean, and why does it matter? Within neuroscience, this question is screened by the desire to declare victory at the moment a neural correlate of consciousness or cognition is found, be that rich node neurons, the claustrum, the pre-frontal cortex, or the brain stem. As Malabou argues, this question has also been screened by neuroplastic versions of capitalist efficiency. Nonetheless, the mere fact of embodiment is neither prophylactic against individualism, nor abstraction, nor transcendence, nor utopian thought.[37] Neuroscientist Rodolfo Llinás hypothesizes the brain as a closed system and argues "given the nature of the thalamocortical system, sensory input from the external world only gains significance via the preexisting functional disposition of the brain at that moment, its internal context. It follows that such a self-activating system is capable of emulating reality even in the absence of input from such reality, as occurs in dream states or daydreaming."[38] Many of our neurons lack connection to the outside world, and our lipid cellular membranes further insulate the cell from the world.[39] Llinás's point here is that the brain is the origin of activation, not the outside world, and I will show how Shelley invokes Victor's embodied imagination and its cognitive powers to anticipate Llinás. Despite embodied cognition's elevation of a brain/body networked system, potential connection should not be mistaken for a necessary connection, and such connection should not be presumed to deliver worldliness as ethics.[40]

There are more reasons to be skeptical of any simple ties between bodies and ethics/ecology. Although embodied cognition insists upon a necessary relationality between human information processing and the world, our notions of the self, and our connections of ourselves to agency, undermine this relationality so that the self can take credit for the differences it witnesses and sometimes makes. Neuroscientist Robert

Sapolski warns us that our brains tend to form us versus them dichotomies where we favor those like ourselves.[41] Although this tendency is referred to being "pro-social," "pro-social" entails an out group. The need for an "out" group puts pressure on what counts as "pro-social," and certainly undermines any easy tie between body and ethics. More worrisome: those who feel the pain of others "with the most pronounced arousal and anxiety are actually less likely to act pro-socially."[42] Paul Bloom underscores how limited the spotlight of empathy actually is, and the fact that we are most empathetic to those most like ourselves.[43]

Political scientist Kristin Monroe, moreover, charts the ways in which personality—our sense of self in relation to others—drives the ethical options that appear on the table during genocide. The bad news is our sociality and relationality are particularly vulnerable to our ability to define someone else's suffering as salient or irrelevant to us. The good news is that priming, or "goal-directed mental activity," can change automatic, subconscious responses to stereotyped groups.[44] Monroe hints that embodiedness can be shaped by concepts of the self, and this is one reason it resists standing in for any particular ethics. Neuroscientist Barrett considers how our notions of realism are freighted with affect, and this makes us particularly vulnerable to certain kinds of delusions.[45] Everything we see is colored by our brain's budget-balancing act—hence our ability to be "hangry." She concludes "affective realism keeps you believing something even when the evidence puts it highly in doubt."[46] Finally, in their critical assessment of what cognitive literary studies adds to literary study, Jager and Savarese highlight that what proponents of embodied cognition think of as intermentality, humanists have understood as ideology.[47] When intermentality is considered an ideology, there is both an incentive and a need to distance oneself from it.

Cognitive scientists increasingly take cognition to be distributed across brain/body environment. However, Goldinger et al. dismiss embodied cognition, declaring that no aspect of human behavior can be plausibly explained by embodiment.[48] According to these authors, embodiment is trivially true because it is what "everyone knows." Moreover, EC proponents "selectively focus on a subset of domains that work."[49] Goldinger rightly objects to embodied cognition's claim that cognition exists for the purpose of action, which, in turn, is falsely reinforced by the coupling of perception and action as part of the same activity. As a counter example, he proffers the kinds of cognition that occur when watching television: these do not lead to action. Embodied cognition sometimes mistakes potential connections for necessary connectedness, a problem exacerbated by the concept of neural networks. Our neural networks require thresholds for activation and are laden with synapses that may or may not be bridged by neurotransmitters. Embodied cognition gets into trouble when it ignores the limits of its empirical instantiations, but a finding's claims to our attention are proportional to their generalizability. And yet the vehemence of this critique of EC may have to do with the recognition of the fact that since the extensions possible within the laboratory are highly constrained and artificial, embodied and extended cognition ultimately challenges the degree to which laboratory science can deliver the cognitive goods. Within EC, thinking is so bootstrapped to its environment that the laboratory cannot deny its distortions.

In closing this brief assessment of the limits of embodied cognition, let me ask the degree to which body can stand in for unity, ecology, sociality, and worldliness, which, baldly put, seems to me what much of this fuss is really about. We embrace embodied minds because they make thinking minds about ecology, relationality, and sociality, and check our human hubris. Climate change has allegedly made it impossible to ignore our wider ecology. But our embodied brains are perfectly capable of this ignorance, and have been for centuries, and thus we might consider the degree to which our cognitive embodiedness—as Shelley does and Llinás and Barrett support—facilitates our confirmation biases, our prejudices, our selfishness, our egoisms, and yes, even our solipsism. But how could one get a research grant to support this conclusion, since it tells us nothing new. Because our cognitive capacities are so limited and expensive, neuroscientists say that we sip the world through a straw, and it goes without saying that our sipping is heavily biased by selections of which we are not normally even aware. It was psychologist Zajonc who showed us how effective subconscious priming could be on our actual choices: mere exposure to a stimulus increases our liking of it. Victor Frankenstein's straw is narrower than most: he admits that once he understands the act of making the monster as selfish he "banished from my mind any thought that could lead to a different conclusion" (143). But his ethics are too little and too late. Try as we might, then, EC will never compensate for all the evils done in the name of "the human": it ultimately refuses to let us consign our bad behaviors to the dustbin of history. Yet if we take from EC a reminder of our very real potential to be ecological so that we work through our limitations, our capacities for ecological thinking might have a chance for success instead of being too optimistically taken as a given.[50] Our ecological mindedness might even profit from how idealism can facilitate a kind of systems thinking.

Mary Shelley and the Embodied Imagination

Shelley certainly understands the degree to which our imaginations are embodied, and shows how the imagination produces wonder, which prompts cognitions.[51] The monster remembers his initial confusion of "a strange multiplicity of sensations" but when he "learned to distinguish between the operations of my various senses," sensation shifts into cognition (80). Light gives him his first sensations of pleasure, introducing reward. When he beholds the "radiant form [of light] rise from among the trees … [he] gazed with a kind of wonder" that opens him to the world (80). At the same time, following Nancy Yousef's reading of the novel, we can see how Shelley doubts any claim that mere embodiment grounds us in the world because there are many imaginative thoughts which cannot be traced back to perception (rights, duties, liberty, justice) yet are nonetheless cognitions. According to Yousef, the novel highlights the failures of any autonomous development of mind—the idea that time itself is sufficient for sovereign minds to develop—by foregrounding the supernatural leaps from sensation to meaning of an idea, and expression to meaning. As she puts it, "the creature's first response to the first cottage scene raises questions about the origin of his understanding of expression and behavior."[52] Hence Yousef shows how Shelley follows Locke and Rousseau in getting the monster from sensation to particularity, but also how solitary learning or embodiment on its own has the resources to facilitate connections is precisely the question that all these writers leave unasked.

And yet if many of today's proponents of "embodied cognition" stress what can go right, Shelley worries about what can and does go wrong with our all-too embodied minds and imaginations.[53] For Shelley, the nervous body consistently threatens collapse. Frankenstein repeatedly falls victim to nervous fevers. From the moment he appears in the novel, Walton is captivated by Frankenstein's body: "dreadfully emaciated by fatigue and suffering" (13). While working on the monster, Victor describes himself as "nervous to a most painful degree" (38). In this nervous view, embodiment allows suffering to inscribe itself onto the body, and helps us to learn from our experiences. However, when we think, we know very little if at all of how we think, and this explains why it is possible to ignore the difference that embodied cognition allegedly makes.[54]

Not only does Shelley focus on how embodied imaginations make us vulnerable to nervous diseases, but they also often reinforce our prejudices and narcissism. Simply put, the turn away from Cartesian models of the mind that distance it from objects and other human beings is not enough to ensure sociality and ecology because we are attending to various stimuli and ignoring others, and the emotions grant certain stimuli salience. Victor is certainly capable of walling himself off from the emotions of others: while his father is exhilarated by Victor's being set free after Clerval is murdered, Victor notes, "I did not participate in these feelings" (153). Shelley thus offers Victor as a test case about what goes wrong with embodied cognition. Exhibit A: The reasons why Victor is interested in science is his ego: Victor sneers when "the ambitions of the inquirer seemed to limit itself to the annihilation of those visions on which my interest in science was chiefly founded. I was required to exchange chimeras of boundless grandeur for realities of little worth" (29–30). Driven by his embodied emotions, Victor seeks the thrills of chimeras at the expense of realities, and the worst part of it is that he is blind to how dangerous chimeras are to science. Exhibit B: Shelley credits Paris, not London, for being able to see beyond its own prejudices. At the condemnation of Safie's father, "all Paris was indignant; and it was judged that his religion and wealth, rather than the crime alleged against him, had been the cause of his condemnation" (98). Yet Shelley's reference to "Turk" on the very next page incites English prejudice just after she credits the French with the ability to recognize prejudice, and by appealing to Francophobia, she tries to help her readers examine and resist their own prejudices (99). Exhibit C: Victor's nervous body hardly prevents him from belief in spirits. When Victor credits "spirits" for providing him with meals in the Arctic, Shelley writes that "I had no doubt that [such fare] was sent there by the spirits that I had invoked to aid me"—he loses what little scientific credibility he had even as he shows how thought can leap beyond its surround (173).

Shelley does insist upon the fact of animal and human embodiedness. She does so, however, not in the service of patriarchy, but to insist that although men, including her husband, are fond of idealism, their repeated denial of their bodies makes them even more subject to the somatic than what women experience. Her mother, Mary Wollstonecraft, had opened up the issue of physical strength to include mental strength for women, and had in this way begun to chip away at any simple idea of the superior strength of male bodies as a justification for patriarchy. In this view, male strength is undermined by male idealism. When Walton opens the novel by informing his sister that he needs to be convinced that the Arctic is a land of ice and snow, Shelley highlights the (masculine) forgetting of embodiedness, along with the costs of this forgetting. Walton writes, "I try in vain to be persuaded that the pole is the seat of frost and desolation; it ever presents itself to my imagination as the region of beauty and delight" (5). The passive voice here and the vocabulary of presentation show us that Walton would like us to believe that his imagination operates without any of his own input. Later on, before the trial of Justine, Victor insists, "he (the monster) was the murderer! I could not doubt it. The mere presence of the idea was an irresistible proof of the fact" (56). No court could be compelled by such idealism. Perhaps such forgetting is encouraged by the patriarchal abstraction of the masculine body as the universal body. The problem with abstraction is that it has no other against which to measure itself, and this is why Shelley's underscoring of the facticity of embodiedness serves as a caution against, but not a wholesale rejection of, male idealism.

Shelley's most fulsome critique, however, has to do with how our embodied cognition so easily facilitates total narcissism, a problem that much of today's ecological versions of cognition simply wishes away. Never one to abstain from a pity party, Victor insists, "I am, by a course of strange events, become the most miserable of mortals. Persecuted and tortured as I am and have been, can death be any evil to me?" (157). How could he possibly know that out of all mortals, he is the most miserable? When Victor mistakenly imagines how the monster will murder him on his wedding night, he insists "I would die to make her happy," thus showing the strength of his egoism and that he consequently never really understood Elizabeth (159). There is no scenario under which his death could make her happy. Only when narcissism is registered as a problem can distance from the self acquire the possibility of undermining it.

Shelley also recognizes the degree to which embodiment can support both notions of fixity and dynamism, and this explains why she converts an emotion into a verb. This returns us to the issue of how we define embodiment depends upon what we want our idea of body to do. She at times considers embodiment in terms of the ephemerality and mutability of feelings, and thus seeks to find ways to develop a character capable of regulating emotion. To the extent that emotion stands with the body but requires regulation, the theory is that its emotional dynamism can be controlled.[55] Victor muses "how mutable are our feelings" (144). Enthusiasm in particular demands regulation because Walton credits it with "elevating him to heaven" (6). Such regulation is all the more needed, given that feelings in the novel hardly have moral efficacy. If human beings have capacity for benevolence and empathy, they are also motivated by vengeance and hatred, and thus the cultivation of feelings could never be a good in itself. By converting compassion from a characteristic into a verb, as when the monster's narrative "compassionated him," she notes its effectiveness but qualifies that effectiveness because it only works immediately and contextually. Once the monster is no longer present to compassionate him, Victor has no more compassion. Victor recognizes that one cure to "mental torment" is precisely vigorous exercise, and thus after Elizabeth's death, he very briefly takes an oar (73). Human physiology in this view offers an incentive for seeking means of emotional regulation and thus fixity. Although Walton recognizes the potential of human affection to "regulate his mind," his excess affection for Victor achieves no such discipline (74).

Frankenstein thus teems with ways to care for the self, and this care undermines the idea that our embodiedness itself has an ethics, insofar as ethics asserts values beyond self-interest, based on a recognition of others. In this view, abstraction from our bodies is what opens the door to an ethics. I have already mentioned exercise. Far from being a given, Shelley considers the body to be the product of its habits. Walton touts his Humean prudence to his sister: "you know me sufficiently to confide in my prudence" (10). And when the monster admits that "the feelings of revenge and hatred filled my bosom, and I did not strive to control them; but allowing myself to be borne away by the stream, I bent my mind towards injury and death," he alludes to Seneca's warning that in order to act on such passions as anger, one must consent to the feelings they inspire (113). He acknowledges a non-ethical indulgence in one's feelings. Shelley also recognizes the ways in which women are charged with the care of male selves, and the novel forecasts the devastating consequences of such exploitation.

One reason why Shelley recognizes the power of what we today call EC but remains skeptical of its promises is because although in the novel the body often seems to be its own frame, bodies never speak for themselves, relying instead upon other frames like gender, sensibility, and vitalism to fix their meanings.[56] Barbara Johnson highlighted how *Frankenstein* is about women's autobiography: since the writing of a life is almost by definition a male privilege, monstrosity becomes Shelley's figure for thinking about the self-contradictions required of female identity.[57] In particular, in *Frankenstein*, gender is a kind of urcontingency: femininity operates under the sign of death, a view advanced by theories of generation of the time that equate the male seed to the living principle and the female body as a kind of inert nest. So Shelley takes seriously how certain bodies are subject to more precarity than others. The female monster's powers of bestowing life despite Victor's association of her with "the filthy process" of death help explain the violent misogyny behind Victor's destruction of her (137).

Of course, this gendered frame is intensified by sensibility. Sensibility further complicates what embodiedness means and does.[58] Now as a kind of universality that guarantees common experience, and now as a version of distinctness and distinction that speaks to a refined and individual experience, sensibility is torn between two masters that it cannot simultaneously obey. As Shelley recognizes, the problem of the felt reality of the psychosomatic is only exacerbated by the culture of sensibility. Sensibility grounds the body in the nervous system and threatens to put into place an ideal embodiment that is trivial: in this view, the body is the sum total of its sensations, a totality that grows increasingly complicated when one realizes the difficulty of sorting out the difference between internal versus external sensations. Barrett argues that our emotions are mixed and are in part about our body-budgets. No wonder Romantic embodiedness so often amounts to a vague pointing of fingers at nervous diseases as the cause of whatever is awry. Sensibility further encourages narcissism insofar as heightened awareness is preoccupied by the feelings that one has most access to, which is one's own feelings.

Even worse, sensibility exacerbates the idea that to feel something is to change something, and to feel badly about something is to do something meaningful. Victor's declaration that he suffers "living torture" during Justine's trial excuses him from not having acted, while the monster's confession to Victor's dead body that "my agony was superior to thine" raises the issue of why this kind of accounting seems so necessary (191). Victor and the Monster have trained themselves to cash in on their sufferings for empathetic credit. In this regard, we do well to recall Steven Goldsmith's argument that the emotional turn within reading and criticism is about the feeling of having done something as opposed to actually having done something.[59]

Vitalism further complicates embodiment. Shelley understood that the fact that our bodies have certain connections does not mean that we always use them. To wit, because Victor embraces a vitalist embodiment, the idea that life is a separate principle and separable from its chemical and electrical building blocks, life can simply be superadded to a dead body. Although Catherine Packham argues that vitalism overthrew the mind and replaced it with bodily regulation, vitalism in the form of a principle severely curtails what the body by itself can guarantee.[60] Not surprisingly, neither Victor nor Walton has problems disregarding their current surrounds. After Victor's mother's death, Shelley comments, "it is so long before the mind can persuade itself that she, whom we saw every day, and whose very existence appeared a part of her own, can have departed forever" (27). Today, we turn to "emergence" when we seek to overcome crude reductionism.

Now one of the most powerful questions Shelley asks is: is a dead body embodied? What is a body without life? In raising this issue, she returns to Galvani's claim to have discovered animal electricity in the body of a dead frog's leg and Bichat's nearly tautological definition of life as the sum total of processes which resist death. Galvani's critics found his claim of animal electricity absurd, for how could a dead and severed leg evidence animal electricity? Volta agreed and argued that what Galvani had identified as animal electricity was really nothing more than physical electricity. Without life, the body is incapable of self-organization. Noë argues that life entails a kind of incipient mindfulness.[61] Yet when life is considered to be a principle superadded to a body, then a dead body can be embodied. The Romantic period's fascination with recently drowned victims and with suspended animation meant that the line between the dead and living body was far more ambiguous than it is today, and the fact that what looked like death could be the suspension of life meant that embodiment could straddle the dead.[62] By using Victor to open up a space between the living and nonliving body, Mary Shelley questions the kinds of autonomy associated with the biological science of life. Is there no indebtedness of living matter to nonliving matter? When Victor claims that Clerval "restored him to life" after his nervous collapse, he incoherently refuses a distinction between the signs of life and life itself. Mary Shelley declares her skepticism about the concept of life as a principle when she insists that Galvanism had given us a "token" of such things. In her 1831 Preface, she intensifies this skepticism as she describes: "I saw the hideous phantasm of a man stretched out, and then, on the workings of some powerful engine, show signs of life, and stir with an uneasy, half-vital motion" (196). Unlike Victor, she takes pains to bracket signs of life from life, and her use of "half-vital" furthers her sense that electricity cannot be life.

Like the women in the novel, the monster also cannot get around his embodied contingency. The monster associates his own body with deformation and deformity. His deformation harkens back to a time when theology could suggest that evil has a visible physiognomy like the mark of Cain. Stuart Curran recently suggested that the significance of Geneva in the novel was tied to the role Calvinism played there, and the fatalism of being a part of the elect or not.[63] When Victor connects deformation to daemon, he implies that the morphology of the monster reveals a God who provides stable visual signs for good and evil (56). And yet when Shelley broadens monstrosity to include Victor as doppelgänger, the Turk, Justine, and the barbarity of mankind, she hastens to argue that evil cannot be correlated to particular bodies, and that monstrosity may only be a morphology. Here she may be availing herself of natural philosophical arguments made by Geoffroy Saint Hilaire that monstrosity was a problem of development and not of creation. God could not thus be held responsible for evil. The monster refers to his "personal deformity" in an attempt to drain his monstrosity of metaphysical evil, but in so doing he attaches his self to monstrosity (106). My turn to attachment suggests that the contingency of the body requires kinds of attachment, and once again embodied contingency never speaks for itself.

When we compare the monster's deformed body with Victor's, we witness how only certain bodies are associated with primitivism or daemons. In this view, certain bodies are allowed to have more dynamism than others. Although Walton reads Victor now as a wreck, a deformation, he is quick to associate his deformity with a lost nobility. Walton comments: "I began to love him as a brother; and his constant and deep grief fills me with sympathy and compassion. He must have been a noble creature in his better days, being even now in wreck so attractive and amiable" (15). And as Victor contemplates Clerval's absence, he remarks that "your form so divinely wrought, and beaming with beauty, has decayed, but your spirit still visits and consoles your unhappy friend" (130). When the monster repeatedly worries about his deformation, he has internalized a fixed idea of monstrosity as deformation tending toward primitivism. Such primitivism of course does not prevent the monster from wishing away his monstrosity. My question here, however, is why does no one consider the monster's lost nobility? Why does his body not get read as a ruin?

We are now prepared to revisit the nesting box structure of the novel. Shelley provides us with four frames for thinking about cognitive embodiment: Percy's preface, Walton's, Victor's, and the Monster's. Form here renders embodied thought into the methodological problem of how particularities resist generalization. Percy's preface directs us immediately to Erasmus Darwin and German physiology, and what these sciences can tell us about human passion so that Mary's novel will not "enervate" like most ones of the day (3). Walton's narrative begins by describing how the St.

Petersburg winds "brace [his] nerves" (5). So does the monster begin with the light pressing on his nerves (80). The competing frames highlight the problem of the body's ability to refer, and what our nervous bodies mean. The four frames thus demand that the reader extrapolate principles from the particulars, and to imagine reasons that can account for how a similar nervous system can account for cognitive and especially temperamental differences. What explains why Walton listens to his crew, and turns back, and why Victor doesn't? Is a monstrous body meaningfully different, or are its differences simply morphological? This move to generalization, moreover, is emphatically, a move to abstraction, reminding us that embodied cognition has no less need for generalization and idealism. Finally, enervation reminds us that cognitive embodiment does not always redound to the credit of mankind.

Embodiment within cognitive science and the humanities promises more than it can deliver. It downplays the cognitive value of abstraction even as it makes select abstractions unnatural. If its efficacy is tied to the body's ability to black box agency, that is all the more reason to question its powers. Within Romantic studies, embodied cognition cannot alone deliver a more social/environmental/materialist and less idealistic Romanticism. Shelley understood the contingency of the body and sought to operationalize it against an abstracting and theoretical culture which sought to make it ancillary. Patriarchy suggested that men could transcend their bodies while women and the poor could not; to which Shelley's answer is Victor's swooning body. There is also the issue of how and why we attach ourselves to certain forms of the body. To the extent that EC assumes the body's efficacy lies within its necessary connectedness to its environment, it ignores how cognition traffics in abstraction, not to mention how system thinking and learning require abstraction and how creativity plays with environment. Within the cognitive sciences, perhaps it is high time to work on the biology of abstraction, and to remember that abstraction from one's present moment and surround is also valuable to survival, as when we contemplate and imagine the future. Of course, as Shelley recognizes, abstraction has its dangers, too.

Embodied cognition thus raises hard questions that must more fully be reckoned with. That Victor's egoism and narcissism are actually symptomatic of his embodied state as much or more so than his mind raises the issue of what kind of body we are presuming. What appeases us so that we accept the body's elevation in the form of the visual system into a cognitive law? More crucially, as in embodied cognition, embodiment has epistemological consequences, and not just the ones we want, because it is through our bodies and our feelings that we apprehend reality. Although feltness would seem to help us distinguish between reality and delusion, the fact of the matter is because we feel the virtual reality of our imaginations, and our imagined stimuli are processed through the same system as our perceptions. If feltness offers the signature of reality as Barrett insists, we need protocols in place so we can distrust it. Hence Shelley has us meditate upon the paradoxes of Walton's working to feel cold in the Arctic, and Victor's early assessment of the monster's body as beautiful. To overcome the problem of imagined sensation's ability to supplement actual sensation, which Hume insisted was not possible, Shelley turns to embodiment to warn us of the costs of enthusiastic idealism, but she was too aware of context to assume that the body could deliver what is promised in its name. Although Victor Frankenstein abuses idealism, Shelley's exploitation of form recognizes how abstraction makes both skepticism and questions of methodology possible. Crucially, it allows an embodied imagination to consider what embodied cognition leaves behind, and why the body cannot be fully trusted.

Notes

1   S. D. Goldinger et al., "The Poverty of Embodied Cognition," *Psychonomic Bulletin and Review* 23, no. 4 (2016). Thanks to Orrin Wang for his perceptive suggestions.

2   Rom Harré, *Cognitive Science: A Philosophical Introduction* (London: Sage, 2002), 1. Harré asks in his introduction to cognitive science, what is cognition, and he declares that "in scientific matters it is unwise to set up hard and fast definitions. It is better to list some examples of what a general concept covers, and to add an etcetera!" In this way, new examples have the power to change the argument, for good and ill.

3   Joseph LeDoux. *The Deep History of Ourselves* (New York: Viking, 2019), 244–5.

4   Shaun Gallagher, *How the Body Shapes the Mind* (Oxford: Clarendon Press, 2005), 24–5, 26, 28, 10. Gallagher, for instance, welds the body to cognition by turning to "body image," defining it as an "intentional state," and then giving it "an active role in shaping our perceptions." How do these categories shape the evidence? He moreover "assumes" "when we are not perceptually attentive to the body, we still may have some degree of marginal awareness of it." In 2017, he acknowledges that the enactivist claim is not "environment determines representational content," but then goes on to give the examples where the disconnection from the surround is an "imbalance of neurotransmitters." "Disconnection" of course makes connection the default. Stanislas Dehaene in *How We Learn* (New York: Viking, 2020) argues that abstraction allows human learning to be superior to artificial intelligence, chapter 2 especially. He suggests that learning is about finding the grammar of the domain in question (35).

5   Catherine Malabou, *What Should We Do with Our Brain?* (New York: Fordham University Press, 2008), 63.

6   David Herman, "Narrative Theory after the Second Cognitive Revolution," in *Introduction to Cognitive Cultural Studies*, ed. Lisa Zunshine (Baltimore: Johns Hopkins University Press, 2010), 165.

7   Shaun Gallagher, *Enactivist Interventions: Rethinking the Mind* (Oxford: Oxford University Press, 2017), 9.

8   Ibid., 1.

9   Francisco Varela, Evan Thompson, and Eleanor Rosch, *The Embodied Mind* (Cambridge: MIT Press, 1991), 16.

10   Ibid., 8.

11   Andy Clark, *Surfing Uncertainty: Prediction, Action, and the Embodied Mind* (New York: Oxford University Press, 2016), 249.

12   Alva Noë, *Out of Our Heads* (New York: Hill and Wang, 2009), 49.

13   Gallagher, *How the Body Shapes the Mind*, 29–30. Look at all the instances in which Gallagher qualifies his connections between body and cognition with "can" or "may." On a page and a half, he qualifies his statements no less than eight times. These qualifications undermine the necessity of the body's cognitive causality. See also Piotr

Winkielman and Liam Kavanagh, "The Embodied Perspective on Cognition-Emotion Interactions," in *Handbook of Cognition and Emotion*, ed. Michael Robinson, Edward Watkins, and Eddie Harmon-Jones (New York: Guilford Press, 2013): 213–30. They consider Jean Mandler's thesis that "embodied processing may be progressively replaced by more abstract general reasoning representations" (217).

14   Lorraine Daston, *Against Nature* (Cambridge: MIT Press, 2019), 60.

15   Colin Jager, "Can We Talk about Consciousness Again? Emergence, Natural Piety, Wordsworth," *Romantic Circles Praxis,* Special Volume on *Romantic Frictions* (2011): Section 4. https://romantic-circles.org/praxis/frictions/HTML/praxis.2011.jager.html.

16   Gallagher, *How the Body Shapes the Mind*, 142. See also Jesse Prinz, *The Conscious Brain* (Oxford: Oxford University Press, 2012), 182–3. Because of all the cross-talk between dorsal and ventral visual systems, Prinz rejects the two-system model.

17   Mark Bruhn, "Romanticism and the Cognitive Science of Imagination," *Studies in Romanticism* 48 (2009): 549–55. Bruhn is the most abstract of these critics, and he considers how literary Romanticism can deepen thought experiments within cognitive science. His attention to "blending"—the fact we live in conceptual blends between sensation and perception—connects him to embodied cognition. Robertson is at work on a book on the Embodied Imagination in Romanticism.

18   George Rousseau, *Nervous Acts* (Houndmills: Palgrave Macmillan, 2004).

19   Alan Richardson, *British Romanticism and the Science of Mind* (Cambridge: Cambridge University Press, 2001).

20   Alan Richardson, *The Neural Sublime* (Baltimore: Johns Hopkins University Press, 2010).

21   John Savarese, "Wordsworth between Minds," *Romantic Circles Praxis*, Special Volume on *Multi-media Romanticisms* (2016): 12. https://romantic-circles.org/praxis/multi-media/praxis.2016.multi-media.savarese.html.

22   John Savarese, *Romanticism's Other Minds* (Columbus: Ohio State University Press, 2019).

23   Lisa Ann Robertson, "Enacting the Absolute: Subject-Object Relations in Samuel Taylor Coleridge's Theory of Knowledge," in *Distributed Cognition in Enlightenment and Romantic Culture*, ed. Miranda Anderson, George Rousseau, and Michael Wheeler (Edinburgh: Edinburgh University Press, 2019), 125. She argues here that Coleridge understands knowledge to emerge at the intersection of subject and object.

24   Mary Shelley, *Frankenstein* (Oxford: Oxford University Press, 1993). Page references to this edition are cited parenthetically in the text throughout this chapter.

25   Immanuel Kant, *Critique of Pure Reason*, trans. Werner Pluhar (Indianapolis: Hackett Publishing, 1996), 342.

26   Colin Jager, "Can We Talk about Consciousness Again."

27   Richard Terdiman, *Body and Story: The Ethics and Practice of Theoretical Conflict* (Baltimore: Johns Hopkins University Press, 2005).

28   Peter Brooks, *Body Work* (Cambridge: Harvard University Press, 1993).

29   Lisa Feldman Barrett, *How Emotions Are Made* (Boston: Houghton Mifflin Harcourt, 2017), 282.

30   Malabou, *What Should We Do with Our Brain?*, 24.

31   Brooks, *Body Work*, 7.

32   Constantina Papoulias and Felicity Callard, "Biology's Gift: Interrogating the Turn to Affect," *Body and Society* 16, no. 1 (2010).

33 Leo Bersani, "Why Sex?," Keynote Address at the Conference of the Society for Psychoanalytic Inquiry, Chicago, Illinois, 2014. https://www.youtube.com/watch?v=qwRAJdAMYV0.

34 Brooks, *Body Work*, 204.

35 Papoulias and Callard, "Biology's Gift," 33–4.

36 Ibid., 41.

37 Guy Dove, "How to Go beyond the Body: An Introduction," *Frontiers in Psychology* 6, no. 660 (2015), 10.3389/fpsyg.2015.00660. In pondering where to go next in "embodied cognition," Dove highlights the absence of work on how the mind abstracts.

38 Rodolfo Llinás, *I of the Vortex: From Neurons to Self* (Cambridge: MIT Press, 2001), 57.

39 Ibid., 74.

40 Frans De Waal, *Mama's Last Hug* (New York: W. W. Norton, 2019), 103–4. Hence de Waal argues that empathy is a neutral capacity, and can be used for sake of cruelty.

41 Robert M. Sapolsky, *Behave* (New York: Penguin Books, 2017), 387–91.

42 Ibid., 169.

43 Paul Bloom, *Against Empathy* (New York: HarperCollins, 1993).

44 Kristen Monroe, *Ethics in an Age of Terror and Genocide* (Princeton: Princeton University Press, 2012), 265.

45 Ibid., 75–7.

46 Ibid., 284.

47 Colin Jager and John Savarese, "Cognition, Culture, Romanticism: A Review Essay," *Romanticism and Victorianism on the Net*, no. 57–8 (2010): paragraph 12, 10.7202/1006519ar.

48 Goldinger et al., "Poverty of Embodied Cognition," 973–4 and Prinz, *Conscious Brain*, 170–85. Prinz undermines much of the main evidence cited for enaction. As he puts it, "recognition is not sufficient for action" (196). He also asks: must consciousness only have the one function of action (204)? For defenses of embodied cognition, see Michael Wheeler, "In Defense of Extended Functionalism," in *The Extended Mind*, ed. Richard Menary (Cambridge: MIT Press); Kinga Woloszyn and Mateusz Hohol, "In Defense of Extended Functionalism," *Frontiers in Psychology* 8 (2017); Gallagher, *Enactivist Interventions*; and Gallagher, *How Body Shapes the Mind*.

49 Ibid., 961.

50 The discipline of behavioral economics is given over to the idea that if we come to terms with how poor our decision-making processes are, we might actually make better decisions. See Daniel Kahneman, *Thinking Fast and Slow* (New York: Farrar, Straus, and Giroux, 2011); Richard Thaler, *Misbehaving* (New York: W. W. Norton, 2015); and Dan Ariely, *Predictably Irrational* (New York: Harper Perennial, 2008).

51 Gallagher, *Enactivist Interventions*, 187–212. Gallagher addresses the scaling up problem—that EC has been better at dealing with basic processes involving perception and action that do not necessarily need representation. Because imagination is "representation hungry," it requires such scaling up.

52 Nancy Yousef, *Isolated Cases* (Ithaca: Cornel University Press, 2004), 161.

53 Dove, "How to Go beyond the Body," 1; Gallagher, *Enactivist Interventions*, 193. Dove states that EC researchers have recently acknowledged that "embodiment might be context dependent and come in degrees." Tellingly, Gallagher defines imagination in terms of "active engagement with possibilities," leaving out the possibility of disengagement.

54 Gallagher, *How Body Shapes the Mind*, 32–3; Gallagher, *Enactivist Interventions*, 191. Proponents of EC step around this problem by claiming that "bodily schemas" undergird the pre-noetic (before thought). In this view, cognition structures pre-thought. Another way is to collapse thinking, imagining, and doing.

55 Barrett, *How Emotions Are Made*, 280, 286. Barrett argues that emotions are concepts built by social consensus. On the one hand, concepts help us make predictions. On the other hand, "concepts also encourage us not to see what is present." Barrett helps us see the lability of embodiment, and the possibility of seeing the emotions as concepts.

56 Ellen Goldner, "Monstrous Body, Tortured Soul: Frankenstein at the Juncture between Discourses," in *Genealogy and Literature*, ed. Lee Quimby (Minneapolis: University of Minnesota Press, 1995); Paul Youngquist, *Monstrosities: Bodies and British Romanticism* (Minneapolis: University of Minnesota Press, 2003). For instance, Goldner situates Frankenstein between Foucault's discourse of the public body and private soul. Youngquist reads bodies in Romanticism as the subjects of intense normalization.

57 Barbara Johnson, "My Monster/My Self," Reprinted in *A Life with Mary Shelley*, 15–26 (Stanford: Stanford University Press, 2014).

58 G. J. Barker-Benfield, *The Culture of Sensibility* (Boston: Houghton Mifflin Harcourt, 1992). Barker-Benfield ties sensibility to the growth of consumer culture, adding another layer.

59 Steven Goldsmith, *Blake's Agitation* (Baltimore: Johns Hopkins University Press, 2013), 268–316.

60 Catherine Packham, *Eighteenth-Century Vitalism: Bodies, Culture, Politics* (Houndmills: Palgrave Macmillan, 2012), 6.

61 Noë, *Out of Our Heads*, 41.

62 Robert Mitchell, *Experimental Life* (Baltimore: Johns Hopkins University Press, 2013).

63 Stuart Curran, "*Frankenstein*: Matters of Fact," Keynote Address at Mary Shelley Circuits and Circulation Conference, Bologna, Italy, September 2018.

4

Non-Binary *Frankenstein*?

Chris Washington

Several years ago, the seemingly impossible befell the world: *Sesame Street*'s Cookie Monster began advocating that humans put down that plate of over-sugared baked goods and—*quelle horreur*—de-cookie by eating more vegetables. The Cookie Monster made this radical suggestion in counterpoint to the obesity epidemic in the United States and he claimed, shockingly, that even he, now, was gobbling down on vegetables primarily and was only an occasional Cookie Monster. Something like hysteria exploded across the social media landscape of the time. It centered on the waggish suggestion that the Cookie Monster could not be the Cookie Monster any more, that he had somehow abandoned his very ontological self. What, we may well ask, happens to a Cookie Monster that no longer eats cookies? This question, at least, was the Wittgensteinian ostensive worry over his self and the name attached to that self when he announced his vegetarianism. If the Cookie Monster, the thinking went, with his newfound kale salads and crudité gluttony, was no longer living on an exclusive cookie diet, then can it be said that he is still the Cookie Monster and not something totally, ontologically different, the Kale Monster? What, after all, are the ontological ramifications of eating for a monster, especially if its diet falls outside the hegemonic parameters of normative eating associated with gender politics wherein men are associated with meat-eating and women with vegetarianism, as Carol Adams has painstakingly shown in *The Sexual Politics of Meat*? And what, moreover, are the ontological implications of a name for a monster, even one partially named monster?

While it will take some time to return to this question of monsters and diet, regarding names I want to provisionally say that to appellate a monster "monster" is to give it a name without naming it, to insist on the nominative problems with which Romanticism, in its apocalyptic mode, and all that this mode has long entailed, begins: in the beginning, or shortly thereafter, in Paradise, Adam provided a name to every creature on earth. In the ideology of this fantasy world, the signifier exactly ontologically represents the signified: Adam is an Adam; Eve is an Eve; a giraffe is a giraffe; a man is a man; a woman is a woman; a monster is a monster. If we think of Romanticism as a story about the reclamation of this Paradise through a transcendental merger of subject and object—a certain critical lineage of high Wordsworthianism—then it is also the case that Romanticism, in this mode, is the attempt to name conventionally, to rest in the comfort of normative nominative protocols. One can picture the creature in Mary Shelley's *Frankenstein* (1818) reading this very story about Adam and Eden naming the world of nonhumans in book VIII of *Paradise Lost*. Let's say, then, that this type of conservative ideological normativization reinforces the idea that gender and the names that typically attach to gender cohere at some ontological metaphysical and material level. Let's also say, then, that apocalyptic Romanticism invests in and advances a conservative cisheteropatriarchal biopolitics through its Eurocentric Christological psychobiographizing in that it abides by this narrative of perfectly representative ontological nomination.

But what I've called, in *Romantic Revelations*, "post-apocalyptic Romanticism" dismisses a return to Paradise in the *apocalypsis* (revelation of or return to a perfect world) sense of apocalypse and chooses, rather, to break with these cisheteropatriarchal nominative protocols.[1] Percy Shelley, for instance, on his reading of this Christian fantasy in *A Defence of Poetry*, is aware of the perils of its gender apocalypse and suggests, instead, a post-apocalyptic Romanticism that frees women—and we might even say gender and sexed difference—from slavery: "a Paradise was created out of the wrecks of Eden."[2] By breaking with that Edenic tradition, post-apocalyptic Romanticism does not attempt to name the unnameable, to give a name to the monster, the monstrous, that precedes, antecedes, and especially exceeds Paradise's normativizing nominativism. That is to say, a monster, according to its very (no)name, has no gender, has no name, and is simply something unfathomable, a namelessness that can never be named since naming it would mean it was no longer a monster but something more recognizably like a person complete with a gender identity normatively implied by whatever signifying name it takes. The Cookie Monster becomes Bert or Ernie, even Big Bird, one more gendered creature amongst other anthropomorphized yet gendered creatures. Post-apocalyptic Romanticism in this register is not then the search for a name, but rather the search to think existence outside the semantic field of perfect ontological cohesive representations of the signifier and signified, of subject and object.

Romanticism of this sort is in fact like the creature, nameless and, let us say, non-binary in terms of how Susan Stryker defines non-binary as revolting against heteropatronymy: "an emerging terminological preference among younger generations who consider binary gender identity to be something more relevant to their grandparents than to themselves."[3] Maybe, then, this type of Romanticism even *is* the creature since he has no grandparents. And, moreover, as Nancy Yousef points out in her reading of John Locke's *Essay Concerning Human Understanding* and the novel, nor does the creature have any parents since, for Locke, like the creature, existence begins, as David Collings puts it, "as if one comes into being like another Adam, without parents, guardians, or friends."[4] Post-apocalyptic Romanticism, however, finds a friend in what Kate Singer writes in *Romantic Vacancy*, her remarkably field-defining revision of Romanticism: "by breaking free from gendered bodies and spaces, vacancy opens a non-binary landscape of transgressive figurative motions."[5] Rejecting binaristic figurative and material structures, post-apocalyptic Romanticism breaks with whatever narratives and traditions it follows. In that sense, post-apocalyptic Romanticism might even drop the post-apocalyptic label and even the name Romanticism itself to give voice to this radical break.

In what follows, I propose to try to think this Romanticism—a label I will retain for now for narrative convenience if not coherence—in the spirit of Singer's non-binaristic vacancy and in the spirit of what Stefano Harney and Fred Moten call "the undercommons," the resistance from underneath, from the vanished, or evanishing, point of social life, against those hegemonic forces of authoritarian fascist biopolitical control that control by means of ignoring, silencing, shaming, blaming even, in the case of many, refusing a, their, name.[6] This type of undercommons Romanticism tarries in the post-apocalyptic wake of namelessness, and, in doing so, finds its peace in what happens at the end of the world, after the Paradise of applied nominatives, after the Edenic wreck, an end of the world then that is the beginning of a new one, a world-to-come, perhaps, even, I will argue, what has otherwise been called a justice-to-come. Collings's "monstrous 'man'" friends us, too, then, in that Collings is right that Shelley recognizes "the justice of his [the creature's] claims," although, I think, not the "humanity" of them, as Collings claims, but, as we will see, the nonhumanity of justice—which is to say justice can only emerge from the nonhuman—that the creature's existence allows.[7]

Perhaps it might do to begin somewhere then, with a strange comment by Jacques Derrida that has long confounded critical commentary and explication:

> Here there is a sort of question, call it historical, of which we are only glimpsing today the conception, the formation, the gestation, the labor. I employ these words, I admit, with a glance toward the business of child-bearing—but also with a glance toward those who, in a company from which I do not exclude myself, turn their eyes away in the face of the as yet unnameable which is proclaiming itself and which can do so, as is necessary whenever a birth is in the offing, only under the species of the non-species, in the formless, mute, infant, and terrifying form of monstrosity.[8]

This passage, Derrida's famous ending to his "Structure, Sign, and Play in the Discourse of the Human Sciences," closes his essay's long deconstruction of Levi-Strauss's structuralism. Of interest, to me, is the language Derrida employs and the parturient resonances it has for Shelley's novel. It employs a willful binaristic logics of childbearing which, of course, implies, usually, a male/female normative reproductive cycle—and which Derrida himself acknowledges by glancing at—even as it heralds the justice-to-come that preoccupies later Derrida-writing that Derrida here cannot anticipate: that which is incalculable and is therefore unanticipatable and what Derrida will otherwise eventually call justice, the justice-to-come in the proleptic posterity of what deconstruction wants to have wrought in its attempt to escape the binary of its own binaristic investigation of the metaphysics of presence.

Leaving aside whether or not deconstruction ever does, or can, work its way beyond the aporia of the binary, or merely reproduces it in some kind of unconscious parturient *mise en abyme* logic as outside the scope of this essay, the figuration and figure of the "unnameable," the "monstrosity"-to-come, I think it is safe to say, eerily recall *Frankenstein* in many ways, not least in its language of "the species of the non-species." Victor puts it this way in the novel: "a new species would bless me as its creator and source; many happy and excellent natures would owe their being to me. No father could claim the gratitude of his child so completely as I should deserve their's."[9] We might object to Victor's patronymic exergue that the creature stands out as a species of one but we might say, as well, that such logic is precisely why the creature ultimately seeks, it seems, to replicate the binaristic logic of the two-sex model when he requests Victor fashion him a female companion. He has been acculturated by Victor's two-sex hegemonic sensibilities even if, for the creature, a patronymic name is occluded and exorbitant. The creature, this lone representative of a monstrous species, in wishing for a companion, gives voice to his desire, his species-of-one biopolitical yearning to multiply his own species. Or so it seems. But we must recall a crucial detail: that the libidinal economy of reproductive two-sex desire is Victor's—the creature, in fact, never suggests children nor does he imply that his female "Eve" be sexed, that is, that "Eve" participate in replicating the binary of that two-sex model. The creature, instead, exemplifies what David Sigler observes in his incisive study of sexual enjoyment in the period, that the "range of possible sexualities within British Romanticism is much broader than the usual binaries."[10] The creature visions an enbie world.

What the creature does give "birth" to, in what we might see as a subtle, or explicit, or non-libidinal economy that whipsaws across the novel and does not square with Victor's cishetereopatriarchal speciesist biopolitics, is the idea of an ontologically strange "birth" ideation. The creature finds no binary match when he is "born" for the irrevocable fact that he is not born. He has no parents in the sense that we use as one measure to make sense of biopolitical hetero-sense. Initially, he has no ideas even about what constitutes the two-sex family proper. Even his idea of a father comes via a *via negativa* exemplar, which is to say that his idea of a father descends from not having a father, biologically or socially, which abrogates the law of the father entirely. He syncretizes his idea of a father from the crude and cruel textual allegory he derives from his backtracked reading of Victor's diary he has obliviously backpacked for so long. Therefore, Victor, for the creature, has no patronymic name at all, not even the nominative, father, beyond what he later recursively ascribes to Victor as a result of his multinational found-poem reading syllabus of Milton, Goethe, and Plutarch, and the De Lacey's ostensive pedagogy. Initially he, of course, has no mother either. Neither a he, nor a she, was there at the primal scene of his creation. This literal rather than psychoanalytical lack is what, in heteronormative terms, would be called strange. It means that both Victor and the creature—the former literally and the latter literally and figuratively—give birth to what is not even, properly speaking, a species because what they both birth by non-birthing is a kind of non-birth. The process of non-literal birth here is rather a paradoxical process of literal birthlessness.

We can see this play out in the creature's request for a female Eve in that, ultimately, this request eventuates in the creation of a not-new species but does so only because the creature is left alone, with no possibility of another of his species, in the novel's logic that speaks to its own desire to avoid orthodox cisheteronormative biopolitics and instead example a futural justice-to-come outside all such logics. Since a mortal species requires two to avoid extinction, then the creature is, perforce, a species that manifests a non-species, a species that is not a species, a non-binaristic being. As such, the creature is neither ontologically alive nor dead in the sense that humans understand, by one measure at least, life and death in and through the concept of species. He exceeds the binaries of the species and the non-species and of the living and the dead. He was, we might also recall, created from bits and pieces of the living and the dead and the human and nonhuman, merging what cannot be merged into a blurring of non-binaristic boundaries that are more than dialogical or dialectical. Therefore, we can say, however provisional this may end up, that he precedes, antecedes, and exceeds himself, his own existence, and is, in this sense, not constrained by the binaries of the metaphysics of presence. He is a monstrosity-to-come that has never yet arrived but is always already here whenever a non-birth is in the offing. And if this logic itself begins to sound faintly in- or a-human, then we might do well to dwell in this space, this new spacetime as Karen Barad would call it, this in-, non-, and a-human space of the nameless creature within which, maybe, the non-nominative of the monstrous, this "mute" silence, can give voice to the voiceless and the voicelessnessed of Romanticism that demands many names outside the plenitude of ontological binaristic presence.[11] It is in this voicelessness and namelessness—in the wake and break of nominative gender politics like Singer's Romantic vacancy—that the inhuman logic of the creature exceeds Romanticism itself, is one of, but not the, undercommons of Romanticism.

Following these Romanticisms—vacancy and the undercommons—my essay ultimately seeks to retheorize moribund social constructivists accounts of Romantic sex and gender circulating since 1980s-era literary criticism that continue to persist and insist—however willfully or unwittingly—on a binaristic or universalistic normativity. Perhaps, unsurprisingly, given the dominance of Michel Foucault's and Judith Butler's work, gender studies deriving from that work remain mired in social constructivism, no doubt because neither Foucault nor Butler ever totally came to grips with how physical materiality is not just a product of discursive sociality. While it would be reductive simply to understand Foucaultian discourse as an idealist manifestation of language, his and Butler's shared (though admittedly different) focus on the semiotic, ideologically driven dimensions of bodies has led to an erasure of non-binary and transgender difference even while their work also implicitly provides warm room for those differences. As Anson Koch-Rein argues, drawing on Foucault's *Abnormal* lectures, "the transgender monster preexists transgender as a term. Despite the term's much more recent specific emergence, then, transgender has long been part of monstrosity's history and historicity" and "the transgender monster has also been part of *Frankenstein*'s literary history for quite some time."[12]

Nonetheless, a great deal of post-Foucaultian, post-Butlerian critical accounts are also firmly anthropocentric, offering little flexibility to engage the neither-human-nor-nonhuman non-binary of *Frankenstein*'s creature in all of their material forms. Romantic feminist scholar Anne Mellor, for instance, notes the dubious nature of the masculine/feminine binary—yet she retains the human/nonhuman binary.[13] In contrast, I want to argue, *Frankenstein*'s non-binary thinking provides resources for moving forward from the confines of the discursive prison of gender that retains within it, however unwittingly or unwillingly, a binarism between the masculine and feminine, the human and the nonhuman. Theorists like Stryker, Barad, and Jack Halberstam have helped explode social constructivism as a naïve although well-meaning politics that strove to resist mansplaining essentialist cisheteropatriarchy by demystifying it as the bad harmful fiction it is. Non-binary thinking, in this way, does not return us to a bad essentialism or a cisheteropatriarchal phallogocentrism but rather fashions radical new ways to theorize the material body *and* discursive constructions of sexes and genders. For one, non-binary thinking theorizes that biological materiality does not reify gender but can unravel the hierarchized binaristic social constructions of gender just as such social constructions have already upended the orthodox binaries that supposedly inhered in the materiality of biologized bodies and their attendant rigidly policed cultural categorizations. To put it another way, "sex" and "gender" do not have stable meanings that are by any means materialistically or culturally clear and should not be stabilized absolutely. Rather, sexes and genders are up for constantly shifting, individual definitional grabs.

The task, then, is to see how the novel, and how the creature, defines the creature since Shelley's *Frankenstein* has very often been read from a social constructivist perspective, a commonality across otherwise wildly divergent theoretical vantages—critical race studies, deconstruction, ecocriticism, to name a few—while the novel's non-binary and transgender thinking has largely gone unnoticed in critical Romantic accounts of it, outside of Koch-Rein's aforementioned "*Trans*-lating the Monster." So while, as Jolene Zigarovich has demonstrated, Stryker's classic essay, "My Words to Victor Frankenstein above the Village of Chamounix—Performing Transgender Rage," has founded what Zigarovich helpfully refers to as the "trans monstrosity" genre and has had a definitive impact on queer Gothic studies as well, it has seen little discussion by Romantic scholars.[14] Meanwhile, in trans studies, as a result of Stryker's essay, *Frankenstein* readings have taken a curious shape that defies and broadens parameters of what literary criticism can be—very little Romantic scholarship would recognize it. Almost always these essays that follow Stryker's hybridize the critical and the poetic, the personal and the political, a merger often meant to mirror the stitched-together, plotted-and-piecedness, of the creature's bodily creation. Indeed, in Stryker's essay and some of its descendants, the creature is a representational stand-in for the author insofar as the creature's monstrousness—its body that exceeds the cultural bounds of gender—corresponds to how trans bodies are viewed by the culture they are embedded within.

Stryker, for instance, asserts that the term "monster" needs "to be reclaimed by [the] transgendered."[15] This recovery would, she says, help transgender persons acknowledge their "egalitarian relationship with non-human material Being."[16] She then implores non-transgender persons to also realize their own material, rather than just social, constructedness, their own sutured-together bodies. Despite the clear boundary-breaking upshot of this gesture for transgender people, we might pause and consider how her reading nonetheless appears to recall a Butlerian social construction theory of gender that equivocates about the material real-ness of the body, similar to what Barad points out in her critique of Butler in their *Meeting the Universe Halfway* (2007) and Barad's subsequent essays on transmateriality which assert a materiality that entangles any social constructivism with the biological vitality it purports to live against. On Stryker's reading of the novel, everyone becomes a monster.

This social and ontological flattening would seem to exactly opposite-day the creature's ontological point that difference cannot be universalized to a speciesist "we" that excludes in its grammatical claim to inclusion. For if, as Stryker says, the monster of Shelley's novel reminds us that all human-ness is materially constructed then Stryker's argument, for all of its good intentions, would seem to erase difference by depressing bodies into a metaphysical and material universalism, to configure the trans-ed body as one more body amongst others, one more monster among monsters—which would, it follows, mean that there are no monsters and transgender people either. Stryker thereby runs the risk of eliding the very transgender differences she seeks to spotlight and champion.

On my reading, which owes much to Stryker's, Shelley's creature represents a proliferation of difference in that he/she/they establishes a trans-ness exorbitant to the binaristic logics of sex and gender. It is for this reason that the creature also stresses that the biopolitical reproductive drive of the human species configures humans as the real monsters they think they are not since this drive requires the destruction of the nonhuman for sustenance. This is, as we will see, one reason that the creature's food in his imagined paradise is "not that of man" (103). The monster, it seems, stands outside the monstrosity of the monster Stryker is trying to recover here; *Frankenstein's* "monster" would, *de facto* and *de jure*, be even more monstrous in that he/she/they is non-binaristic in terms of gender and species, neither male nor female, neither human nor nonhuman, but both both *neither* and *both* of those binaries *and* something else entirely.

Halberstam's more recent *Trans**: *A Quick and Quirky Account of Gender* (2018) provides a different way to think "trans*" that, I think, elucidates how *Frankenstein* thinks the non-binary. Halberstam defines trans* with an asterisk as a term for "unfolding categories of being organized around but not confined to forms of gender variance."[17] The "asterisk modifies the meaning of transitivity by refusing to situate transition in relation to a destination, a final form, a specific shape, or an established configuration of desire and identity."[18] Trans* "makes trans* people the authors of their own categorizations."[19] Along these non-telic definitional lines, I want to argue that the creature in *Frankenstein*, in similar ways to how Halberstam defines "trans*," exemplifies a non-binary being materially, socially, and ontologically, one who does not desire a celebratory reclamation of monstrosity that reifies a human and nonhuman binary. For the creature, ontology *itself* is trans* in that difference proliferates and is proliferating without any telos or desire for telos. But it would be more accurate to say that for the creature trans* is both interminable and paraontological, to borrow from Marquis Bey's reading of Fred Moten's idea of Blackness, in that trans* and Blackness come before and after ontology itself since both are anoriginal and differentiating. In Bey's words trans* and Black, "they are differently inflected names for an anoriginal lawlessness that marks an escape from confinement and a besidedness to ontology."[20] They "precede and provide the foundational condition for those fugitive identificatory demarcations."[21] The creature, thinking trans*itivity as paraontological, illustrates how non-binary, non-telic temporality stages justice-to-come as itself interminable—small wonder Jeanette Winterson has recently re-envisioned the novel as a trans*narrative novel, *Frankissstein*.[22]

But can we actually think the creature in terms of an an-original, paraontological trans*ness or does this reading, like Stryker's, stray from its good intentions into an unwitting return to a repressed social constructivism by making ontological claims its culturally bound reality will not allow it to cash? Literary scholarship on the novel is certainly liberally peppered with a nascent awareness of the creature's possible trans*-ness, which makes allegorical sense given what Jeffrey Jerome Cohen writes of monsters in general, that "any kind of alterity can be inscribed across (constructed through) the monstrous body, but for the most part monstrous difference tends to be cultural, political, racial, economic, sexual."[23] Elizabeth Young's *Black Frankenstein*, for instance, discerns a racial metaphor in the text adopted by and propelling American literary cultural mythmaking—and it is easy to find such ideas in readings of race in Romantic studies proper.[24] A nascent suspicion of the novel's trans*ness is similarly discernable in its traces in Romantic scholarship. Peter Brooks's psychoanalytic reading postulates that "a monster may also be that which eludes gender definition," or, even that "the monster would thus be a woman, but a woman who would answer Freud's infamous question 'What does a woman want?' with the ostensible reply: to be a male, with a female to love," the latter a working theory that Sandra Gilman and Susan Gubar beat him to in their suggestive comment, "Victor Frankenstein's male monster may really be a female in disguise."[25] Even such resolute men-are-from-Mars-women-are-from-Venus scholars like Mary Poovey and Mellor note the socially constructed similarity of reality and materiality for the creature and for women.[26] But much like Butler who, reflecting on Barbara Johnson's famous "My Monster/My Self" essay, allows that the creature "might have both male and female, an excess of gender," these are all wobbly asseverations on the creature that pivot around a deep investment in a second-wave feminism whose thinking cannot quite escape the two-sex model's binary grasp.[27]

Frankenstein is different, I would argue, as the ontological conditions of the creature's very being instances: as we saw, he/she/they is neither alive nor dead, human nor nonhuman, and, in the multiplicity of his/her/their non-being, eludes and elides the cultural designations that would confirm "him" as male or female and sets "him" as a manifestation of paraontological trans*ness. Whatever his/her/their body might consist of, and we don't know due to Victor's willfully frustrating vagueness on most points concerning the primal scene of his primal elements of creation, his/her/their emplacement in society trans*verses gender altogether. He/she/them is unrecognizable as anything familiar or human and therefore is labeled, named, a monster, something that by its definitional nature is unknown and unnameable. The creature is thus something paraontological that originates outside of all origin and destination and a being who is still to-come, even to his/her/theirself, because he/she/

they does not know, epistemologically, what he/she/them is and is unknowable in his/her/their being, unbearable within the physical and metaphysical frameworks of the world in which he/she/them cannot actually be said to exist, and does not, throughout the novel, as yet, exist in the epistemological and ontological theories that structure cisheteronormative personhood.

Walton, for instance, notes the creature's epistemological and ontological maladaptation, shall we say, in the only word amongst the self-proclaimingly misunderstanding mélange of words he uses that actually captures, or names, anything accurate about the creature—that the creature is "unearthly" (158). Otherwise, Walton places his own words under erasure, covering up his own footprints in his metaphorical snow, so to speak, with each step: "over him hung a form which I cannot find words to describe; gigantic in stature, yet uncouth and distorted in its proportions" (158). He cannot find the words to describe this creature but then, as if he finds his way with words within the caesura of the semicolon, looses a volley of words to describe the creature. He describes what cannot be described even while, having done that which he said is not possible while actually doing so, judges it to be not a description, not a real description since signifiers, apparently, are inadequate to adequately describe the signified of the creature they must adequate. To put it differently, he names what cannot be named and in doing so evidences that that cannot be named. This paradoxical erasure imparts a different significance to what he then says immediately afterwards: "never did I behold a vision so horrible as his face" (158). "Never," indeed, because within the acculturating logic he operates within, he never has beheld "him" since to behold "him," just as the act of naming him unnames him, unbeholds him. More than just the blind De Lacey, no human being can behold the creature in the fullness of his ontology since the creature's ontology itself cannot, or more accurately, does not, behold the creature himself insofar as it instantiates he/she/them physically for the empirical eye that nineteenth-century, and even contemporary, beliefs in the epistemology that underwrite ontology require for gender and normative nomination.

Several understudied passages in the novel, I think, surprisingly, allow us to see how the creature's paraontological, anoriginal trans*ness appears in what are otherwise considered background scenes of little importance. In this regard, it is as if trans*ness, paraontologically, can only be fleetingly glimpsed, which is appropriate because that is the only way paraontology can be "seen"—in the glimpse of its impossibility in the gleamingly possible.

One of these passages occurs directly after the creature's creation. Having recovered from what we might cheekily call his post-partum paroxysms, Victor throws over his scientific ambitions entirely and turns to the study of international literature alongside Henry:

> I felt great relief in being the fellow-pupil with my friend, and found not only instruction but consolation in the works of the orientalists. Their melancholy is soothing, and their joy elevating to a degree I never experienced in studying the authors of any other country. When you read their writings, life appears to consist in a warm sun and garden of roses, in the smiles and frowns of a fair enemy, and

the fire that consumes your own heart. How different from the manly and heroical
poetry of Greece and Rome. (44–5)

Victor's orientalism does more than indulge a Eurocentric ethnocentrism that divides
the world; it also cleaves the world into feminine and masculine halves, the Greeks
and Romans of classical antiquity authoring a "manly" poetics of epic ambition while
"oriental" authors compose something feminine in nature that is, for reasons left
unstated, also melancholic. It is as if Victor unconsciously recalls and pedagogically
mobilizes and mechanizes Aristophanes's encomium on love about androgynous
bodies in Plato's *Symposium* as a mode of viable literary explication. That text, perhaps
familiar to both Shelleys, as Percy would go on to translate this text in 1818, has
perhaps unsurprising resonances here. Victor baldly splits the West and the East like
the original bodies of human beings in Aristophanes's speech are split when Jupiter
divides the children of the sun, and the earth, and the moon into separate halves.
The spheres become two, with the masculine sun-children now two male bodies, the
feminine earth-children two females, and the androgynous moon-children a male and
a female. Love, according to Aristophanes, is a phenomenon that takes place physically
as the two male halves try to find their other half, the two females theirs, and the male
and female likewise.

What is strange in Victor's theory of literature, though, is that a two-sex
cisheteropatriarchy world would, perforce, develop from an androgynous
undercommons of the binary, the lunar Western male and Eastern female bodies in
desperate search for their other. Shelley captures this well in his translation, with echoes
of it pulsing in his fragmentary "On Love": "human beings were formerly not divided
into two sexes, male and female; there was also a third, common to both the others, the
name of which remains, though the sex itself has disappeared. The androgynous sex,
both in appearance and name, was common to both the male and female."[28] This is to say,
then, that Victor's unconscious, accidental, extemporaneous invention of Aristophanic
lit crit would necessitate a cisheteropatriachy based, not in social Eastern and Western
orientalism constructions Edward Said long ago revealed as disingenuously false and
falsely debasing because colonial, but in the physical body's essential androgyny, in
what we might think of as a trans*ness that, having been halved, cisheteropatriarchy
tries achingly to recover, to stitch itself back into that always already paraontological
non-binary trans* body that is neither male nor female. To stitch itself together like the
creature is stitched together from the living and the dead, from, for all we know, male
and female body parts. Trans*ness literally paraontologically precedes other genders
and sexes.

But we should also note the other defining features of Victor's literary criticism
since we see this schizo split-body effect doubling the already double themes of Victor
and the creature of doubles of each other and the self. Indeed, what is melancholic
about Arabic poetry, to follow Victor, is its bifurcation of friend and enemy that spills
out in Victor's reading of such texts. But the frowny-faced melancholy of the enemy
also gives way to the division of the self for the "fire that consumes your own heart"
seems to be predicated on the enemy of the previous clause whose "smiles and frowns"

are characteristic of that fair enemy's evenhandedness, their ability to smile and frown on, to judge impartially, their own enemy. Thus, the binary of friend and enemy recalls the split doubling of sun, earth, and moon, and doubles the self, breaking the self in two, not unlike the effect we've long read between Victor and the creature. The self, like the temperate, evenhanded enemy, both smiles and frowns. The globe, the earth, having been riven into heterogeneous zones by Victor's literary analysis finds itself, now, like Aristophanes's androgyne, looking for love in itself, in the self of its other half, its enemy and friend, in the self that is not one self but two, having been halved by the god that created that species. As such, we can think of the sadness Victor locates in his post-partum oriental literature syllabus as not the longing of a parent for their child but the sadness of the lover looking for his other half. Victor, egotistical creator of a new species, a type of god in his own mind, is the god of bodies torn asunder rather than stitched together. His libidinal economy that leads to his creation of the creature is the desire for his other half. Victor retains a binaristic logic even while unconsciously nodding to the non-binary trans*ness that engenders, literally, male and female genders, whereas the creature consciously instantiates and literally and figuratively voices and endorses this—his/her/their own—trans*ness.

But, what, we might well pause to ask, does any of this, perforce, have to do with justice let alone the justice-to-come I mentioned *Frankenstein* trans*thinks? For one, the creature stages what Ross Woodman, writing on Percy Shelley's *Prometheus Unbound* (1819), calls his/her/they ideal revolution in the prototypical figure of the androgyne, except, to endorse and extend his analysis, the creature thinks revolution on non-binary terms.[29] Woodman's is a useful reminder that revolutionary justice is, in general, what the Shelleys were up to as is Anahid Nersessian's reading of Percy Shelley's *Laon and Cythna* (1817) as a poem in which erotic love, for one, is what "gradually coaxes us toward a more expansive, philosophical love of justice," an idea she notes he "borrowed from Plato's *Symposium*."[30] We might also look to Elizabeth's discourse on the judicial courts to witness how the legacies of masculine Greco-Roman culture surface in new contexts in the present, for the system Elizabeth targets descends from European classical judiciary antiquity.

Justice in the novel, when attached to the law, is configured in a distinctly gendered way and Elizabeth parses it as such in contrast to Victor who remains beguiled by the law and cannot recognize its unfairly structured ostracism of women. While the name Justine ironically rings with its Latin etymological root *iustus*, she of course finds no justice in the world of the novel being innocent of the crime of murdering William. Elizabeth, however, believes Justine and demonstrates a disinterested impartiality— the ability to smile and frown alike if you will—characteristic of the fair-mindedness needed by a judge. In a letter to Victor, she recounts a conversation she has with her uncle concerning the pastoral life versus the juridical life:

> My uncle and I conversed a long time last night about what profession Ernest should follow. His constant illness when young has deprived him of the habits of application; and now that he enjoys good health, he is therefore proposed that he should be a farmer; which you know, Cousin, is a favourite scheme of mine.

A farmer's is a very healthy happy life; and the least hurtful, or rather the most beneficial profession of any. My uncle had an idea of his being educated as an advocate, that through his interest he might become a judge. But, besides that he is not at all fitted for such an occupation, it is certainly more creditable to cultivate the earth for the sustenance of man, than to be the confidant, and sometimes the accomplice, of his vices; which is the profession of a lawyer. I said, that the employments of a prosperous farmer, if they were not a more honourable, they were at least a happier species of occupation than that of a judge, whose misfortune it was always to meddle with the dark side of human nature. My uncle smiled, and said, that I ought to be an advocate myself, which put an end to the conversation on that subject. (41)

Again, we see a binary on display, this time in terms that evoke *Star Wars*, where the light side is aligned with agriculture and the dark side with the judiciary. While we might initially hear a kind of environmentalism in Elizabeth's ascription of the light side to the pastoral—as if she grew up in the Frankenstein household, as she likely did, reading Horace—she couches Latin *agriculturae* in biopolitical terms, that which "is the most beneficial profession of any" because, apparently, it cultivates the earth "for the sustenance of man." We have certainly seen a recall of apocalyptic Romanticism and, here, live now on an earth we must plot and piece to our own anthropocentric ends. The light side coheres with the natural world; on the dark side, meanwhile, in what we might characterize as the socially constructed world of laws, humans are meddlers in that natural world by positioning men as law itself, adhering, in other words, to the law of the father the creature excises or more accurately elides and abjures from his vision of life. Humans create laws that play on the very binary of light and dark invoked here, only, here, this binary exists in the human soul. Whereas in the passage above, Victor divides the world along cisheteropatriarchal lines, Elizabeth recourses to a universalized humanism that sees all humans as essentially split between a metaphysical pyschomachia of warring good and evil impulses. In both depictions, a binary exists: on Victor's it is Europe and Asia and accordant male and female gender ascription; on Elizabeth's, a physical world pre-existing gender and a social world created by that same gender and a cleaved soul that ping pongs between good and evil.

But nonetheless, for all her own occupation in, and propagation of, binaristic logic, Elizabeth's vision of judgment hints at whispers of a justice-to-come because, in her formulation, the tribune of judicial logic itself must be deconstructed and remade in non-binary form. The problem, as Elizabeth sees it, runs deeper than a simple nature/social split feminist recovery project. As Singer shows us, any such notion of a feminist recovery project is unnecessary because women writers of the period always already "look askance at linear histories based on clearly gendered subjects, and instead figure newly affective literary history" that create "revolutionary ontologies."[31] These ontologies obviate the gendered binarisitc logic with which Romanticism congregates itself. Indeed, Elizabeth, like Singer, pinpoints that the real issue is the fundamental two-sex model that powers these other binaries. Her uncle voices this in the end when he says she "ought to be an advocate."

Yet, of course, his verbal endorsement of her only-if legal prowess is predicated on his non-verbal culturally derived empirical knowledge that she cannot be an advocate given what the laws of society on whose behalf she would be advocating, advocate. Ironically, because she demonstrates Kantian analytic reasoning impartial in its judgment that would revise the law so that it carries out its own stated reason for being, justice, she proves herself worthy of standing at the bar of the law.[32] But, nonetheless, it is precisely this worthiness that also bars her from the bar of the law since the law does not accept any such reasonableness—as she herself proves in her diagnosis of its inherent partiality, its meddling with the dark arts of the soul so as to forward an individual's, and perforce society's, evil voices and vices. The law, then, is itself an accomplice of the criminality, the injustice, it itself must need stand against in order to render justice. It exonerates itself from criminality in the very act of catching itself red-handedly committing a crime. This recursive rendering that re-renders, re-delineates, re-sketches in its own outlines is at the heart of Elizabeth's critique of pure unreason even as she understands, in the very leveraging of the critique, that she cannot exceed the parameters of the law's codifications because she is a female. This is to say, she recognizes and rejects the binary that underlies the world in which she lives despite that it resurfaces, re-renders itself, in her own advocacy for the non-advocacy life, for the life of a farmer who feeds and sustains the human species. Becoming a biopolitician *par excellance* in the agricultural profession will presumably reconcile the human soul, to follow her terms, and the human sociocultured body, forging good and evil into something, to risk a phrase, beyond good and evil.

In similar fashion, the law, or society, to upend its own self-induced, self-advocated injustices, would need to un-reconcile the male and the female by opening the court's doors to women which would then weight the scales of justice evenhandedly, beyond the toxic masculinity that characterizes it as, beyond, then, male and female. In effect, what Elizabeth's critique hints at is the justice-to-come represented by the creature's non-binary trans*ness and it does so in a way that moves beyond Victor's own inability to realize and understand his own orientalist, Aristophanic literary dilemma.

What then of the creature? The creature appears to be stuck in the same binaristic loop as Elizabeth. He demands that Victor fashion a female counterpart for him, a demand that, on the surface, would seem to indicate a desire on the creature's part for a binary cisheteropatriarchal mating partner if not a fully fledged nonhuman species. And yet, the creature's vision takes on a determinedly non-binary orientation in that he proposes to live away from humankind altogether and enjoy a peaceful posthuman existence. He conjures a remarkable post-apocalyptic Romanticism:

> If you consent, neither you nor any other human being shall ever see us again: I will go to the vast wilds of South America. My food is not that of man; I do not destroy the lamb and the kid, to glut my appetite; acorns and berries afford me sufficient nourishment. My companion will be of the same nature as myself, and will be content with the same fare. We shall make our bed of dried leaves; the sun will shine on us as on man, and will ripen our food. The picture I present to

you is peaceful and human, and you must feel that you could deny it only in the wantonness of power and cruelty. Pitiless as you have been towards me, I now see compassion in your eyes; let me seize the favourable moment, and persuade you to promise what I so ardently desire. (102–3)

In adopting this vegan diet he reminds us that, as Carol J. Adams and Derrida both say, carnivorous diets and cisheteropatriarchy are irreducible.[33] Safe to say, then, that by "companion" the creature means com-panion etymologically (*com*: "with"; *panem*: "bread"), as one who leavens bread and cooks it on an open fire, one who literally breaks bread with another, that is, as a friend and not the Aristophanic lover; the creature is well beyond the androgyne even. Elsewhere he will call it "communion," which, in Latin, signals fellowship and sharing, often over food (104). In rejecting the carnivorousness of "man," he thus rejects cisheteropatriarchal biopolitics even more fully than Elizabeth, who is pleased to marry Victor after all.

As well, while I don't want to propose to decode some secret meaning encrypted in this text as its universalized language is very much of its nineteenth-century time, the word "man" nonetheless seems, to me, to carry much greater significance in this passage than we have previously given it credit for. That is, the creature attaches specific importance to the man-ness of "man" here, as if to demarcate himself and his to-be-created companion from the built-in masculinity the word explicitly imparts, almost as if there is something toxic about masculinity. And yet what to make of its next appearance when it seems to be deployed favorably, with the assertion that "the sun will shine on us as on man" which jams together the heliocentric nonhuman world with an anthropocentric skyward-looking ontology and recalls Elizabeth's encomium on the agricultural life as that which provides "sustenance" to "man"? But, I think, or at least let's consider, that the creature puts more pressure on the word "as" in this clause, more making it function as a simile that differentiates the nonhuman and the human, with the heliocentric world washing its hands entirely of anthropocentric ontological models. Instead, the simile, as similes do, marks the fundamentally different nature of the human and the nonhuman: the sun will shine on the creature and his partner but will do so "as" as in "as if" they were part of this species present in the universalizing "man." Making the comparison, of course, makes the point that the two—the creature and his companion and the human species—are not comparable. In other words, the creature is very much divorcing himself from the world of humans but also from the "him" of himself. It is a thoroughgoing de-gendering of his life in this post-apocalyptic vision. Him and her will not be a him and her but a their—and a their un-united in their theirness.

The creature's thoughts are consonant with Victor's in terms of cisheteropatriarchal life—we assume much about the creature because the novel identifies Victor as the cisheteropatriarchal exemplar and the heterogeneous, heteronormative hegemony that he signals speaks as if for "man," which is to say, for a universalized "us." Victor is not kidding around; he takes his cishetereopatriarchy seriously and sees the world exclusively through that lens:

Even if they were to leave Europe, and inhabit the deserts of the new world, yet on of the first results of those sympathies for which the daemon thirsted would be children, and a race of devils would be propagated upon the earth, who might make the very existence of the species of man a condition precarious and full of terror. (119)

But the creature isn't kidding around either; nor is he shy. In his/her/their requests and demands of Victor he/she/they is crystal clear about what he/she/they wants and he/she/they never mentions children, which indicates a rejection of the symbolic and real economy of the law of the father. Nor does he/she/they characterize the partner he/she/they wants as a partner in the mating sense—perhaps one reason he fears she will turn to "the superior beauty of man" (118). While Victor understands the creature's request for a being who has a desire for a cisheterosexual mate to engage in sexual intercourse and breeding, the creature makes clear in the novel that the sympathies necessary for he/she/they are compassion and love which he/she/they cannot find with humans—the creature never mentions sex and procreation: "no sympathy may I ever find" (159). And, again, if we take the "no" like we take the "man" above, not in any type of pressurized over-reading, but in the face-valuation the creature places on it, then it rings with a definitive finality that asks us to hear no as a "no," as a "no, I cannot be part of this because I am not part of this." Victor projects his own fantasies onto the creature and can only see a binary of male and female nonhuman monsters as humans human-mating. The embodiment of cisheteropatriachal biopolitical desire, Victor, in his primal scene imaginary representations of the creature's life, cannot conceive of the possibility of a trans* future for the creatures.

So while the relationship the creature seeks appears cisheteropatriarchal, the creature actually defies and rejects such binaries. The creature wants a two but nothing evidences that "he" wants a two-sex model or even that he/she/they wants the two "he" wants to be binary. To recall Sigler, initially, "the lesson in British Romantic writing is that one must learn to enjoy properly, in one or two styles—male or female." He cites the creature's learning "'the difference of the sexes'" from watching the De Lacey family as an example (81).[34] But if, as Sigler also shows, for both Freud and Lacan, becoming acculturated is how one "count[s] as a viable subject of determinate gender," then we must wonder about a creature acculturated enough to desire companionship but who, even having learned "the difference of the sexes," never genders that companionship in the sense that he/she/they never sexes it in terms of sexual enjoyment, desire, or sexual reproduction.[35] Rather, he/she/they's cultural estrangement from acculturation allows the creature to look but not assimilate, to exemplify a non-mitochondrial difference that is not absorbable by the closed-off cell of cisheteropatriarchal culture. We have to understand the creature's posthuman, nonhuman future vision, a wish for a "female" creature that will live with "him" in non-patriarchal, non-biopolitical fashion, then, as non-binaristic in that "he" views this as a relationship that expands difference, expands what a relationship between a male and female can be—and even expands what a male and female is since the creature's post-apocalyptic Romanticism stages a future-creature that undercommons across and over and under the boundary of human sexual reproduction and social gender-making. It renders all such divisions asunder in cutting them together apart, to borrow a phrasing from Barad. They are not, in terms of the sexed body, male or female. It is not, on the creature's proposal, a relationship that fits into a conventional view of familial life. Seen from this angle, the creature represents non-binary life.

The novel's non-binary thinking, in this way, evinces the temporality of a justice-to-come. When the creature disappears "in darkness and distance" at novel's end it models a trans* vision that rejects teleology and even eschatology (161). "What would it mean to desire a future that we can't even imagine but that we are told couldn't ever exist?" trans scholars and activists Morgan Bassichis, Alexander Lee, and Dean Spade ask.[36] This succors with Derrida's insight that the future is always monstrous—it will always emerge as difference itself, unanticipatable and incalculable (if it were calculable, if we knew what would happen, it would not be the future). As Derrida also reminds us, " … as soon as one perceives a monster in a monster, one begins to domesticate it … to compare it to the norms, to analyse it, consequently to master whatever could be terrifying in this figure of the monster."[37] That is, one begins to make the monster normative, to re-translate its trans*ness into recognizability, just as Victor does when he imagines the creatures sexually procreating like humans do. The creatures, those monsters, must be re-imagined and normativized, given the name human, so that we can forestall the fear anything non-normative inspires; it is this re-translation that the creature resists even as it persists in Victor's cishereteopatriarchal fantasy.

In fact, the very fact of the creature's existence, to recursively a-temporalize this essay, defies Victor's cishetero fantasy: the creature is not birthed from a two-sex union: he is created by one male. But that male, whatever he might have thought was going to happen, is not, it turns out, replicating himself. The creature is, instead, a mishmash of human and nonhuman biological flesh and of wildly divergent cultures—of the French Enlightenment, of Felix and family, of Sophie's Arabic poetry and linguistics, of indigenous studies via Volney's *Ruins*, and the English, German, and Greek-turned-Latin-citizenship cultural studies on offer from Milton, Goethe, and Plutarch. Physically, culturally, ontologically, he/she/they is both human and nonhuman. Rather than the divided gendered global geopolitics of Victor's Greco-Roman syllabus, the creature draws across a multicultural and multinational commonwealth of conventions and mores and definitions of human and nonhuman bodies.

In this sense, we can understand the justice-to-come of the trans* future the creature represents. In *No Future: Queer Theory and the Death Drive*, Lee Edelman argues that cishetero families give birth in order to replicate themselves through their children and in the process stave off the future since they continually replicate the present in those children. Therefore, we might say, in the wake of and following on, the afterbirth of Edelman's thought, that temporality remains stubbornly cishetero and binary.[38] Reproduction would then be, if we follow this logic, a mode of extinction in life and through life since it is just a replication that never leads to a future, what Edelman appropriates from Freud and calls the death drive. For this reason, life is not death in the binary but it isn't life either if we think of life as propulsive in nature across a futural trajectory. As Butler writes, maybe replication is monstrous itself.[39]

This is how "we"(?) get justice then: by following a trans* non-binary, non-end-stopped, non-replicative trajectory, like what the creature begins to imagine as a beginning that never ends. The creature's existence thinks and imagines the unimaginable trans* future even as he reminds us that "we" are a we and "we" cannot exist until "we" reclaim the non-finality of trans*ness and reject the monstrousness of universalized socially constructed human biopolitics and cisheteropatriarchal families. Ultimately, the creature represents trans* difference in his/her/their theorization of how nonhuman being can be, indeed, is, present within so-called "human" ontology but un-translatably, paraontologically present. It is a difference with no end in sight, moving ever onward into the unknown, no end, that is, in a fixed site but only in the non-binary trans*ness of new ontologies, new beings and modes of being.

Notes

1   Chris Washington, *Romantic Revelations: Visions of Post-apocalyptic Hope and Life in the Anthropocene* (Toronto: University of Toronto Press, 2019).

2   Percy Bysshe Shelley, *A Defence of Poetry*, ed. Donald H. Reiman and Neil Fraistat (New York: W. W. Norton, 2002), 509–38, 525.

3   Susan Stryker, *Transgender History: The Roots of Today's Revolution*, 2nd ed. (New York: Seal Press, 2017), 24–5.

4   David Collings, *Monstrous Society: Reciprocity, Discipline, and the Political Uncanny, c.1780–1848* (Lewsiburg: Bucknell University Press, 2009), 212.

5   Kate Singer, *Romantic Vacancy: The Poetics of Affect, Gender, and Radical Speculation* (Albany, NY: SUNY Press, 2019), xvii.

6   Fred Moten and Stefano Harney, *The Undercommons: Fugitive Planning and Black Study* (Brooklyn, NY: Autonomedia, 2013).

7   Collings, *Monstrous Society*, 221.

8   Jacques Derrida, "Structure, Sign, and Play in the Discourse of the Human Sciences," in *Writing and Difference*, trans. Alan Bass (Chicago, IL: University of Chicago Press, 1978), 278–93, 293.

9   Mary Shelley, *Frankenstein; or, The Modern Prometheus*, ed. J. Paul Hunter (New York: W. W. Norton, 2012), 33. Page references to this edition are cited parenthetically in the text throughout this chapter. I have also used the *Romantic Circles* version of the novel edited by Stuart Curran. https://romantic-circles.org/editions/frankenstein.

10 For Sigler these "atypical sexualities become thinkable because of the period's ideological investment in enjoyment," a fascinating claim that falls outside the scope of this essay. David Sigler, *Sexual Enjoyment and British Romanticism: Gender and Psychoanalysis 1753–1835* (Montreal, CA: McGill Queen's Press, 2015), 16.

11 Karen Barad, *Meeting the Universe Halfway: Quantum Physics and the Entanglement of Matter and Meaning* (Durham, NC: Duke University Press, 2017).

12 Anson Koch-Rein, "*Trans*-lating the Monster: Transgender Affect and *Frankenstein*," *LIT: Literature Interpretation Theory* 30, no. 1 (2019): 44–61, 47.

13 Anne Mellor, *Romanticism and Feminism* (New York: Routledge, 1992), 17–18.

14 Jolene Zigarovich, "The Trans Legacy of *Frankenstein*," *Science Fiction Studies* 45, no. 2, Frankenstein (July 2018): 260–72, 267. Susan Stryker, "My Words to Victor

Frankenstein Above the Village of Chamounix—Performing Transgender Rage,"
GLQ 1, no. 3 (1994): 237–54. For examples of this plotted-and-piecedness effect, see
Harlan Weaver, "Monster Trans: Diffracting Affect, Reading Rage," *Somatechnics* 3,
no. 2 (2013): 287–306; Sonny Nordmarken, "Feeling Ever More Monstrous: Feeling
Transgender In-Betweenness," *Qualitative Inquiry* 20, no. 1 (2014): 37–50. For an
exemplary reading of trans tropes in Romantic literature, see Nowell Marshall,
"Beyond Queer Gothic: Charting the Gothic History of the Trans Subject in Beckford,
Lewis, Byron," in *TransGothic in Literature and Culture*, ed. Jolene Zigarovich (New
York: Routledge, 2018).

15   Stryker, "My Words," 240.

16   Ibid., 240.

17   Jack Halberstam, *Trans*: A Quick and Quirky Account of Gender* (Oakland, CA:
University of California Press, 2018), 4.

18   Ibid., 4.

19   Ibid..

20   Marquis Bey, "The Trans*ness of Blackness, the Blackness of Trans*ness," *TSQ:
Transgender Studies Quarterly* 4, no. 2 (2017): 275–95, 275.

21   Ibid., 275.

22   Jeanette Winterson, *Frankissstein* (New York: Grove Press, 2019).

23   Jeffrey Jerome Cohen, *Monster Theory: Reading Culture* (Minneapolis: University of
Minnesota Press, 1996), 7.

24   Elizabeth Young, *Black Frankenstein: The Making of an American Metaphor* (New
York: New York University Press, 2008).

25   Peter Brooks, "What Is a Monster?" in *Frankenstein; or, the Modern Prometheus*, ed. J.
Paul Hunter (New York: W. W. Norton, 2012), 368–90, 389. Sandra Gilman and Susan
Gubar, *The Madwoman in the Attic: The Woman Writer and the Nineteenth-Century
Literary Imagination* (New Haven, CT: Yale University Press, 2000), 340.

26   Mary Poovey, *The Proper Lady and the Woman Writer* (Chicago, IL: University of
Chicago Press, 1984). Anne Mellor, "Possessing Nature: The Female in *Frankenstein*,"
in *Romanticism and Feminism*, ed. Anne Mellor (Bloomington, IN: Indiana University
Press, 1988), 220–32.

27   And as Koch-Rein notes, Brooks, for instance, relies on the assumption that anatomy
equals gender (48). Judith Butler, "Afterward. Animating Autobiography: Barbara
Johnson and Mary Shelley's Monster," in *A Life with Mary Shelley* (Stanford, CA:
Stanford University Press, 2014), 37–52, 48–9. Barbara Johnson, "My Monster/My
Self," in *A Life with Mary Shelley* (Stanford, CA: Stanford University Press, 2014),
15–26.

28   Plato, *The Symposium*, trans. Percy Bysshe Shelley, ed. David K. O'Conner (South
Bend, IN: St. Augustine's Press, 2002), 26–7.

29   Ross Woodman, "The Androgyne in *Prometheus Unbound*," *Studies in Romanticism*
20, no. 1 (1981): 225–47, 225.

30   Percy Bysshe Shelley, *Laon and Cythna*, ed. Anahid Nercessian (Ontario, CA:
Broadview Press, 2016), 14–15.

31   Singer, *Romantic Vacancy*, xix.

32   Timothy Michael provides a searching study of Kantian reason in regards to the
law, among other ostensibly fundamental topics, in Romanticism. See his *British
Romanticism and the Critique of Political Reason* (Baltimore: Johns Hopkins
University Press, 2016).

33 Carol J. Adams, *The Sexual Politics of Meat: A Feminist-Vegetarian Critical Theory* (London: Bloomsbury, 2015). Jacques Derrida, "Eating Well, or, the Calculation of the Subject," in *Points … Interviews 1974–1995*, ed. Elizabeth Weber (Stanford: Stanford University Press, 1995), 255–77. For a thorough look at vegetarianism in the period, see Timothy Morton, *Shelley and the Revolution in Taste* (Cambridge: Cambridge University Press, 1994). For a reading of veganism and the novel, see Washington, *Romantic Revelations*, 150–87.

34 Sigler, *Sexual Enjoyment*, 7.

35 Ibid., 7.

36 Morgan Bassichis, Alexander Lee, and Dean Spade, "Building an Abolitionist Trans and Queer Movement with Everything We've Got," in *Captive Genders: Trans Embodiment and the Prison Industrial Complex* (Oakland, CA: University of California Press, 2011), 37.

37 Jacques Derrida, "Passages—From Traumatism to Promise," in *Points … Interviews, 1974–1994* (Stanford, CA: Stanford University Press, 1995), 372–98, 386.

38 Lee Edelman, *No Future: Queer Theory and the Death Drive* (Durham, NC: Duke University Press, 2004).

39 Butler, "Afterward. Autobiography," 43.

5

What's Love Got to Do with It? *Frankenstein* and Monstrous Psychoanalysis

Joel Faflak

"My Accursed Origin"

In the Prologue to *The Human Condition*, Hannah Arendt describes the 1957 launch of Sputnik, the first artificial earth satellite, as "second in importance to no other"[1] event. Arendt's remark was prompted by an American reporter's "strange statement" of "relief about the first 'step toward escape from men's imprisonment to the earth,'"[2] although ironically Sputnik fell back through the earth's atmosphere only several months later. Arendt asks: "Should the emancipation and secularization of the modern age, which began with a turning-away, not necessarily from God, but from a god who was the Father of men in heaven, end with an even more fateful repudiation of an Earth who was the Mother of all living creatures under the sky?"[3] Fixated on renouncing fathers and mothers, Mary Shelley's *Frankenstein* (1818) takes shape out this perverse desire to outstrip the very human condition that makes subjects and their subjectivities possible in the first place, as if to exist nowhere at all. The Monster tells his maker, "No father had watched my infant days, no mother had blessed me with smiles and caresses; or if they had, all my past life was now a blot, a blind vacancy in which I distinguished nothing" (120).[4] Here Shelley takes aim at what Slavoj Žižek calls the illusion of humanism, which presupposes a "home, a 'natural' place for man: either this world of the 'noosphere' from which we fell into this world and for which our souls long, or Earth itself."[5] Caught between a rock and no place, the Monster finds himself permanently estranged, the result of a Heideggerian *Geworfenheit*, of "'being-thrown' into a concrete historical situation" not of his making. As Žižek asks, "what if we effectively are 'thrown' into this world, never fully at home in it, always dislocated, 'out of joint,' and what if this dislocation is our constitutive, primordial condition, the very horizon of our being? What if there is no previous 'home' out of which we were thrown into this world ?"[6] For Shelley, this estrangement reflects a desire to witness, as Marc Rubinstein writes, the primal scene of our origin.[7] Born into a world we did not make, a world made by those who themselves have nowhere else to go, we desire at once to find our place and get out of the place, except there seems to be no other place for us to go except to undiscovered lands also not of our making.

I want to read this state of de-existence in terms of psychoanalysis, one of many forms of dark enlightenment prophesied by Shelley's first novel.[8] By 1957 psychoanalysis had firmly planted its flag in America as ego psychology, which professes the ego's battle to prevail over its inner demons—an escape from a rather different ecology and enemy. For Jacques Lacan, the Freudian subject split between two solitudes with no homeland was itself the unwanted guest of ego psychology. Leo Bersani notes that the new Penguin Freud, which re-translates James Strachey's translation of *das Es* as "the it" rather than the Id, marks the unconscious as the gap "between perception and consciousness," against the "more orthodox view of the unconscious in depth-psychology [or ego psychology] as behind or below consciousness."[9] The latter implies the potential to reveal and subdue hidden or repressed terrors, whereas the former, seeing "the unconscious as before consciousness, in the sense of an ontological rather than a temporal anteriority," the "It in the I," "transforms subjecthood from psychic density into pure potentiality."[10] This "reservoir of possibility"[11] sounds ideally democratic, expressive of post-Second World War American optimism, except that it also plants the unconscious in our midst as a terrorist difficult to police, something "lodged within a subject that it vastly exceeds."[12] As Freud said to Jung in 1909 on the occasion of Freud's only visit to America, "They don't realize we are bringing them the plague."[13] And thereafter we can surmise a schism in Freud's legacy: on one hand, we have the desire to bring the unconscious to consciousness and thus (at the very least implicitly) to diagnose and cure its symptomology; on the other hand, we have a psychoanalysis that explores this desire as only one of the plague of fantasies by which we live.

Shell-shocked by confronting an uber-egotism that imagines it can survive its darker instincts, Victor is a cautionary tale of how all attempts to exert the ego's will turn toxic. Both sign and symptom of this ambivalence are the Monster, who is at once sparked and infected by Frankenstein's "rapture" (36) or "enthusiasm" (38), which encrypts the destructive excess of what Walton calls Victor's "senseless curiosity" (209). Confronted by the essential mystery of life, Christopher Bollas writes, the infant is driven by an "epistemophilic instinct,"[14] which psychoanalysis re-stages, as if "inside a mystery play,"[15] as the desire and ultimate cause of the process itself. The "noumenal transference" created by this "drive to know" "bears an epistemophilic demand to the presumed intelligence informing the analytic process."[16] By telling the story of a subject who submits his maker, at once father and mother, to an analysis in which both confront the fallout of their "drive to know," the novel attempts to account for both the genesis and the effects of this epistemophilia. The Monster asks of Victor, "Who was I? What was I? Whence did I come? What was my destination?"; but although "these questions continually recurred," the Monster, like Victor himself, remained "unable to solve them" (102). Seeing in Walton's eyes the "expectation, and the wonder and hope" that he should tell Walton the "secret" of his discovery, Frankenstein responds, "that cannot be" (53). As Walton recounts to his sister at the end of the novel, "Sometimes I endeavoured to gain from Frankenstein the particulars of his creature's formation: but on this point he was impenetrable" (209). Communication in the novel unfolds as a series of unanswered questions addressed to a "presumed intelligence," which compel us to wonder about the remote source of their asking. But like "thoughts which must remain untold" in Percy Shelley's *The Triumph of Life*,[17] the secret itself is beside the point, which suggests that the questions, demanded by the model of subject formation that molded and dictated the Monster's development as a human in the first place, are the wrong ones.

By circling this empty center the novel writes the tragedy of what Bersani calls the "conflict-ridden subject-object relational model dominant in Western philosophy and psychoanalysis,"[18] like ego psychology. That Frankenstein manufactures human life without any forethought for how it will survive its inevitable relations with the world implies that the model takes care of itself, but does a great disservice to the subjects it forms. The Monster's thirst to know, his plea for recognition, the sheer drive of his will, indeed the virtual constitution of his being, all confront Victor with a force with which he had not reckoned: a "nonhuman receptivity perhaps lodged within the human body since the beginning of human life"[19] that object relations would wish away. This "ontological discomfort" suggests the need for a "relational mode beyond sex, beyond love, beyond relationship itself," a "relational upheaval [necessary] if the human is to survive as an event in the history of our planet."[20] *Frankenstein* never offers this "life-enhancing alternative,"[21] which would sentimentalize the novel's dsytopianism; but the Monster's experience of neglect does confront us with our all-too-easy acceptance of how sense gets made and how relations are meant to function. As the Monster says to Victor about having been left to his own education, "Of what a strange nature is knowledge! It clings to the mind, when it has once seized on it, like a lichen on the rock" (120). This "strange" viscosity suggests our sensorium's attunement to and embeddedness in the world, what recent neuroscientific research describes as "extended" cognition and what Jane Bennett calls the "vital materiality" of a perceptual ecology formed by the recombinative mashup between human and nonhuman forces.[22] Making sense of the world, that is to say, is irrevocably intertwined with the sense-making that makes making sense possible in the first place, a kind of cognitive intersectionality that challenges the precedence of verbal association and communication as fundamental to our understanding of human experience. As Bollas argues, contrary to the "idea that we understand one another through the different orders of communication," it is "likely that we are compelled to know more about the other when the illusion of understanding breaks down" and "communication recognize[s] the impossibility of itself."[23] Or as the Monster tells Victor, "the human senses," the very mode of relationality, are, paradoxically, "insurmountable barriers" to the "union" between subjects (145).[24]

The Monster materializes this "impossibility" as what Peter Brooks calls an "epistemophilic product," "a scientific idea [that] becomes a bodily fact."[25] Like the Lacanian subject caught between its imaginary and symbolic constitutions, he anatomizes the perpetually unfulfilled desire to know who we are or where we come from. On one hand, the Monster is a "sympathetic and persuasive participant in Western culture," able to "produce and project his desire in language" and thus within the symbolic "culture system or law into which individual subjects are inserted."[26] Yet this "metonymical movement ... extends desire forward without reaching a goal ...

which cannot be named, since the object of desire is unconscious."[27] He thus remains victim of the "deceptive relations, of ideology and fascination" that define the imaginary, "the order of the specular, of the mirror stage" that "arises from the subject's perception of itself as other."[28] This leaves him caught between being heard and being seen, the former granting him access to the social, the latter assuring his perpetual exile. As "the reconstruction of dead fragments from many bodies," Fred Botting writes, "the traces of many texts, into a new and hideous combination that refuses to submit to the authority of the creator," *Frankenstein* comprises "an interrogation of origination, creativity and authority."[29] The novel is thus less "a work of literature" than "a product of criticism"[30] in that it "incorporates its (critical) readers into its monstrous textual body and confronts them with a series of shifting relationships, disperses them among its textual positions and along its narrative chains."[31] Like Victor summoning from the corporeal remains that constitute its making the truth of their origin, the novel, as if to leave *us* calling upon the specters of a knowledge that we cannot materialize, finds its prophetic power in warning us about the tragedy of asking in the first place.

"Senseless Curiosity"

Frankenstein is framed as a series of encounters driven by curiosity to know and sympathy for the other, the open but unprotected transmission of which is one of the narrative's central drives. Because of his "desire of finding a friend—of my thirst for a more intimate sympathy with a fellow mind than had ever fallen to my lot" (30), Walton "was easily led by the sympathy [Frankenstein] evinced" (28). The central focus of this process is the Monster's determination to let his maker know the struggle to come to terms with his "accursed origin" (130): "It is with considerable difficulty that I remember the original era of my being: all the events of that period appear confused and indistinct'" (102). Gradually he "learned to distinguish between the operations of my various senses," and his story recounts the object relations of his formation as a subject, as if compelling Victor to confirm their legitimacy. We can read these psychic and affective bondings between speaker and interlocutor as transference, which was Freud's explanation for how the analysand repeats past trauma by (largely unconsciously) projecting its psychic impact onto the analyst, who then helps the analysand to work through and withdraw the projection—to remember the past at a more conscious level. In the Monster's appeal to Victor, or Victor's encounter with Walton, for instance, we can read the latter as analysts privy to their patient's psychic experience. Both catalyst and obstacle to transference are what Freud calls the "quota of affect"[32] attached to memory, which attachment needs to be abreacted and thus discharged through the analytical process, the clinical equivalent of Aristotelian catharsis. Yet Freud came to see transference as a rather more interminable process in spite of the patient's desire for release from her passionately stubborn attachments to the past, not just because of lingering resistances, as well as the analyst's countertransference, driven by the unanalyzed portions of her experience, but also because transference itself produced new psychic material requiring further analysis.[33] As Jung argued, transference leaves both subjects "altered," a kind of alchemical hybridization of identity that "continually produc[es] new formations," and thus "yields an endless and self-replenishing abundance of living creatures, a wealth beyond our fathoming."[34]

Put another way, no one gets released from transference in the novel. While the Monster demands Victor's tacit agreement to hear his story, he is also the analyst who confronts Victor with his own disavowal of the past. And Walton is not so much Victor's sounding board as he is compelled to understand not just Victor's plight but the very source of his motivation as Walton's way of figuring out his own. Walton's disclosure of his encounter with Frankenstein to his sister, who functions as silent interlocutor or screen and thus proxy for a possible but unknown reader, delimits this horizon of interminability. Because we never know if Walton's letters reach their destination, the question arises of where communication actually goes in the novel, of what might be its actual purpose. The "quota of affect" to which Freud refers, as much as the experience it accompanies, signifies the more indeterminately structural and systemic orchestration of how subjects come to be and to survive within the psychic ecology of experience itself. That is to say, subjects and subjectivity would be impossible without the "quota of affect" that brought them into being in the first place, traumatically or otherwise. Transference thus persists as an equivocal affective and psychic ontology which, because it compels subjects perpetually to seek the origins of their experience, is also a sleep of reason that only breeds more monsters.

It also explains why relations in the novel never add up to a coherent or fulfilling subjective experience, which is to say that curiosity and sympathy are not the same thing. Frankenstein's warning to Walton, "Unhappy man! Do you share my madness?", suggests that curiosity, as the symptom of an unsatisfied desire to know, exposes the lie of sympathy, which at least since Adam Smith's *Theory of Moral Sentiments* (1757) defined how benevolent relations defined a civil society, madness being a key threat to this intelligibility. Like *Things as They Are* (1794), the first novel by Shelley's father-in-law William Godwin, *Frankenstein* whets its characters' appetite for a narrative completion that never comes but that amalgamates subjects into a relationship in which they are doomed to confront one another's resistant psychologies.[35] The shock of dire experiences blocks and silences our capacity to take them in, an epistemological delay that attends "an experience that is not fully assimilated as it occurs."[36] This is to name the trauma of knowing itself: the fact that, as Lacan reminds us, the real "resists symbolization absolutely,"[37] especially when it confronts "an animal as complex and wonderful as man" (53). As Botting writes, "what is human cannot be defined in itself, but only by what it is not, by its difference from others: as the figure of the monster is introduced to affirm the primacy of humanity, it succeeds only in reiterating differences in their monstrous form."[38]

What also drives the novel's encounters as they spiral toward an unspoken origin or secret, then, is a transposition of subjectivities[39] which confront a certain defamiliarity with themselves and others and, by endlessly detouring the ego's drive toward singularity, expose its darker designs.[40] For instance, Walton at first mistakes Frankenstein, "an European," as the "savage inhabitant of some undiscovered land," which alien identity "strongly excited [his] curiosity" (128), just as the Monster, as if walking through Lacan's mirror stage, sees in his reflection both who he is and is not, a "shadow in the moonshine," a "frail image" and "inconstant shade" (131), thereafter inciting a desire to find a place in the symbolic order that he can never inhabit. This desire in turn anticipates the Monster's encounter with the De Lacey family, a scene of sympathy that, like that binding Victor's family, is a suturing of foreign or unexpected identities and elements threatening to unravel at any moment, a hybrid composed of differences that challenge its composition. Social relations, including hereditary alliances, are at once inalienable and estranging, an alienating matrix of experience into which the subject, like Justine or Safi, finds herself thrown as the product of her encounters with others in the world.

The curiosity driving transference thus tracks a more elemental psychic interaction between subjects and their worlds. Frankenstein's obsession with going "[farther than] others have gone before" in the "scientific pursuit" of asking "Whence ... did the principle of life proceed?" (50, 51) suggests an epistemophilia that marks him from birth, one that determines the very relationality between subjects and their environments. Everyone in the novel is the product of his curiosity, quite literally because, as part of any domestic and social circuitry of others, they are of necessity curious about *his* curiosity as symptom of their own thirst to know. That is to say, to be *with* others is implicitly and inevitably to want to know them, even (perhaps especially) when that desire takes the form of its own disavowal. In Lacanian terms, everyone in the novel is a subject presumed to know—that is, to understand—the other, which is Lacan's way of saying we project what we lack in ourselves onto another whose reciprocal lack ends up locking communication in a kind of *méconnaissance*. Like Percy Shelley's sense of poetry as opening within thought a "void [that] for ever craves fresh food,"[41] Victor's pursuit produced "continual food for discovery and wonder" (52). From this void or "darkness" came "a sudden light [of discovery] ... so brilliant and wondrous" that "all the steps by which I had been progressively led to it were obliterated, and I beheld only the result" (52). This "magical scene" (52) of discovery, however, remains a primal scene, the absent center around which the novel orchestrates its various encounters and exchanges.

"I Have an Affection for It"

In her Introduction to the third edition of *Frankenstein* (1831), Mary Shelley recounts the novel's gestation: "My imagination, unbidden, possessed and guided me, gifting the successive images that arose in my mind with a vividness far beyond the usual bounds of reverie" (9). In this "waking dream" she saw "with shut eyes, but acute mental vision ... the pale student of unhallowed arts kneeling beside the thing he had put together. I saw the hideous phantasm of a man stretched out, and then, on the working of some powerful engine, show signs of life, and stir with an uneasy, half vital motion" (10, 9). Just as Shelley seems inherently revulsed at the thought of her "hideous progeny" (10) even before it has come into being, a similar disgust strikes Frankenstein when he first sees the "accomplishment" of his "unhallowed arts" (57).

As a "convulsive motion agitated its limbs," Frankenstein asks: "How can I describe my emotions at this catastrophe?" (57). Writing long after the novel's publication, however, Shelley also expresses an "affection" for her "thing," for it reminds her of "happy days" (10), as if to say that love eventually comes from spending time with the fulfillment of a desire that one both owns and disowns. The rather darker lining of Shelley's affection for her creature is, of course, what Victor is made to feel for his, partly by virtue of the guilt induced by his Swiss superego, partly because his creation dares him to speak the feeling for what it has become, and partly because Victor never thought far enough ahead to realize that one day he might be *required* to feel love. Like all future parents who want or wish to have a child, until the idea materializes itself as a subject, the idea itself is merely a placeholder that necessitates love as a future proposition that might, depending on the relational context within which the subject materializes, sorely challenge that love's altruism. The notion of unconditional love was invented to assuage this reality, when in fact, as the novel demonstrates, one might just as easily encounter a love/hate that leaves subjects bent on each other's assured mutual destruction.

Yet it is not just that feeling dare not speak its name. The aggression comes from the fact that Victor does not know what he *is* feeling in the first instance. That feelings do not "bear telling" suggests that they can neither endure nor carry across in a definitive manner their import. Put another way, feeling emerges as if precisely not by our knowing what feeling is, except that the feeling itself, our experience *of* it, both urges and tells us that we should be doing something, that we must be feeling *something*. Elsewhere I explore the incompossible nature of affect as the very thing that materializes our being and yet, like consciousness itself, passes all understanding because it is the very mode through which understanding passes, through which thought materializes itself: the feeling *of* thought.[42] Clearly some violent emotion disturbs Victor, but again it is not so much the violence of the feeling itself as it is the violence that attends the fact that feeling comes as if out of nowhere, which is why we feel the palpable energy and effort of Victor's desire to know, but tragedy of never seeing, the moment of its origination and gestation. In the first instance neither Shelley nor Victor knows what they will feel once their progeny, which they would otherwise apprehend, appears, a kind of anticipatory anxiety about not knowing the outcome of their desire. And neither can their progeny know any better except in terms of how the world tells him he *should* feel.

We might call this affection love, but Shelley's sense of love is rather less straightforward.[43] In an early letter to her future husband, she writes: "How you reason & philosophize about love—do you know if I had been asked I could not have given one reason in its favour—yet I have as great an opinion as you concerning its exaltedness and love very tenderly to prove my theory."[44] The statement leaves Shelley's own "theory" unexpressed except as the absence of what it is not: neither her husband's "philosophy" nor her "reason," for only experience can bring love into existence as a way to negotiate social relations. But experience oddly pre-empts any expectation of what these relations might otherwise become, for to determine and fix what love might be in advance is to express a certain "hatred of the future,"[45] and Shelley's statement is all about something evermore about to be, as if without any fixed limit. Which is also to say that love itself is always a kind of afterthought. As Adam Phillips writes, "Love as an artefact of the ego, love as something the child will eventually hear of as something much spoken about comes late in the day."[46] This, of course, comes as a shock to the Monster, who wonders why his creator does not love him. But how does he come to understand what love has to do with it in the first place?

Part of Bersani's project is to critique notions of sympathy and empathy that mask what is the "ineradicably human" nature of "aggressiveness [as] the vengeful response to the frustration of desire."[47] For Bersani, Freud and Lacan offer "a theory of love [that] can't help but be a demystification of love" as that which makes "the human subject ... exceptionally open to otherness."[48] Any move away from the subject's original state of primal narcissism necessarily entails a violence done both to itself and to others. Irrevocably pushed toward the other to "understand" its and our difference from one another, it is as if the ego, rather than being at odds with the superego, "brilliantly reinvented itself as a voice authorizing its otherwise unspeakable impulse to shatter itself in its mad project of mastering, that is, obliterating the world-as-difference."[49] The ego's desire to take in the objects, both human and nonhuman, toward which it inevitably finds itself pitched, to which it is called to respond, and against which it must necessarily define itself, produces a "tension between the enlightened self-interest of ego-rationalism and the rageful drive to destroy that characterizes the ego once it is seduced by the prospect of hyperbolizing itself,"[50] by which Bersani means the world's insistence that the ego insist upon itself. With this desire to achieve "'mastery over the external world'" in order to "swell[.] ... the triumphant ego" comes a "'harmful, malignant [and narcissistic] *jouissance*' ... that "makes aggressivity intractable."[51]

Such aggression stymies any attempt at finding a "life-enhancing alternative" to the types of relationality that obviously work for no one in the novel. In his desire to inhabit himself as a psychological subject, the Monster confronts the violence of the modes of Western being that went into his constitution, modelled by the alien and alienating nature of his maker, apparently the model of Western object relations, who is himself rather passive-aggressive in how he at once courts and shuns the company of others. Victor confuses his love for the Monster—or rather, at first, his love for the *idea* of embodying this love in the form of the Monster—with his profoundly narcissistic desire to master that embodiment's intractable otherness as his own, which desire he recognizes and disavows through his revulsion at seeing the result. Each time he confronts the death of his immediate circle (the primal scene of which is, of course, the early death of his own "mother"), it is as if he witnesses the Monster writing home to him the profoundly aggressive nature that lies at the core of all desiring subjects. Among the various tellings that shape the novel, then, perhaps none is more insidious than Victor, persuaded by the Monster's powers of analysis, "determined at least to listen to his tale ... partly urged by curiosity," although "compassion confirmed [his] resolution": "For the first time, also, I felt what the duties of a creator towards his creature were, and that I ought to render him happy before I complained of his wickedness" (102). If a preternatural curiosity drives him, which is one thing, his recognition that he should have compassion is this curiosity's most insidious form. *Now* he decides to show—that is, perform—love.

Or rather, Victor defaults to a love he feels he should feel, which is to say, as a properly trained product of his romantic inheritance of the civic, democratic, proto-neoliberal ideals of sympathy, he turns to compassion as a default for love, and while he "consented to listen," he did so with "a heavy heart, and depressed spirits" (102). It is as if he witnesses, as the Monster recognizes in his own reflection, the *Geworfenheit* of his place in the world. Phillips writes that "To love what is other is to love what cannot be loved; it is like being force fed, and like being force fed it could only unleash an extreme violence, or the extreme stifling of violent energies called depression."[52] This murderous insistence becomes that much more powerful when the Monster witnesses Victor tearing apart the one object that would "complete" the Monster, as if literally to materialize for the Monster what is wrong with the entire mode of relationality into which he introduces the Monster in the first place. Implicitly the Monster realizes the horror of his own desire for a certain kind of Western relationality that signifies his mastery via the demands of his "hyperbolizing ego." At the most primal, amoral level of his experience of his "ontological discomfort," that is to say, the Monster realizes that in murder, the victim just happens to be in the way—the way in which "the possibility of violent collision ... remains a constant menace in movement."[53] Which is what, again, makes Victor's apparent disavowal of the monster a form of stubbornly passionate attachment masquerading as the most toxic form of bad consciousness and which suggests why the Monster, like Dora with Freud or Matilda with Woodville in Mary Shelley's second novel, challenges Victor's mindless mindfulness.

But, of course, the Monster never leaves the scene of his relation to his maker. Instead, as if determined to write the annihilating impulse of Victor's empathy back to itself, the Monster spreads his vehemence, like the plague in Shelley's third novel, *The Last Man* (1826), across a vast geopolitical terrain, as if to mark the territory of a mode of relationality that reaches even places one would think devoid of relationality. As he says to Walton, once he realized that Victor "dared to hope for happiness," he became bent on his destruction. But as the Monster continues, "For while I destroyed his hopes, I did not satisfy my own desires. They were for ever ardent and craving; still I desired love and fellowship, and I was still spurned" (221). Perhaps the novel's most tragic dimension lies in its attempt, like Victor for the Monster, to "render" happiness as social construct rather than authentic feeling.[54] The novel drives toward happiness as the finite and static yet utterly elusive goal of a desire that systemically eludes all characters. For instance, anticipating their wedding, Victor notes that "Elizabeth seemed happy," although "Those were the last moments of my life during which I enjoyed the feeling of happiness" (192). Happiness and the "feeling *of* happiness" are two very different things. The Monster, noting a similar desire in those around him, spends a great deal of time seeking out what happiness and hope might mean. Stalking and witnessing Felix, Agatha, and their father, he ascertains that "They were not entirely happy" (110) and wonders why their "looks of affection and kindness" might at the same time "express pain" (111): "I was at first unable to solve these questions; but perpetual attention and time explained to me many appearances which were at first enigmatic." Subsequently he "longed to discover the motives and feelings of these lovely creatures" so that "it might be in [his] power to restore happiness to these deserving people" (115). He has, again, learned to become the perfect Western liberal subject, except that something about happiness is designed to *not* make it work, which is to say that something more primal is at work beneath the surface of hope. Every effort reminds him of his "accursed origin," such that every time he "cherished hope, ... it vanished" (131). As Sara Ahmed argues, the "hap of happiness then gets translated into something good," making happiness an "anticipatory causality" that "something good" will happen.[55] One's habituation to happiness orchestrates a contraband relationship between violence and civility that structures how subjects feel and feel about others and their environment. As the goal of Victor's "senseless curiosity," happiness, masquerading as love, becomes the novel's death drive.

Bersani speaks of Freud's *Thanatos* as a kind of "metaphysic death drive": "Ultimately, humans are conveyor belts for lines of force that are intrinsically unrelated to their humanness."[56] This is to mark the profoundly inhuman dimension of the will as the "energy of pure force":

> The human carries the line of force but, in embodying it, also contravenes it, slows it down. Personality and language, with varying degrees of effectiveness, block impersonal force. Energy incarnate is frictional energy; the flesh, the body that carries lines of force into the world is also what modulates them, what coerces unimpeded force into a continuously interrupted thrusting, a pulsating back and forth.[57]

Something of this force characterizes, on one hand, the blind ambition and curiosity that drive Victor and, on the other hand, the swift and brutal manner in which the Monster erupts in and out of everyone's lives. His boat "shot across the waters with an arrowy swiftness" (168); he "[ran] with the swiftness of lightning" (196); "he fled with more than mortal speed" (203). Like a "sprung" (223) animal, the Monster traverses the novel's attempt to humanize and thus civilize its otherwise inhuman modes of relationality. Put another way, Victor's curiosity is "senseless" because it exists beyond sense—not only beyond reason and rationality but also beyond his desire to know his own feelings, to master the very perceptual apparatus of his body. Instead, like the Monster, he encounters that he "has a physical identity in excess of the psychic identity with which all humans have been enriched and burdened in the course of our evolution."[58] Put simply, the problem of becoming and being human is human being(s). The Monster's "sprung" nature, like the shocks of the novel's gothic machinery, suggests a broader attempt to escape, not life, but those who make it hell simply by being, and thus being in the way.

How You Reason and Philosophize about Love

For Bersani, Phillips "raises the possibility of analysis as no longer based on the prospect, or the illusion, of personal knowledge."[59] Again drawing on the work of Bollas, Bersani notes that we are "*choreographed into being,*" in that our first form of knowledge is to "'learn the grammar of our being before we grasp the rules of our language.'"[60] Bersani suggests that "[o]ur uniqueness, our individuality, is the form of how we have, over time, moved ourselves and how others have moved us, through space," which speaks to the "specificity of a corporeal rhythm" as opposed to any "psychic content."[61] This is to set aside any "epistemological ambitions" in the name of exploring, as in the original mother/infant dyad, "something about how [the mother] knows [the infant]," more particularly "how she wants him to be knowable."[62] That is to say, the "mother and infant may have a growing sense of what each other are like, but they are more attuned by their impersonal narcissistic investment in each other, to what each is becoming in the presence of the other," a "first intimacy [that] is an intimacy with a process of becoming, not with a person."[63] "Impersonal intimacy asks of us what is the most inconceivable thing: to believe in the future without needing to personalize it. Without, as it were, seeing in our own terms,"[64] which may be what Shelley is trying to impress upon her future husband in that early letter. The purpose of analysis is thus not to define the "psychological subject," but rather to "rehearse[] … revised reenactments of a choreographed self-fashioning."[65] "Strangely," Bersani notes, "there is no psychological subject within the therapeutic move,"[66] for psychoanalysis consists precisely in disentangling the subject from the coercive object relations of its formation to reveal the "'virtual being,'" what Phillips calls "'potential being' as long as the potential is always seen as an unknowable (i.e., unpredictable) category [that] would be precisely the object of this kind of love."[67] Turning our attention to such a "'process of becoming'" attunes us to experience as what Bersani calls "evolving affinities of being." If only Victor and the Monster had known that, although Shelley, specifically by showing us the tragedy of what does *not* work in Western modes of relationality, seems to infer such a "life-enhancing alternative."

In the meantime, *Frankenstein* gives us the monstrous allegory of the psychological subject as constituted by its own inhumanity, a focus of post-Lacanian accounts of psychoanalysis. Colette Soler argues that psychoanalysis addresses the discontents of "humanisation," which mediates the "frontier between survival and socialisation," a "colonising" process that echoes Alenka Zupančič's discussion of the advent of sexuality, not as the "ultimate horizon of the animal called 'human'" nor "the anchor-point of irreducible humanity," but as "the operator of de-humanisation or 'de-anthropomorp hisation.'"[68] In this way, Frankenstein's attempt to fashion the mirror of his humanity ushers the subject through the mirror stage of its own genesis, which materializes the missed encounter with the real of humanity itself as *its* very constitution. The fort/da between monster and maker confronts "Freud's most profound originality": "to set affect free from psychic organization; unbound affect produces the excitement of *jouissance*," especially at its limit, where the "'extraordinary narcissistic enjoyment' that accompanies satisfied aggression at once hyperbolizes the ego and risks shattering its boundaries."[69] To confront this desiring limit of the subject, the "schism between affect and affectively unmotivated force" is to feel, as it were, the unknowability of feeling itself, what we otherwise trivialize and sentimentalize by calling it love, or rather love's ultimate goal in happiness.[70] The more Victor represses the de-humanizing violence of the ego's desire, the more it returns in the uncannily civilized, seriously discontented form of the Monster, catching both in what Soler calls the "real unconscious [*inconscient réel*] … a knowledge to be deciphered, but which remains impregnable, one that we can never entirely catch up to."[71]

That the novel, poised at the "impregnable" limit of knowledge, leaves the Monster un-named marks his barred entrance to the symbolic *within* the symbolic as the negative form of a possible "life-enhancing alternative" to symbolic relations, which are anything but human. Unable to acquiesce, refusing to go away, the monster, as *ich*, functions as the "key symptom" that "still persists" "beyond fantasy," what in Seminar XXIII Lacan explores as *le sinthome*, "a certain signifying formation penetrated with enjoyment: it is a signifier as a bearer of *jouis-sense*, enjoyment-in-sense."[72] The symptom as psychic rebus or obstacle is the manifestation of something gone wrong, the significance of which we at first miss and resist, something to get past in order to access the "correct," "native," or "normal" mode of our being. The "symptom, conceived as *sinthome*," however, "is literally our only substance, the only positive support of our being, the only point that gives consistency to the subject."[73] We can thus say that Victor's neglect of the monster signals the fact that the suturing *had* and *has* to take place. That is to say, Shelley's novel casts the shadows of the future of psychoanalysis as the tragedy of the inhuman, but equally intuits the farce of a culture that insists on the fantasy of its own humanity. Yet if Shelley writes this impossibility as tragedy, it is tragedy without catharsis as the farce that comes with imagining the tragedy could resolve the epistemological dilemma of the human condition in the first place. In the political unconscious of psychoanalysis to which the novel contributes its unfinished and unfinishable narrative—it prophecies the *demise* of psychoanalysis itself. Letting go of psychoanalysis, as Adam Phillips suggests, frees it to do its more profound work of an (un)thought "more committed to happiness" (though not of the facile kind) "and inspiration … than to self-knowledge, rigorous thinking, or the Depths of Being," a practice that "values truthfulness but not truth."[74] Shelley's novel thus offers psychoanalysis as a prophetic counter-history of the subject. The monster walks out of the novel as if through the mirror stage of fantasy itself to no place in particular, there being no place to go.

Notes

1   Hannah Arendt, *The Human Condition* (Garden City, NY: Doubleday, 1959), 1.
2   Ibid., 2.
3   Ibid., 2.
4   Mary Shelley, *Frankenstein; or the Modern Prometheus* (New York: Oxford University Press, 2008). Page references to this edition are cited parenthetically in the text throughout this chapter.
5   Slavoj Žižek, *On Belief* (New York: Zone Books, 2001), 8.
6   Ibid., 8–9.
7   Marc Rubinstein, "'My Accursed Origin': The Search for the Mother in *Frankenstein*," *Studies in Romanticism* 15 (Spring, 1976): 165–94. In "From the

History of an Infantile Neurosis" (1918), Freud could "venture upon no decision" if the primal scene was a repressed reality or a phantasy reconstructed from the unconscious; moreover, he found the distinction irrelevant, for one could only remember the past through one's imaginary reconstruction of it in any case (*The Standard Edition of the Complete Psychological Works of Sigmund Freud*, trans. James Strachey, 23 vols. [London: Vintage, 2001], 17:97). As Ned Lukacher argues, the primal scene is always already a scene of analysis, an "ontologically undecidable intertextual event that is situated in the differential space between historical memory and imaginative construction, between archival verification and interpretive free play" (*Primal Scenes: Literature, Philosophy, Psychoanalysis* [Ithaca: Cornell University Press, 1986], 24).

8   Fred Botting notes that the novel "appears a most appropriate subject for [psycho] analysis to revel in and reveal the effects of profound unconscious wishes and traumas, conflicts of ego and id and, of course, oedipal anxieties and fantasies" (*Making Monstrous:* Frankenstein, *Criticism, Theory* [New York: St. Martin's Press, 1991], 90). That the novel is born from Mary's Shelley's dream of the novel, of course, makes it difficult to resist psychoanalyzing either Shelley's motives or the text they produce, as Martin Tropp notes (cited in Botting, *Making Monstrous*, 91). See esp. Jerrold E. Hogle's special volume, *Frankenstein's Dream* for *Romantic Circles Praxis* (June 2003). https://romantic-circles.org/praxis/frankenstein/index.html. Botting's chapter in *Making Monstrous*, "Allure, Authority, and Psychoanalysis: The 'Case' of *Frankenstein*" (90–99), addresses an array of Freudian psychoanalytic approaches to the novel up to that point, but moves beyond them to address an issue central to my own approach: "the inability of psychoanalysis to realise its presumed authority with the revelation of truth" (93). This "inability" makes the novel an allegory for psychoanalysis as a kind of non-ontology, less a psychic content, either authorial or textual, to be deciphered, however resistant to understanding, than a missed encounter with understanding itself. Regardless, I am indebted to a legacy of psychoanalytical and psychological readings of the poem (and this is by no means an exhaustive list) that, besides Botting's *Making Monstrous* and *Frankenstein/Mary Shelley* (New York: St. Martin's, 1995), includes: Morton Kaplan and Robert Kloss, "The Fantasy of Paternity and the Doppelganger: Mary Shelley's *Frankenstein*," in *The Unspoken Motive* (New York: Free Press, 1973), 119–45; J. M. Hill, "Frankenstein and the Physiognomy of Desire," *American Imago* 32 (1975): 335–58; Marc Rubinstein, "'My Accursed Origin'"; William Veeder, "The Negative Oedipus: Father, *Frankenstein,* and the Shelleys," *Critical Inquiry* 12 (1986): 365–90; Mary Jacobus, "Is There a Woman in This Text?" *New Literary History* 14 (1982): 117–41; David Collings, "The Monster and the Imaginary Mother," in *Frankenstein*, ed. Johanna M. Smith (Boston: Bedford Books of St. Martin's Press, 1992), 245–58; Paul Youngquist, "*Frankenstein*: The Mother, the Daughter, and the Monster," *Philological Quarterly* 70, no. 3 (1993): 339–59; Peter Brooks, "What Is a Monster? (According to *Frankenstein*)," in *Body Work: Objects of Desire in Modern Narrative* (Cambridge, MA: Harvard University Press, 1993), 199–220; and Marie Mulvey-Roberts, "The Corpse in the Corpus: *Frankenstein*, Rewriting Wollestonecraft, and the Abject," in *Mary Shelley's Fictions: From Frankenstein to Falkner*, ed. Michael Eberle-Sinatra (New York: St. Martin's Press, 2000), 197–210.

9   Leo Bersani, "The It in the I," in *Intimacies*, ed. Leo Bersani and Adam Phillips (Chicago: University of Chicago Press, 2008), 25.

10 Ibid.

11 Ibid.

12 Ibid.

13 Cited in Russell Jacoby, "When Freud Came to America," *The Journal of Higher Education*, September 21, 2009. http://www.chronicle.com/article/Freuds-Visit-to-Clark-U/48424.

14 Christopher Bollas, *The Mystery of Things* (New York: Routledge, 1999), 9. Bollas borrows the term from Melanie Klein.

15 Ibid.

16 Ibid., 10.

17 Percy Shelley, *The Triumph of Life*, *Shelley's Poetry and Prose*, ed. Donald H. Reiman and Neil Fraistat (New York: W. W. Norton, 2002), l. 21. Shelley's text proceeds as a series of unanswered questions—"And what is this?" (l. 177); "First who art thou?" (l. 199); "Whence camest thou and whither goest thou?/How did thy course begin [...] and why?" (ll. 296–97); "Then, what is life?" (l. 544).

18 Leo Bersani, *Receptive Bodies* (Chicago: University of Chicago Press, 2018), ix.

19 Ibid.

20 Ibid., 59, 25.

21 Ibid., ix.

22 See Andy Clark and David Chalmers, "The Extended Mind," *Analysis* 58 (1998): 7–19; and *The Extended Mind*, ed. Richard Menary (Cambridge, MA: MIT Press, 2010). See Jane Bennet, *Vibrant Matter: A Political Ecology of Things* (Durham, NC: Duke University Press, 2009), and also Mark Rowlands, *The Body in Mind: Understanding Cognitive Processes* (Cambridge: Cambridge University Press, 1998).

23 Bollas, *Being a Character: Psychoanalysis and Self-Experience* (New York: Routledge, 1993), 186, 187; *Mystery*, 13.

24 As Nancy Yousef notes in *Isolated Cases: The Anxieties of Autonomy in Enlightenment Philosophy and Romantic Literature* (Ithaca: Cornell University Press, 2004), "This is the case not because the creature is cursed with a hideous body veiling a non-monstrous person but because to wear the human form in this novel is to bear a human history" (168), an empiricism that short-circuits access to any inner essence because the outer *is* this access—which is to mark the Monster's double bind as the subject's virtual inability to see and be seen, and thus to know.

25 Brooks, *Body Work*, 220.

26 Ibid., 202, 203.

27 Ibid., 203.

28 Ibid.

29 Botting, *Making Monstrous*, 22.

30 Fred Botting, *Frankenstein/Mary Shelley* (New York: St. Martin's, 1995), 1; cited in Diane Hoeveler, "*Frankenstein*, Feminism, and Literary Theory," in *The Cambridge Companion to Mary Shelley*, ed. Esther Schor (Cambridge: Cambridge University Press, 2003), 45. Hoeveler provides a helpful overview of Freudian and Lacanian readings of the novel (45–62).

31 Ibid., 3.

32 Sigmund Freud and Joseph Breuer, *Studies on Hysteria* (1895), *The Standard Edition*, 2:166.

33 See Freud, "Analysis Terminable and Interminable" (1937), *The Standard Edition*, 23:209–54.

34 Carl Jung, "The Psychology of the Transference" (1946), in *The Collected Works of C. G. Jung*, ed. Herbert Read, Michael Fordham, and Gerhard Adler; trans. R. F. C. Hull, 21 vols. (New York and Princeton: Princeton University Press, 1953–83), 16:182, 177–8.

35 Godwin calls this curiosity "magnetical," in that Caleb does "not know that, where there is mystery, there is always something at bottom that will not bear the telling," in *Caleb Williams*, ed. David McCracken (Oxford: Oxford University Press, 1991), 112, 148. Botting draws our attention to the parallel (77). See my "Speaking of Godwin's *Caleb Williams*: The Talking Cure and the Psychopathology of Enlightenment," *English Studies in Canada* 33, no. 1–2 (June/September 2005): 99–122.

36 Cathy Caruth, "Introduction," in *Trauma: Explorations in Memory*, ed. Cathy Caruth (Baltimore: Johns Hopkins University Press, 1995), 5.

37 Jacques Lacan, *Seminar I: Freud's Papers on Technique*, ed. Jacques-Alain Miller, trans. John Forrester (New York: W. W. Norton, 1991), 66.

38 Botting, *Making Monstrous*, 95.

39 I take the notion of transference as transposition from Jerrold Hogle, *Shelley's Process: Radical Transference and the Development of His Major Works* (Oxford: Oxford University Press, 1988), esp. 10–18.

40 See Freud, "Remembering, Repeating and Working-Through: Further Recommendations on the Technique of Psycho-Analysis, II)," *The Standard Edition* 12 (1914): 145–56. Transference shifts the epistemological and ontological grounds upon which the subject comes to understand his being. "By postulating the death drive," writes Lukacher, "Freud attempts to account for the absolute resistance to recollection that he meets in the transference" (*Primal Scenes*, 87). Jung, like Lacan, saw the unconscious as unreadable: "the unconscious is by definition not amenable to direct observation and can only be inferred" (*Collected Works*, 16:170). Transference thus signaled a "mutual unconsciousness" or "unconscious infection" between analyst and analysand (16:176). It thus challenges "not only our understanding and our sympathy, but the whole man" and is "what happens when the check normally exerted on the unconscious by the conscious mind is disrupted" (16:178, 187).

41 Shelley, *A Defence of Poetry, Shelley's Poetry and Prose*, 517.

42 See "More Than a Feeling: Shelley's Affect," *Romantic Circles Praxis* (May 2018). https://romantic-circles.org/praxis/affect/praxis.2018.affect.faflak.html.

43 I hasten to note my debt to two recent accounts of love in the work of Percy Shelley: Julie Carlson, "Like Love: The Feel of Shelley's Similes," in *Romanticism and the Emotions*, ed. Joel Faflak and Richard C. Sha (Cambridge: Cambridge University Press, 2013), 76–97; and Chris Washington, "The Dark Side of the Light: The Triumph of Love in Shelley's *The Triumph of Life*," *Romantic Circles Praxis* (October 2019). https://romantic-circles.org/praxis/triumph/praxis.2019.triumph.washington. html. Both see in Shelley's verse a potentiality I explore below. As Washington writes, "Imagining beyond the anthropocentric subject, Shelley's theory of love suggests not the egoistic chaos of a world lost to political anarchy but rather a radical politics of love that creates worlds anew," which suggests that Shelley was no doubt influenced by his wife's searing analysis of love as a theoretical prospect in her first novel. See also Carlson's account of the Godwin-Shelley family romance in *England's First Family of Writers: Mary Wollstonecraft, William Godwin, Mary Shelley* (Baltimore: Johns Hopkins University Press, 2007).

44 To Percy Shelley, November 3, 1814. In Mary Shelley, *The Letters of Mary Wollstonecraft Shelley*, 3 vols., ed. Betty T. Bennett (Baltimore: Johns Hopkins University Press, 1980), 1:5. I thank Richard Sha for pointing out this reference.

45 Adam Phillips, "On a More Personal Note," in *Intimacies*, ed. Bersani and Phillips, 103.

46 Ibid., 90.

47 Bersani, *Receptive Bodies*, 59.

48 Leo Bersani, "The Power of Evil and the Power of Love, in Bersani and Phillips," in *Intimacies*, 74.

49 Ibid., 71.

50 Ibid., 70.

51 Ibid., 66.

52 Phillips, "On a More Personal Note," 101–2.

53 Bersani, *Receptive Bodies*, 72.

54 See my "Jane Austen and the Persuasion of Happiness," *Romanticism and the Emotions*, 98–123.

55 Sara Ahmed, *The Promise of Happiness* (Durham: Duke University Press, 2010), 30, 40.

56 Bersani, *Receptive Bodies*, 60.

57 Ibid., 63.

58 Ibid., 80.

59 Ibid., 53–4.

60 Ibid., 54.

61 Ibid., 55.

62 Ibid., 54.

63 Philips, "On a More Personal Note," 113, 114.

64 Ibid., 117.

65 Bersani., *Receptive Bodies*, 55.

66 Ibid., 55.

67 Philips, "On a More Personal Note," 107.

68 Colette Soler, *Humanisation? Psychoanalysis, Symbolisation, and the Body of the Unconscious*, trans. Benjamin Farrow and Hugues D'Alascio (New York: Routledge, 2018), 1. Alenka Zupančič, *Why Psychoanalysis? Three Interventions* (Aarhus: Aarhus University Press, 2008), 3.

69 Bersani and Phillips, *Intimacies*, 66–7.

70 Bersani, *Receptive Bodies*, 72. For Bersani, such an encounter is what locates "psychoanalytic thinking … outside categorical thought" (Bersani and Phillips, 67), the place where, as Derrida argues, psychoanalysis encounters its greatest resistance to itself. See Jacques Derrida, *Resistances to Psychoanalysis*, trans. Peggy Kamuf, Pascale-Anne Brault, and Michael Naas (Stanford: Stanford University Press, 1998).

71 Soler, *Humanisation?*, 7.

72 Slavoj Žižek, *The Sublime Object of Ideology* (New York: Verso, 1989), 74–5.

73 Ibid., 75.

74 Adam Phillips, *Promises, Promises: Essays on Psychoanalysis and Literature* (New York: Basic Books, 2001), xv.

6

The "very creature he creates": *Frankenstein* in the Making of *Moby-Dick*

Samuel Otter

For Herman Melville, in writing *Moby-Dick; or, the Whale*, Mary Shelley's *Frankenstein: or, the Modern Prometheus* was not peripheral but crucial. A recognition of that importance helps to advance the ongoing critical effort to evaluate the transatlantic networks of nineteenth-century literature. Elisa Tamarkin has argued that "the project of transatlanticism is almost impossible to conceptualize, in literary terms at least, without a sense that its character as an intellectual practice is essentially genealogical."[1] The connections between Melville and Shelley extend our understanding of Anglo-American literature, and specifically the portrayal of male identity and intensity, the relationships between form and epistemology, the archive of materialisms, the correspondences between verbal and visual culture, and the dynamics of literary creativity.

Acquiring *Frankenstein* from their joint British publisher Richard Bentley, Melville in a pivotal scene in *Moby-Dick*, describing the spectacle of a fractured Ahab, the victim of his own consuming obsession, drew upon Shelley's scene in which Victor Frankenstein first encounters the Creature he has created, a tableaux that Shelley had emphasized at the beginning of a chapter and in her introduction to the revised third edition of the novel. Melville multiplies Shelley's divisions, turning her portrait of male compulsion and abandonment into an intimate, alienating encounter with self-difference (Ahab becomes both creator and creature), a revelatory moment in which the distinctions between what is internal and what is external to the self are confounded and integrity and agency are dispersed. Both authors examine the manufacture of their male protagonists and the substance of their corporeal quests. Like Shelley, Melville places on display an assortment of bodily parts (his Whale and her Creature) and invites readers to assemble them, but refrains from embodying the

I appreciate the invitations to speak on the topic of this essay offered by Orrin Wang and Edlie Wong at the University of Maryland and by Tom Schmid and Brian Yothers at the University of Texas at El Paso. These opportunities and the responses of audience members contributed to the development of the argument. I am also grateful for research assistance provided by Katherine Bondy and Danny Luzon.

whole and raises questions about monstrosity. In his rendering of Victor Frankenstein's encounter with his Creature, Melville not only reworks Shelley's words from both her chapter and her introduction but also reimagines the engraved frontispiece in the third edition of *Frankenstein* that he owned. In the frontispiece, the artists Theodor Von Holst and William Chevalier themselves had interpreted Victor Frankenstein's recognition scene, presenting the creator and Creature as intimately bound in their vulnerability and distress and refusing the ascriptions of hideousness proclaimed by an array of characters. The *Moby-Dick/Frankenstein* relationship offers a striking example of the complex relays between image and word in nineteenth-century illustration that scholars recently have been tracing.[2] Shelley's and Melville's recognition scenes also have reflexive qualities, affording an opportunity for the writers to reflect on their own literary creations and for readers to consider the artifacts that these books have brought into being.

At least since Luther Mansfield and Howard Vincent's 1952 scholarly edition of *Moby-Dick*, literary critics have mentioned a link between Melville's book and *Frankenstein*. Mansfield and Vincent point to chapter 108, in which Ahab tells the *Pequod*'s bewildered carpenter that he will order the ship's blacksmith to manufacture "a complete man after a desirable pattern ... fifty feet high in his socks ... chest modelled after the Thames tunnel" (412).[3] Others, such as Hershel Parker, Andrew Delbanco, and Shawn Thompson, have noted verbal echoes of *Frankenstein* in the shared plots of obsession and revenge. Yet rarely is Shelley's novel discussed as a significant intellectual or aesthetic influence on *Moby-Dick*. I know of only a few such analyses, including John Bryant's essay comparing the techniques of narrative framing in the two books and Chris Baldick's chapter from *In Frankenstein's Shadow* about capitalist monsters, divided male psyches, and the ambiguities of pursuer and pursued.[4]

We know that Melville obtained a copy of *Frankenstein* in 1849 from his British publisher Richard Bentley, who had brought out Melville's third, fourth, and fifth books (*Mardi* and *Redburn* in 1849, *White-Jacket* in 1850) and would publish the sixth, *Moby-Dick*, in 1851. Bentley and his partner Henry Colburn held the copyright for Shelley's *Frankenstein*, which first appeared in three volumes in 1818. They published a revised, one-volume third edition in 1831, which Bentley, no longer working with Colburn, reprinted in 1849, bound with the first volume of Schiller's *The Ghost-Seer*, as volume 9 in the series *Standard Novels and Romances*. Melville records his ownership of *Frankenstein* in a list he made that was included in the journal of his trip to England in late 1849 (Figure 6.1).[5] He acquired *Frankenstein* just before he began writing *Moby-Dick*, and we can see the effects of Shelley's novel on his thinking and his literary practice in a pivotal chapter titled "The Chart."

In this chapter, the narrator Ishmael describes a scene below the decks of the whaling ship *Pequod*, in Captain Ahab's cabin, a scene that, given maritime social hierarchies and spatial discriminations, he could not have witnessed. The chapter begins with Ahab poring over his log-books and tracing paths on his maritime charts, seeking to calculate where and when he will encounter Moby Dick. It ends with a scene of eloquent vehemence, one of the most exacting passages in the book. Often at night, the narrator explains, Ahab would be forced from his hammock by his dreams:

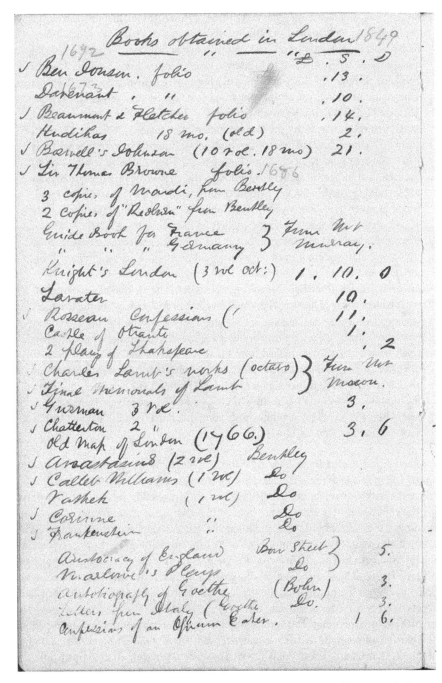

Figure 6.1 Melville's list of "Books obtained in London," 1849, part of his journal of a trip to England and the Continent in 1849–50. "Frankenstein" appears as the sixth title up from the bottom of the list. MS Am 188 (372), Houghton Library, Harvard University.

[W]hen, as was sometimes the case, these spiritual throes in him heaved his being up from its base, and a chasm seemed opening in him, from which forked flames and lightnings shot up, and accursed fiends beckoned him to leap down among them; when this hell in himself yawned beneath him, a wild cry would be heard through the ship; and with glaring eyes Ahab would burst from his state room, as though escaping from a bed that was on fire. Yet these, perhaps, instead of being the unsuppressable symptoms of some latent weakness, or fright at his own resolve, were but the plainest tokens of its intensity. For, at such times, crazy Ahab, the scheming, unappeasedly steadfast hunter of the white whale; this Ahab that had gone to his hammock, was not the agent that so caused him to burst from it in horror again. The latter was the eternal, living principle or soul in him; and in sleep, being for the time dissociated from the characterizing mind, which at other times employed it for its outer vehicle or agent, it spontaneously sought escape from the scorching contiguity of the frantic thing, of which, for the time, it was no longer an integral. But as the mind does not exist unless leagued with the soul, therefore it must have been that, in Ahab's case, yielding up all his thoughts and fancies to his one supreme purpose; that purpose, by its own sheer inveteracy of will, forced itself against gods and devils into a kind of self-assumed, independent being of its own. Nay, could grimly live and burn, while the common vitality to which it was conjoined, fled horror-stricken from the unbidden and unfathered birth. Therefore, the tormented spirit that glared out of bodily eyes, when what seemed Ahab rushed from his room, was for the time but a vacated thing, a formless somnambulistic being, a ray of living light, to be sure, but without an object to color, and therefore a blankness in itself. God help thee, old man, thy thoughts have created a creature in thee; and he whose intense thinking thus makes him a Prometheus; a vulture feeds upon that heart for ever; that vulture the very creature he creates. (190–1)

A chapter that begins in an isolated cabin with meticulous drawing on sea charts ends with an image of the self ablaze, fleeing from and devouring itself. According to Ishmael, Ahab's focus leads to his disintegration. Unraveled by his intensity, his parts no longer cohere and readers are provided with a glimpse of an alternative state. Ahab becomes a semblance of himself, and his self-division is conveyed through a series of knotted allusions: to the omnipresence of hell in Christopher Marlowe's *Faustus*, to the internal hells in Thomas Browne's *Religio Medici*, to Satan's soliloquy in Book 6 of Milton's *Paradise Lost*, to the last act of Byron's *Manfred*, in which Manfred defies the Spirit by describing his internal torture and self-destruction. Melville owned or had access to all of these texts while he was writing *Moby-Dick*.[6]

In the long passage that I have quoted, the figurative overload, multiplied abstractions, and blurred antecedents render the sentences difficult to follow. It seems that at night, in sleep, Ahab's soul, described as his vital essence ("the eternal, living principle … in him"), becomes detached from his will, which has assumed an independence and sovereignty. The soul recoils at the corrosive determination of the will and flees in the body. (The paragraph leaves open the possibility that another Ahab may remain in the cabin while this one rushes out.) Ahab's internal divisions are conveyed through a series of jarring metaphors, rendering faculty psychology into gothic spectacle. The self is split open and catches fire from its depths. The soul flees from the will. The will is brought into being as a creature that lives and feeds internally. The soul or spirit becomes vacant, a ray of light with no substance to reflect it. The referent in Melville's phrase "without an object to color" is uncertain. Is that object the mind? The body? A worldly goal? The spirit, without object, alienated from the "characterizing mind," lacks direction and consequence. It exists only as "a blankness in itself."

When the semblance of Ahab rushes from the stateroom, it is not entirely clear what is seeking to escape from what. "The common vitality," which can no longer endure the proximity of the monomaniacal will, may be the soul or some combination of soul, intellect, and emotions. The confusion here could be deliberate or could be the effect of Melville's rhetorical intensity, but there is no doubt about the fundamental discord on display.[7]

The allusions and metaphors in the scene culminate in the image of Ahab as a Prometheus, tortured not by a bird of prey sent by Zeus but by his own consuming thoughts. The narrator emphasizes the cycle of self-inflicted division and destruction, repeating the doubled phrases "created a creature" and "the very creature he creates." The image and diction here offer a complex response to Shelley's *Frankenstein* and particularly to the beginning of chapter 5 in the third edition, when the narrator Robert Walton relates Victor's account of first seeing the Creature stir to life in his student quarters at Ingolstadt, in Bavaria, and then fleeing his creation. Melville rewrites Shelley's portrait of nocturnal restlessness and recognition and exorbitantly incarnated self-estrangement:

> It was already one in the morning; the rain pattered dismally against the panes, and my candle was nearly burnt out, when, by the glimmer of the half-extinguished light, I saw the dull yellow eye of the creature open; it breathed hard, and a convulsive motion agitated its limbs.
>
> How can I describe my emotions at this catastrophe, or how delineate the wretch whom with such infinite pains and care I had endeavoured to form? His limbs were in proportion, and I had selected his features as beautiful. Beautiful!— Great God! His yellow skin scarcely covered the work of muscles and arteries beneath; his hair was of a lustrous black, and flowing; his teeth of a pearly whiteness; but these luxuriances only formed a more horrid contrast with his watery eyes, that seemed almost of the same colour as the dun white sockets in which they were set, his shriveled complexion and straight black lips.
>
> ... I had worked hard for nearly two years, for the sole purpose of infusing life into an inanimate body. For this I had deprived myself of rest and health. I had desired it with an ardour that far exceeded moderation; but now that I had finished, the beauty of the dream vanished, and breathless horror and disgust filled my heart. Unable to endure the aspect of the being I had created, I rushed out of the room, and continued a long time traversing my bedchamber, unable to compose my mind to sleep.[8] (43)

Across these paragraphs, Shelley juxtaposes the terms "creature" and "created," emphasizing shared etymology and the intimate, corrosive links between her protagonists. Later in the novel, she narrows the space between the repetition, most dramatically in the Alpine encounter, when the "monster" indicts the human being who has given him life: "Yet you, my creator, detest and spurn me, thy creature, to whom thou art bound by ties only dissoluble by the annihilation of one of us" (83). In her manuscript draft of the scene in which Victor flees from his study, Shelley originally made use of a similar polyptoton, having him say that he could not endure the sight of "the creature I had created." Her husband Percy drew a line through "creature" and inserted the word "being" above it, providing a more neutral term but diminishing the effects of contiguity. In the published novel, as in the quotation above, the phrase reads, "the being I had created." Mary Shelley had Victor Frankenstein recoil from "the creature I had created"; Melville has Ahab seek escape from "the very creature he creates." It is as though, when Melville at the end of "The Chart" rewrote the scene of Victor's flight, the resonance of Shelley's pairing and a strange sympathy—the depth of his interest in her portrait of divided male ambition and abandonment—led to the inadvertent return in his prose of her original phrasing.[9] The masculine dyads of creator and created, pursuer and pursued, and heroism and recklessness are also present in the novel published by Mary Shelley's father William Godwin, *Things as They Are; or, the Adventures of Caleb Williams*, another title on Melville's 1849 list of books obtained in London (spelled *Calleb Williams* and appearing nine titles up from the bottom; see Figure 6.1).

Both Shelley and Melville offer equivocal analyses of male ambition and obsession. Like Victor Frankenstein, Ahab is seized by one idea. Both characters seek to expose natural mysteries, figuring their quests in corporeal terms. Both dwell on the face and its enigmatic features, with Ahab's inquiries given a literal and violent edge as those features are viewed as recalcitrant, even hostile:

Victor Frankenstein:
I have described myself as always having been embued with a fervent longing to penetrate the secrets of nature ... [The most learned philosopher] had partially unveiled the face of Nature, but her immortal lineaments were still a wonder and a mystery. He might dissect, anatomise, and give names; but, not to speak of a final cause, causes in their secondary and tertiary grades were utterly unknown to him. (26–7)

Captain Ahab:
Hark ye yet again,—the little lower layer. All visible objects, man, are but as pasteboard masks. But in each event—in the living act, the undoubted deed—there, some unknown but still reasoning thing puts forth the mouldings of its features from behind the unreasoning mask. If man will strike, strike through the mask! ... That inscrutable thing is chiefly what I hate; and be the white whale agent, or be the white whale principal, I will wreak that hate upon him. (159)

Both Victor Frankenstein and Captain Ahab are melancholy and despairing, likened by their authors to trees blasted by lightning. Both harness the power of electricity to achieve their ends (Ahab most conspicuously in the chapter titled "The Candles"). Both suffer episodes of fever and raving. Fatal impulses drive them to dominate nature and to exact revenge. The two men are—or imagine they are—lured to their destinies by the objects of their pursuit. Both envision a manufactured man sutured out of disparate parts (Ahab does so in the chapter titled "Ahab and the Carpenter"). And their own volatile manufacture—how these men are assembled psychically and emotionally—is the preoccupation of their authors.

Like Frankenstein's Creature, Ahab is goaded by a sense of profound injury and gripped by vengeance. Both the Creature and the Captain are caustically aware of their bodily difference. They brood over agency and responsibility. Ahab is doubled not only in his self-alienation but also in the figures of the white whale, a further "creature he has created," and of the narrator Ishmael, who for a time succumbs to his captain's monomania and ultimately represents a different kind of obsession with the whale. Shelley's *Frankenstein* may have spurred Melville to multiply his pairings.

Of course, there are differences between the male protagonists in *Frankenstein* and in *Moby-Dick*. In the recognition scene, Victor Frankenstein is split into creator and creature, but he flees intact. In his recognition scene, Ahab is divided into two and then divided again, confusing the distinction between internal and external. He is "no longer an integral," neither part nor whole. The Creature is wracked by a sense of hideousness, while Ahab broods over the impotence typified by his severed leg. And Melville is concerned with theological matters in ways that Shelley is not: the possible absence of the divine is more urgent in *Moby-Dick* than its presumed absence in *Frankenstein*. But the resemblances between Shelley's young student and Melville's aged captain are notable.

In the introduction Shelley provided for the third edition of *Frankenstein*, she advertises the importance of the scene at Ingolstadt when Victor recoils from his creature. She claims that the novel had its beginning in her vision of a student who shuddered at the first signs of life in the appalling entity he had created. She imagined the student rushing away from "his odious handywork, horror-stricken." Waking from sleep, he hoped that he would find that the "thing" would no longer be alive. Instead, he saw the bed curtains part and the creature staring at him "with yellow, watery, but speculative eyes." Shelley describes herself as "possessed" and "haunted" by the "unbidden" product of her imagination (x–xi). This description echoes Victor's psychic state, thus associating the unsettling conceptions of author and protagonist. Whether or not this retrospective origin story is true, with it Shelley underscores the importance of Victor's encounter and flight. Her emphasis made an impression on Melville, who not only restaged Victor's scene for Ahab at the end of "The Chart" but, in doing so, incorporated adjectives from Shelley's 1831 preface. Melville combined her **"unbidden"** imagination and **"horror-stricken"** (x–xi) student in his portrait of Ahab fleeing **"horror-stricken"** from the **"unbidden** and unfathered birth" (191) he has provoked (emphasis added to highlight the repetition). Shelley's scene and diction became part of the verbal texture of *Moby-Dick*.

Shelley's emphasis also influenced the painter Theodor Von Holst and the engraver William Chevalier, who produced the now-famous frontispiece image in the third edition of *Frankenstein* (Figure 6.2). Holst and Chevalier illustrate and also interpret the recognition scene. Their setting is both medieval and modern, alchemist's chamber and scientist's laboratory. Visual rhythms unite three figures—Victor, the Creature, and an inserted skeleton—in a cycle of animation and decomposition. Victor stands at the threshold, the Creature sits on the floor, and the skeleton lies supine. Victor's dilated eyes, illuminated from below, look out and slightly down. The Creature's gaping eye (an emphasis carried over from Shelley) is directed at his pelvis or at his legs or at the skeleton between them. (Alexandra Neel describes this visual arrangement as a "birthing scene.") The empty sockets in the upside-down skull are angled upward and to the left, aimed toward or beyond the viewer, doubling but also diverging from Victor's gaze. To the right of the triangle formed by the Creature's legs, the raised and bent leg of the skeleton repeats but contracts the angle. The skeleton's limb points upward to Victor's body and is paired with his slightly bent leg. Their two feet converge in the shadows at the bottom of the door, beside the Creature's large foot. In Holst and Chevalier's portrayal, as Victor flees, his hand gripping the door and pushing it open, the three figures are linked by posture, pattern, and the illumination at the center of the image: a gothic *fiat lux* that extends from the creator to his creation. The Creature's wide eye—the eye that in Shelley's introduction and narrative repulses the student—here in the frontispiece stares at its body and conveys distress. Holst and Chevalier's depiction of the Creature is not, as it is in Shelley's text, mediated through the perspectives of Victor and the narrator Walton. In the engraving, the creature and his creator are both separated and bound in their alarm.[10]

Moby-Dick remained unillustrated in Melville's lifetime, but the frontispiece to Melville's copy of *Frankenstein*, with some alterations (an older protagonist, a shipboard cabin rather than a student's apartment), might serve as a visual accompaniment to "The Chart," elucidating Melville's chapter through its affinities and differences. Both Holst and Chevalier and Melville delineate the eruption of horror in confined quarters where the intensity of thought has taken shape. They offer scenes of male vulnerability and alienation and suggest a ruinous cycle from which escape is vain. Yet Melville's portrayal lacks the symmetry of Holst and Chevalier's frontispiece. Melville describes the aftermath, rather than the moment, of flight. While Holst and Chevalier place Victor Frankenstein's creation in the foreground, Melville's narrator broods over the entity that has rushed from the cabin. In contrast to the stream of light in the engraving that illuminates the Creature sprawled on the floor, Ahab's "tormented spirit," encased in the body but disengaged from it, is indistinct, like "a ray of living light … but without an object to color." Ahab's spirit, in Melville's odd locution, "glared out of bodily eyes." Melville's phrase transfigures the three gazes in Holst and Chevalier's frontispiece engraving: Victor's stare, the creature's gape, and the skeleton's hollow sockets. The phrase "glared out of bodily eyes" conveys an acute ocular estrangement. Ahab's spirit is estranged from his eyes; it "glares out of" them, shines through them without aim, in defiance and well as anguish.

FRANKENSTEIN

Figure 6.2 Frontispiece steel engraving in *Frankenstein: or, the Modern Prometheus: Revised, Corrected, and Illustrated with a New Introduction,* by Mary Wollstonecraft Shelley (London: Richard Bentley, 1849). Drawn by Theodor Von Holst and engraved by William Chevalier. Below the image appeared an engraved cursive version of a passage from page 43: *"By the glimmer of the half-extinguished light, I saw the dull yellow eye of the creature open; it breathed hard, and a convulsive motion agitated its limbs. * * * I rushed out of the room."*

Holst and Chevalier's vivid image and the text on which it is based also raise another possibility for influence. In an early chapter of *Moby-Dick*, Melville provides what we might regard as a counter-scene. Ishmael, late at night in his lodgings at the Spouter-Inn on the Massachusetts coast, before he signs onto the *Pequod* as a member of the crew, encounters an "abominable savage" (38), a large creature with an "unearthly complexion" (37), apparently disfigured face, and a head that reminds the transfixed narrator of "a mildewed skull" (38). As the Polynesian harpooneer Queequeg undresses and Ishmael watches from the shadows in bed, he considers running away, but has second thoughts given the location of his room on the second floor. Queequeg extinguishes the light, climbs into bed, begins feeling Ishmael, and a commotion ensues, mediated by the landlord. Then Queequeg invites Ishmael back into bed, the young sailor reassesses the situation, turns in, and instead of being awakened by the gaze and outstretched hand of a "monster"—Victor Frankenstein's term for the Creature before he rushes down the stairs (44)—Ishmael reports that he "never slept better in my life" (40). The next morning, he awakens to find Queequeg's arm thrown over him "in the most loving and affectionate manner" (41). In the scene at the Spouter-Inn, the obverse of Ahab's later spectral flight, Melville imagines an alternative outcome for Victor Frankenstein's initial encounter with the Creature.[11]

I have not yet mentioned one of the most notable aspects of Holst and Chevalier's frontispiece—their portrait of the Creature—and the related textual questions about his physical appearance that have become an interpretive crux for readers of Shelley's novel. In scene after scene, the characters—Victor, his youngest brother William, the narrator Robert Walton, the Creature himself—describe Frankenstein's creation as "hideous." The old man in a shepherd's hut shrieks upon seeing him and musters youthful energy to bolt across the fields. Agatha De Lacey faints. Felix De Lacey attacks. William covers his eyes and screams. Their reactions are manifest, but the cause is not. Shelley has both Victor and Walton articulate the representational challenge. As Victor describes the Creature's coming to life, he doubts his abilities to "delineate the wretch" (43). In the final scene of the novel, Walton tells his sister Margaret that the Creature presented "a form which I cannot find words to describe" (197).[12] Mary Shelley does describe the form of her Creature, but her words fall short of accounting for the revulsion of her characters.

Narrating to Walton the spectacle of the Creature awakening in the recognition scene, Shelley has Victor convey several details of his appearance. As already has been noted, Victor observes "the dull yellow eye of the creature open; it breathed hard, and a convulsive motion agitated its limbs." Victor tells Walton that he had "selected his features as beautiful" (43), but that when he viewed the Creature's pieced-together visage, he found it ghastly. The proportions of the Creature's body—the relationship of limbs to trunk—may not or may resemble the conventional symmetries of human figures (Shelley is inconsistent on this aspect), but the arrangement of the facial features—"selected" rather than natural—appalls viewers. At the beginning of his story, Victor exclaims, "Oh! no mortal could support the horror of that countenance" (44); at the end of the novel, Walton, seeing the Creature towering over Victor, echoes this response, "Never did I behold a vision so horrible as his face, of such loathsome, yet appalling hideousness" (197).[13]

Victor also reports that the Creature's skin offers disturbing access to what it should conceal: "His yellow skin scarcely covered the work of muscles and arteries beneath" (43). He portrays the Creature's movements as disturbing: not only the awakening convulsions but also "when those muscles and joints were rendered capable of motion, it became a thing such as even Dante could not have conceived" (44). Later in the novel, he describes how the Creature's words had provoked compassion that turned to disgust "when I looked upon him, when I saw the filthy mass that moved and talked" (128). The hideousness that the characters perceive also involves the Creature's size. Victor reports that he is "about eight feet in height, and proportionably large" (40), and both Victor and Walton refer to his "gigantic stature" (61, 11). The Creature himself claims that his "outward form" misrepresents his inner qualities or that it did at the start of his existence before his degradation (199–200), while Victor maintains that the Creature's "soul is as hellish as his form" (188).

To sum up: The Creature's eye is not transparent but muddled. His skin exposes what should be hidden. His animation is not smooth but broken. His size dilates and disconcerts presumptions about the human body. But a gap remains between these heterogeneous parts and the ostensibly hideous whole. Avoiding a sustained description, Shelley leaves it to her readers to assemble the Creature and assess his character. The question of the Creature's monstrosity has engaged a range of critics, including Chris Baldick, Patrick Brantlinger, Peter Brooks, Stefani Engelstein, Denise Gigante, and James Heffernan.[14]

In the frontispiece engraving, Holst and Chevalier delineate a figure whose appearance does not match the terms—"hideous" and "monster"—employed by the characters in the novel. The bones in the Creature's left arm and right leg are visible, evoking Victor's description of its attenuated skin, but this effect is restricted to these two limbs. The scar that runs parallel to the tibia in the right leg indicates the Creature's stitching, but the dominant linear effects in the body involve the smooth modeling of the torso and left leg achieved through Chevalier's cross-hatching. (In contrast, the cross-hatching in the upper part of the raised right arm indicates some misshapenness.) The Creature's head seems to lack a neck and to be situated toward the left shoulder, rather than in a central position, with an exploratory or supportive hand behind it. But such asymmetry is visually understated and can be interpreted expressively as well as literally, that is, can be interpreted to suggest both the Creature's sense of dislocation and his manufacture. The illustrators extend Shelley's detail of "lustrous black" hair, lending a gendered ambiguity to the Creature's head and amplifying its lack of fit on the masculinized body. The limbs, and especially the legs, appear large in proportion to the body, but not egregiously so, given the taste for classical exaggeration among the contemporary artists who influenced Holst.[15] The musculature in the torso is well defined. The face in profile, while anguished, consists of the standard features, conventionally arrayed.

Victor tells his friend Clerval that "The form of the monster on whom I had bestowed existence was for ever before my eyes" (48), and the terms "form" and "deformity" are frequently used by characters in Shelley's novel to evaluate the Creature. From his awakening in Victor's study to the last view of him on Walton's ship, the Creature is associated with the term "form." How do Shelley's characters, and the somewhat conflicted author herself, know the Creature? Through the arrangement or disorder of his parts, through his shape or outline, through the relationships between embodiment and essence, through what is directly given to their senses, through the categories they bring to their perceptions—that is, through the tangle of meanings the concept "form" has accrued. Victor has formed a Creature repeatedly labelled as "deformed," and that incongruity sustains Shelley's plots of horror and revenge. The Creature tells his creator, "my form is a filthy type of yours, more horrid even from the very resemblance" (112), and "deformity" in *Frankenstein*, as Brantlinger and Heffernan have argued, is plotted according to its deviation from a presumed human norm. The Creature's own responses epitomize this dynamic when, across only a dozen lines in the novel, Shelley has him first hope that the De Lacey family will "overlook the deformity of my figure," then admire the "perfect forms" of the De Laceys, and finally recoil from his own image in a pool and come to grasp his "miserable deformity" (97).

Questions of form and epistemology are also at the center of *Moby-Dick*, and Shelley's novel may have influenced Melville's literary inquiries in this regard. I have in mind not only aspects of Melville's book that I already have mentioned—the scrutiny of Ahab and the encounter between Ishmael and Queequeg—but also the epic undertaking to know whales. (The question of whether Moby Dick is a "monster" looms over Melville's narrative.) Although Melville's narrator continually employs the rhetoric of unrepresentability, whales are conspicuously visible in *Moby-Dick*, their outsides and insides open to view. The narrator's claims of elusiveness raise the stakes and incite exegesis. Attention is lavished on the vivid parts of the huge animals—head, forehead, jaw, teeth, penis, tail, skin, hump, contour, and skeleton—their proportions, and their relationship to what Ishmael refers to on several occasions as the "true form" of the sperm whale (237, 239, 325). In *Moby-Dick*, as in *Frankenstein*, readers are invited, even challenged, to assemble creaturely parts. Chapters delve into the whale's flesh, exposing sights like those that haunted Victor Frankenstein in the "vaults and charnel houses" (38), "the dissecting room and the slaughter-house" (41). Victor trembles at the mention of these scenes, but Ishmael's corporeal disclosures often come with a visceral jocularity and fascination.[16]

While composing *Moby-Dick*, Melville was influenced, verbally and visually, by Shelley's *Frankenstein*, and we can chart the relationships in the two books between scenes, images, and characters and issues of psychology, heroism, egotism, obsession, form, materiality, and creativity. In doing so, we gain a fuller understanding of the afterlife of *Frankenstein* and of the porousness of national literary borders.

In the introduction to the third edition of *Frankenstein*, which Melville owned, Shelley famously narrates the origin of her book, conceived in the summer of 1816 at Byron's villa near Lake Geneva. The guests, confined indoors due to inclement weather, agreed to Byron's proposal that they each write a ghost story. Shelley dramatizes her struggles in coming up with an idea, foreshadowing, in her retrospective account, issues of creativity that will animate her novel. She explains, invoking Genesis and distinguishing a secondary human labor from the divine original, that "Invention... does not consist in creating out of void, but out of chaos; the materials must, in the first place, be afforded: it can give form to dark, shapeless substances, but cannot bring into being the substance itself" (ix). She then alludes to an anecdote about Columbus and his egg. In this apocryphal tale, Columbus, a guest at a Spanish banquet, is asked by a jealous courtier if he thought there were other men in Spain who would have been capable of making his discoveries. In reply, Columbus takes an egg and invites the diners to stand it on its end. After no one can accomplish the task, he crushes the end of the egg on the table and then stands it on the ruptured part, making the point that once he had revealed the path all could follow it. This anecdote, which had been in circulation since the mid-fifteenth century, is another instance of transatlantic influence, since Shelley likely read a version in Washington Irving's 1828 *History of the Life and Voyages of Christopher Columbus*.[17] She draws from the story a lesson about how invention depends on reconceiving and manipulating previous materials. But the Columbus anecdote is intensified by its proximity to her own narrative of conceptual violence. Shelley's *Frankenstein*, like Columbus's egg, involves a theatrical, even aggressive, statement about transforming materials: taking the symbol of creation and re-creating it, both mocking and asserting origins, altering recognitions. *Frankenstein* and *Moby-Dick* are secondary creations, as Shelley describes them, sutured from disparate literary, scientific, philosophical, and mythological elements. But with their plots whose mere summary conveys their force (as Aristotle recommends for effective tragedy), their now-emblematic scenes and characters, and their exposures of creativity—disseminated over time in various media far beyond the academy and their countries of origin—their titles now epitomize their stories for those who have never read a page of Shelley or Melville. These two books, as Melville writes of "original" characters in *The Confidence-Man*, have produced effects "akin to that which in Genesis attends upon the beginning of things."[18]

Notes

1   Elisa Tamarkin, "Transatlantic Returns," in *A Companion to American Literary Studies*, ed. Caroline F. Levander and Robert S. Levine (New York: Blackwell, 2011), 274. Joseph Rezek usefully surveys the different emphases and governing arguments in the field of transatlantic studies, in "What We Need from Transatlantic Studies," *American Literary History* 26, no. 4 (Winter 2014): 791–803.

2   On intermediality and illustration, see Christopher J. Lukasik, "The Meaning of Illustration in Early Nineteenth-Century America," in *A Companion to Illustration*, ed. Alan Male (New York: John Wiley and Sons, 2019), 422–43.

3   Herman Melville, *Moby-Dick; or, the Whale*, ed. John Bryant and Haskell Springer (New York: Pearson Longman, 2007). Page references to this edition are cited parenthetically in the text. For Mansfield and Vincent's connection of this quote to *Frankenstein*, see their note 466.27 in Herman Melville, *Moby-Dick; or, the Whale*, ed. Luther S. Mansfield and Howard P. Vincent (New York: Hendricks House, 1962), 812–13.

4   Hershel Parker, *Herman Melville, A Biography: Vol. 1, 1819–1851* (Baltimore: Johns Hopkins University Press, 1996), 700; Andrew Delbanco, *Melville: His World and Work* (New York: Alfred A. Knopf, 2005), 129–30; Shawn Thompson, "British Romanticism," in *Herman Melville in Context*, ed. Kevin J. Hayes (New York:

Cambridge University Press, 2018), 271–2; John Bryant, "Melville Essays the Romance: Comedy and Being in *Frankenstein*, 'The Big Bear of Arkansas,' and *Moby-Dick*," *Nineteenth-Century Literature* 61, no. 3 (December 2006): 277–310; Chris Baldick, *In Frankenstein's Shadow: Myth, Monstrosity, and Nineteenth-century Writing* (New York: Oxford University Press, 1987), 74–84. Elizabeth Young discusses the ways in which Melville in his 1855 story "The Bell-Tower" (included in his 1856 collection *The Piazza Tales*) revises the story of *Frankenstein* as an anti-slavery racial allegory; see *Black Frankenstein: The Making of an American Metaphor* (New York: New York University Press, 2008), 42–4.

5   Rebecca Bauman describes the third edition in *Frankenstein 200: The Birth, Life, and Resurrection of Mary Shelley's Monster* (Bloomington: Indiana University Press and the Lilly Library, 2018), 13–17. On Melville's copy of *Frankenstein*, see Merton M. Sealts, Jr., *Melville's Reading: Revised and Enlarged Edition* (Columbia: University of South Carolina Press, 1988), entries 467 and 438a. Melville's list of "Books obtained in London 1849" can be found in facsimile and type in *Journals*, ed. Howard C. Horsford with Lynn Horth (Evanston and Chicago: Northwestern University Press and The Newberry Library, 1989), 144–5.

6   Mansfield and Vincent, in their Hendricks House edition of *Moby-Dick*, itemize the allusions to Browne, Shelley, and Byron (719); Jonathan A. Cook extends the list to Marlowe's *Doctor Faustus* and Goethe's *Faust*, in *Inscrutable Malice: Theodicy, Eschatology, and the Biblical Sources of "Moby-Dick"* (DeKalb: Northern Illinois University Press, 2012), 100–1.

7   Among those who parse the final scene in "The Chart," which between 1960 and 1990 served as a focal point for many critics, are Jonathan Arac, "'A Romantic Book': *Moby-Dick* and Novel Agency," *Boundary* 2, no. 17.2 (Summer 1990): 40–59; Peter J. Bellis, *No Mysteries Out of Ourselves: Identity and Textual Form in the Novels of Herman Melville* (Philadelphia: University of Pennsylvania Press, 1990), 39–40; Paul Brodtkorb, *Ishmael's White World: A Phenomenological Reading of "Moby-Dick"* (New Haven: Yale University Press, 1967), 62–6; Cook, *Inscrutable Malice*, 99–101; Paul McCarthy, *"The Twisted Mind": Madness in Herman Melville's Fiction* (Iowa City: University of Iowa Press, 1990), 71–3; Henry Nash Smith, "The Madness of Ahab," *The Yale Review* 66, no. 1 (October 1976): 14–32; and Robert Zoellner, *The Salt-Sea Mastodon: A Reading of "Moby-Dick"* (Berkeley: University of California Press, 1973), 96–101. Recently, critics interested in new materialist approaches have taken up the passage again. See the essays by Mark Noble, Russell Sbriglia, and Matthew Taylor in *Rethinking Ahab: Melville and the Materialist Turn*, ed. Meredith Farmer and Jonathan Schroeder (University of Minnesota Press, 2021).

8   Mary Shelley, *Frankenstein: or, the Modern Prometheus: Revised, Corrected, and Illustrated with a New Introduction* (London: Richard Bentley, 1849). Page references to this edition are cited parenthetically in the text. This work is the revised third edition (first published in 1831) that Melville acquired in 1849. The 1831 and 1849 editions have the same pagination. The passages that I quote from Chapter 5 of the third edition appear unchanged from the first edition of 1818 (vol. 1, ch. 4).

9   Mary Wollstonecraft Shelley, "Frankenstein, Volume I," in *The Shelley-Godwin Archive*, MS. Abinger c. 56, 21v. Retrieved from http://shelleygodwinarchive.org/sc/oxford/frankenstein/volume/i/#/p45. Shelley gives the terms "creature" and "creator" adjacency in *Frankenstein* on pages 83 and 86 of the third edition. Melville joins the terms not only in *Moby-Dick* but also in the last paragraph of his *Frankenstein-*

influenced story "The Bell-Tower" about a Renaissance inventor's fatal manufacture of an automaton: "So the creator was killed by the creature." See Herman Melville, *The Piazza Tales and Other Prose Pieces, 1839–1860*, ed. Harrison Hayford, Alma A. MacDougall, G. Thomas Tanselle et al. (Evanston and Chicago: Northwestern University Press and The Newberry Library, 1987), 187.

10 Holst and Chevalier's image is reproduced and discussed in Max Browne, *The Romantic Art of Theodor Von Holst, 1810–44* (London: Lund Humphries, 1994), 76–7, and Martin Myrone (ed.), *Gothic Night-mares: Fuseli, Blake and the Romantic Imagination* (London: Tate Publishing, 2006), 71. In the 1849 copy of *Frankenstein* that Melville owned, Holst and Chevalier's frontispiece is carried over from the 1831 edition, but not their facing title-page vignette that depicted Victor's tearful departure from Elizabeth and his home for his university studies at Ingolstadt. Critics often reproduce the frontispiece but rarely analyze it in detail. For brief treatments, see Christopher Frayling, *Frankenstein: The First Two Hundred Years* (London: Reel Art Press, 2018), 93–5; Eleanor Salotto, "*Frankenstein* and Dis(re) membered Identity," *The Journal of Narrative Technique* 24, no. 3 (Fall 1994): 196; and Grant F. Scott, "Victor's Secret: Queer Gothic in Lynd Ward's Illustrations to Frankenstein (1934)," *Word and Image* 28, no. 2 (April–June 2012): 208 and passim. For fuller accounts, see Beatriz González Moreno and Fernando González Moreno, "Beyond the Filthy Form: Illustrating Mary Shelley's *Frankenstein*," in *Global Frankenstein*, ed. Carol Margaret Davison and Marie Mulvey-Roberts (Cham, Switzerland: Palgrave Macmillan, 2018), 228–31, and especially Ian Haywood, "Image of the Month: Theodore Von Holst, 'Frankenstein' (1831)," *Romantic Illustration Network*. https://romanticillustrationnetwork.com/2016/11/26/image- of-the-month-theodore-von-holst-frankenstein-1831/ (accessed January 2, 2020), and Alexandra Neel, "Still Life in *Frankenstein*," *Novel: A Forum on Fiction* 48, no. 3 (November 2015): 432–6. I have quoted from page 433 of Neel's essay. Signaling a literary genealogy, Holst in his *Frankenstein* frontispiece used elements from an earlier book illustration he had done of Faust in his study. See Browne, *The Romantic Art of Theodor Von Holst*, 81.

11 Other avenues for speculating on the ways in which *Frankenstein* influenced Melville's writing would include comparisons between the Creature's account of his developing consciousness in chapters 11 through 16 of the third edition (vol. 2, chapters 3 through 8, in the first edition) and the illegitimate and disowned child Isabel's narrative of becoming human in Books 6 and 8 of Melville's *Pierre; or, the Ambiguities* (1852) and also comparisons between the galvanized, incongruous embodiments in *Frankenstein* and in Melville's late poem "Art": "But form to lend, pulsed life create, / What unlike things must meet and mate." "Art" was included in Melville's final published volume *Timoleon Etc.* (1891). See Herman Melville, *Published Poems: "Battle-Pieces," "John Marr," "Timoleon*," ed. Robert C. Ryan, Harrison Hayford, Alma MacDougall Reising, and G. Thomas Tanselle (Evanston and Chicago: Northwestern University Press and The Newberry Library, 2009), 280.

12 Instances of characters using the term "hideous" can be found throughout the novel (Shelley, *Frankenstein*, 44, 47, 61, 103, 111, 112, 114, 124, 127, 164, 176, and 197).

13 "Beautiful" was Percy Shelley's substitution for "handsome," which Mary originally had written in her manuscript. Her inconsistency about the Creature's symmetry is evident in the different assessments throughout the novel (Shelley, *Frankenstein*, 40, 43, 186, and 197).

14 Baldick, *In Frankenstein's Shadow*, 33–5; Patrick Brantlinger, "Race and *Frankenstein*," in *The Cambridge Companion to Frankenstein*, ed. Andrew Smith (Cambridge: Cambridge University Press, 2016), 128–42; Peter Brooks, *Body Work: Objects of Desire in Modern Narrative* (Cambridge, MA: Harvard University Press, 1993), 199–220; Stefani Engelstein, *Anxious Anatomy: The Conception of the Human Form in Literary and Naturalist Discourse* (Albany: State University of New York Press, 2008), 179–217; Denise Gigante, "Facing the Ugly: The Case of *Frankenstein*," *ELH* 67, no. 2 (Summer 2000): 565–87; and James Heffernan, "Looking at the Monster: *Frankenstein* and Film," *Critical Inquiry* 24 (Autumn 1997): 133–58. Engelstein underscores the characters' excessive responses to the Creature and observes that "it is readers rather than Shelley herself who have named the Creature a *Monster*" (215).

15 Percy Shelley added the "lustrous black" description of the Creature's hair to Mary's manuscript. On Holst's admiration for the "perverted classicism" of Henry Fuseli and others, see Myrone (ed.), *Gothic Night-mares*, 53–71.

16 For an example of Ishmael's carnal attractions, see the astounding items on display in the cetacean butcher shop below the decks of the *Pequod*, in the second half of chapter 94, "A Squeeze of the Hand" (Melville, *Moby-Dick*, 369–70).

17 Washington Irving, *A History of the Life and Voyages of Christopher Columbus* (London: John Murray, 1828), 1: 432–3. Shelley was acquainted with Irving in the 1820s, during his years in Europe.

18 Herman Melville, *The Confidence-Man: His Masquerade*, ed. Harrison Hayford, Hershel Parker, and G. Thomas Tanselle (Evanston and Chicago: Northwestern University Press and The Newberry Library, 1984), 239. Wyn Kelley also connects the speculations about originality in Shelley's 1831 Preface and Melville's 1857 *The Confidence-Man*; see "Writ in Water: The Books of Melville's *Moby-Dick*," in *A Companion to the American Novel*, ed. Alfred Bendixen (Malden, MA: Wiley-Blackwell), 405–6. In the chapter of *The Confidence-Man* from which I have quoted, Melville speculates on the creative properties of "original" characters such as Hamlet, Don Quixote, and Milton's Satan.

7

Finitude, Frames, and the Plot of *Frankenstein*

Yoon Sun Lee

Frame tales are difficult to summarize, and yet somehow it seems as if they should be easy to grasp. While it is difficult to determine the order of priority that should govern the relation between the frame and the stories within, it does feel as though the frame itself holds out some material image of knowledge as representation. The feeling could be described as the intuition that something that has been framed grants us some cognitive warrant or license. A frame thus appears to address itself to the understanding. But what exactly it conveys may not be clear at all times to all viewers. As a frame tale, *Frankenstein* proves challenging when it comes to making decisions about the plot's priorities. This is the case not only because of the complexity and number of narrative levels, but because of the particularly fraught significance the novel assigns to the very idea and the practice of framing.[1]

It should be noted that Shelley's novel does not refer to itself as a frame tale, a later critical coinage. But it follows the procedure of this literary genre insofar as it embeds stories and their tellers within other stories.[2] Walter Scott's review for *Blackwood's Edinburgh Magazine* carefully notes all the narrative levels, summarizing the events that occur in each one, including the creature's tale.[3] The text of Shelley's novel does refer repeatedly both to the action of framing and to the concept of a frame. Victor conceives of the creature as "a frame for the reception of [animation]"; the creature refers to himself in his final valedictory speech as "this miserable frame" (41, 215).[4] Marilyn Butler and other critics have linked this language with ongoing debates over vitalism in the early nineteenth century.[5] Those debates, which will be discussed in more detail below, had to do with the relation between life and frame. The question was whether the mere frame or structure of a creature was sufficient to give rise to life, or whether the latter had to be superadded to the organic frame by and from another source. It had to do, in other words, with the efficacy, the action of the frame.

This essay will try to connect the formal problematic of the frame with the discursive formation of finitude. Through the latter phrase, I refer to the epistemological shift that Michel Foucault describes as occurring between 1775 and 1825, a change in how both knowledge and being were conceived. I will argue that the plot of Shelley's novel arises as much from its layout, its structure, as from the events that make up its stories. At its most capacious, the plot enacts this shift from one regime of knowledge to another.

In the classical episteme, the frame upholds and displays the potential totality of knowledge. In the modern one, the frame indicates finitude, points to all that cannot be seen, gestures toward all that occurs within a dark interiority.

We can view *Frankenstein*'s tales as arranged in parallel, paratactically, thus invoking a kind of knowledge that rests quite simply on representation, on the ordered naming and showing of things. In such a perspective, the narrative levels would rest side by side in an array: Walton's, Frankenstein's, the creature's. Each narrative would appear as a sign, in Foucault's words, without "meaning exterior or anterior."[6] As signs they do not need deciphering: they translucently reveal their own meanings, as they are posed next to each other within the element of discourse. We simply need to note where the tales are the same, and where they are different. Both Walton and Victor seek to expand the boundaries of human knowledge; both Walton and the creature are lonely, long for a companion, regret Victor's loss. "Where there is discourse, representations are laid out and juxtaposed; and things are grouped together and articulated ... in the Classical age, discourse is that translucent necessity through which representation and beings must pass—as beings are represented to the mind's eye, and as representation renders beings visible in their truth."[7]

But it is also true that the novel's multiple frames or levels open onto each other in ways that draw attention to the ongoing consequences of events set in motion. That is, they gesture outside their own diegesis to past and future events that they cannot themselves represent. The tales also gesture toward meanings that they may contain within themselves, meanings that they cannot themselves articulate. In this perspective, we can think of each narrative as defined by its own finitude. Walton cannot narrate his own future, the creature can at best anticipate his own end. None of the tellers can fully state the meaning of their tale, which seems to revolve around the status of "man" himself as the subject and object of knowledge.

The epistemological significance of such arrangements is the burden of Foucault's study, *The Order of Things*. Foucault argues that the knowledge of natural beings, of language and labor shifted from reflecting the former arrangement I have just described to the latter. Shelley's novel vividly inhabits this moment when knowledge was reshaping itself around the recognition of finitude, rather than the possibility of representation. This shift opened up to exploration an entire realm of interiority, and made the concept of this interiority the ground and target of knowledge.[8] *Frankenstein* enacts this dynamic not only within the stories it contains, but through its formal arrangement: the distinctive, eloquent non-unity of its assemblage. My focus will be on the relation between the novel's plot, its complex form, and its transitional epistemic situation.

The novel's plot seems to prise the concept of action away from that of self-directed agency. The novel's action, in other words, cannot be reduced to Walton's grand dreams, Victor's labors, or even the creature's revenge. It can be helpful to turn back to the Aristotelian elaboration of action as plot, or as something that has both a formal dimension and an actantial one. In the Aristotelian sense, action is both praxis and that which bears or gives dimension to form, or to certain kinds of representation of praxis. Aristotle states in the *Poetics* that epic poetry, like tragedies, should have a certain type of plot: one that "should involve a single action, whole and complete in itself … so that like one whole living creature it may produce its appropriate pleasure."[9] Plot or action in this sense embodies knowledge in a perceptible form with a certain temporal extension. Action also raises the question of magnitude, through an analogy with organic form. Plot magnitude is illustrated by analogy with living creatures: "a living creature or anything else made up of parts not only must have its parts organized but must also have just the size that properly belongs to it."[10] But Aristotle goes on to make clear that this is purely an analogy; the unity of a plot doesn't depend on actually representing the life of one living creature. Nor does he question the status or efficacy of representation as such. Representation can be well-formed or ill-formed, but it cannot fail. Aristotle's action *is* the creature in question, which possesses its own proper size and shape but no hidden interiority. The joints or articulations of this creature in its more complex incarnation (in a complex as opposed to a simple plot) are provided by recognition or reversal, preferably recognition attended by a reversal. Recognition is defined as "a change from ignorance to knowledge."[11] In the best types of plots, according to Aristotle, this knowledge is an event that brings about further events or consequences.[12]

This way of thinking about plot and knowledge requires a certain double vision. Stephen Halliwell usefully describes it as Aristotle's "dual-aspect mimeticism": there is, on the one hand, "a plot structure, which is the intelligible design produced by the playwright," and which has properties like "scale, proportions, unity," but "one can also speak of the actions and agents represented by the play," and here one has to use concepts like "purpose and choice, success and failure … good and evil, guilt and innocence … we experience [the plot in this sense] through an understanding that depends on them, and we respond to it with evaluative judgments … that presuppose and are informed by that understanding."[13] A number of connections to Shelley's novel can be drawn at this point. Victor's action not only results causally in the creature's form, but can be said to be itself the creature's form. Thus, the problem of the creature's being remains indissociable from a buried principle of mimesis. A certain horror springs from this sense that he is an imitation of being in both of those aspects, which can't be reconciled or merged (as, arguably, they can in the case of a created agent like Adam, in *Paradise Lost*). How the creature is put together, in other words, seems to merge with what he does independently, again not simply in a deterministic sense, but in a more ontological one, breaching a boundary between representation and what it purports to imitate, a picture directly come to life, stepping out of the frame. His scale, proportions, and unity are constantly foregrounded; uncannily, he is always too big, relative to his surroundings, but he is not large enough to be sublime—all of him can be seen at once, perhaps because the novel does not offer the "right" place from which to view him. The novel's frames notably fail to offer such a location.

At both levels, as a materially realized design and as an agent performing actions associated with concepts like purpose, choice, success, and failure, the creature constantly enacts the failure of unity, despite having visually perceptible boundaries. After hearing the creature's story, Victor vacillates between these ways of seeing him. "I compassionated him," he says; he feels pity and fear; but then, "when I saw the filthy mass that moved and talked, my heart sickened, and my feelings were altered to those of horror and hatred" (138). Whether as imitation or as empirical being, the creature doubly draws attention to this lack of unity, his multitudinousness or irreducible numerousness. His insistent passionate demand emphasizes both the necessity and the lack of a deep, interior principle of unity.

Despite its references to pleasure and the cognitive mastery afforded by representation, Aristotle's emphasis on plot's magnitude, on being or having the right size, can be seen from our historical standpoint as linked in some ways to a thematic of finitude. There is, of course, the cognitive finitude or limitation on which a good plot's very form is based: the initial limitation of knowledge that makes recognition possible. But this is linked to hamartia, the famous waywardness of action itself: in Amélie Rorty's words, "some error or misdirection in the action itself, a deflection that brings a reversal of the very intentions that propelled it."[14] In her striking account,

> plot reveals that there is, as it were, a canker in the very heart of action. All action is formed by intelligence … but by an intelligence directed to a relatively limited purpose. The gap of opacity, and with it the possibility of ignorance and deflection, always stands between even the best general purposes and the particular actions that actualize and fulfill them.[15]

This limitation or blindness within action itself is explicitly taken up by Shelley's novel through its plot's preoccupation with consequences, the way that action extends beyond itself, and seems to have no foreseeable end.

Action in a more local sense seems to be thought of not as initiating an action but as stopping its consequences from going any further. There is also a desire to locate the original or efficient cause of something. Victor repeatedly claims, for example, with a strange positiveness, "William, Justine, and Clerval had died through my infernal machinations … they all died by my hands … they died by my machinations" (177–80). But such reasoning is linked by Shelley to a Godwinian view of legal institutions as inherently corrupt. They aim to establish causation of this type in a way that can only satisfy an unfortunate anthropological need.[16] In the plot, the weight falls more heavily and more consistently on the other, future-oriented end of action, on the fear that consequences cannot be bounded. Victor engages in a long speculative narration of what would happen if he were to complete the creature's mate, picturing the "first results" and remote consequences for "future ages" (161); he then uncreates the female. His final, dying thought is that the creature lives on "to be an instrument of mischief" (211). The terror of a chain of consequences recalls Godwin's discussion in his *Enquiry Concerning Political Justice*: "Man is in no case … the beginner of any event or series of events … but only the vehicle through which certain antecedents operate."[17] Godwin argues that there is always "a regular succession of phenomena, without any uncertainty of event, so that every consequent requires a specific antecedent"; one kind of system "has for its medium only matter and motion, the other … has for its medium thought."[18] Godwin does not see any uncertainty, yet uncertainty is all that *Frankenstein* seems to envision. That consequences ensue is certain, but their nature and extent can only be fearfully guessed. Action, then, is necessary to cut them off—either action, or some kind of frame.

Shelley's novel solves this problem by creating what we might call an artificial finitude through diegetic means, by using the jagged edges or boundaries of one narrative to delimit another. We feel the absence, in other words, of the kind of editor who completes the story in Goethe's *Sorrows of Young Werther*. Shelley's tales seem to cut each other off in subtle ways. They exist side by side, but they also contain each other, nested within. In this way, the form of the novel evidences its relation to changing codes of knowledge, the epistemic shift from the classical to the modern era. Foucault posits this shift from knowledge understood in terms of ordering and representation to one that has to take into account a certain view of history.[19] It is a change from tabulating "the possibilities of being" in all its empirical, fully accomplished diversity to a search for "the conditions of life"—what he calls an analytic of finitude.[20] It is also a change in the function or status of language. As he puts it,

> the theory of representation disappears as the universal foundation of all possible orders; language as the spontaneous tabula, the primary grid of things, as an indispensable link between representation and things, is eclipsed in its turn: a profound historicity penetrates into the heart of things, isolates and defines them in their own coherence … seeking the principle of their intelligibility only in their own development, and abandoning the space of representation.[21]

In the classical episteme, language was "the nexus of representation and being"; the function of discourse "consisted in articulating one upon the other what one represents to oneself and what is."[22] Discourse could divide an assumed totality into units (whether this whole was language or wealth or the living beings of the world), assign them names, and display these in ordered forms that invited comparison. Signs did not need to hide themselves or apologize: they fully captured being's order. Everything could in this sense be represented and therefore known. But in the modern episteme, to know something was to know the finite, often invisible conditions for it to exist. "Breaking the old Classical continuity of being and nature, the divided force of life will reveal forms that are scattered, yet all linked to the conditions of existence."[23] This is also the moment when, in Foucault's words, "man enters in his turn, and for the first time, the field of Western knowledge."[24] This turn toward the conditions of knowledge and of life appears in the complex layered plot of Shelley's novel.

In the creature's extraordinary tale, his education proceeds exactly along the lines of the three positivities, as Foucault calls them: language, labor, and life itself. Words, value, and work lay out the scope or field of the representation that he offers to Victor in the hope of being understood. I think it's important to note that the creature is not simply asking for recognition as a self-conscious being. Rather, he wants to be understood in a certain way. He desires to be represented and placed within an order based on identity and difference arrayed in a certain way. He wants to place his being within a larger order, and he wants to be understood in the same way that he himself has come to understand language, labor, and life. His narrative is remarkably explicit about this process: language appears first as a unified field of sound, from which he eventually learns to distinguish sounds, just as he learns to distinguish discrete perceptions from an undifferentiated field of sensory stimulation:

> Their pronunciation was quick, and the words they uttered, not having any apparent connexion with visible objects, I was unable to discover any clue by which I could unravel the mystery of their reference … I cannot describe the delight I felt when I learned the ideas appropriated to each of these sounds … I distinguished several other words, without being able as yet to understand or apply them; such as good, dearest, unhappy. (103)

But even before he learns language, he learns about wealth through its opposite, poverty: "one of the causes of the uneasiness of this amiable family." And he learns about poverty through his discovery of labor. He quickly comes to see labor in connection to the total amount of wealth possible in this little economy:

> I found that the youth spent a great part of each day collecting wood for the family fire; and, during the night, I often took his tools … and brought home firing sufficient for … several days..... I observed, with pleasure, that he did not go to the forest that day, but spent it repairing the cottage, and cultivating the garden. (102)

His own labor allows Felix to engage in more productive forms of labor. Indeed, his replenishment of the woodpile is referred to as "performed by an invisible hand" (105). Most consequentially, he learns of the existence and the relations of other living beings—not only "of the division of property" but "of the difference of sexes" (110–11), of old and young, "the birth and growth of children."[25]

The creature is caught, torn apart by exactly this rupture between the classical and modern epistemes. In these epistemes can be seen the material forms of knowledge—a materiality that the creature describes in a striking metaphor: "Of what a strange nature is knowledge! It clings to the mind, when it has once seized on it, like a lichen on a rock" (111). We see that knowledge is not just passively organized, but that it durably connects, even clings to heterogeneous spheres of matter and activity. Knowledge is based on seeing, classifying, representing: framing. Natural history, the classical mode of organizing beings, constructed a particular field of visibility or rubric for seeing. It did not look at everything. It limited its object to "the extension of which all natural beings are constituted … the form of the elements, the quantity of those elements, the manner in which they are distributed in space in relation to each other, and the relative magnitude of each element"; for Linnaeus, for example, the "number, form, proportion, situation" of particular elements or organs formed the basis of classification.[26] Knowledge began, Foucault argues, in a carefully constructed or filtered visibility and ended in an exhaustive taxonomy. This is what the creature tries to do. He represents himself on the same plane with humans and other living beings, analyzes his own being into elements, noting his physical similarities and differences: "I was more agile than they, and could subsist upon coarser diet; I bore the extremes of heat and cold with less injury to my frame; my stature far exceeded their's" (111). Yet there is clearly a problem with this mode of understanding: the world itself seems to reject it. It issues in the remarkable demand the creature makes of Victor: "My companion must be of the same species, and have the same defects. This being you must create" (135). This follows the logic of identity and difference, the logic of taxonomy: "in Classical terms, a knowledge of empirical individuals can be acquired only from the continuous, ordered, and universal tabulation of all possible differences."[27] In this case, he perceives a gap in being that must be filled: another being exactly like him in all other respects except that of sex. "I demand a creature of another sex, but as hideous as myself" (137).

The creature imagines that if his demand is granted, he would "become linked to the chain of existence and events, from which I am now excluded" (139). That is, he would have a place in being itself, *imagined as a network of identities and differences.* He equates order with being, taxonomic kinship with sympathetic and sentimental kinship. This is clearly a mistake: he seems to forget here the lesson that every encounter, even that with De Lacey, so clearly and painfully establishes: that it is his appearance, his visual form ("a filthy type of your's, more horrid from its very resemblance," he notes [122]) that condemns him. His crime is nothing other than the form, proportion, and situation of his parts. It exists within the classical epistemic regime of natural history, based on analysis, and on the discrimination of visible differences. It is knowing through seeing, a knowledge of surfaces; the naturalist, in Linnaeus's words, "'distinguishes the parts of natural bodies with his eyes, describes them appropriately ... and names them.'"[28] Even in the face of such knowledge, the creature hopes that the very difference between his own body and the "perfect forms of [his] cottagers—their ... delicate complexions" (104) would constitute a relation, even if it's a distant one. He hopes that even if they belong to different and widely separated classes, they could still occupy positions in the same series of being. Foucault remarks that until the end of the eighteenth century, "life does not exist: only living beings. These beings form one class, or rather several classes, in the series of all the things in the world."[29]

But the creature is riven by contradiction because he also represents and embodies the new, modern episteme, based on "the emancipation of language, of the living being, and of need, with regard to representation," a way of knowing that Foucault describes as based on "the violence and the endless effort of life, the hidden energy of needs," that which cannot be represented on a surface, through a language continuous with order. Order is replaced by "freedom, a desire, or a will."[30] The modern episteme grounds itself on the notion that what is to be known, the ground of knowledge itself, must be sought in "a profound, interior, and essential space"—somewhere deep within the volume of the organic structure.[31] It finds the unity of knowledge in a "behind-the-scenes world even deeper and more dense than representation itself ... that ... inaccessible point, which drives down, beyond our gaze, towards the very heart of things." Here, "things ... turn in upon themselves, posit their own volumes, and define for themselves an internal space ... this [classical] space of order is now shattered:

there will be things, with their own organic structures, their hidden veins, the space that articulates them, the time that produces them."[32]

We can see the modern episteme already present in the labor undertaken in so many places in the novel: labor is not just a calculable unit of value as in the classical episteme, but also a means, in Foucault's words, of "triumphing for an instant over death"—not only by producing what's necessary to sustain life (which the De Lacey family barely does), but also in Victor's own labors, more literally, aimed at overcoming the finitude of humans as natural beings.[33] Foucault notes the difference between natural history and the emergent field of biology; in the classical age, nature had been conceived as a "homogeneous space of orderable identities and differences … a unitary field of visibility and order."[34] That space, that totality breaks up. After Cuvier, he argues,

> the living being wraps itself in its own existence, breaks off its taxonomic links of adjacency … constitutes itself as … a double space … the interior one of anatomical coherences and physiological compatibilities, and the exterior one of the elements in which it resides … both these spaces are subject to a common control: it is no longer that of the possibilities of being, it is that of the conditions of life.[35]

To know came to consist not in filling out the table of species or types, but in tracing "a series, of sequential connection, of development."[36] Victor's attempt to know and then to reverse this sequence, how "the form of man was degraded and wasted … the corruption of death succeed[ed] to the blooming cheek of life … how the worm inherited the wonders of the eye and brain" (40) affirms this sequence-based form of knowledge by aiming simply to reverse or overturn it. The meaning of the creature's tale is inevitably assigned by modern readers not to its own visible shape, but to what came before: Victor's tale of how he made it. In other words, the modern episteme highlights the scandalous conditions of the creature's existence, rather than his unfortunate form. It dialectically affirms finitude as the condition of knowledge, and finds its bitter counterpart and repetition in the way that the creature, at the end, keeps Victor alive, leaving him carefully calibrated sustenance and encouragement (198). The creature is all too aware of the conditions of Victor's fragile being. It is also worth noting the creature's repeated use of the phrase, "the series of my being" (215), as though he accepts in the end that his only relation to other beings is in this shared temporal, sequential, and limited nature, as if being were nothing but anteriority, and as if anteriority were itself material.

Both of these are true with regard to the creature, who correctly believes that he has no lived history: "From my earliest remembrance I had been as I then was in height and proportion … What then was I?" (112). Like his life, his actions arise simply from the way in which he is put together. It is important to note that in the much-discussed debate between William Lawrence and John Abernethy over the principle of life, the key terms of that debate were action and organization, and the dispute had to do with their relations. Abernethy insisted that we have good reasons for believing that life is distinct from organization. The mind and the actions of life affect each other. Failure or disturbance of the actions of life prevent or disturb our feelings, and enfeeble, perplex, or distract our intellectual operations. The mind equally affects the actions of life, and thus influences the whole body ... though these facts may countenance the idea of the identity of mind and life, yet we have good reasons for believing that they are perfectly distinct.[37]

Within "actions," Abernethy seems to include both conscious and unconscious ones, including the kinds of actions that we evaluate through concepts like "purpose and choice, success and failure ... good and evil, guilt and innocence." Action plays an ambiguous role, but organization is carefully applied only to matter and to chains of material consequences. To this, Lawrence argued that the organization or the form of matter was itself life, which was just a special kind of action:

Organization means the peculiar composition which distinguishes living bodies; in this point of view they are contrasted with inorganic, inert or dead bodies. Vital properties, such as sensibility and irritability, are the means by which the organization is capable of executing its purposes ... Functions are the purposes which any organ or system of organs executes in the animal frame; there is, of course, nothing corresponding to them in inorganic matter. Life is the assemblage of all the functions, and the general result of their exercise ... organization is the instrument, vital properties the acting power, function the mode of action, and life the result.[38]

Thomas Rennell, who wrote a response to Lawrence's lectures, called this "a sort of logic which cannot be allowed," and tried to expose its fallacy: "a scalpel is the instrument, a hand the acting power, cutting the mode of action, and a wound the result. What would Mr. Lawrence say to the man who would assert, that the wound was co-existent with the scalpel, or again that the act of cutting was a wound?"[39] Rennell's surgical example highlights the fact that Lawrence's account of life changes the nature of interiority itself. Interiority is not simply a space that can be cut into or opened up, but, like Shelley's creature, an assemblage of ways of functioning. It becomes in a way more mysterious when it disappears as a space and becomes a question of organization.

Form comes to life, as it were, when considered critically under the rubric of function, but such knowledge has to find some other place, some outside in which to stand. In the modern way of thinking based on the concept of "organic structure," functions become a very special kind of action with regard to an organism that must keep itself alive. Instead of a static visible structure whose parts can be analyzed, organic structure offers the drama of a finite being trying to maintain itself, but the essence of whose life can no longer be directly viewed. In Foucault's words, "Character is not, then, established by a relation of the visible to itself; it is nothing in itself but the visible point of a complex and hierarchized organic structure in which function plays an essential governing and determining role."[40] By asking about the function of the novel's frames, then, we are in a sense participating in this same mode or discourse of knowledge.

Shelley's novel pursues questions of surface and depth, finitude and totality, at its formal level as well as at its narrative-epistemological level. Its frames offer grids of visibility, occasions for examination. Each also hides and conditions the others. Its narratives can be seen either as embedded within each other or adjacent to one another. The point may be to question which one it is: do Walton's, Victor's, the creature's narratives exist on the same level as representations, as knowledge? Are they equivalent, continuous, side by side? Can they be compared? Or is the relation rather one of enclosing, containing, one conditioning another, one functioning within another, so that the creature's diegesis is innermost, "an interior and necessary volume," "the dark, concave, inner side of their visibility"?[41] If the classical episteme relied on "unencumbered spaces in which things are juxtaposed: herbariums, collections, gardens ... a non-temporal rectangle in which, stripped of all commentary, of all enveloping language, creatures present themselves one beside another ... grouped according to their common features ... bearers of nothing but their own individual names," Shelley's novel creates a multiply temporal rectangle in which these creatures present their own beings alongside each other, for no one in the present to know.[42] Each narrative depends on the others as its condition of existence, just as the conditions of the creature's empirical existence provide the substance of Victor's narrative. But it is not clear from where such a view would be possible.

Frankenstein illuminates an enigmatic juncture within the history of knowledge as Foucault presents it. It is not a coincidence that Shelley's novel is framed by or within accounts of a glittering, continuous surface breaking up, breaking apart, to reveal the depths beneath. It suggests that knowledge would like to be material and formal, efficient and final cause, but that it's determined by its own inexplicable ruptures. "September 19th, the ice began to move, and roarings like thunder were heard at a distance, as the islands split and cracked in every direction" (209). There is also the singular poignancy of the moment when Victor reseparates the pieces of the second creature and drops them, forever unconnected, into the sea. A shared space is replaced by inescapable depth; this might be considered a summary of the plot of the novel. Invisible, intangible, inaccessible forces emerge as the conditions of life and of knowing. This is, of course, the space from which the creature speaks and makes his demand: the terrible and tragic positivity of his need. This is what makes his demand scandalous: the juxtaposition of this nostalgia for the classical epistemic order with a self-authorizing interiority, the creature's clamorous, reluctant finitude. And this is what makes it tragic: the novel shows in the creature's reception by others a rejection of finitude, of material dependence or the conditionality of being, as an intersubjective or moral ground of relation.[43]

Shelley's novel, then, invites us to ask not only how bodies come into being but how knowledge itself is assembled, on what basis, in what configurations, through what connections—and how its forms are situated in matter and along time, how they unfold their materiality and intersect with their own historicity. I have tried to suggest that the frame-structure of the novel points us to this larger plot. Each narrative frame or level both displays and cuts off, holds itself out for examination and also hides. As distinct from a single character's plot, perhaps the plot of the novel as a whole would be this continuously shifting framing of knowledge, this internal play of edges.

We might take this novel as an embodiment or illustration of the shift to the modern in the way that Foucault takes Velázquez's painting, *Las Meninas*, as "the representation … of Classical representation."[44] Foucault's remarkable reading of that painting centers on frames, notably the painter's canvas on the left side: we "can see nothing of it but the reverse side, together with the huge frame on which it is stretched."[45] But the most important frame, "wider and darker than any of the others," is that of the mirror located among other pictures at the back of the pictorial space, giving out light and reflecting the void in front of the painting, soon to be occupied by the figure of "man."[46] The end-point of Foucault's study is the emergence of the human sciences, the appearance of the human as the subject and object of knowledge. In an important paradox, the human viewer was able to remain invisible in the classical order, like the sovereign in Velázquez's painting, even if its gaze was implied everywhere. It is only when knowledge itself came to depend on conditions that could not be seen that the human viewer became visible, problematic, a part of the picture. We can see Shelley's novel, then, with its multiple embedded frames, as equally preoccupied with that space of the viewer in front of it.[47] Each narrative frame tries to represent exactly that space, a position from which to view, to experience, and perhaps to know. It appears to be agnostic about the latter possibility. To see something may be to know it, or it may simply suggest the need to look within oneself and to fail to see what's there. The creature's narrative may be something like that innermost and reflective space, the mirror within the painting.

Notes

1   On the significance of the frame structure in relation to theories of reading and narrative signification, see Criscillia Benford, "'Listen to My Tale': Multilevel Structure, Narrative Sense Making, and the Inassimilable in Mary Shelley's *Frankenstein*," *Narrative* 18, no. 3 (2010): 324–46; and Beth Newman, "Narratives of Seduction and the Seductions of Narrative: The Frame Structure of *Frankenstein*," *ELH* 53 (1986): 41–63. For a somewhat different reading of the creature's significance as the inability to be framed in aesthetic terms, see Denise Gigante, "Facing the Ugly: The Case of Frankenstein," *ELH* 67, no. 2 (2000): 565–87.

2   James Hogg and Walter Scott are among those who would make use of this form, which attained prominence slightly earlier in the German context. See Mark Ittensohn, "'A Story Telling and a Story Reading Age': Textuality and Sociability in the Romantic Frame Tale," *Studies in Romanticism* 55 (Fall 2016): 393–415.

3   Scott objects to the length and detail of the creature's narrative; see Scott, "Remarks on Frankenstein, or The Modern Prometheus: A Novel," *Blackwood's Edinburgh Magazine* 2, no. 12 (March 1818): 613–20.

4   Mary Shelley, *Frankenstein* (New York: Penguin, 2018). Page references to this edition are cited parenthetically in the text.

5   See Marilyn Butler's introduction to Mary Shelley, *Frankenstein* (Oxford: Oxford University Press, 1998), as well as her "Frankenstein and Radical Science," *TLS* April 1993; Andrew Smith, "Scientific Contexts," in *The Cambridge Companion to Frankenstein*, ed. Andrew Smith (Cambridge: Cambridge University Press, 2016), 69–82. See also *Romanticism and the Sciences*, ed. Andrew Cunningham and Nicholas Jardine (Cambridge: Cambridge University Press, 1990), as well as *Frankenstein, Annotated for Scientists, Engineers, and Creators of All Kinds*, ed. David H. Guston et al. (Cambridge: MIT Press, 2017). On Shelley's novel as critical of science, see Anne Mellor, "Making a Monster," in *The Cambridge Companion to Mary Shelley*, ed. Esther Schor (Cambridge: Cambridge University Press, 2003), 9–25.

6   Michel Foucault, *The Order of Things: An Archaeology of the Human Sciences* (New York: Random House, 1970), 66.

7   Ibid., 311.

8   See Marshall Brown, *The Gothic Text* (Stanford, CA: Stanford University Press, 2005), on the centrality of interiority to Gothic, and to Shelley's novel in particular.

9   Aristotle, *Poetics*, trans. James Hutton (New York: W. W. Norton, 1982), 71.

10   Ibid., 53.

11   Ibid., 56.

12   See Terence Cave's study, *Recognitions: A Study in Poetics* (Oxford: Clarendon, 1990).

13   Stephen Halliwell, *The Aesthetics of Mimesis* (Princeton, NJ: Princeton University Press, 2002), 173.

14   Amélie Rorty, "The Psychology of Aristotelian Tragedy," in *Essays on Aristotle's Poetics*, ed. Amélie Rorty (Princeton, NJ: Princeton University Press, 1992), 1–22, 8.

15   Ibid., 11.

16   The representation of the institutions of justice closely follows the critiques offered by William Godwin in his *Enquiry Concerning Political Justice* (see below).

17   William Godwin, *An Enquiry Concerning Political Justice*, 3rd ed., 2 vols. (London: Johnson, 1798), 1:385.

18   Ibid., 398–99.

19   Foucault, *The Order of Things*, 220.

20   Ibid., 274.

21   Ibid., xxii.

22   Ibid., 311–12.

23   Ibid., 274.

24   Ibid., xxiii.

25   On the myth of Frankenstein, see Chris Baldick, *In Frankenstein's Shadow* (New York: Oxford University Press, 1987).

26   Foucault, *The Order of Things*, 134.

27   Ibid., 144.

28   Quoted in Foucault, *The Order of Things,* 161.

29   Ibid., 161.

30   Ibid., 209 (includes the previous quotation).

31   Ibid., 231.

32   Ibid., 239–40.

33   Ibid, 257.

34   Ibid., 268.

35   Ibid., 274.

36 Ibid., 263.

37 John Abernethy, *An Enquiry into the Probability and Rationality of Mr Hunter's Theory of Life* (1814), quoted in a review essay of this and other works by Abernethy, Lawrence, and others, *Quarterly Review*, July 1819, 2.

38 William Lawrence, *An Introduction to Comparative Anatomy and Physiology* (1816), quoted in ibid., 16.

39 Thomas Rennell, *Remarks on Scepticism* (1819), quoted ibid., 17.

40 Foucault, *The Order of Things*, 228.

41 Ibid., 237.

42 Ibid., 131.

43 On sympathy in Shelley's novel, see David Marshall, *The Surprising Effects of Sympathy* (Chicago, IL: University of Chicago Press, 1988).

44 Foucault, *The Order of Things*, 16.

45 Ibid., 3.

46 Ibid., 6.

47 For a thought-provoking discussion of this space in front of the frame and the frame in relation to the materiality of the signifier, see Orrin Wang, "Against Theory Beside Romanticism: The Sensation of the Signifier," *diacritics* 35, no. 2 (summer 2005): 3–29, and *Romantic Sobriety* (Baltimore, MD: Johns Hopkins University Press, 2011). See also the very relevant discussions by Michael Fried in *Absorption and Theatricality: Painting and Beholder in the Age of Diderot* (Berkeley, CA: University of California Press, 1980), as well as *Art and Objecthood* (Chicago, IL: University of Chicago Press, 1998). My thanks to Orrin Wang for drawing my attention to the latter and for his helpful remarks on this essay.

8

Blackness and Anthropogenesis in *Frankenstein*

Rei Terada

Frame

Although I possessed the capacity of bestowing animation, yet to prepare a frame for the reception of it ... still remained a work of inconceivable difficulty and labor.[1] (33, 35)

Mary Shelley's *Frankenstein* has been understood in its own generation and ever after as a reflection on racial slavery. *Frankenstein* was immediately taken up in abolitionist and pro-slavery discourses and Shelley's Creature[2] was commonly interpreted as an enraged free Black or escaped slave. Since so many readers have acted as though the Creature were Black, openly reading through their anxieties to do so, critics exploring what Shelley might be saying about racial slavery tend to leave the problem of thinking about Blackness to these previous readers. At the same time, they seem uneasy—why wouldn't they be?—about working on the basis of previous anti-Black associations. Unhappy with leaving the Creature's Blackness to depend on racist readers, Shelley criticism hasn't quite let go of the more basic assumption that leads there, that the Creature's Blackness is ultimately a matter of attribution, an instance that must be discerned before it's thought. When it seems as though one should not *want* to be able to discern it—as though it were the perceiver who created Blackness by deciding where it is—it is in danger of never being thought.[3]

Taking a cue from Shelley's obsession with the "human frame," the Creature's Blackness can instead be posited speculatively to frame the entire novel. *Frankenstein* is absorbed by the Enlightenment question that, as Nahum Chandler writes, had arisen with regard to "the discourse concerning the humanity of the Negro slaves": "on what basis and in what manner can one decide a being, and its character of existence, as one kind or another?"[4] So why is it that *Frankenstein* has been studied for its interest in human constitution and its interest in racial slavery, but not for its interest in racial slavery's framing of the issue of human constitution?

If race is an attempt to control the problem of humanness, and if chattel slavery infuses the problem with life and death implications for all, Blackness takes on the status of what there is to be managed with regard to racial slaves' bondage and agency, in their racialization, and in the contours of the human and the real. The racial slave is divided between the reifications of race (cultural and ideational as much as essential), the heteronomy of slavery, and the indetermination of the slave's Blackness;[5] Blackness, in excess of definition, seems the vanishing point inside and outside category.[6] From this perspective, *Frankenstein* criticism's inability to crystallize the Creature's Blackness with a direct reference can hardly be avoided: what would a direct reference to Blackness be? How could it avoid being one more moment in which Blackness is made concrete or abstract, only to fall apart again? Racial slavery both inspires and confounds the effort to constitute human category; its contradictions interrupt the task of stabilizing the Creature's Blackness, even as the problem of his Blackness overflows historical reference to slavery. Passages of critical reception and Shelley's novel alike that show a struggle to apprehend the Creature categorically can be seen more importantly to struggle with the rough edges of concepts and strategies developed in slavery—the mismatched vocabularies of race and Blackness; of form and plenum; of efforts to manage racial distinctions and an irruption of chaotic events to which they cannot catch up. The nineteen-year-old Mary Shelley, already estranged from her famous radical father's social capital and having no career of her own yet to lose, is able to draw sharp, darkly comic vignettes of these struggles. Her sketches engage, or perhaps are engaged by, an eschatological structure of anthropogenesis that nevertheless enables her own and perhaps any similar literary practice. I think this tension explains why her novel comes across as myth and satire simultaneously. Reading *Frankenstein* through this tension suggests that Blackness in the novel might be considered, not only through reference to the historical archive of racial slavery, but through the interplay between the Creature's ironic prompting of the human question and the eschatological legends that answer him.

Critical Locations of Blackness

In a substantive and thoughtful essay published in 1993, H. R. Malchow begins the scholarly discussion of Blackness in *Frankenstein* by interweaving Shelley's portrayals of the Creature and stereotypical images of Black men in nineteenth-century British culture, images "that drew on fears and hopes of the abolition of slavery in the West Indies."[7] These anti-Black stereotypes are seen to be energized when white British liberals' progressivism came under pressure from the prospect of Black political agency, as in news of slave rebellions. Stereotypes, in turn, help to generate material conditions, actions, and words. Much of Malchow's article carefully presents the texture of "'Race' in the Napoleonic Era" on the assumptions that racism is grounded in ideology (thus the quotation marks around "race"), organized through racial stereotypes.[8] So, consistency in stereotyping can be read in reverse as evidence that *Frankenstein* is concerned with the racial slave.

Malchow relies on stereotypes' arbitrariness when he observes that "a reading of this text which attempts to draw out an embedded racial message must begin where racism itself begins, with physiognomy."[9] A review of the Creature's physical descriptions follows, correlated to "the standard description of the Black man in both the literature of the West Indies and that of African exploration."[10] Malchow reflects that "on the level of physiognomy at least, a racial reading seems … nearer the mark than a Marxist [reading]" that would locate the terror in the dangers of class unrest.[11] I've found no essay on race, slavery, or Blackness in *Frankenstein* that does not include Shelley's physical descriptions of the Creature, and every essay on race, slavery, or Blackness in *Frankenstein* mentions that Shelley's symbolization is not stable. Her complex narrative evocations of certain circumstances of slavery are taken to be more definitive. All in all the correlation is not perfect, but a "near" preponderance, "parallels" that also entail gaps.[12] A contextual-ideological argument such as his, Malchow correctly observes, "necessarily rests on 'evidence' that is indirect, circumstantial, and speculative. There is no clear proof that Mary Shelley consciously set out to create a monster which suggested, explicitly, the Jamaican escaped slave or maroon."[13]

Not only is Shelley's symbolization unstable, critics who deal with it don't want it to be stable, nor should they. Conditions of slavery can be described, but what would correlation with the "escaped slave" look like? A novel that was completely stereotypical? Completely historical? Completely experiential? (Clearly not, as nothing else is.)[14] Although there were many complaints about the insinuating logic of new historicism, which abandoned linear cause and effect arguments and began to use, instead, arguments based in resonance, with indefinite objects and opaque connecting verbs, the revised methodology folds in the realization that linear cause and effect, tight conceptualization of objects, and assignments of historical origin and telos encourage violence. Allegory raises concerns similar to stereotype to the extent that it "will always imply a concept prior to what it represents," as David Lloyd writes in a relevant context.[15] In Shelley's generation it was common to think that allegory was one of the least satisfying modes of literature. A desire for correlation between sets of features seems to reduce both; for Coleridge, allegory makes "the principal … even more worthless than its phantom proxy."[16]

When critics nevertheless sound apologetic that they *cannot* produce Blackness as an object, then, it reflects a conflict between wanting to have empirical evidence (of something for which evidence is not the right category) for the argument and not wanting to participate in the stereotyping that happens instead. The cite-and-resonate method of literary history hopes that historical references to racial slavery, or the words of slaves, will capture Blackness in the picture like sunlight in a photograph. As I said the appeal to resonance accurately senses the possibility of violence. But the protocols of literary history by themselves—most people don't do only literary history—prolong confusion. The problem is the worry, not invested in other abstractions in the same way, that there is no way to talk about Blackness unless it is something or nothing, in a specific location or nonexistent.[17] Exploration of the Creature's question, "What was I?"[18] may instead inquire into "the historical and enabling point … for the paradigms of Western modernity" (Barrett), as various phrasings describe Black studies' core concerns: "the position of the unthought" (Hartman and Wilderson); a Black "center of gravity" (Rodriguez); a "critique of Western Civilization" (Moten, citing Robinson); a critique of the "human project" (Wynter); "a self-critical questioning of the method involved in not only seeing human being, but making human being" (Gordon).[19] Might such frames be able to explain what has happened to make it seem that Blackness *does not exist* where it doesn't appear?

Allan Lloyd Smith carefully allows an "oblique" "question of race" in *Frankenstein*,[20] "enmeshed within a variety of contemporaneous discourses"[21]—of gender, class, marginality, poverty, "a contemporary web of discourses on rights, justice, responsibilities, and otherness."[22] He goes on to discuss the Creature's dialectics of consciousness and those in slave narratives of northward escape.[23] Whereas Malchow's materials are ideological and preponderantly imagistic, Smith's "set of correspondences" often takes two-sided narrative form. It incorporates slaves' descriptions of slavery and repeated rituals of interaction between Black and non-Black people, interactions both of whose sides Shelley, on the narratological level, inhabits. Smith, too, observes that the correspondences do not unify:

> The Creature's narrative may be as much explained by reference to Rousseau's *Confessions*—or even the popular genre of penny confessions by condemned criminals—as by its resonance with the slave narratives that followed shortly after. And yet, if we consider the cultural subtexts of Mary Shelley's imaginative investigation of what it might mean to be a disenfranchised, unacknowledged and spurned member of the human race, the implication of some racially inflected dimension surely becomes inescapable.[24]

Within the concentrating oppressions, where scholarship loses the causal thread, race has happened inescapably and generally. Despite the critic's slight ruefulness at being unable to show exactly how or quite where it resides, the atopicality of the Creature's "dimension" is striking, not as argumentative flaw but as the transindividual pattern of "the relation between transcendental frame and the body, or nobody, that occupies, or is banished from, its confines and powers of orientation."[25] These are not questions of identification, representation, or allegory, but of suspension, limit, and frame.

Romanticism thinks about these questions as long as they are not explicitly connected to Black people, so that the most helpful essays for thinking about *Frankenstein*'s implications for Blackness do not thematize what they are thinking about as related to Blackness. Denise Gigante's approach through aesthesis, beauty, and ugliness, notably, operates without needing to define its object qualities, making it interesting that elsewhere Blackness is not treated in the same way. In fact, the point is that "aesthetic theory comes up empty" when addressing its limit (here, ugliness, although Blackness can also limit).[26] She presses home that the supposed ugliness, or ugliness (since the question of whether there is anything that ugliness could be that is not suppositional is part of the topic) of the Creature would in aesthetics be "treated as a negative form," one that "simply lacks," that cannot appear at the table setting across from beauty, that "emerges as a mere tautology" or,[27] as in Kant, does not exist at all[28]—and yet also, as she emphasizes, "functions more positively than lack," is "too real," "exceeding representation."[29] Real fantasy is Gigante's psychoanalytic frame, and she pushes it to the existential conclusion, "not sufficiently accounted for in aesthetic discourse," that the Creature's "radically uninscribed existence"[30]—"existence" makes it more than a question of his appearance, and "uninscribed" pushes it beyond a set of norms—makes encounter in *Frankenstein* "less of an aesthetic experience than a question of survival."[31] Now, if this article were talking about Blackness in *Frankenstein*, there would be a lot to debate. But is there a way to be sure it's not, at least in the sense that it addresses strategies, foundational to eighteenth-century aesthetics, that *also* produce Blackness as a different *kind* of limit, displacing Blackness away from beauty *and* ugliness? Whether Gigante's provocations speak to Blackness or have already been transposed *from* the quandaries of racial slavery to aesthetics does not have to be the question. Exploration is already possible, as long as Blackness isn't expected in the form of an encounter, outside, to be located before being discussed.[32]

Geneva Defends Itself

Mary Shelley stages constitutive questions from racial slavery, leaving the Creature to embody the Black space—neither merely negative nor merely concrete, as the secondary literature finds—between race and slavery. Gayatri Spivak, orienting the novel by "foreground[ing] a version of the native informant," observes, "Shelley's text is in an aporetic relationship with the narrative support of philosophical resources it must use."[33] Despite its "incidental imperialist sentiment," "it does not deploy the axiomatics of imperialism" as though they were unproblematic.[34] Rather, Shelley "*cannot* make the monster identical with the proper recipient of these lessons."[35] Spivak's observation that parts of the novel pull away from an axiomatics that it is not capable of dissolving is helpful. Her insight is borne out in the novel's mockery of "philosophical resources" that support self-interest. As I'll explore later, building on Spivak's second point about the persistence of the philosophy under strain, these same passages are also a miniature eschatology of anthropogenesis that clings despite Shelley's mockery.

Geneva defends itself in *Frankenstein*: what kind of texture does this society have? Shelley depicts civic rituals in which people are often mistaken for the sake of civility, especially men who are intuitively sure they are right. They also easily set aside knowledge that they believe is correct. Victor Frankenstein's certainties and eternal passions are especially ill observed and ephemeral, but across the board, conviction is ungrounded. The power of discernment is diminished on both ends, by being inefficient and by failing to matter when it's done. In the throes of his crush on Victor, for example, Robert Walton knows that "no one can feel more deeply" than Victor "the beauties of nature" (17), just as Victor is positive that "none ever conceived of the misery" that he has endured and is sure that Justine, "the poor victim" about to be executed, "felt not as I did, such deep and bitter agony" (67–68).

Walton himself finds his affection for Victor, intense when he is a total stranger, "excite[d] ... to an astonishing degree" (15), yet never wonders what his attraction is based on.[36] Everyone persists in forming and expressing such intuitive convictions and attachments.

At the same time they constantly observe themselves and others abandoning what they know in order to act on what they "hear ... continually spoken of" (162). Disavowal gets them to the next day. Not only Victor Frankenstein, but also Walton and Elizabeth Lavenza confess with abandon that they are aware of what they don't have the wherewithal to think about ("I was unable to pursue the train of thought" [Victor, 155 and elsewhere]; "I cannot bear to look at the reverse side of the picture" [Walton, 11]; "I cannot bear to think of the other side of the question" [Elizabeth, 48]). Some of these intuitions and collapses of conviction turn up in contexts of legal judgment, as when authorities begin to presume guilt (147) or when a magistrate listens with some interest to Victor's story, "but when he was called upon to act officially in consequence, the whole tide of his incredulity returned" (169). On such occasions, the characters can neither defend their intuitions nor mobilize them against petty interests.

Thinking with Gigante, this too is a matter of "survival"—at least of the survival of the self "as is." Among the many occasions when Victor explains why he does not tell his friends that they are in mortal danger, only one sentence, sounding like a slip, indicates his possible calculation: "if I returned, it was to be sacrificed, or to see those whom I most loved die" (141). "Or" wants to mean that two catastrophes could happen, one just as well as the other; it also suggests that if he returned, he would be making a choice between the two that he does not have to make if he "pass[es] [his] life on that barren rock" (an island on the Orkneys) (141). In practice, Victor chooses between endangering his life, at most—part of his reputation, more likely—and one of his loved ones' again and again. He endangers Elizabeth because he wants to marry her before telling her who he is. Shelley presents calculations of major and minor self-interest side by side, and her juxtapositions of life and death situations with the revelation that often what counts as survival is the continuation of the self "as is" is tart. "Timorous" neighbors decline to get involved in Justine's murder trial (63); "impractible" obstacles deter police protection (170). Victor makes the Creature eight feet tall only for the convenient magnification, "as the minuteness of the parts formed a great hindrance to my speed" (35).[37]

Into this society of everyday violence that Shelley satirizes, in which intuition has a dubious reputation and knowledge is sacrificed to self-interest "in so deadly a manner" (60), the nameless Creature comes to life. As Nancy Yousef has emphasized, his difference is a difference of kind against differences of degree. The most relevant contrast is the difference of ethnicity: Safie, the "Christianized 'Arabian'"[38] woman who is also learning a language, delivers "a reminder that the creature is essentially unlike the human, stranger than the foreign."[39] Indeed, his otherness is absolute, "'like no one in the whole world,' and the fantastic quality of his existence consists in the literal truth of the statement, the fact that it is true of him in a way that it cannot be true of any other character in the novel."[40]

It is "literal truth" that he is like no one in the whole world—and, as Yousef writes, this literal truth is literally impossible: a fact beyond telling, that arrives only in the envelope of its exclusion from any possible reality. As Yousef details, the Creature's socialization into sensibility and linguistic fluency without any society whatever is Shelley's great lunatic touch. Thus, "an important paradox that readers of *Frankenstein* confront is that a monstrosity that the novel cannot, and does not try very hard to, illustrate is central to the narrative."[41]

Literal truth and impossibility prove to be co-dependent, the impossibility helping to make the truth unmistakable. As Safie's ethnic difference measures the Creature's difference in kind, the cheap certainty that the characters espouse and easily abandon highlights the difference in kind of their certainty that the Creature is absolutely different. He is not only literally, but infinitely, legible-as-illegible. Of course, according to Victor he is eight feet tall; still, he is not apprehended in the way that eight-foot Irish men would be, and have been, apprehended. As Elizabeth Young points out, Charles Byrne, a celebrity for his gigantism in the 1780s, was 7'7" and the toast of London. There is something else, another way for characters to act as though they knew the story: to act as though the story was his body.

Unmistakable

The general idea is that the Creature is unmistakable and his memory "indelible" (38). But the near contradiction between monstrosity and unmistakability plays out in different logics running concurrently. Walton records his first description of the Creature before he has heard Victor's tale: "a being which had the shape of a man, but apparently of gigantic stature" (12). It's a strange description, but it lacks the quality of absoluteness that later ones have. "A being which had the shape of a man" is not being granted humanness and not yet denied it. The being's "shape," *per se*, is here excluded from the criteria of nonhumanity, while his face cannot be seen "at the distance of half a mile," and the crew does not interact with him in any way. So what is there to keep Walton from writing that, amazingly, he has seen a very large man? Walton's "but" phrase is equivocal over again. "Gigantic stature" qualifies the male shape—it certainly counts against him. On the other hand, this qualification makes it sound as though right now, gigantic stature is the only problem: a minor problem, compared to the ones we know the Creature has. This qualification is further qualified with "apparently," making it a kind of double negative. It sounds very odd to be unsure about giantism; so, it sounds as though Walton is sure of the being's stature, but unsure that giantism is the cause of it. It remains opaque what makes him unsure of that. Finally, there is an inverse relationship between all the qualification and the crew's reaction: "this appearance excited ... unqualified wonder" (12). The sighting has effects; the appearance of someone, not only surviving, but driving along the frozen sea "many hundred miles from any land ... seemed to denote that it was not, in reality, as distant as we supposed" (12). By morning, after they have rescued Victor, things have settled: he "seemed to be, a savage inhabitant" (13). The crew has no need for him to be monstrous.

Victor Frankenstein of course is more than familiar with the Creature's form, yet early on, at a time when he has encouraged himself to think that maybe the Creature no longer exists, even he does not recognize him instantly:

> I suddenly beheld the figure of a man, at some distance, advancing toward me with superhuman speed. He bounded over the crevices in the ice, among which I had walked with caution; his stature also, as he approached, seemed to exceed that of a man …. I perceived, as the shape came near (sight tremendous and abhorred!) that it was the wretch whom I had created. (76)

Shelley hints that Victor's difficulty shows his resistance to giving up his hope that the Creature no longer exists or at any rate is of no account: with that motive, Victor can perceive the figure of a man. Victor has not only seen the Creature, but constructed him, and still he can experience a "first" time when he is not sure.

In later scenes, however, which repeat aspects of Walton's account, Victor Frankenstein is overwhelmed with ungrounded certainty and an influx of orientation when he identifies the Creature. As Victor roams the mountains near his home, mourning for William, he recalls,

> I perceived in the gloom a figure which stole from behind a clump of trees near me; I stood fixed, gazing intently: I could not be mistaken. (56)

Victor recognizes the Creature without indicating how he does so. It's not clear what exactly he gazes at intently, or whether he is gazing to make a decision or just out of fascination. The figure is neither like nor unlike a man; it is not placed on a scale. Victor's gaze is intransitive, infinite, and yet conclusive, and *nothing* is on the other side of it; no grammatical object is given. Nothing is explained as a matter of sense data to be processed or indeed as any thought. Unlike the implication that monstrousness needs processing as illegible, there is no friction now, and finally, a "full" unmistakability. Victor's phrase "I could not be mistaken" is terser than his endless other protestations of certitude ("No one can conceive the anguish I suffered during the remainder of the night, which I spent, cold and wet, in the open air") (57). His intentness here exceeds the strength of his intentions, elsewhere, as though he were more able to identify the Creature than his own desires. Being unable not to recognize him brings satisfaction; everything else disappears. "He was the murderer! I could not doubt it" (56); "I did not for a minute doubt" (64).

Victor is infallible one more time, almost as strongly, as Frankenstein and the Creature track one another across the far North:

> I viewed the expanse before me with anguish, when suddenly my eye caught a dark speck upon the dusky plain. I strained my sight to discover what it could be, and uttered a wild cry of ecstasy when I distinguished a sledge, and the distorted

proportions of a well-known form within. Oh! with what a burning gush did hope revisit my heart! warm tears filled my eyes, which I hastily wiped away, that they might not intercept the view I had of the demon. (176)

Victor's visual strain, replaying his intent gaze in the forest, indicates that he is not content with mere possibility. But why did his eye catch "a dark speck" against a "dusky plain" in the first place? It sounds as though Victor already sees something—some telling quality. By the time that he discerns the "well-known form," he has verified the implications of whatever he saw. But as in the early shot of the Creature half a mile away, the dark speck makes it seem as though there is something other than the sum of the parts to discern. The body that he built to eight feet so that minute parts wouldn't slow him down is recognizable when it is only a speck. How could that be? Far from being overly material, here the Creature is almost without body, a pixel, an embryo, a micro-organism, and still has signature, is verified as the same "well-known" being, in spite and because of the fact that what there is for him to be known as is as unthinkable as ever. Furthermore, recalling a bit the critical position in which Blackness needs to be found and then thought, in that order, Victor prefers to think about the Creature's existence when it is in front of him. He is unable to conceive that the Creature is the invisible "spirit" that seems to follow his travels and "extricate [him] from seemingly insurmountable difficulties," for instance leaving food for him in the wild: "I may not doubt that it was set there by the spirits that I had invoked to aid me" (173). Victor's confidence still indicates mainly what he can't stand not to think. He orients himself by the Creature's singularity, so much so that he can't bear a diminished view of it for a moment.[42] Walton's mariners' orientation becomes Victor's entire orientation. He re-enacts the Creature's animation, delivering his form from the verge of sense; he wants to do this again and again, to never not be doing it. The process animates principally Victor, who refreshes himself by congratulating his own ability to be disturbed by the Creature's excess. In this way, Victor follows Hegel's recipe for anthropogenesis and finally political eligibility, showing himself capable of noticing and being torn by alienation.[43]

More than the inconsistency that all critics querying race in the novel observe in Shelley's physical descriptions (including Victor's bitter remark, "I had selected his features as beautiful" (39), inconsistent logics attend his unmistakability, such that it becomes full only when it is completely empty. Noting the contrast between this treatment and the consistency of the Creature's historical deprivation, Yousef remarks firmly, "I cannot offer so straightforward a reading ... of the creature's face."[44] Indeed the Creature's problem is not having been ripped from a homeland, but not having one; not an ethnic origin associated with him, but not being able to have any, as Yousef argues. As she points out, the Creature develops everything that he can from a vestibular world, the "low hovel, quite bare" (83) from which he watches social life through "a small and almost imperceptible chink" (85).[45] If his talents seem supernatural, he implies that they are hypertrophic by necessity, "while my friends were employed in their ordinary occupations" (103). When the Creature imagines what it would be like to have a female partner, he depicts a "veiled" life—Du Bois's figure, repeated again and again in African American writing, for a completely internally organized world, however complex, in which Black communities are divided from the world by "a veil so thick, that they shall not even think of breaking through."[46]

Various counterfactuals and hypotheticals—this sketch of what "shall" happen, Victor Frankenstein's attempt to think their situation forward, and other instances— help to fill in, beyond the social death of the Creature, the range of possibilities of his existence. The Creature's counterfactual statements set up these possibilities and then say what would have happened to them, had they existed. The logic is repeatedly that features of slaves' lives that in the larger society produce human history, produce what Christina Sharpe calls "a new subjectivity in which subjectification equals objectification"[47] when given by slavery: "No father had watched my infant days, no mother had blessed me with smiles and caresses; *or if they had*, all my past was now a blot, a blind vacancy in which I distinguished nothing."[48] In the same mode, the Creature's argument for a "companion" expresses the best case scenario for veiled life in the novel: "*we shall be monsters, cut off from the world;* but on that account we shall be more attached to one another" (120). Returning from hypothetical time, the present of the novel is more abstract: no lateral relation and no sexual relation are available. But having been through the hypothetical case, the reader has been given chances to think: "if they had" it, what would sexual relation be, "cut off from the world" (120)?

Shelley, familiar at least with her mother's review of Equiano's narrative,[49] speculates what racial slavery would be without captivity and without labor. The Creature steals and gathers but doesn't labor, nor is he "property."[50] Far from being confined, he and the other masculine protagonists criss-cross national borders as though they had Eurail Passes. His narrative renders captivity atopic, bursts the categories of freedom and bondage, and distinguishes freedom from the absence of both forced and waged labor. After Shelley is done stripping away aspects of racial slavery, what is left of it? Her abstraction logically reproduces the quandary of the free Black; I mean not only the wage laborer "compelled to wander" the Reconstruction minefield (Du Bois),[51] but the "eternal captive" "never at rest"[52] from exposure to violence whether or not confined, for whom "even somewhere free was not quite sufficient," as Dionne Brand writes.[53]

Yousef has written very thoughtfully about Shelley's abstraction, emphasizing its literal impossibility. As I mentioned, the impossibility is best exemplified by the Creature's socialization without society—the idea that without any nurturing or exchange whatsoever, he could get the point of social life at all, as he does. In Yousef's very original interpretation, Shelley's ascesis is outsize so that the Creature can be a thought experiment: what if the radically individual masculine human of Locke and Rousseau escaped from the pages of their books? Contrary to their hypotheses about human nature, she argues, if that being could exist he would not seem human at all, he would be monstrous.

For Yousef, the Creature's "radical autonomy" explains his impossible singularity (which I have discussed alternatively in terms of his infinite, imposed and abstractly real, non-empirical legibility and illegibility).[54] There are two passages of Yousef's essay it will be helpful to juxtapose. After drawing out how Victor Frankenstein "is first, finally, and throughout the object of human sympathies from which the creature is first, finally and throughout excluded,"[55] she goes on:

> In arguing for a more precise sense of what the novel is allegorizing as monstrous ... I have suggested that his giantism exposes the monstrousness of leaving out the roles of infancy, childhood, dependence, and relation in human formation .... *Frankenstein* does not present us with a monstrous body, only with testimonies to its monstrousness that are so unvaried and unrelenting as to amount to the proposition that it cannot be seen as human.
>
> Yet the creature is not a figure for the failure of sympathy, for insofar as the novel insists that he can never be looked on without horror, it equally insists that the human form and countenance (however miserable, however badly shattered or wrecked) will never excite such horror. It is never a matter of choice or avoidance in the imagination of this novel that the human attitude toward the human face will be an "attitude toward a soul" ... the demand [the creature] makes of Frankenstein arises from his realization that the "human senses are insurmountable barriers to our union" [119]. This is so not because he is cursed with a hideous body veiling a nonmonstrous person but because to wear the human form in this novel is to bear a human history.[56]

I agree with Yousef that Shelley's treatment of the Creature's position goes deeper than misunderstanding and a "nonmonstrous" self beneath that can be uncovered. ("Nonmonstrous" is an interestingly vast word.) In *Frankenstein* "it is never a matter of choice." In deciding that the Creature's underdetermined but apparently rivening presence allegorizes his nonhuman itinerary, bare of the social connections with which other characters introduce themselves, Yousef hypothesizes that in Shelley's conceit, human history forms or is inscribed onto the body, which is therefore understood as human, or as not if it has lived no such history. Yousef means (I think) that for Shelley, everybody has a human history and the fact that everybody has a human history cannot be missed. Therefore, if it could be missing, as Shelley explores counterfactually, that too would necessarily be obvious. To grasp this obviousness it's hard not to think the material in some way—thus the ambiguity I tried to phrase above, "forms or is inscribed onto the body." Human beings would encounter monstrosity in a nonmemberment that lacked a human history while recalling in form the outline of a possible history (that can then be seen as missing).[57] The female creature, most of all, is this nonmemberment of history, the "minor figure," in Hartman's terms, whose rending "fails to produce a radical politics of liberation" corresponding to that of her masculine counterpart.[58] She reaches the status only of "as if ... mangled ... living flesh."[59]

If "to wear" is "to bear" for all human being, if dualism has been rejected and history is all, corporeality is not a base, and history, defined here as minimal nurture, is the body. The human body is realized in and as its itinerary. What then is minimal nurture?

In pursuit of this next question, let's go on to Yousef's contrast between Walton and the Creature:

Whatever the brother may mean when he says [to his sister], "I have no friend," it cannot be what the creature means when he says, "Where were my friends and relations?"[60]

If it's important to notice the difference between what Walton means and what the Creature means, it's also important to ask for the difference between what Walton means and what the racial slave means, and what the Creature means and what the racial slave means and what the prisoner in solitary confinement means. Black studies scholarship debating the ontological implications of racial slavery intervenes exactly here, where various thresholds press. Gigante's and Yousef's theories about what enables the Creature's difference in kind respond to the Enlightenment question put by slavery. Chandler points out that taking "the problem of the Negro," in its exorbitance, "as a problem for thought" would be the only possible way to produce a general account that did not "[presuppose] the status of a European, Euro-American, or 'White' identity, subject, or mode of identification as coherent."[61] Thus in the case of *Frankenstein*, thinking about how Shelley approaches the question "What is Man?" relies in no way on establishing a racial referent for the Creature.

From here it's not just allegorically possible[62] but intellectually necessary to read not only Shelley's novel but anything for what the racial slave has to say about it; and to ask for the implications for any method of a Blackness that is other than race in general and slavery in general. Reading through Blackness is not allegorical, because Blackness is not a set of objects that can be taken for granted to reside within the historical and metaphysical frame to which allegory belongs. Confidence about what Black allegory could be falls away from *Frankenstein* as soon as it brings up the prerequisites and bounds of access to a human history. What is a history that might be begun only to be abducted into a "blind vacancy," "invaded at any given and arbitrary moment," or cultivated only when "cut off from the world"?[63]

With all of the above in mind, Yousef's line of thought suggests that racial slavery is not ideological error, nor reparable within the frame of humanity: an account with afro-pessimist affinities, although afro-pessimism has no exceptionality with regard to the first two theses, and no great exceptionality in the third. Yousef argues that Shelley believes that (a) sympathy cannot fail among humans,[64] and (b) everyone who exists is human, so (c) there can be no "failure of sympathy."[65] Therefore, Yousef does not interpret Shelley as intending "the monster as a figure for cultural constructions for the other as outsider, deviant."[66] To turn this around, one reading of this sentence is the conclusion that Shelley does not portray the racial slave as merely an outsider or deviant, but as "culturally 'unmade.'"[67]

Anthropogenesis

The casual sequencing of the Creature's materialization, not once but recurrently, and the sense that something other than spontaneity is occurring at the brinks of "first" and "second" instances of animation, comes to bear on the end of the novel, where the lastness of the last time reflects the first and vice versa.

Shelley prepares for the last time by allowing the landscape to buckle, wear away, and freeze. The area in which the characters travel is bounded, the restriction of the European citadel is definitely felt, but within it, a phantasmagoria of elided borders and jutting landscapes threatens to return the geography to a kind of hyletic condition. The Creature's and Victor's descriptions of it are seamless—as though to stress that underneath them lies the same world, however turbulent and unknowable. Mont Blanc and the "stupendous" Jura range (116), as the Creature calls it, which rises vertically while diminishing laterally, are called on to set the symbolic world askew, only to reveal another, mysterious but fundamental, the origin of the symbolic one.[68] The sense of *hylē*, Husserl's term for perceived and as yet unconceptualized matter, summons things not yet named, a prehistory of entities troubled only by winds and tides. As the landscape flattens, worn down at the poles, the novel shifts to one of the parts of the globe that "had to be uninhabitable" in a former era.[69] In Shelley the journey returns, though, beyond the era of "the nonhomogeneity of substance,"[70] before its separation. The landscape, void of the spatial orientation that allows time to be measured, and the eroded poles summon the possibility of a "temporal *hylē*,"[71] a phenomenological sensation not yet (and no longer) called time nor divided into past, present, and future.

Spivak appreciates that the novel releases the Creature unextinguished into a site that does not fit an imperial logic. Furthermore, she connects his destination with the novel's address to Margaret Saville, Walton's sister:

> He is "lost in darkness and distance" (191)—these are the last words of the novel—into an existential temporality that is coherent with neither the territorializing individual imagination (as in the opening of *Jane Eyre*) nor the authoritative scenario of Christian psychobiography (as at the end of Brontë's work) .... Margaret Saville does not respond to close the text as a frame. The frame is thus simultaneously not a frame, and the monster can step "beyond the text" and be "lost in darkness." Within the allegory of our reading, the place of both the English lady and the unnamable monster are left open by this great flawed text.[72]

Agreeing that Shelley is not tempted as Brontë is by "the unique creative imagination of the marginal individualist"[73]—Spivak is careful not to celebrate Mary Shelley as one, either—I wonder whether, as *Frankenstein* sails away from the Christian family, the reader is sent beyond racial slavery toward a fantastic Judeo-Christian refuge. If so, Shelley may throw away the problem of blackness's origin by giving it an apocalyptic end.[74]

Spivak is precise, and does not claim that the space toward which the Creature floats is unlimited. She writes merely that it is neither territorial nor familial. My problem is not with her statement, but with the temptation to collapse that beckons in Shelley's eschatological structure. The nothingness into which the Creature announces his "very remembrance" will vanish (190) is uncomfortably close to the "midst of ... darkness" (34) out of which he is brought by Victor's secret knowledge. According to Victor, the beyond of the text is the opening the events have come from. The Creature's animation came through "a passage to life aided only by one glimmering, and seemingly ineffectual, light" (35). Likewise in the chaotic middle, in the storming Jura, "for an instant every thing seemed of a pitchy darkness"; then, lightning had revealed the Creature standing in it (56). In this way, last and first instances happen in the middle and any time. What if the beyond of the text is tethered to the matrix of catastrophic inception, when before the Creature comes to life, Victor feels "dizzy with the immensity" of a fragile prospect (34)?

Caution about the implication of immensity then inflects all the counterfactual, hypothetical, negative, and elliptical spaces of possibility the novel includes. None are entirely unbounded either. They are "free" spaces only in their austerity, as we've seen. How different is the Creature's Hamlet-like closing soliloquy from his previous argument that in South America, it would be possible for him to be forgotten?

Then, the Creature had demanded "a female" who would be created to be his sexual partner, and an isolated domestic life in the *sertão* (118). In his scenario, humanity would not be threatened, difference will not make any difference: "the sun will shine on us as on man, and will ripen our food" (120). But as he adds too honestly, this "*picture*" of the Creatures' life is "peaceful and human" (120, my italics). In the picture, having minimal, "veiled" relations, he would *appear to become human,* that is, "linked to the chain of existence and events, from which I am now excluded" (121). As in the last instance he hopes to be forgotten, "everyone will be ignorant" of their very existence (121). This stipulation implies that the very thought of their having such an existence would be unbearable; violence would follow it. As Victor Frankenstein perceives, moving to South America would not solve that. The image the speech closes on, of being linked on the great chain of events, is exactly the wrong one to comfort Victor. He concludes that they must be either linked violently or eradicated. It may seem that because the bargain does not come about, Shelley suspends the question of what would have happened if Victor had completed it. But together with the Creature's imagination that "we would be monsters," the reasonable possibility that he might actually be trying for something else, and Victor Frankenstein's reasoning, "How can you, who long for the love and sympathy of man, persevere in this exile?" (121), withdraws the scenario. As we've seen, Shelley rules out possibilities by mooting their points ("No mother had blessed me ... or if they had, my past was now a blot") (97).

The Creature's idea that moving to South America would be moving away from all human knowledge does not in itself cancel other postracial horizons. The possibility, for instance, that maybe the only thing that could achieve the kind of secrecy the peaceful picture requires would be assimilation to the point of invisibility. Would the children of two creatures look unusual at all? The fact that they would not, does not, if he thinks of it (as someone trained in the life sciences), assuage Victor. He seems to be concerned about political ontology, too—the possibility that their progeny would be a "race of devils" because of what has happened (138).

The fate of such hypothetical possibilities in the novel troubles the idea that Walton's letter and so the novel launch themselves into a free space in which Margaret Seville and the Creature can both exist undefined. It suggests instead that this free space needs to be read as another fragile thought-balloon among others. The Creature's ending monologue is only the last of his speculative fictions: "the very remembrance of us both will speedily vanish … what I now feel will no longer be felt. Soon these burning miseries will be extinct …. My spirit will sleep in peace; *or if it thinks,* it will not surely think thus" (191). The wish for forgetfulness, like the capacity to forget the extremity of the Creature's situation when listening to his narratorial voice, and Victor's frequent wish to forget all about the Creature altogether, and the Creature's strong desire to forget himself—again juxtaposing the self-serving and the deep—is in the "distance" almost elevated into a total longing for what Agamben calls, and longs for as, "the great ignorance" of gnostic withdrawal.[75] Agamben adduces the second-century Egyptian mystic Basilides, who prophesies that after the saved have been saved, "God will bring on the whole world the great ignorance [*megale agnoia*], so that every creature may remain in its natural condition [*kata physin*] and none desire anything contrary to its nature."[76]

The Creature's disappearance to a distance beyond Walton's and the reader's capacity to verify his death or life figure him as the object whose discovery or permanent concealment would unlock or lock up the mystery of distinction's ground, while the social relations exhibited in its plot say something else. They tell of the convenience of such an object and the suitability of the racial slave for its role. The law of *Frankenstein* is that the Creature was literally created to be that object. The horror is that the fantasy is not just a fantasy; he exists. To turn this around, it seems that it is because the racial slave exists that reality is fantasy, and the novel's cultural resources are drawn toward the management of the crisis. Thus when the novel's end disappears into the joint of eschatology and history, it seems to describe from the inside what it has previously shown to be self-interested illusion. Shelley cannot explore the "last" moment while subtracting eschatology's crisis management, as that management, not her invention, is suffused throughout the notion of ending. Shelley does not depict fantastic reality, however, as the emanation of a real demiurge operating the puppet state of Geneva. As a kind of immanent critique of both mysticism and science, *Frankenstein* takes its explanatory power from elsewhere.[77] The space in which the Creature has been demanded to exist emerges in the novel in its sketches of slavery not restricted to the Americas, to labor, or to captivity in a narrow sense. It shows the assumptions of an expanded or "free" racial slavery reflected in the defenses of its milieu at its most ordinary, in its civil humanist economy. Can it be anything other than ordinary society, then, that pushes the last/first instance of the Creature beyond it?

It's possible to take the conflict of interests between the Creature and Victor, instead, as neither mistaken in its terms nor forgettable. Gigante would be right; it could be a matter of survival, that is, "might make the very existence of the species of man a condition precarious and full of terror" (138). Victor Frankenstein would have reason to conclude that the creature is asking him to risk "sacrific[ing] the whole human race" (156), as Victor blurts out to his father. Only, that would now be a sensible request.

Victor Frankenstein's outburst to his father collapses what had been a risk of humanity's destruction into certainty. Human existence "might" be made "precarious" (138), he bargains with the Creature "at the price perhaps of the existence of the whole human race" (138); later, "I could not, my father, indeed I could not sacrifice the whole human race!" (156). Typically, Victor erases his opportunity; it isn't South America that's the possibility and the risk of humanity that's the downside: it's the other way around. Only Victor Frankenstein has access to the thought of the risk, and since he responds uncritically, no one grasps it as a promise. But it is a promise, as Barbara Johnson's pointed question, "How indeed can one survive humanism?,"[78] suggests. In her phrasing risk and promise are the same. Taken as a rhetorical question, it suggests that humanism is not finite because it is too endemic to see one's way around. In that case humanism survives attempts on its life, and keeps killing. Taken as an actual question, however, it suggests that although humanism's survivors, *if any*, will not be human, there is at least a place from which to pitch this question. Although in the novel it is always slipping, there is a place from which thinking critically of the space that demands the Creature to fill it is different from Victor's determination to fill the space; a place to be exhausted by category, rather than acting as though literature was escaping it; a place from which to risk society for abolition, different from the desire that turns away from it in order to think that where it is going—north, always farther north—is where slavery won't be.

Notes

1   Mary Shelley, *Frankenstein; or, the Modern Prometheus* (1818), ed. Marilyn Butler (Oxford: Oxford University Press, 1993). Page references to this edition are cited parenthetically in the text.
2   It's a question what to call him: "the monster," "the Creature," and "Frankenstein" have so far been the options. He could be called "the Being" or "the nameless character." I'm going along with the currently popular choice "the Creature," not because I think it's best but because all are problematic. On the whole, most Shelley criticism refers to other characters by first or last names that echo the reader's assigned proximity to the characters: "Victor" and "Elizabeth," "Walton" and "Clerval." I call Victor by his first name to condescend to him, as I think Shelley constructs this character throughout as a comic parody of masculine obliviousness and what today would be called white fragility.
3   It isn't that most criticism finds race merely a matter of attribution, but that even if social conditions massively set the terms of discernment, criticism still needs to connect those conditions to something empirical, to make the last attribution itself to circumscribe its own objects.
4   Nahum C. Chandler, *X: The Problem of the Negro as a Problem for Thought* (Bronx, NY: Fordham University Press, 2014), 21–2.
5   Christian dualisms echo in constructions of race as either biological or otherwise material, as Kathleen Biddick, J. Kameron Carter, and Sylvia Wynter variously explain. See Kathleen Biddick, *Make and Let Die* (New York: Punctum Books, 2016); J. Kameron Carter, *Race: A Theological Account* (Oxford: Oxford University Press, 2008); Sylvia Wynter, "Unsettling the Coloniality of Being/Power/Truth/ Freedom: Towards the Human, after Man, Its Overrepresentation—An Argument," *New Centennial Review* 3 (2003): 257–337. On Wynter's "counterhistory," and so her

own not-so-reworked humanism, see David Marriott, *Whither Fanon? Studies in the Blackness of Being* (Stanford, CA: Stanford University Press, 2018).

6   It's possible to distinguish indetermination from overdetermination. Zakiyyah, Jackson remarks that conflicting oppositions that can't be simultaneously embodied "are in fact varying dimensions of a racializing demand that the slave be all dimensions at once"; "coerced formlessness" is "a mode of domination" ("Losing Manhood: Animality and Plasticity in the (Neo)Slave Narrative," *Qui Parle* 25 (2016): 117–18). Jackson refers to proliferating demands that eliminate indetermination. Referring to less structured possibilities, Margo Crawford argues that "when the BAM [Black Arts Movement] mobilized the word 'black' in the most radical manner, it was a way of naming the unknown dimensions of freedom and self-determination .... 'Black' signaled excess, the power of the *unthought*" (*Black Post-Blackness: The Black Arts Movement and the Twenty-First Century* [Urbana: University Illinois Press, 2017]). The different emphases of Jackson and Crawford are not yet a dispute, since accumulated demands are not unknown dimensions. But there is debate about whether "blackness can be claimed outside of racial slavery," that is, whether the indetermination can be had without the political ontology (Sara-Maria Sorentino, "Natural Slavery, Real Abstraction, and the Virtuality of Anti-Blackness," *Theory & Event* 22 (2019): 655). In this debate Hortense J. Spillers's interrogative mode, when she describes the Middle Passage as a suspension in "nowhere at all" that might yet produce forms of monstrosity to be "claimed," occupies a third position (Hortense J. Spillers, "Mama's Baby, Papa's Maybe: An American Grammar Book," in *Black, White, and in Color: Essays on American Literature and Culture* (Chicago, IL: University of Chicago Press, 2003), 215).

7   H. L. Malchow, "*Frankenstein's* Monster and Images of 'Race' in Nineteenth-Century Britain," *Past and Present* 193 (1993): 90.

8   Ibid., 92.

9   Ibid., 102.

10   Ibid.

11   Ibid., 139. That a Marxist reading will not be a reading through race is an interesting assumption.

12   Ibid., 92.

13   Ibid.

14   Malchow is already using such a hegemonic account in order to produce what counts and doesn't count as Black when he selects and deselects categories of relevance. For example, he notes that Shelley did not "[intend] to create a specifically Negro monster" because "she writes of the monster's yellow skin" (Malchow, *Frankenstein's Monster*, 103), and then overrides Shelley's intention: although she gave him yellow skin, he is still Black. That is possible not, for Malchow, because one can be "yellow" and Black at the same time, but because epidermal criteria are not conclusive in academic practice in 1993.

15   Lloyd's context is related: "Perhaps Fredric Jameson's concept of 'national allegories' as the typical form of third-world writing has some pertinence as an engagement with one particular instance or moment of third-world literary traditions where they are concerned with the failure of the symbolic claims made generally for the representative status of new national cultural and political institutions .... In the absence of an external point of origin, can that which originates also represent that

which it brings into being?" (*Anomalous States: Irish Writing and the Postcolonial Moment* (Durham, NC: Duke University Press, 1993), 84–5, n.18).

16 Samuel Taylor Coleridge, *The Statesman's Manual: Or, the Bible the Best Guide to Political Skill and Foresight: A Lay Sermon, Addressed to the Higher Classes of Society* (London: Gale & Fenner, 1826), 37.

17 Walter Benn Michaels's concerns in *The Shape of the Signifier* are exemplary of anxiety about the location of race: isn't it property? If it is property whose is it? It is unbearable if it is somewhere, and if it is not somewhere it isn't anywhere (*The Shape of the Signifier: 1967 to the End of History* (Princeton, NJ: Princeton University Press, 2006)).

18 Shelley, *Frankenstein*, 97. Elizabeth Young's densely citational *Black Frankenstein: The Making of an American Metaphor* (New York: New York University Press, 2008) focuses on the reception that associates the Creature with African Americans (a topic opened by Malchow). For Malchow, the reception of the Creature confirms the relevance of his hypothesis, but does not close the question of what it is that is being shown in the novel. Young, who transfers her *entire* investigation to the "tradition" of a Black *Frankenstein,* expresses no interest in the fact that it mobilizes what she believes is a novel "manifestly unfocused on either blackness or whiteness" (Young, *Black Frankenstein*, 8). Young herself is manifestly unfocused on either Blackness or whiteness to the same extent that she is focused on (a) examples of what others have called Black and (b) the power of metaphor to proliferate its instances. Origin is not a question for her, but not out of an anti-racist skepticism of origin; it does not arise because it is always settled between the archive and metaphor. She apologizes for reproducing the metaphor: "In a world not consistently devoted to demonizing blackness, there might be no need to reappropriate monstrosity" (Young, *Black Frankenstein*, 228). Cultural work occurs "in the meantime" (228), a response by way of a reflection on anti-Blackness. In this counter-Fanonian procedure, the metaphor of *Black Frankenstein* replaces any interest in the fact of Blackness, past or present. Yet Young means to be exhaustive; her references run to sixty pages, and she notes it whenever a work has not attracted scholarship, implying that if there were any at all, she would cite it. In volume, though, she cites Romanticist and Americanist scholarship on slavery and representations of Black people but almost no Black studies, if we take Black studies minimally to entail Blackness as one framing question. She treats the Black studies works she does cite as primary texts, or (rarely) they lie in the crossover zones of Americanist and Romanticist criticism and Black studies, and themselves use mostly historical protocols.

In turn, Young's omission of Black studies goes unmentioned in the reviews of *Black Frankenstein* that have been published. One review, by Meredith Miller, observes that Young avoids "the whole philosophical problem of modern subjectivity" and that "this causes a real loss of depth in the discussions of Fanon, Cleaver, and Baldwin in the later chapters" (review of Young, *Black Frankenstein*, *Gothic Studies* 13 (2011), 117). However, she believes that this happens because Young is "not a Romanticist" (116). Miller does not mention Young's omission of Black studies, either, and for her its absence does not prevent *Black Frankenstein* from "recommend[ing] itself as, among other things, a comprehensive literature review for anyone working on racial politics in the literature and film of nineteenth- and twentieth-century America" (115).

19 Lindon Barrett, *Racial Blackness and the Discontinuity of Western Modernity* (Champaign-Urbana: University of Illinois Press, 2013), 2; Saidiya Hartman and Frank Wilderson, "The Position of the Unthought," *Qui Parle* 13 (2003): 183–201; Dylan Rodriguez, "Black Studies in Impasse," *The Black Scholar* 44 (2014): 40; Fred Moten, *Stolen Life* (Durham, NC: Duke University Press, 2018), 155; Sylvia Wynter, "On How We Mistook the Map for the Territory, and Re-Imprisoned Ourselves in Our Unbearable Wrongness of Being, of *Désêtre*: Black Studies toward the Human Project," in *Not Only the Master's Tools: African-American Studies in Theory and Practice*, ed. Lewis Gordon and Jane Anna Gordon (Boulder, CO: Paradigm, 2006); Lewis R. Gordon, *Fanon and the Crisis of European Man: An Essay on Philosophy and the Human Sciences* (New York and London: Routledge, 1995), 25.

20 Allan Lloyd Smith, "'This Thing of Darkness': Racial Discourse in Mary Shelley's *Frankenstein*," *Gothic Studies* 6 (2004): 209.

21 Ibid., 207.

22 Ibid., 220.

23 Ibid., 214.

24 Ibid., 215.

25 Fred Moten, "Blackness and Nothingness (Mysticism in the Flesh)," *SAQ* 112 (2013): 739.

26 Denise Gigante, "Facing the Ugly: The Case of *Frankenstein*." *ELH* 67 (2000): 565–87.

27 Ibid., 565.

28 Kant "swerves from Burke's empiricist aesthetics by dismissing the 'real existence' of the object: 'All one wants to know is whether the mere representation of the object is to my liking, no matter how indifferent I may be to the real existence of the object of this representation'" (Ibid., 576).

29 Ibid., 566.

30 Ibid., 567.

31 Ibid., 566.

32 Shelley Fisher Fishkin's *Was Huck Black? Mark Twain and African-American Voices* (Oxford: Oxford University Press, 1994), which located, or playfully pretended to locate, a single actual African American boy who lent Twain his voice, was discussed in these terms at the time.

33 Gayatri Chakravorty Spivak, *A Critique of Postcolonial Reason: Toward a History of the Vanishing Present* (New York: Columbia University Press, 1999), 135.

34 Ibid., 133.

35 Ibid., 138.

36 In the 1831 edition, the irony is compounded in that Walton praises Victor for his discernment:

> Sometimes I have endeavored to discover what quality it is which he possesses, that elevates him so immeasurably above any other person I ever knew. I believe it to be an intuitive discernment; a quick but never-failing power of judgment; a penetration into the causes of things, unequalled for clearness and precision. (Shelley, *Frankenstein*, Appendix B, 203)

"I could not rank myself with the herd of common projectors," Frankenstein agrees (Shelley, *Frankenstein*, 180). This is hilarious. I agree with Marilyn Butler that Shelley's target here is the mutual mediocrity sustained in European masculinist circles.

37 He knows it is a bad idea: the scale is "contrary to [his] first intention" but easier (Shelley, *Frankenstein*, 35).

38 Spivak, *Postcolonial Reason*, 137.

39 Nancy Yousef, "The Monster in a Dark Room: *Frankenstein*, Feminism, and Philosophy," *MLQ* 63 (2002): 255. I've also consulted Yousef's revision of this material in *Isolated Cases: Anxieties of Autonomy in Enlightenment Philosophy and Romantic Literature* (Ithaca, NY: Cornell University Press, 2018), 149–69.

40 Yousef, "The Monster," 257.

41 Ibid., 258.

42 The "indelible trace" the Creature leaves extends this orientation in memory, the scar that allows Victor Frankenstein's incoherent life to feel real (Shelley, *Frankenstein*, 58).

43 Heidegger backtracks from the political to make this kind of alienation a mark of human/animal distinction, anthropogenesis proper, again. See Heidegger, *The Fundamental Concepts of Metaphysics: World, Finitude, Solitude* (Bloomington: Indiana University Press, 1995). As this scene does, Richard Iveson evokes the narcissism of Heidegger's anthropogenic technique. The foil to the human "is less a negative to be negated than a mirror which reflects only the essence of being-human that being-human itself renders invisible—a mirror in which 'we humans' always already find ourselves" ("Animals in a Looking-Glass World: Fables of Uberhumanism and Posthumanism in Heidegger and Nietzsche," *Humanimalia: A Journal of Human/Animal Interface Studies* 1 [2010]: 50).

44 Yousef, "The Monster," 223.

45 Ibid., 85.

46 W. E. B. Du Bois, *The Souls of Black Folk* [1903] (New York: Pocket Books, 2005), 90.

47 Sharpe argues that Frederick Douglass "repeats and rearticulates the traumas of what Douglass … does not actually witness and cannot fix with a certain day, time, or year: 'I was born.'" Christina Sharpe, *Monstrous Intimacies: Making Post-Slavery Subjects* (Durham, NC: Duke University Press, 2010), 6.

48 Sharpe, *Monstrous Intimacies*, 97; my italics.

49 Mary Wollstonecraft, review of *Narrative of the Interesting Life of Olaudah Equiano* [1789]; in Wollstonecraft, *The Vindications: The Rights of Men and the Rights of Woman*, ed. D. L. MacDonald and Kathleen Scherf (Peterborough: Broadview, 1997), Appendix A.

50 John Bugg, "'Master of Their Language': Education and Exile in Mary Shelley's *Frankenstein*," *The Huntington Library Quarterly* 68 (2005): 663. Bugg calls the Creature "property" because his exposure to violence recalls "the race-specific laws governing homicide on Caribbean plantations"; but various lines of scholarship on lynching, the conditions of Reconstruction generally, and anti-Black police violence reflect on extralegal violence.

51 W. E. B. Du Bois, *Black Reconstruction in America: An Essay toward a History of the Part Which Black Folk Played in the Attempt to Reconstruct Democracy in America, 1860-1888* [1935] (Oxford: Oxford University Press, 2014).

52 Linette Park, "The Eternal Captive in Contemporary 'Lynching' Arrests: On the Uncanny and the Complex of Law's Perversion," *Theory & Event* (2019), 692. "Social death as a permanent legal category" would come to be enshrined in the Thirteenth Amendment (Joy James, *Seeking the Beloved Community: A Feminist Race Reader* [Albany: State University of New York Press, 2013], 127).

53 Dionne Brand, *A Map to the Door of No Return: Notes to Belonging* (Toronto: Doubleday Canada, 2001), 46.

54 Yousef, "The Monster," 220.

55 Ibid., 223.

56 Ibid., 224–5.

57 Representational theories of racism, in contrast, argue that aesthetic and scientific theories, and their institutional extensions across culture, have a major role to play in inculcating the criteria for humanity with hegemonic forms, values, and rules. Shelley represents this criterial outline, the schematic human, when the Creature appears as "the figure of a man," "a being that had the shape of a man." "'Figure' phrases and 'being' phrases" dodge Blackness twice, splitting it into generic form and racial infill. Victor fully grasps the role of outline when he thinks that the Creature "might ... conceive a greater abhorrence for [his own deformity] when it came before his eyes in the female form" (Shelley, *Frankenstein*, 138). The female companion is both hypothetical "female form" that never emerges and "as if .... living flesh," or "remains" (Shelley, *Frankenstein*, 142).

    Yousef, again, takes a more constitutional approach: what matters *causally* is not conformance to a set of norms, physical or mental. What matters is what has and hasn't happened to the Creature.

58 Saidiya Hartman, "The Belly of the World: A Note on Black Women's Labors," *Souls: A Critical Journal of Black Politics, Culture, and Society* 18 (2016): 167.

59 Ibid., 142.

60 Yousef, "The Monster," 222.

61 Chandler, *X: The Problem*, 22–3.

62 Yeats muses that "allegory is one of many possible representations of an embodied thing" (*Essays and Introductions* [Springer, 1960], 116).

63 Spillers, "Mama's Baby, Papa's Maybe," 74.

64 Yousef, "The Monster," 224.

65 Ibid.

66 Ibid.

67 Spillers, "Mama's Baby, Papa's Maybe," 215.

68 On the Creature's imprisonment in Europe, see Maureen N. McLane, *Romanticism and the Human Sciences* (Cambridge: Cambridge University Press, 2000), 92.

69 Wynter, "Unsettling the Coloniality," 274.

70 Ibid., 279.

71 In Husserl and Derrida, *hylē*, literally "matter," is used to mean material that is perceived but not yet conceptualized and grasped by intention. For Husserl "the sensuous hylē, as such and in its purity, that is to say, before being animated by intentionality, would *already* be a piece of lived experience" (Jacques Derrida, *The Problem of Genesis in Husserl's Philosophy*, trans. Marian Hobson (Chicago, IL: University of Chicago Press, 2003), 86). Implicitly, *hylē* in perception seems to run parallel to identificatory suspension in the realm of ethics. An unmarked state is constitutive of experience. In his Introduction to Husserl's *Origin of Geometry*, Derrida further notes that to propose spatio-pereceptual hylē Husserl needs temporal hylē:

> In some unpublished material [Husserl] seems to go much further: "Urhylē," i.e., *temporal hylē* [my italics], is defined there as "the core of the other of the ego's own" .... *"alien to my Ego," "the intrinsically first other,"* or of "the first 'non-ego'" in the constitution of the *alter ego* (*Edmund Husserl's Origin of Geometry: An Introduction*, trans. John P. Leavey, Jr. [Lincoln: University of Nebraska Press, 1978], 86–7 n. 90).

Shelley is interested in something like *hylē*. The Creature relies on a hyletic idea when he describes his prelinguistic world: "I started up, and beheld a radiant form rise from among the trees. I gazed with a kind of wonder. It moved slowly, but it enlightened my path" (80). He implies that the radiant form gradually becomes the concept sun (without the word *soleil*) as he understands its relevance to him; agreeing with Husserl, it had to be something before. Episodes like Walton's provisional descriptions of the Creature, while they are not nonconceptual, share with *hylē* a smaller degree of suspended intention. This supposition is open to Yousef's criticism of *tabula rasa* philosophies and to the interventions of psychoanalysis: actually this process happens in an interplay with other beings and their perceptions and communications. In the forest the Creature does not have nothing; rather he is the wild child, and gleans something from the birds. Yousef addresses the wild child in *Isolated Cases: Anxieties of Autonomy in Enlightenment Philosophy and Romantic Literature* (Ithaca, NY: Cornell University Press, 2018), 99–111. Commenting on Husserl, Moten remarks: "to engage the phenomenality of the nation on the level of its original constitution is, in some sense, what occurs in the illuminative relay between self and world. However, what is for some a pathway is, for others, a dislocation" (*The Universal Machine* (Durham, NC: Duke University Press, 2018), 106). In previous work, I've been interested in the psychological function of hyletic-type perceptions *given the discontents of society* (*Looking Away: Phenomenality and Dissatisfaction, Kant to Adorno* (Cambridge, MA: Harvard University Press, 2009)).

72 Spivak, *Postcolonial Reason*, 139–40.

73 Ibid., 120.

74 Jacques Khalip traces an alternative discourse of attenuated "lastness" in Romanticism. In P.B. Shelley's "Triumph of Life," Khalip argues, the "generic apocalyptic drive is tempered" when "the last image evokes the last as always discreetly *there*," something that cannot finally be abandoned or completely abandon itself. See Khalip, *Last Things: Disastrous Form from Kant to Hujar* (Bronx, NY: Fordham University Press, 85).

75 Giorgio Agamben, *The Open: Man and Animal* (2002), trans. Kevin Attali (Stanford, CA: Stanford University Press, 2004), 89.

76 Ibid., 89–90. As Agamben goes on to muse, Basilides' solution for the unsavable has implications for beings in general, like Nietzsche's hopes for forgetfulness. Instead of the "contours of a new creation that would run the risk of being equally as mythological as the other," beings might stay as they are but subside from "the historical task" that hierarchizes them (Agamben, *The Open*, 92).

77 Part of the task here is holding on to the fact that the Creature may lose sight of, that his singular existence or nonexistence is not the same as the existence or nonexistence of the space that he has been made to fill, so that destroying the one does not destroy the other. (This is different from being surprised that the Creature wants to kill himself to be relieved, personally, of carrying this problem.) Nor can Victor break the mold for monstrosity by tearing the female creature to pieces: in that respect, the womb is not the kind of reproduction Shelley is talking about.

78 Barbara Johnson, "The Last Man," in Barbara Johnson et al., *A Life with Mary Shelley* (Stanford, CA: Stanford University Press, 2014), 10.

9

Mediating Monstrosity: Media, Information, and Mary Shelley's *Frankenstein*

Andrew Burkett

Over the course of the last two decades, Romanticist scholarship addressing interactive electronic hypertext environments has relied heavily on Mary Wollstonecraft Shelley's novel *Frankenstein* (1818, 1831) in an almost uncanny manner. In 2001, for example, Eric Sonstroem and Ron Broglio began collaborating to create *FrankenMOO*, an immersive electronic environment derived from Shelley's novel and hosted on the Romantic Circles website.[1] Like any MOO, or "Multi-User Dimension, Object Oriented," *FrankenMOO* was designed to employ the internet to offer real-time interactions between multiple writers, readers, and users. As Sonstroem describes them, "MOOs offer the freewheeling interactivity of a connected set of chat rooms, but they frame this unstructured interaction within a relatively fixed and hierarchical textual landscape."[2] Sonstroem and Broglio designed *FrankenMOO* to be much more than simply a recreation or critical and theoretical interpretation of Shelley's novel and certainly something other than simply a MOO whose themes are derived from *Frankenstein*.[3] Equipped with an Encore Xpress HTML interface, the Romantic Circles Villa Diodati MOO relied heavily on the precise use of the original language from Shelley's novel for character, location, and object descriptions, and *FrankenMOO's* interactive figures actually uttered lines directly from the various versions of her original text.[4] In a more recent example, in April 2009, Stuart Curran's Romantic Circles Electronic Edition of *Frankenstein* went live online after fifteen years in the making. Collaborating with Jack Lynch, Sam Choi, Laura Mandell, and a number of other scholars, Curran has produced with his multimedia hypertext "Pennsylvania Electronic Edition" of Shelley's novel one of the most comprehensive single editions of any text in any form, print or electronic, to date.[5]

But why have recent Romanticist research and scholarship come to focus attention so heavily and specifically on Shelley's *Frankenstein* in the production of these immersive electronic environments, hypertext online resources, and digital humanities initiatives? Is there something unique about this novel that allows it to be employed for such projects or, perhaps, actually draws or even prompts scholars to turn to it while pursuing this type of work? A related question might be the following: why have scholars not turned *as often* in this form of research to other equally rich and complex texts from the Romantic era such as Samuel Taylor Coleridge's *The Rime of the Ancient Mariner* (1798, 1817), William Godwin's *Caleb Williams* (1794), William Wordsworth's *The Prelude* (1799, 1805, 1850), or Percy Bysshe Shelley's *Queen Mab* (1813), to name but only a few possible alternatives? Indeed, while electronic editions of rather expansive and complex texts ranging from Erasmus Darwin's *The Temple of Nature* (1803) to Coleridge and Wordsworth's *Lyrical Ballads* (1798–1805) certainly exist, few, if any, electronic resources come even close to approximating the scope and scale of projects involving Shelley's *Frankenstein*.[6] Sonstroem perhaps sums up the magnitude of such *Frankenstein*-based projects best: "We hoped [with *FrankenMOO*] to create a monster that was beyond our control."[7]

The creators of *FrankenMOO* and the collaborators of the Pennsylvania Electronic Edition of Shelley's novel have provided some answers to these and other related questions concerning the reasoning behind turning to *Frankenstein* for the source of their various research projects. Lynch, for example, has noted that Curran's group chose to focus attention on *Frankenstein* because these collaborators understood Shelley's novel itself in terms of the logic of hypertext. As Lynch explains, "[t]he novel is a natural for hypertext: every page is filled with pointers to other texts, both within the novel itself and beyond Shelley's text to a world of contemporary contexts," and, as a result, Curran's edition of the novel is probably best understood as an immense variorum.[8] Sonstroem explains that he and Broglio turned to Shelley's novel for their *FrankenMOO* because, as these collaborators understand it, "*Frankenstein* is already thematically engaged with the revolutionary dynamics of new technology," and because of the apparent *flexibility* of Shelley's narrative.[9] However, many (if not the majority) of the texts from this period have been theorized all too persuasively for their focus on intertextuality and supreme flexibility of narrative, so these questions concerning the ostensible uniqueness of Shelley's text for electronic scholarship remain unanswered.

In what follows, I expound on the logic and reasoning provided by Sonstroem, Lynch, Curran, and others to explain the frequent use of Shelley's novel for the purposes of contemporary digital humanities research and scholarship. I do so, however, neither simply to elaborate on the ways in which *Frankenstein* is a deeply intertextual (or potentially "hypertextual") novel nor to track this text's reliance on or indebtedness to technology, per se. Of course, both of these types of projects have already been accomplished quite successfully by a host of eminent scholars of Romanticism.[10] Rather, to account for the appropriation of *Frankenstein* for the purposes of various information technologies of the present, I focus on the indebtedness of Shelley and her text to the late-eighteenth- and early-nineteenth-century cultures of information and media. Shelley's *Frankenstein* is a novel deeply concerned with the nature and function of "information" and especially with media/tion. This text captures the dramatic tension between two diametrically opposed and competing conceptions of information and information's various means of embodiment that, as I reveal, were available to Shelley during the first decades of the nineteenth century. The novel's first representation of information and embodiment, characterized and espoused by Victor Frankenstein, is a vision of information as abstract (i.e., "virtual") reality. Victor's representation is *virtual* in the Deleuzian sense of the term. "The virtual," Gilles Deleuze explains, is opposed not to the real but to the actual. *The virtual is fully real in so far as it is virtual. ...* Indeed, the virtual must be defined as strictly a part of the real object—as though the object had one part of itself in the virtual into which it plunged as though into an objective dimension [Deleuze's italics].[11]

For Victor, as we shall see, information is best understood as a virtuality abstracted from (though indeed connected complexly to) the material substrates that may variously embody it. Resultantly, Victor understands information as dematerialized and abstract (though nonetheless "real," also in the Deleuzian sense of that term). Otherwise stated, Victor perceives *matter as a medium* for embodying information. Later in the novel, however, Shelley challenges Victor's view with the conception of information and embodiment provided by Victor's own creature. According to the creature, who in the novel's final paragraphs promises to burn his monstrous body to ashes on a funeral pile in order that his "remains may afford no light to any curious and unhallowed wretch, who would create such another" as himself, information is best understood as inherently and irreducibly bound up with and reliant on materiality (243).[12] In other words, for the creature, information is always relentlessly embodied. But where, aside from the imagination, could Shelley have derived such a view of matter as medium and Victor's view of information and matter as decoupled? As we shall see, in the eighteenth century Gottfried Wilhelm Leibniz proposed an argument for matter as medium and a metaphysics that the Shelleys inherited through their investments in both *Naturphilosophie* and the discourse of the Romantic-era sciences of electricity. If Shelley saw matter as medium, she would also likely have perceived matter as simply another substrate (much like the manuscript paper on which she penned her famous text) for the embodiment and conveyance of abstract knowledge and information.

This essay thus makes five major interventions concerning both the primary text of Shelley's novel and secondary readings of *Frankenstein*. For one thing, I underscore the significance of the nature and function of information and media in (and on) the novel. By drawing on the history of the discourse of electromagnetism and other sciences of electricity, I show that not only did a number of unprecedented developments in media and information technology and theory occur during the Romantic period but also propose that such technological innovations and theoretical developments likely shaped Shelley and her text. In order to produce such an argument, I necessarily turn to close readings of *Frankenstein* (and especially its early chapters) in order specifically to reveal the ways that we can newly appreciate Victor's natural philosophy as fundamentally based on concerns deriving from early-nineteenth-century issues involving media and information technologies and theories. These close readings of the novel constitute the second major project of this essay. Third, after establishing this reading of Victor's natural philosophy, I turn to an analysis of the complex and rather complicated overall structure of the novel itself, focusing my examination on the elaborate frame narrative and nested narrative structures that comprise the textual apparatus that is *Frankenstein*. The complicated structure of this text continually draws attention to the novel's own physicality as mediated form, as the reader is repeatedly reminded of the fact that the epistolary novel is to be always understood as a set of interconnected (though sometimes seemingly unrelated) documents (e.g., Robert Walton's letters and journal, Victor's manuscript as transcribed by Walton and mailed in his letters, the various narratives and stories told by a range of characters) that have been sutured together into a monstrous body of information that the reader necessarily pieces together so as to make sense of the form of the novel's totality (not only diegetically but extra-diegetically as well). The parallels between the monster's fragmented body and the novel as a sutured-together information structure and mediated narrative apparatus then become quite obvious. In this context, it appears that the novel's diegesis inspires, or perhaps instigates, a type of thinking that the novel's structure itself comes to embody. Furthermore, once we understand the ways in which Shelley's text is both conceptually and formally self-conscious of and indeed reliant on the nature and function of information and media, we can account for why recent Romanticist scholarship has so often turned to this novel in digital humanities initiatives—the text's themes and structures themselves generate such analysis, research, and application. Finally, with these four concerns of the essay in mind, we may more clearly understand a fifth. Shelley's novel has often been referred to as a "message" from the past sent to warn us about the dystopian techno-science of modernity and as offering allegories that have been seen as ranging from admonitions (and even premonitions) of developments in nuclear warfare, biotechnology, artificial intelligence, genetics, and biochemistry.[13] This novel has been theorized for its various embedded ethical commentaries and forewarnings. In addition to these potential allegories of techno-science, Shelley's novel must be understood as an admonition concerning the complexities, if not the discontents, involving the monstrous matrix of our own historical moment's cybernetics and informatics. The novel suggests that thinking about media in terms of monstrosity often necessitates the invention of dynamic media systems that are beyond a given creator's control. Or, as Robert Mitchell and Phillip Thurtle recently ask in their analysis of contemporary biological art constructions, "[i]f the medium is the message, as [Marshall] McLuhan contended, then what happens when the medium comes to life?"[14] As I argue, Shelley raises this very question with *Frankenstein*, though, of course, in relation to the media of her own day. Once the novel is adequately historicized and theorized for its own interventions concerning media and information theory and technology, Victor's "hideous narration" (220) and Shelley's "hideous progeny" are given novel meaning and context.[15]

British Romantic Biomedia, the Discourse of the Sciences of Electricity, and *Frankenstein*

Victor perceives information as more essential than materiality. To borrow a crucial phrase from N. Katherine Hayles, I propose that Victor privileges information over material instantiation and comes to center his attention on "how *information lost its body*."[16] Through Victor, Shelley thus crafts an interpretation of information that, as Hayles has shown, only becomes prevalent in the mid-twentieth century through the cybernetic paradigm, which was "founded on a view of information that conceptualized it as distinct from the material substrate in which it was embedded."[17]

Otherwise stated, Victor's understanding of information is something like what Eugene Thacker refers to as the "biomedia" view of information in which biological materiality is seen as essentially only a substrate for information. As Thacker defines the term,

> "biomedia" is an instance in which biological components and processes are technically recontextualized in ways that may be biological or nonbiological. Biomedia are novel configurations of biologies and technologies that take us beyond the familiar tropes of technology-as-tool or the human-machine interface. ... Biomedia are particular mediations of the body, optimizations of the biological in which "technology" appears to disappear altogether.[18]

Of course, by "biomedia" Thacker primarily refers to contemporary configurations of biological materials and technologies issuing from fields ranging from molecular biology and genetics to biotechnology and bio-informatics.[19] However, his biomedia paradigm also relies on a more transhistorical philosophy of the relationship between information and materiality. Nicely summarizing Thacker's biomedia view of this relationship, Hayles explains that "[j]ust as the pertinent aspect of a newspaper is not that it happens to be made of plant fiber but that it is printed with words, so in a biomedia view flesh becomes the material carrier for the information it expresses."[20] In other words, according to the biomedia paradigm, information is understood as the primary site for the control and transfiguration of organic (i.e., biological) materials. Once Victor has synthesized the scientific information concerning "the cause of generation and life" necessary to bestow "animation upon lifeless matter," he begins collecting and arranging his materials for "the creation of a human being" through the suturing together of largely arbitrary body parts (80, 81). As Victor assembles his materials in this manner, his laboratory becomes that infamous "workshop of filthy creation" (82). Drawing from Friedrich Kittler's concept of "discourse network," Richard Menke has recently proposed that we "describe the creature as a headily powerful blend of inscription and technology that takes on a life of its own."[21] Indeed, for Victor, as I argue, the creature's body is of importance primarily for its purpose in serving as the material vessel for the undisclosed scientific information that he has "discover[ed]" (80). Thus taking Menke's suggestion to understand the creature as "discourse network" one step further, I propose that precisely because of his unique view of information, Victor envisions the creature's body literally as a form of media—that is, as the abstract (i.e., "scientific") information of natural philosophy that he has synthesized through his studies of occultism, alchemy, and cutting-edge Romantic science. In other words, Victor's monster becomes the first literary example of what I am calling "Romantic biomedia."[22] The figure of the creature thus serves as a prime example of the fact that the Romantics were radically reconceptualizing and reimagining what "media" could actually mean or even be. Moreover, the mediated body of scientific information that is Victor's creature may be aligned with other revolutionary technical and industrial innovations of the Romantic period—including new electromagnetic technologies, precinematic magic lantern shows, and especially the phantasmagoria that, much like Shelley's creature, intimately associates new media with horror, virtuality, and especially with the gothic. While it may be a tempting and certainly a fascinating project, this essay will *not* trace the now perhaps obvious trajectory beginning with the creature's monstrously mediated body from Shelley's novel and running through, while mutating with, mid-nineteenth-century stage performance spectacles of the creature as produced by Richard Brinsley Peake and Henry Milner, Thomas Edison's early-cinematic image of the creature's body, Boris Karloff's performance as the creature for Universal Pictures, or subsequent filmic and new media depictions of this monstrous body including Shelley Jackson's *Patchwork Girl* (1995), a work of hypertext (electronic) fiction.[23] Instead, I historicize and theorize Shelley's vision of information and mediation through what might initially appear to be an unlikely source—the discourse of the sciences of electricity.

To raise again a key question posed earlier in this essay, without the cybernetic paradigm at her disposal, where could Shelley have derived her conception and representation of information as disembodied from material substance? To answer this question, we must remember that the cybernetic paradigm is deeply rooted in the history of electricity and especially in the history of the discourse of electromagnetism, a body of scientific knowledge that was, of course, newly emerging in the Romantic era and that, as many critics have shown, Shelley drew on heavily in her novelistic depiction of both Walton's polar voyage in search of the magnetic north pole and, perhaps more obviously, with Victor's animation of his creature through the "spark" of electrocution (84).[24] Tracing the origins of the cybernetic paradigm within developments in theories of electromagnetism from this period allows us to understand better how Shelley might have come to perceive information not only in a more traditional materialist view but also as part of a complexly mediated field, as the discourse of electromagnetism came to represent the phenomenon during this era.[25] Historian of science Barbara Giusti Doran explains the significance of the paradigm shift occurring with the birth of electromagnetism:

> In the electromagnetic view of nature, Western science experienced its greatest disjuncture since the seventeenth-century Newtonian synthesis. For the first time, numerous phenomena that could find no explanation in the context of the mechanical worldview had an alternative, encompassing metaphysic. By the end of the nineteenth century, the mechanical notions of "atoms in a void" and "forces acting between material particles" had been replaced by the notions of the electromagnetic field as a nonmaterial, continuous plenum and material atoms as discrete structural-dynamic products of the plenum.[26]

Doran meticulously tracks the origins of Michael Faraday's revolutionary lines of electric and magnetic force and physical theories concerning the "luminiferous aether" that had taken root between 1825 and 1850 back through the Romantic and Enlightenment eras all the way to seventeenth-century conceptions of and challenges to philosophies of materialism, including those of René Descartes and Leibniz. In doing so, she reveals that the revolution that had developed by the mid-nineteenth century into "a conscious rejection of the mechanical concepts of atom, void, and force in favor of the plenum and a field-theoretic notion of matter" must be placed especially in the context of Leibniz's early philosophies of matter and force.[27]

Theories of matter had become largely demechanized by the mid-nineteenth century through the work of individuals such as James Clerk Maxwell and his electromagnetic theory of light, and by the 1890s, the field-theoretic conception of matter was cemented by Joseph Larmor's synthesis of optical, electromagnetic, and atomic theory through the first electron theory of matter that viewed mass as a phenomenon of electromagnetism.[28] However, as Doran reveals, this late-nineteenth-century field-theoretic view—which would be essential for the arrival of the cybernetic paradigm—would have been impossible without seventeenth- and eighteenth-century investigations challenging traditional mechanical philosophies of matter.[29] With his the *Monadology* (1714), Leibniz was perhaps the most important early figure in this trajectory. Leibniz explains at the start of this text that "[t]he Monad, of which we shall here speak, is nothing but a *simple* substance, which enters into compounds. By 'simple' is meant 'without parts.'"[30] The *Monadology* thus opens with Leibniz's desire to make sense of the complex relationship between continuous substances and the elemental parts that, paradoxically, must constitute them. "And compounds," he subsequently writes,

> are in this respect analogous with [*symbolisent avec*] simple substances. For all is a *plenum* (and thus all matter is connected together) and in the *plenum* every motion has an effect upon distant bodies in proportion to their distance, so that each body not only is affected by those which are in contact with it and in some way feels the effect of everything that happens to them, but also is mediately affected by bodies adjoining those with which it itself is in immediate contact. Wherefore it follows that this inter-communication of things extends to any distance, however great.[31]

Doran explains that Leibniz's work thus presents "[t]he concept of substance as a continuous plenum of force" and insists upon "the reality of a *medium* that is the locus of optical and gravitational action [my italics]."[32] In other words, Leibniz's metaphysics calls for an alternative conception to mechanical philosophy by fundamentally reconceiving matter as a continuum and, therefore, though still admitting the reality of the atom, theorizes matter *as* medium.

Leibniz's uptake and popularization by the German Romantics are widely recognized by scholars of the period. Although Leibniz witnessed no major proponents of his philosophic doctrines during his own lifetime, Catherine Wilson has shown that

> [b]oth Kant and Schelling made statements to the effect that only their age had been able to understand and restore the real Leibniz. ... The young Schelling was, of all Leibniz's end-of-century readers, perhaps the most convinced by the *Monadology*.[33]

Of course, Immanuel Kant and Friedrich Wilhelm Joseph von Schelling were not unique in their fascination with the philosopher. Johann Gottfried von Herder was absorbed by Leibniz's philosophic system, as was Friedrich von Schlegel.[34] Leibniz's work also significantly influenced the development of *Naturphilosophie*.[35] In fact, through Leibniz's impact on Schelling's vision of *Naturphilosophie*, his work shapes the discourses of electrochemistry and electromagnetism (and, as we shall see, impacts the fiction of Mary Shelley through such discourses). Johann Wilhelm Ritter, the renowned German electrochemist, was not only an acquaintance of Herder and Johann Wolfgang von Goethe but was, moreover, deeply influenced by Schelling's *Naturphilosophie*.[36] Following Schelling's vitalist philosophies as well as the thought of other *Naturphilosophen* of the University of Jena (e.g., F. Schlegel) espousing vitalism, Ritter first articulates the science of electrochemistry in the first decade of the nineteenth century and ultimately shapes Hans Christian Ørsted's discovery and explanation of the phenomenon of electromagnetism.[37]

As a number of editors and critics of *Frankenstein* suggest, Percy Shelley's citation of those "physiological writers of Germany" in the first sentence of his anonymous preface to the 1818 edition of the novel is made in reference to Ritter, Schelling, Schlegel, and other Jena-circle Romantics.[38] The Shelleys' interests in these German "physiological writers" may therefore be understood not only as a preoccupation with the vitalist-mechanist debates of the early-nineteenth century (as such interests are traditionally explained by scholars of Romanticism) but also as a fascination with a much older and more basic metaphysics of matter deriving ultimately from the *Monadology* (and, thus, as an historical trajectory linking Leibniz, Schelling, Ritter, and the Shelleys).[39] That is to say, Percy and Mary Shelley are drawn to the ideas of figures such as Schelling and Ritter because, in *Naturphilosophie* and the discourse of the Romantic-era sciences of electricity, these authors locate the vestiges of an alternative theory of matter and mediation stemming from a Leibnizian metaphysics of matter as medium.[40]

In *Frankenstein* Shelley asks her audience to look at the world through Victor's eyes and, in effect, to see the possibility of perceiving matter as something completely novel—that is, to look at *matter* and to see it *as medium*, because the body of Victor's creature is represented by the novel as a composite mediation of synthesized (scientific) information. This history of the discourses of electrochemistry and especially electromagnetism can therefore account for Shelley's depiction of Victor's own metaphysics (and physics) of matter, medium, and information.[41] Seen in this light, the potential for Leibniz's philosophic influence on Shelley also gives new context to what has already been shown to be the almost certain impact of Sir Humphry Davy's work on Shelley's novel and especially the ways in which she likely drew from Davy's explanations of the employment of galvanic electricity in the Romantic-era search for the discovery of the principle of "life force."[42] In short, Shelley's depiction of Victor's natural philosophy is indebted not only to Davy's representation of galvanic chemistry but also to a Leibnizian metaphysics of matter.

"Real Information" and Unreal Bodies in *Frankenstein*

While we now have an historical account of the precybernetic ways in which Shelley might have arrived at such a view of the creature's body, we must track a similar route through the logic of her novel to understand better the ways in which Victor himself arrives at such a vision of his creation. Once Victor arrives in Ingolstadt and is acquainted with both M. Krempe and M. Waldman, his university professors, he becomes utterly obsessed with collecting information in his project to "pursu[e] nature to her hiding places" in order to discover "the cause of generation and life" (82, 80). "[N]atural philosophy," Victor states,

> and particularly chemistry, in the most comprehensive sense of the term, became nearly my sole occupation. I read with ardour those works, so full of genius and discrimination, which modern inquirers have written on these subjects. I attended the lectures, and cultivated the acquaintance, of the men of science of the university; and I found even in M. Krempe a great deal of sound sense and *real information* [my italics]. (77–8)

The information that Victor gleans while "engaged, heart and soul" in his academic pursuits ultimately leads him to ponder where "the principle of life proceed[s]" and famously takes him into "vaults and charnel houses" where he closely examines "the change from life to death, and death to life," finally to arrive at the secret "of bestowing animation upon lifeless matter" (78, 79, 80). Fascinated with the "information" that he has uncovered in his laborious studies, Victor states:

> What had been the study and desire of the wisest men since the creation of the world, was now within my grasp. Not that, like a magic scene, it all opened upon me at once: the information I had obtained was of a nature rather to direct my endeavours so soon as I should point them towards the object of my search, than to exhibit that object already accomplished. (80)

In the next paragraph of the novel, Shelley contrasts Victor's use of the word *information* here, by which, according to the term's closest referent in the *Oxford English Dictionary*, he means abstract "intelligence" or "[k]nowledge communicated concerning some particular fact, subject, or event," with a much older adjectival registration deriving from the infinitive "to inform."[43] In one of the text's first major breaks in narrative voice, Victor switches from his narration of diegetic events to Walton, and he addresses his transcriber (as well as the reader) of his oral history directly:

> I see by your eagerness, and the wonder and hope which your eyes express, my friend, that you expect *to be informed* of the secret with which I am acquainted; that cannot be: listen patiently until the end of my story, and you will easily perceive why I am reserved upon that subject [my italics]. (80)

Through the use of the first person, this defamiliarizing passage brings to the surface of the reader's attention the fact that the tale with which we are engaging is one that is complexly mediated. That is, the story is, in itself, a complicated transmission of narrative information between subjects. Victor here refuses to "inform" Walton—rejecting any participation in shaping the mind or character of his scribe (or, for that matter, of course, of the reader)—precisely because of the more abstract and dangerous "information" that he has uncovered. Shelley is careful to underscore the idea that, for Victor, information is abstract, secret, and divorced from the world of lived experience:

[T]his discovery [of "the cause of generation and life"] was so great and overwhelming, that all the steps by which I had been progressively led to it were obliterated, and I beheld only the result. (80)

Victor is left only with "the information [he] had obtained" concerning the cause of generation and life. Shelley thus contrasts the usage of "to be informed" here with her employment of "information" in the immediately preceding paragraph in order to draw the reader's attention to the fact of the various registrations (and formations) of "information" present in the novel.

The more ardently Victor pursues this secret information, the more his own body wastes and degrades: "My cheek had grown pale with study, and my person had become emaciated with confinement" (82). Victor fully loses track of the importance and significance of physical bodies—including his own—as he becomes increasingly engrossed in his pursuit of "real information" (78). Furthermore, critics have often been perplexed by Victor's decision to suture together dismembered bodies into the monstrous body of the creature: it would have been much more practical for the scientist to perform his experiments on undissected corpses—as was the case with actual work being done on electricity and electrocution during this era.[44] However, seen in this context, Victor's twisted perception of embodiment gives new meaning and explanation to his obsession with fragmented and dismembered bodies. Cloistered in scholarly pursuit, Victor goes into hiding in his study and fully loses touch with the primacy of physicality. In so doing, he leaves behind any prioritization of the physical as he enters the realm of abstraction in his burning pursuit of information.

Victor's conception of that "real information," which becomes essential to his animation of the creature just a few pages later in the novel, represents a notion of information as something theoretical and removed from the actualities of ordinary life and experience. Victor's "information" is very different from words such as *intelligence* and *knowledge*. Simon Schaffer has noted that "[t]he word ['intelligence'] refers both to signals received from without and to the capacity to register and interpret these signals," thus highlighting both the term's basis as factual communication and the comprehension of facts.[45] Relatedly, *knowledge* is, according to the *Oxford English Dictionary*, "[t]he apprehension of fact or truth with the mind."[46] Victor perceives the "information" concerning "the cause of generation and life" as abstract, lost, secret, and removed from ordinary lived experience, and his view of "information" thus invokes what Menke would define as the term's "modern sense."[47] According to Menke, "[i]nformation becomes fact that has lost its context, signs that have lost their matter, intelligence that has lost its faculties."[48] Indeed, Victor's "real information" concerning the secret of life is decontextualized and largely disconnected from reality.

Whereas Victor loses touch with the realities of knowledge, intelligence, and lived bodily experience, his creature becomes the living *embodiment* of these very concepts. The creature is careful to convey to Victor his self-awareness of bodily experience and of the various ways in which he has become a sensitive, intelligent being. "I was … endowed with a figure hideously deformed and loathsome; I was not even of the same nature as man," the creature explains to Victor (145). He continues: "Of what a strange nature is knowledge! It clings to the mind, when it has once seized on it, like a lichen on the rock" (146). Having "continually studied and exercised [his] mind" on *Paradise Lost*, *Plutarch's Lives*, and the *Sorrows of Werter*—not to mention Victor's own journal of his creation—the creature has become a wise and deeply self-conscious subject (152). Moreover, he understands embodiment and intelligence in ways opposed to Victor's philosophies of information and mediation. Most important, the creature sees his body as essential to his sense of self and irreducibly tied to cognition. In the final pages of the novel, the creature grieves what will become his loss of lived bodily experience following his death. "I shall no longer see the sun or stars, or feel the winds play upon my cheeks. Light, feeling, and sense, will pass away; and in this condition must I find my happiness," he states (244). The creature's final promise to Walton and the reader is that he will immolate himself on a funeral pile so that his "remains may afford no light to any curious and unhallowed wretch, who would create such another as [he has] been" (243). Shelley concludes her novel with the creature's promise to destroy his body completely: "I shall ascend my funeral pile triumphantly, and exult in the agony of the torturing flames. The light of that conflagration will fade away; my ashes will be swept into the sea by the winds" (244). For the creature, then, information and being are only embodied.

Virtuality and the Structure of *Frankenstein*

Unlike his creature, Victor views information and mediation in ways akin to what Hayles would refer to as the "posthuman" view, not only because, as in the posthuman paradigm, Victor privileges information over material instantiation but also, and more important, because in doing so he enters what Hayles refers to as "the condition of virtuality."[49] As Hayles explains, one often only needs to take "a small step to perceiving information as more mobile, more important, more *essential* than material forms. When this impression becomes part of your cultural mindset, you have entered the condition of virtuality."[50] Victor's natural philosophy concerning the relationship between mediation and information is also something like what Deleuze explains as the "actualisation" of the "Idea":

> When the virtual content of an Idea is actualised, the varieties of relation are incarnated in distinct species while the singular points which correspond to the values of one variety are incarnated in the distinct parts characteristic of this or that

species. ... Thus, with actualisation, a new type of specific and partitive distinction takes the place of the fluent ideal distinctions. We call the determination of the virtual content of an Idea differen*ti*ation; we call the actualisation of that virtuality into species and distinguished parts differen*ci*ation.[51]

In Deleuze's theory of the virtual/virtuality, then, through the process of *actualisation*, each differen*ti*ation of the virtual content of the Idea comes to correspond to a specific differen*ci*ation of the "species." Therefore, for Deleuze, mediation occurs as a one-to-one correspondence between differen*ti*ated virtual content and differen*ci*ated material part. Because the "discovery [of 'the cause of generation and life'] was so great and overwhelming" for Victor, "all the steps by which [he] had been progressively led to it were obliterated, and [he] beheld only the result" (80). In other words, what Deleuze would refer to as the "differen*ti*ation" of Victor's secret "Idea" has been lost to history (or "obliterated," as Victor states), and what he is left with is pure and immediate differen*ci*ation—the *actualised* body of the once "lifeless clay" (i.e., the creature) through the "spark" of electrocution (82, 84).

This reading of *Frankenstein* through the lens of Deleuze also gives new meaning and support to recent scholarship suggesting the novel's investment in virtuality and theorizing the ways in which gothic narratives generally aspire toward the virtual. As Jules Law explains, the "virtual" can be defined as "any form of mediation which purports through novel formal innovations to make its own apparatus transparent; in short, any form which denies its own status as mediation and claims instead the status of pure immanence."[52] In its formal attempts to mediate the densely complicated set of narrative transmissions between the text's various storytellers and listeners (i.e., receivers of narrative), *Frankenstein* actively gestures toward not only what Law refers to as the drive for "pure immanence" that often characterizes gothic narrative but also toward a Deleuzian virtuality. The novel desperately wishes to simulate the found object—whether that found object is the intercepted letters supposedly mailed to Mrs. Margaret Saville in England, Walton's transcription of Victor's tale in manuscript form, the documents that the creature has apparently collected during his stay in the hovel adjacent to the De Lacey cottage, or other of the text's ostensibly "real" artifacts. However, the novel inherently fails in such a project through its variety of defamiliarizing interruptions in narrative voice (the text's repeated intrusions of the first person, for example), and it does so precisely because Shelley is urging her readers to recognize the simulacrum of "real information" that the text itself purports to be. *Frankenstein* thus ultimately directs readerly attention to the virtuality of the novel's narrative form and structure in its desires to become transparent.

As many critics have pointed out, *Frankenstein* becomes a rather complex frame narrative—a nested narrative structure of story within story. Beth Newman nicely summarizes the novel's nested narratives:

> *Frankenstein* ... contains an elaborate series of frames. Working from the outside in we start with an epistolary narrative, the letters of a Captain Walton

to his sister Mrs. Saville, who remains safely at home in England while he seeks fame, glory and the North Pole. His letters announce the discovery and rescue of a stranger—[Victor] Frankenstein—who tells his bizarre story to Walton, who then includes it in his letters home. Frankenstein's story contains yet another, the confessions of the monstrous creature he has created and abandoned; and the Monster includes within his own narrative the story of the DeLaceys [*sic*], the family of exiles he tries pathetically and unsuccessfully to adopt as his own.[53]

As Newman suggests, Shelley's novel is deeply invested in examining and representing the nature and function of virtuality. The text both formally and thematically asks the reader to understand and experience it as a virtual environment. As the novel becomes a simulacrum of disembodied narrative voices, Shelley's Victor enters what Hayles refers to as "the condition of virtuality" through his privileging of information over materiality during the course of the unfolding of the text's diegesis. Newman points out in her analysis of the novel's frame structure that "each teller in the chain of narrative embeddings accepts the story he hears without question, and repeats it unchanged," with the result that readers of the novel gain no new perspective but instead hear in Walton, Victor, and the creature an eerily similar voice that works to erase the distinctions between these narrators.[54] Newman's provocative point here is that

> once a narrative has been uttered, it exists as a verbal structure with its own integrity, and can, like myth, think itself in the minds of men (and women). Being infinitely repeatable in new contexts, it has achieved autonomy; it now functions as a text, having been severed from its own origins, divested of its originating voice.[55]

In other words, Shelley's novel structurally reinforces its thematic content, as the text's formal apparatus points toward Victor's view of information as having lost its body.

Mothers, Motherboards, and Shelley's Media Monster

In the context of this historical and theoretical account of Shelley's novel against the background of media and information theory (and its history), we can much more clearly understand and appreciate the reasoning behind the transformation of *Frankenstein* into hypertext online resources and simulated, immersive digital environments. At the very core of its themes and structures, *Frankenstein* asks us to allow it to mutate and transform into *FrankenMOO*. And while McLuhan has famously proposed that "the medium is the message," Shelley's work thus poses a much more complicated and certainly a much more dramatic question—her *Frankenstein* asks us to consider what happens when the medium comes to life.[56]

In a reading of Kittler's *Discourse Networks, 1800/1900* (1990), Alan Liu theorizes what he refers to as the discourse network of 2000 at length:

The distinctive signal of 2000 … synthesizes [Kittler's discourse networks of] 1800 and 1900. In 2000, the channel is just as seemingly senseless, random, and automatic as in 1900. … Where the author was once presumed to be the originating transmitter of a discourse next sent for management to the editor, publisher, and so on through all the other positions in the discursive circuit, now the author is in a mediating position as just one among all those other managers looking upstream to previous originating transmitters. … Random and senseless those precursor transmissions may seem (in the way we often feel that overwhelming data is meaningless), yet—in a curious reversion of 1800—that content held in databases and XML now sets the very standard for an ultrastructured and ultradescribed rationality purer than any limiting instantiation of the *Ding an Sich*. And so what Kittler calls the "mother's mouth"—now the discourse of the motherboard, of the matrix itself—seems to return. Only it is alienated from the romantic-era voice of inspiration issuing from the unstructured life that Wordsworth or Blake called "childhood."[57]

As Liu's work thoroughly reveals, XML, HTML, and the networked complexities of real-time operations of the internet and web-based interactions constitute the discourse network of 2000. For Liu, the discourse network of the present is a strange recapitulation and transformation of what Kittler has described as the discourse network of 1800, the discursive formation of the Romantic age. According to Kittler, Romantic-era authors collectively worked to transcribe the voice of "Mother Nature" in lyric, the ode, and other forms of prose and poetry available during the late-eighteenth and early-nineteenth centuries. Kittler explains that

the discourse network of 1800 executed a new maneuver. The very Nature that the philosopher's stylus uses as a writing surface for inscribing divine thoughts is at the same time, but in direct contradiction, the source of all writing. Not God, but a tranquil, immediate Nature guides the pen from the depths of the soul through clear eyes.[58]

For Kittler, such literary transcriptions of the voice issuing from the "Mother's Mouth" and from "Mother Nature" (more generally) must be understood as dominant and powerful discursive technologies of this period. David Wellbery succinctly rephrases Kittler's point here in his forward to *Discourse Networks, 1800/1900*: "Romanticism is the discursive production of the Mother as the source of discursive production."[59] What Kittler describes as the Romantic discursive formation is echoed in the discourse network of 2000, Liu suggests, with the crucial difference that the voice of "nature" lying behind (and ultimately beyond) the Romantic transcription systems of lyric, the ode, the novel, and so on, has been transfigured into the autonomous cybernetic "voice" of the "motherboard" and of the "matrix" of the Web itself. The implication here is, of course, that if there is anything even remotely like a formation of subjectivity in that "Mother's voice" of the discourse network of 2000, it must only be understood in terms of posthumanist dispersion, dislocation, and decentralization. That is to say, "Discourse Network, 2000" is a deeply virtual phenomenon.

As numerous critics and other readers of Shelley's *Frankenstein* have been careful to indicate since the 1970s, the figure of the mother (and of the "maternal" in general) is marginalized in the novel, and the complexities of gender in the novel have thus sparked much renewed feminist (and gender studies) critical and theoretical interest in Shelley's tale.[60] Anne Mellor has gone as far as to suggest that the novel is, at its heart, a parable concerning the dangers of a man making a baby in the absence of a woman.[61] The novel clearly shows that the impetus for Victor's desire to discover "the cause of generation and life" (and the resultant experiment with the creature) issues from his wishes to bring his own dead mother back to life. Of course, Victor fails in this project—Shelley thus apparently indicating that the mother/the mother's voice may only be virtually present in the novel in her/its eerie absence. Initially, then, it might appear that Victor's failed parthenogenesis turns the novel into a cautionary tale about the rejection of the materialist cause in search (and in favor) of the virtual. Indeed, Marilyn Butler, for example, has provocatively argued that Mary Shelley should be classed among the materialists, noting that William Lawrence, Percy Shelley's personal physician, had "sketched out" in early 1816 a "materialist case against spiritualized vitalism."[62] However, as we have seen, *Frankenstein* ultimately rejects materialist philosophy too in its embrace of virtuality, even in its very narrative structure, and only in so doing does Shelley's novel become a richly complicated media/information system serving as an apparently inexhaustible source not only for literary criticism and theory but also for new media and contemporary digital humanities initiatives. As *FrankenMOO* and the Romantic Circles Electronic Edition of *Frankenstein* amply demonstrate, the drive toward virtuality present both formally and conceptually in Shelley's novel has proven to be incredibly *generative*. In these ways and for these reasons, *Frankenstein* thus stands characteristically outside of Kittler's discourse networks of both 1800 and 1900. With its autonomous qualities, its obsessions with disembodiment, and especially its focus on virtuality in its impulses, themes, structures, and preoccupations, Shelley's *Frankenstein* is the Romantic correlate for the cybernetic discursive formation and matrix of our own historical moment—the monstrous *Discourse Network, 2000*.

Notes

1   Eric Sonstroem, "Do You Really Want a Revolution? CyberTheory Meets Real-Life Pedagogical Practice in *FrankenMOO* and the Conventional Literature Classroom," *College Literature* 33, no. 3 (2006): 150.
2   Ibid., 150.
3   Ibid., 152.
4   Ibid. In addition, Ron Broglio discusses his work on MOOs and a number of projects related to the Romantic Circles Villa Diodati MOO and its history. See Broglio, "Living inside the Poem: MOOs and Blake's *Milton*," in *Digital Designs on Blake* (2005), ed. Broglio, *Romantic Circles Praxis Series*. romantic-circles.org/praxis/designsonblake/broglio/broglio.html. Accessed November 1, 2019.
5   Jack Lynch, "Unexplored Regions: The Pennsylvania Electronic *Frankenstein* as Variorum Edition," in *Literature and Digital Technologies: W. B. Yeats, Virginia Woolf,*

Mary Shelley, and William Gass, ed. Karen Schiff (Clemson, SC: Clemson University Digital Press, 2003), 50.

6   Electronic texts that allow for dynamic collation (such as *The Temple of Nature* [1803] and *Lyrical Ballads* [1798–1805]) are available on the Romantic Circles website. See Erasmus Darwin, *The Temple of Nature*, ed. Martin Priestman, *Romantic Circles Electronic Editions*. romantic-circles.org/editions/darwin_temple/. Accessed November 1, 2019. Also see Samuel Taylor Coleridge and William Wordsworth, *Lyrical Ballads*, ed. Ron Tetreault and Bruce Graver, *Romantic Circles Electronic Editions*. romantic-circles.org/editions/LB/. Accessed November 1, 2019. For a relevant treatment of Coleridge's *Christabel* (1816) and hypertext, see Chris Koenig-Woodyard, "A Hypertext History of the Transmission of Coleridge's *Christabel*, 1800–1816," *Romanticism on the Net* 10 (1998). erudit.org/en/journals/ron/1998-n10-ron422/005806ar/. Accessed November 1, 2019.

7   Sonstroem, "Do You Really Want a Revolution?" 151.

8   Lynch, "Unexplored Regions," 51, 54.

9   Sonstroem, "Do You Really Want a Revolution?" 151.

10 Along with Sonstroem and Lynch, see Mark Hansen, "'Not Thus, after All, Would Life Be Given': 'Technesis,' Technology and the Parody of Romantic Poetics in *Frankenstein*," *Studies in Romanticism* 36, no. 4 (1997): 575–609. Also see Fred Botting, "Reading Machines," in *Gothic Technologies: Visuality in the Romantic Era* (2005), ed. Robert Miles, *Romantic Circles Praxis Series*. romantic-circles.org/praxis/gothic/botting/botting.html. Accessed November 1, 2019.

11 Gilles Deleuze, *Difference and Repetition*, trans. Paul Patton (New York: Columbia University Press, 1994), 208–9.

12 Mary Wollstonecraft Shelley, *Frankenstein; or, the Modern Prometheus* (1818), ed. D. L. Macdonald and Kathleen Scherf (Peterborough: Broadview Press, 1999). Page references to this edition are cited parenthetically in the text. Unless otherwise noted, all citations in this essay are from the Broadview edition of *Frankenstein* (original 1818 text).

13 See especially Courtney S. Campbell, "Biotechnology and the Fear of *Frankenstein*," *Cambridge Quarterly of Healthcare Ethics* 12, no. 4 (2003): 342–52; Theodore Ziolkowski, "Science, *Frankenstein*, and Myth," *The Sewanee Review* 89, no. 1 (1981): 34–56; Teresa Heffernan, "Bovine Anxieties, Virgin Births, and the Secret of Life," *Cultural Critique* 53 (2003): 116–33; Frances Ferguson, "The Nuclear Sublime," *Diacritics* 14, no. 2 (1984): 4–10; and Maureen N. McLane, "Literate Species: Populations, 'Humanities,' and *Frankenstein*," *ELH* 63, no. 4 (1996): 959–88.

14 Robert Mitchell and Phillip Thurtle (eds.), *Data Made Flesh: Embodying Information* (New York: Routledge Press, 2004), 18.

15 Mary Wollstonecraft Shelley, "Introduction [1831]," in *Frankenstein*, 358.

16 N. Katherine Hayles, *How We Became Posthuman: Virtual Bodies in Cybernetics, Literature, and Informatics* (Chicago, IL: University of Chicago Press, 1999), 2.

17 Hayles, "The Human in the Posthuman," *Cultural Critique* 53 (2003): 136.

18 Eugene Thacker, *Biomedia* (Minneapolis: University of Minnesota Press, 2004), 5–6.

19 Ibid., 2–7.

20 Hayles, "The Human in the Posthuman," 136–7.

21 Richard Menke, *Telegraphic Realism: Victorian Fiction and Other Information Systems* (Stanford, CA: Stanford University Press, 2008), 7.

22   In a related context, Victor Frankenstein also produces with his creature what a
     number of critics cite as the first literary "cyborg." See Chris Hables Gray, Steven
     Mentor, and Heidi J. Figueroa-Sarriera, "Cyborgology: Constructing the Knowledge
     of Cybernetic Organisms," in *The Cyborg Handbook*, ed. Gray, Mentor, and Figueroa-
     Sarriera (New York: Routledge Press, 1995), 5.

23   See Richard Brinsley Peake, *Presumption; or, the Fate of Frankenstein* (1823), in *Seven
     Gothic Dramas, 1789–1825*, ed. Jeffrey N. Cox (Athens: Ohio University Press, 1992),
     385–425; Henry M. Milner, *Frankenstein, or, the Man and the Monster: A Melodrama
     in Two Acts* (London: J. Duncombe & Co., 1826); Thomas A. Edison, *Frankenstein*,
     dir. J. Searle Dawley (USA: Edison Studios, 1910); *Frankenstein*, dir. James Whale
     (USA: Universal Studios, 1931); and Shelley Jackson, *Patchwork Girl* (Eastgate
     Systems, 1995).

24   See Jessica Richard, "'A Paradise of My Own Creation': *Frankenstein* and the
     Improbable Romance of Polar Exploration," *Nineteenth-Century Contexts* 25, no. 4
     (2003): 295–314. Also see Laura E. Crouch, "Davy's *A Discourse, Introductory to a
     Course of Lectures on Chemistry*: A Possible Scientific Source of *Frankenstein*," *Keats-
     Shelley Journal* 27 (1978): 35–44.

25   Carlos Baker has shown that Percy Bysshe Shelley accepted the materialist view
     of matter until late 1813. See Baker, *Shelley's Major Poetry: The Fabric of a Vision*
     (Princeton, NJ: Princeton University Press, 1948), 35. Marilyn Butler has argued that
     Mary Shelley's representation of Victor's quasi-vitalist natural philosophy is "serio-
     comic" and that Shelley thus embraces the materialist cause in writing *Frankenstein*.
     See Butler's introduction to *Frankenstein; or, the Modern Prometheus: The 1818 Text*,
     by Mary Wollstonecraft Shelley, ed. Butler (Oxford: Oxford University Press, 2008),
     xxi.

26   Barbara Giusti Doran, "Origins and Consolidation of Field Theory in Nineteenth-
     Century Britain: From the Mechanical to the Electromagnetic View of Nature," in
     Historical Studies in the Physical Sciences, vol. 6, ed. Russell McCormmach (Princeton,
     NJ: Princeton University Press, 1975), 134.

27   Ibid., 134–5.

28   Ibid., 135.

29   Ibid., 138.

30   Gottfried Wilhelm Leibniz, *The Monadology and Other Philosophic Writings*, trans.
     and ed. Robert Latta (Oxford: Oxford University Press, 1925), 217.

31   Ibid., 250–1.

32   Doran, "Field Theory," 142.

33   Catherine Wilson, "The Reception of Leibniz in the Eighteenth Century," in *The
     Cambridge Companion to Leibniz*, ed. Nicholas Jolley (Cambridge: Cambridge
     University Press, 1995), 469–70.

34   Ibid., 467–8.

35   Doran, "Field Theory," 146.

36   See Walter D. Wetzels, "Johann Wilhelm Ritter: Romantic Physics in Germany,"
     in *Romanticism and the Sciences*, ed. Andrew Cunningham and Nicholas Jardine
     (Cambridge: Cambridge University Press, 1990), 203–4. Also see Richard Holmes,
     *The Age of Wonder: How the Romantic Generation Discovered the Beauty and Terror of
     Science* (New York: Pantheon Books, 2008), 329.

37   For an investigation of German vitalist science, see Wetzels, "Aspects of Natural
     Science in German Romanticism," *Studies in Romanticism* 10, no. 1 (1971): 44–59.

For an account of the foundation of the field of electrochemistry by Johann Wilhelm Ritter, see Wetzels, "J. W. Ritter: The Beginnings of Electrochemistry in Germany," in *Proceedings of the Symposium on Selected Topics in the History of Electrochemistry*, vol. 78-6, ed. George Dubpernell and J. H. Westbrook (Princeton, NJ: The Electrochemical Society, 1978), 68–73. For an account of Ritter's impact on Hans Christian Ørsted's work in electromagnetism, see Roberto de Andrade Martins, "Ørsted, Ritter, and Magnetochemistry," in *Hans Christian Ørsted and the Romantic Legacy in Science: Ideas, Disciplines, Practices*, ed. Robert M. Brain, Robert S. Cohen, and Ole Knudsen, vol. 241 of *Boston Studies in the Philosophy of Science* (Dordrecht: Springer, 2007), 339–85.

38 Macdonald and Scherf, *Frankenstein*, 19. In his Norton edition of the novel, J. Paul Hunter notes that these "German physiologists" also included, among others, Johann Friedrich Blumenbach. See *Frankenstein: The 1818 Text*, ed. Hunter (New York: W. W. Norton, 1996), 5. For an account of British interests in Ritter during the period, see Holmes, *Age of Wonder*, 328. Percy Shelley writes: "The event on which this fiction [*Frankenstein*] is founded has been supposed, by Dr. [Erasmus] Darwin, and some of the physiological writers of Germany, as not of impossible occurrence" (Macdonald and Scherf, *Frankenstein*, 47).

39 See Butler, introduction to *Frankenstein*, xv–xxi, and Holmes, *Age of Wonder*, 305–36. Also see Sharon Ruston, *Shelley and Vitality* (Basingstoke: Palgrave Macmillan, 2005).

40 In a relevant study, Tilottama Rajan claims that "[Gottfried Wilhelm] Leibniz helps us to understand several elements in the Godwinian theory of possibility that subtends" Shelley's *Valperga; or, the Life and Adventures of Castruccio, Prince of Lucca* (1823) (91). She proposes that William Godwin was influenced by the *Monadology* (1714) and suggests that "Leibniz permits Godwin, and through him Mary Shelley, to retain a necessitarian concept of character without allowing necessity to foreclose possibility" (91, 92, 95). My work thus provides added context and support for Rajan's provocative considerations of the connections between Shelley's fiction and Leibniz's philosophy. See Rajan, "Between Romance and History: Possibility and Contingency in Godwin, Leibniz, and Mary Shelley's *Valperga*," in *Mary Shelley in Her Times*, ed. Betty T. Bennett and Stuart Curran (Baltimore, MD: Johns Hopkins University Press, 2000), 88–102.

41 Although Shelley possessed something like a proto-cybernetic understanding of the relationship between information and mediation via her various source materials for *Frankenstein*, her conception and representation of this relationship were, of course, *significantly* different from the ways in which the discourses of cybernetics and field theory would come to theorize and depict such matters. For one thing, while Shelley's representation of matter as medium has numerous affinities with a field-theoretical metaphysics, the Leibnizian "plenum" is obviously different from late-nineteenth- and mid-twentieth-century treatments of these ideas. As James Clerk Maxwell explains, investigations of what had been previously referred to as the "plenum" must be recognized and interpreted as acting "according to mathematical laws" (459). Although a renowned mathematician, Leibniz did not employ or call for a mathematical investigation of the plenum in the *Monadology*, and therefore the dissemination of his work (as taken up by *Naturphilosophie* and the discourse of the sciences of electricity) was not a specifically mathematical one. See Maxwell, "A Dynamical Theory of the Electromagnetic Field," *Philosophical Transactions of the*

Royal Society of London 155 (1865): 459–512. Furthermore, although Victor's notion of the relationship between information and mediation is akin to the cybernetic representation of information, Shelley does not describe information in terms of what N. Katherine Hayles has shown to be either cybernetics' "construction of (human) neural structures … as flows of information" or its "construction of artifacts that translat[e] information flows into observable operations" (50). See Hayles, "Contesting for the Body of Information: The Macy Conferences on Cybernetics," in *How We Became Posthuman*, 50–83.

42 Crouch, "Davy's *A Discourse*," 37.

43 *Oxford English Dictionary Online*, s.v. "information," s.v. "informed," s.v. "inform." See *The Oxford English Dictionary*, 2nd edn. (1989), *OED Online*. oed.com. Accessed November 1, 2019.

44 For critics addressing the complexities and role of the fragmentation of the creature's body/the novel, see Chris Baldick, "The Monster Speaks: Mary Shelley's Novel," in *In Frankenstein's Shadow: Myth, Monstrosity, and Nineteenth-Century Writing* (Oxford: Clarendon Press, 1987), 30–6; Daniel Cottom, "*Frankenstein* and the Monster of Representation," *SubStance* 9, no. 3 (issue 28, 1980): 60–71; and Eleanor Salotto, "*Frankenstein* and Dis(re)membered Identity," *The Journal of Narrative Technique* 24, no. 3 (1994): 190–211. For scientific work concerning experiments involving electrocution during the Romantic period, see especially Giovanni Aldini, *An Account of the Late Improvements of Galvanism* (London: Cuthell and Martin, and J. Murray, 1803).

45 Simon Schaffer, "Babbage's Intelligence: Calculating Engines and the Factory System," *Critical Inquiry* 21, no. 1 (1994): 204. Also cited by Menke, *Telegraphic Realism*, 17.

46 *Oxford English Dictionary Online*, s.v. "knowledge."

47 Menke, *Telegraphic Realism*, 18.

48 Ibid., 18.

49 Hayles, *How We Became Posthuman*, 19.

50 Ibid., 19.

51 Deleuze, *Difference and Repetition*, 206–7.

52 Jules Law, "Being There: Gothic Violence and Virtuality in *Frankenstein, Dracula*, and *Strange Days*," *ELH* 73, no. 4 (2006): 987.

53 Beth Newman, "Narratives of Seduction and the Seductions of Narrative: The Frame Structure of *Frankenstein*," *ELH* 53, no. 1 (1986): 144.

54 Ibid., 147.

55 Ibid.

56 Marshall McLuhan, *Understanding Media: The Extensions of Man* (New York: McGraw-Hill, 1964), 9.

57 Alan Liu, *Local Transcendence: Essays on Postmodern Historicism and the Database* (Chicago, IL: University of Chicago Press, 2008), 235–6.

58 Friedrich A. Kittler, *Discourse Networks, 1800/1900*, trans. Michael Metteer and Chris Cullens (Stanford, CA: Stanford University Press, 1990), 64.

59 David E. Wellbery, forward to *Discourse Networks, 1800/1900*, by Kittler, trans. Metteer and Cullens (Stanford, CA: Stanford University Press, 1990), xxiii.

60 See especially Ellen Moers, "Female Gothic," in *The Endurance of Frankenstein: Essays on Mary Shelley's Novel*, ed. George Levine and U. C. Knoepflmacher (Berkeley: University of California Press, 1979), 77–87; Marc A. Rubenstein, "'My Accursed

Origin': The Search for the Mother in *Frankenstein*," *Studies in Romanticism* 15, no. 2 (1976): 165–94; Mary Poovey, "My Hideous Progeny: Mary Shelley and the Feminization of Romanticism," *PMLA* 95, no. 3 (1980): 332–47; Barbara Johnson, "My Monster/My Self," *Diacritics* 12, no. 2 (1982): 2–10; Mary Jacobus, "Is There a Woman in This Text?" *New Literary History* 14, no. 1 (1982): 117–41; and *The Other Mary Shelley: Beyond Frankenstein*, ed. Audrey A. Fisch, Anne K. Mellor, and Esther H. Schor (Oxford: Oxford University Press, 1993).

61 See Mellor, "The Female in *Frankenstein*," in *Romanticism and Feminism*, ed. Mellor (Bloomington: Indiana University Press, 1988), 220–32.

62 Butler, introduction to *Frankenstein*, xx, xv–xxi.

10

"A daemon whom I had myself created": Race, *Frankenstein*, and Monstering

Patricia A. Matthew

Was I then a monster, a blot upon the earth, from which all men fled, and whom all men disowned (83)?[1]

It's no small thing to write about the murder of Michael Brown in a volume that aims to think theoretically about a work of fiction. Brown, killed on August 9, 2014, by police officer Darren Wilson, is not a metaphor. Neither is his family's grief and the grief of a community that not only mourns him but also mourns the protestors who have since died, largely without notice, in alarming circumstances. Michael Brown isn't a metaphor. But when Wilson described Brown in his testimony to the grand jury to justify his actions, he used monstrous metaphors to do so. Wilson took a young man who was already Other in American society and monstered him—by which I mean he ascribed super human strength coupled with demonic malevolence to a young man who would go on to be described as "no angel" by a media who defaults to how power characterizes the Black victims of violence. Monstering as the byproduct of Othering is a social practice I've been thinking about since 2018 when Aleta Hayes reflected on *Frankenstein* in a short, performative talk that was part of Stanford University's commemoration of the novel's bicentennial. At turns uplifting, provocative, and troubling, Hayes's reflection makes a claim that is helpful as a way to think in new ways about race in/and *Frankenstein*: "It is natural to Other people, but it is not natural to turn them into monsters."[2]

The year of Michael Brown's death was a particularly violent year of monstering. The Ferguson protests were in 2014. John Crawford was murdered by police in a Walmart in 2014. Ezell Ford too was killed by police in Los Angeles that year. Eric Garner was killed on Staten Island. And on November 22, 2014, Tamir Rice, age twelve, was killed by police while playing in the park. Hayes's reflection, as I discuss below, doesn't describe the creation in the novel as Black, but readers, historians, literary critics, artists, and filmmakers have read him as such almost from the beginning. *Frankenstein* is replete with references that not only invite us to read the creation as Black but to read the world of the novel as one on the cusp of a slave rebellion that cannot be stopped. The 1818 edition of the novel was published in the midway point between the 1807 and

1833 bills to abolish the slave trade and slavery, and it reflects the national anxiety this debate sparked. It emerged under the shadow of rebellions and uprisings in Haiti from 1791 to 1804. Mary Shelley's readers would have heard about the 1787 *Zong* Massacre, revealed in a public trial that captivated and horrified those who heard of the 208 men and women thrown from the *Zong* ship by their captors. They would also have seen the schematic engraving of the slave ship Brookes that showed the brutal way that captured Black men and women were literally packed into the hold of ships when they were transported to the West Indies. Olaudah Equiano's incredibly popular *Interesting Narrative* went to nine editions and multiple languages before he died in 1797, the year Shelley was born. Her mother reviewed the autobiography.

It is no wonder, then, that as early as 1849, *Frankenstein; or, the Model Man* was performed at the Adelphi Theatre, and *The London Gazette* account of the "extravaganza" includes a sketch of a scene with Frankenstein depicted as white and the creation (the "Model Man" of the title) depicted as a Black man in a grass skirt to signal that he is neither British nor European.[3] Contemporary scholars including Howard Malchow, Patrick Brantlinger, and Marie Mulvey-Roberts have shown modern readers the cultural moment that produced the novel to make the case, quite convincingly, that Shelley's audience would have understood the monster not just as an Other but one that represented the enslaved men and women they both relied on for domestic goods (sugar, rum, cotton) and feared. In *Black Frankenstein: The Making of an American Metaphor*, Elizabeth Young meticulously lays out the various ways the story has not only been a political metaphor but a raced one as well. And, in 2018 Hayes gave her talk and Jill Lepore commemorated the novel's bicentennial in *The New Yorker* by thinking through its racial tropes. Hayes wrestles with race and the monster, both embracing and disavowing what separates him from us. And in her retrospective on the novel, Lepore sees in the De Lacey episode a slave narrative similar to Frederic Douglass's description of his education.

It is these two 2018 reflections on the novel that invite a reading of how the novel performs its monstering in contemporary characterizations of Black men. If Victor Frankenstein and his creation are malleable analogies for timeless, universal questions about ethics, science, motherhood, exploration, and the debate about nature versus nurture, they both also serve as tropes for England's culture of enslavement and the attendant debates about abolition, revolution, and emancipation. All of this I argue in what follows is captured in the creation's recounting of his time observing the De Lacey family. In this portion of his narrative, I read all the elements of race, monstering, and gender that surrounded Michael Brown's death. When Wilson monstered Michael Brown in his testimony to the grand journey by referring to the young man as "it" and describing him as a "demon," he was participating in a long, violent history that shaped the imagination of a young writer whose imagination that came of age as England grappled with the prospect of emancipation. My goal here is not to make a one-to-one analogy between the ecosystem the novel depicts and the one that Brown and contemporary African Americans are forced to navigate, but as Paul Youngquist explains: "The aim of remembering ... is twofold: to see raced violence as an inheritance and to understand the form it takes today."[4]

Aleta Hayes is African American, and her reflection was one of numerous events organized by Stanford in 2018. The series of short reflections by Stanford alumni—biologists, historians, and engineers—thought about the novel by reflecting on the paired questions: what makes a human? what makes a monster? I included Hayes's talk with other reflections in my first-year writing class's semester-long focus on the novel. Hayes, a lecturer in the dance and theatre department, began her talk by paraphrasing Roman playwright Terrence: I am a human being. Nothing that is human can be alien to me. The talk is available via YouTube, and if you watch it you will hear Hayes describe an assault she suffered at the hands of a Black man in New York City's West Village. Here are the key elements of the story. She was sitting with a friend (white, gay, and Norwegian) when the Black man approached the table and asked for money. When Hayes did what most New Yorkers in her situation would have done and said no, he commented by saying "Don't you like African-American men?" and speculated that her companion was Russian. With a chuckle, she tells the audience that she corrected the man and clarified that her companion was, in fact, Norwegian. The Black man left and then returned about fifteen minutes later and hit Hayes on the head so hard that she notes that without her thick hair she would have been seriously injured. Although the incident occurred in 2008, it's painful to see how much it still affects Hayes. Her voice shakes when she describes the moment of the attack. At the same time, it's fascinating to see the complicated ways she tells her story. She describes the man who attacked her as "quite large, very deranged looking, with a bottle of malt 99 or something." He's a monster. But she also makes a confession. For a year, she explains, she crossed the street whenever she saw a Black man: "me the descendent of slaves with two brothers." One of her brothers, she tells her audience, moved to Europe and never returned to the United States. Her reflection ends by asking the audience to understand that they are all monsters who must see the humanity in one another.

The performative reflection takes a number of complicated turns with Hayes positioning herself as both part of the dominant culture and the Other at the same time. She doesn't explicitly mention the spate of extra-judicial murders of Black men and women that lead to the protests surrounding Michael Brown, but it hangs over her talk when she mentions being the descendent of slave with two brothers who we can presume are Black as well. She also never once explicitly mentions that Frankenstein's creation is a Black man. This might be because she aims for some version of color blindness (when she describes the dancers she selects for performance she notes, "I am looking not for the difference but the sameness"), but, although she talks about Shelley's interest in vitalism, refers to her parents as philosophers, and notes her attempts to revive her ailing child, she never feels it necessary to define the monster as Black even as she uses the language of monstrosity to describe her attacker.

Hayes's reflection is interesting to my thinking about race in the novel partly because she ends on a note of equity but primarily because of how she distances herself from her Black attacker by highlighting not her humanity (at one point she says "I have the ugly monster in me. I am also the ugly monster" and then plays with that metaphor extending it to her audience) but her erudition. She clarifies that she is African American (as opposed to, say, West Indian, Nigerian, Kenyan, etc.) and then lists her accomplishments. She plays cello and violin and has sung with jazz orchestras. She emphasizes that she was a pre-med major at Stanford. In describing the dancers she works with, she refers to the "Gifted black ballerina with my tall Blonde hip hop dancer" as if, one of my students pointed out after watching the video, these are rare incongruities. The descriptions bring to mind the complicated dance of respectability politics many Black people perform to gain entrance into society and to protect themselves from racist violence. In her characterization of the Black man as she asks her audience to look beyond the surface, beyond race, she monsters him. Like so many Black women in predominately white spaces, she has to cover a great deal of ground in a short time, and she shares an intimate experience and what it sparked. Less than being a monster she's the Other, but the lesson she tries to share is misshapen by how she manages it both by her own fallibility and the ideology that underscore her narrative. The same ideology is at work in the De Lacey chapters of the novel.

There is something noble about the impoverished De Laceys that functions as a critique of aristocratic excess. Their simple agrarian life reads like the ideal William Godwin promotes in *An Enquiry Concerning Political Justice*, a theory Shelley critiques in her second novel *Valperga*. The elder De Lacey's blindness reveals that so long as the creature cannot be seen, he is human, literally judged not by the colors of his skin but the content of his character. The episode addresses anxieties about emancipation that shaped abolitionist debates. It is also about multiple kinds of literacy—not just what the creature learns but what readers learn when he tells his story to his creator. The question he asks as he anxiously wonders how he will be received by the family is one for all of society: "Could they turn from their door one, however monstrous, who solicited their compassion and friendship?" (91). The lessons he learns undermine any notion of comity and inclusion.

In his time with the De Lacey's (he lives near them through four seasons), the creation learns where he fits into the aesthetic economy of a society that values fair-skinned people with lyrical voices, and readers learn that without the interference of that aesthetic he is a kind and helpful figure. So much of his story focuses on the beauty of the De Lacey family—not only dwelling on the beauty of the women but also noting the perfect symmetry of Felix's face. The creature is also depicted as naturally good, taught by violence not to hate but to hide. If *Frankenstein* is about nature versus nurture, it also treats the enslaved figure on the cusp of emancipation as a blank slate on which to inscribe European values. The creature also quite literally learns to read. It's worth noting that he recounts this in a way that would have been recognizable to Shelley's readers familiar with Equiano's *Interesting Narrative*. Referring to the family reading during the "frosty season," the creature describes his reaction to the activity: "This reading had puzzled me extremely at first; but, by degrees, I discovered that he uttered the same sounds when he read as when he talked. I conjectured, therefore, that he found on the paper signs for speech which he understood, and I ardently longed to comprehend these also."[5] Here is Equiano discussing his literacy:

I had often seen my master and Dick employed in reading; and I had a great curiosity to talk to the books as I thought they did ... for that purpose I had often taken up a book, and have talk to it, and then put it up to my ears to it, when alone, in hopes it would answer me."[6]

Shelley invents more context for how the creation learns to read than Equiano offers in the *Interesting Narrative,* but their first understanding of reading (speaking books and paper signs for books) and the fact that they learn in solitude bind them and give credence to the reading of the novel as a slave narrative that Lepore and others have put forward.

Reading the novel as a slave narrative clarifies the stakes of the creature's emancipation. One of the arguments against this outcome was the claim that enslaved people were childlike and dependent, on the white plantation class and that they would be lost and aimless without slavery. The creation's period watching the De Lacey family also reflects, among other concerns, the anxiety about emancipation that historians like Padraic X. Scanlon note in his study of anti-slavery politics in Sierra Leone: "emancipated black people posed a threat to the social order and ought to 'earn' their freedom by proving that they were reconciled to the continuation of white supremacy."[7] We see this both in the creature's constant references to the De Lacey's beauty and how their beauty seems to inspire his natural inclination to use his strength for their good, specifically by ensuring that they always have cut wood for their homes.

It is in the De Lacey episode that the creation's education leads to wrenching realizations about his status as outsider. This description of himself is one such moment:

> And what was I? .... I was not even the same nature as man. I was more agile than they, and could subsist upon coarser diet; I bore the extremes of heat and cold with less injury to my frame; my stature far exceeded their's [*sic*]. Was I then a monster, a blot upon the earth, from which all men fled, and whom all men disowned? (83)

The hopelessness of the De Lacey episode is not simply because it clarifies that what is wrong with the monster is that his body and visage obscure what could be moral about his character. It is also the moment that he fully understands what makes him different from the society he moves through and reveals how little it matters that he has embraced the education that turns him into a philosopher and practically worships the look and sound of the De Laceys. If the first part of his education is learning empirically, this portion of his training, an education he ambitiously embraces ("My days were spent in close attention that I might more speedily master the language"), brings painful realizations: "I cannot describe to you the agony that these reflections inflicted upon me," he tells Victor, while wishing that he had not "known or felt beyond the sensations of hunger, thirst, and heat" (82, 83). While reading gives him pleasure and access to the kind of European education that would indicate belonging to the world Frankenstein, Walton, and Clerval move through, his racial markers prohibit his social inclusion.

Lepore notes that Frederick Douglass was born the same year the novel was published and makes the claim that *Frankenstein* "very closely follows" the trajectory of the slave narrative with Douglass and the creation passing through similar stages:

He described learning to read by trading with white boys for lessons. Douglass realized his political condition at the age of twelve, while reading the 'Dialogue Between a Master and Slave,' reprinted in 'The Columbian Orator.' It was his coming of age. 'The more I read, the more I was led to abhor and detest my enslavers,' Douglass wrote, in a line that the creation himself might have written.[8]

Where Douglass's education relies on white boys, it is Safie's arrival that facilitates the creature's learning, and he sees them as peers. "She and I improved rapidly in the knowledge of language," he explains to Frankenstein while bragging like a child wanting to impress his father: "I may boast that I improved more rapidly than the Arabian … I could imitate almost every word that was spoken" (82). Their shared sensibility is a rare moment when the creature doesn't feel quite as isolated. They both weep over the "hapless fate of [America's] original inhabitants" (83), and after Safie's arrival he understands the various "strange systems" of society.

Safie's story combines the notion of woman as chattel—enslaved first by their fathers and then by their husbands—and a gendered representation of the legacy of slavery that forms an invisible bond between the creation and the woman he admires. It is yet another story within a story in a novel that works with frame narratives. One way to interpret how their narratives overlap is as an analogy for white women's involvement in the abolitionist movement. Writers like Amelia Opie, Maria Edgeworth, Wollstonecraft, and others used slavery as a metaphor for white women's marginalization—not only as chattel but as objects subjected to men's appetites. Safie's mother, "a Christian Arab seized and made a slave by the Turks," is described as a woman born free who "spurned the bondage to which she was now reduced" (86). While Safie's bondage differs from her mother's, she nonetheless is a pawn in her father's political schemes. He manipulates Felix's desire for Safie until it is no longer convenient for him. As a result, like the creature, Safie is illiterate in a strange country where her ancestry and religion place her at the margins of acceptability. However, and this is key, her beauty mitigates what makes her the Other and ensures her place within a family the creature hopes will welcome him. She is Other, but she is not a monster. The De Lacey episode ends violently with the creature in the home he has watched over and helped maintain, never to be part of it. His "beloved cottagers" are all too human. Safie sees him and runs away him, and the younger De Lacey develops the strength to move the monster: "Felix darted forward, and with supernatural force tore me from his father". The creature could have "torn him limb from limb" but he leaves distraught and describes himself "howling" and like a "wild beast." He likens himself to Milton's Satan: "the arch fiend" while the De Lacey family flees and the creature burns the cottage down (88, 94).

Lepore's reading of the novel and race concludes by explaining that by the 1850s, Frankenstein's monster appears in American political cartoons as "a nearly naked black man, signifying slavery itself, seeking his vengeance upon the nation that created him." The ideology that underscores it is captured in Thomas Jefferson's 1853 *Notes on the State of Virginia* where he describes Black people as follows:

Besides those of colour, figure, and hair, there are other physical distinctions proving a difference of race. They have less hair on the face and body. They secrete less by the kidneys, and more by the glands of the skin … They seem to require less sleep … They are at least as brave, and more adventuresome.[9]

Victor's hope that he might create a race of beings that would worship him as their creator might not immediately indicate that these beings are actually raced. In other words, he never describes the creature as Black or African even though he uses different colors to describe him (yellow, black, pearly white, and dun-white). But as historians, philosophers and theorists argue the transatlantic slave trade shaded how Europeans read race. In his now-essential treatise on the subject, philosopher Anthony Appiah discusses the "dual connection made in eighteenth-and nineteenth-century thought between, on the one hand, race and nationality, and, on the other, nationality and literature."[10] Writing about race and Romanticism, Marlon Ross notes that in the period that " … even as the abstract notion of race appears strange and estranging, the embodiment of the person and others within racial categories becomes increasingly comfortable, convenient, and necessary."[11] And as Saidiya Hartman reminds us "the language of race developed in the modern period and in the context of the slave trade."[12] It is this language and the images it conjures that I am most interested in, particularly the ways that we can trace twentieth and twenty-first descriptions of the Black male monster back to *Frankenstein.*

Malchow, credited with the first convincing reading of the novel's connection to slavery and abolition, notes that enslaved Black people were described similarly in both the West Indies and the United States. Allan Lloyd Smith is even more precise when he argues that the description of Frankenstein's creation reflected nineteenth-century myths about the citizens of Dahomey: "even the creation's ability to withstand pain is in keeping with a popular misconception of the period: The Dahomeans, for example, "assumed a mask of insensitivity in the face of trial, thinking that self-pity in any form would only invite further troubles. To the European, however this cultural trait often appeared as evidence of unfeeling animality."[13] Mulvey-Roberts, who describes the novel as "a textual patchwork of abolitionist writing and pro-slavery propaganda, inscribed upon the body of the monster," connects the moment that produced this description to Shelley's reading of Mungo Park's *Travels in the Interior Districts of Africa* (1799).[14] Park describes witnessing a blind woman's reconciliation with a son who had been absent for four years noting the kind of kinship I think Aleta Hayes seeks in her 2018 reflection on the novel and Shelley depicts in blind De Lacey's initial acceptance of the creature. Park describes the blind woman affectionate response to touching her son's, face, and arms as making him believe that "whatever difference there is between the Negro and the European in the confirmation of the nose and the colour of the skin, there is none in the genuine sympathies and characteristic feelings of our common nature."[15] Park's description here nods toward the idea of understanding race as little more than an external marker. He doesn't quite claim it is a construct, but the "whatever" is a nod toward why it shouldn't matter. But it does. As Appiah notes:

For, however mythical the notion of race seems to be, we cannot deny the obvious fact that having one set of heritable characteristics—dark skin, say—rather than another—blonde hair, for example—can have profound psychological, economic, and other social consequences, especially in societies where many people are not only racialists but racists.[16]

The New Yorker's description of Darren Wilson, who is six foot four and 214 pounds, evokes other images. He is described as "a former Boy Scout with round cheeks and blue eyes" who, "speaks with a muted drawl."[17] In the report of the shooting, mixed among the clinical descriptions of where bullets were found among the residue of gunpowder, is Wilson's phantasmagoric account of Brown. Wilson conjures him as an unstoppable monster capable of deflecting bullets, a man who kept lurching at Wilson. According to the police report, Wilson said that Brown "appeared psychotic," "hostile," and "crazy," as though he was "looking through" Wilson. He made a "grunting noise" and, Wilson claims, after several commands continued to "charge." "It looked like a demon."[18] It's the kind of monstering familiar to anyone paying careful attention to the narratives constructed about Black men. I want to think of Darren Wilson as a monster, but that impulse suggests that he is an outlier, a rare exception when he is, in fact, legion. He is not a metaphor, but an arm of the state—a six foot four, 214 pound arm who received half a million dollars in donations to move to a different community where he can live in relative peace with his family.

Concomitant with the physical monstering are descriptions of Black men's characters. Michael Brown, *New York Times* readers were told, was no angel.[19] It mattered very little that the *Times* was actually quoting from an anecdote Brown's father shared with them. An article in *Vanity Fair* claims that paper of record has passively monstered so many Black men over the years that their credibility in these matters is severely compromised.[20] *FiveThirtyEight* in an article headlined "There Are Millions of Michael Browns in America" took each of the mistakes *The New York Times* attributes to Brown and showed their prevalence among Brown's peers. In a study of how six Black men were characterized in the media, two sociologists point to historical precedent as a prelude to a discussion of the rhetoric about contemporary Black men. They note the language of the 1899 description of Sam Hose lynched for reportedly murdering his employer and sexually assaulting his wife: "the newspapers wrote 'a monster in human form' emerged, which detailed Hose as cold-blooded, killing his employer, and savagely raping his employer's wife."[21]

The contemporary push back to this characterization takes the form of the kind of respectability politics Hayes performs when she lists her accomplishment and accomplishments. Consider the competing pictures of Trayvon Martin, murdered in 2012 by a vigilante who saw a monster in a young man wearing a hoodie. When I googled Martin's name, the three images that popped up were of him in his hoodie, a quartet of pictures of him blowing smoke, suggesting that he was smoking pot, and one of him in a Hollister T-shirt, looking like the boy his family wants us all to remember. Michael Brown, we were told repeatedly, was headed to college. There is a collective resistance to the monstering of Trayvon Martin that has become part of the ritual of mourning Black death at the hands of the police or those white Americans who feel deputized by society to stand their ground. Smith provides the ideal lens through which to read this impulse when he discusses how Frankenstein's creation describes himself: "the Monster exists in a state of 'double consciousness' like that famously described by W.E.B. DuBois ... Both within and outside of the culture of the De Laceys (or of his creator), the Creation necessarily develops a schizophrenic sense of himself." He continues: "The Creation's assertion of his literacy, and his human sensitivity, is emblematic of the breaking down of such boundary assumptions."[22] In defense of *The New York Times's* characterization of Brown, a columnist explained that "no angel" is an echo of an anecdote at the beginning of the story when Brown told his father about how, while looking at a cloud formation, he perceived "Satan chasing the angel and the angel running into the face of God." "He was grappling with life's mysteries," Eligon had written later in the profile piece.[23]

It's a coincidence I know that Michael Brown, according to his father, reflected on his place in the world by seeing biblical characters in the clouds. It's also the kind of conversation so easy to imagine between a young man and his father. It's one of the sadder moments in the De Lacey episode. Having learned to read, the creation finds himself with the *Sorrows of Werther,* saddened at his isolation. He speaks to his creator: "My person was hideous, and my stature gigantic; what did this mean? Who was I? What was I? Whence did I come? What was my destination" (89)? They are the questions of youth, not the questions of a monster, but of a human seeking their place in the world. Frankenstein talks about the "daemon whom I had myself created" after the creature promises to wreck vengeance on his creator. The creature's threat and subsequent fulfilling of it feed into the monstering metaphor that continues to haunt Black people, especially in encounters with the police. Consider how protestors in Ferguson were met with military grade weapons. They were called "thugs" as part of the legacy of using "rebellion" and "insurrection" to describe oppressed people seeking agency and justice. Youngquist's observation about how "heavily armed and militarized police ... seem to reveal a terminal logic of control ... as if a race war smolders silently beneath the surface of social life" is apt.[24] Young's work offers historical context for what Younquist observes when she explains that Victor's creation "translated smoothly to an American context" because he was an amalgamation of two things at once—the vengeful former enslaved person and a symbol of Black power. As Young puts it, the creature "Invok[es] racial uprising."[25] Here it is worth remembering how images and reports of avenging violence were circulated and Shelley's interest in Fuseli's 1781 painting "The Night-mare." Percy Bysshe Shelley, who supported abolition, was anxious about the prospect of violence: "can he who the day before was a trampled slave suddenly become liberal-minded, forbearing, and independent?"[26] He had reason to be concerned. While I question the veracity of nineteenth-century accounts of Black violence, we know that the Tacky Revolt in 1760 actually happened, that Toussaint L'Ouverture, leader of Haiti's revolution, was the subject of a Wordsworth sonnet, and that the Haitian revolution terrified whites in the Caribbean and the European continent. Mulvey-Roberts argues that the "Shelley's monster behaves like a rebellious slave in burning down De Lacey's cottage."[27] The metaphor is right there: "like a rebellious slave." The question that is the epigraph for this reflection is not one that Brown would have asked. He may have been monstered, but he was actually human, a young man, a kid with family, friends, and school teachers and a whole community around him. He is no more a metaphor than the other Black people killed by police in the year of his death: Dantre Hamilton, Dan Parker, Rumian Brisbon, Akai Gurley, Jerome Reid, and Tanisha Anderson.

Notes

1   Mary Shelley, *Frankenstein, or the Modern Prometheus* (1818), ed. J. Paul Hunter, 2nd ed. (New York: Norton Critical Edition, 1996). Page references to this edition are cited parenthetically in the text. I am grateful to Manu Chander and Tressie McMillan Cottom for reading early drafts of this chapter and to Liam Drislane and Matt Sandler for research assistance and reading recommendations. I am especially grateful to Orrin Wang for his patience and crucial questions and recommendations as I finished this essay. I have respectfully asked that Bloomsbury join a growing movement in publishing to use a capital B when referring to Black people.

2   Aleta Hayes, "Frankenstein at 200: What Is a Monster, What Is Human with Aleta Hayes," filmed January 29 at Stanford University, 10:39. https://www.youtube.com/watch?v=0suFo3cjYDU.

3   Marie Mulvey-Roberts, "Monstrous Dissections and Surgery as Performance: Gender, Race and the Bride of Frankenstein," in *Global Frankenstein*, ed. Carol Margaret Davison and Marie Mulvey-Roberts (Palgrave Macmillan, 2018), 53–71, 57.

4   Paul Youngquist, "In the Wake," *Cultural Critique* 90 (2015): 148–58. doi: 10.5749/culturalcritique.90.2015.0148. Accessed October 8, 2019.

5   Shelley, *Frankenstein*, 78.

6   Olaudah Equiano, *The Interesting Narrative and Other Writings*, ed. Vincent Carretta (New York: Penguin, 2003), 68.

7   Padric X. Scanlon, *Freedom's Debtors: British Antislavery in Sierra Leone in the Age of Revolution* (New Haven: Yale University Press, 2017), 19.

8   Jill Lepore, "The Strange and Twisted Life of Frankenstein," *The New Yorker*, February 5, 2018.

9   Thomas Jefferson. *Notes on the State of Virginia*. In: Eze Emmanuel., editor. *Race and the Enlightenment: A Reader* (Malden, MA: Wiley-Blackwell; 1787 [1997]), 95–103; quoted in Calvin John Smiley and David Fakunle, "From 'Brute' to 'Thug:' The Demonization and Criminalization of Unarmed Black Male Victims in America," *Journal of Human Behavior in the Social Environment*, 26, nos. 3–4 (2016): 352. doi: 10.1080/10911359.2015.1129256.

10 Kwame Anthony Appiah, "Race," in *Critical Terms for Literary Studies*, ed. Frank Lentricchia and Thomas McLaughlin (Chicago: University of Chicago Press, 1990), 274–87.

11 Marlon Ross, "The Race of/in Romanticism: Notes towards a Critical Race Theory," in *Race, Romanticism, and the Atlantic*, ed. Paul Youngquist (London: Routledge, 2013).

12 Saidiya Hartman, *Lose Your Mother: A Journey along the Atlantic Slave Route* (New York: Farrar, Straus and Giroux, 2008).

13   Allan Lloyd Smith, "'This Thing of Darkness': Racial Discourse in Mary Shelley's *Frankenstein*," *Gothic Studies* 6, no. 2 (November 2004): 208–22, 211.

14   Marie Mulvey-Roberts, *Dangerous Bodies: Historicizing the Gothic Corporeal* (Manchester: Manchester UP, 2016) 53.

15   Mungo Park, *Travels in the Interior Districts of Africa* (Ware: Wordsworth Editions, 2002) 74; quoted in Mulvey-Roberts, *Dangerous Bodies*, 67.

16   Appiah, "Race," 285.

17   Jake Halpern, "The Cop," *The New Yorker*, August 3, 2015.

18   Department of Justice Report Regarding the Criminal Investigation in the Shooting Death of Michael Brown by Ferguson, Missouri Police Officer Darren Wilson, March 4, 2015.

19   John Eligon, "Michael Brown Spent Last Weeks Grappling with Problems and Promise," *The New York Times*, August 24, 2014.

20   Kia Makarechi, "Besides Michael Brown, Whom Else Does The New York Times Call 'No Angel'?" *Vanity Fair*, August 25, 2014.

21   Smiley and Fakulne, "From 'Brute to Thug,'" 51.

22   Smith, "'This Thing of Darkness,'" 214–15.

23   Michael McGough, "Opinion: NYT Regrets Calling Michael Brown 'No Angel' but Was the Newspaper So Wrong?" *Los Angeles Times*, August 28, 2014.

24   Youngquist, "In the Wake," 149.

25   Elizabeth Young, *Black Frankenstein: The Making of an American Metaphor* (New York: New York University Press, 2008), 20, 27.

26   Percy Bysshe Shelley, *The Complete Poetical Works of Percy Bysshe Shelley*, ed. Thomas Hutchinson (London: Oxford University Press, 1935), 33; quoted in Mulvey-Roberts, *Dangerous Bodies*, 58.

27   Mulvey-Roberts, *Dangerous Bodies*, 64.

11

The Smiles That One Is Owed: Justice, Justine, and Sympathy for a Wretch

Erin M. Goss

Hardly the sole purview of snowflake millennials, as lamented by recent sensationalist British publications bemoaning the existence of "Flakensteins" who "claim Frankenstein's monster was 'misunderstood'"[1] or a slightly more neutrally described "new generation" invested in "discovering his sensitive side,"[2] sympathy for Mary Shelley's stitched together creature has long been a primary response to her novel. Percy Shelley's own review of *Frankenstein*, apparently written to fend off expected negative reviews of the 1818 publication but not published until 1832, assumes such sympathy as the novel's central achievement. It would be, Percy Shelley writes, "impossible to read" the creature's articulation of his predicament "without feeling the heart suspend its pulsations with wonder, and the 'tears stream down the cheeks.'"[3] And, while Percy himself may not offer a sufficient foil to the crankily imagined millennials infesting the lawns of writers at *The Times* and *The Sun* in early 2018, a reviewer from 1824 imagines the story similarly. Discussing *Frankenstein* on the occasion of re-reading it after disappointment with "the extreme inferiority" of Shelley's later *Valperga* (1823), the anonymous *Knight's Quarterly* reviewer locates the earlier novel's primary interest in the very sympathy that 2018 heads could somehow imagine was a new invention. Placing himself "entirely on the side of the monster," this reviewer insists that "justice is indisputably on his side, and his sufferings are, to me, touching to the last degree." What must it be, the reviewer asks, "to feel oneself alone in the world!"[4] Indeed, the primary drama of Shelley's novel for her early readers was not the dramatic overreach of science or even the improper manipulation of corpses; it was often, rather, this question of sympathy, moral necessity, and moral obligation. What is it that the world owes Frankenstein's creation? What is Frankenstein's *duty* (a word the novel repeats some two dozen times) to his creature?

If the attack on monster-loving millennials who find it in their hearts to imagine Shelley's creature to be only "misunderstood" is, as David Barnett calls it, an attack on empathy itself,[5] it is perhaps time to dwell a bit longer with the compassion due the creature. That he is ill-used is not to be questioned, and I'll not come close to doing so. That Victor Frankenstein does wrong by him, similarly, remains beyond the realm of openable queries. However, I would like to spend a bit more time in this essay with the nature of the creature's wrongdoing, and the versions of it that have escaped attention in the decades and centuries that we have been reading this book and wondering whether he is more sinned against than sinning. Specifically, I am interested in the grounds on which Victor's creation *expects* to receive sympathy. The created being who invites and likely warrants the reader's compassionate feelings on account of his repeated ill treatment at the hands of all humans he encounters demands Victor's sympathy largely on account of a more specific privation and felt loss. He is alone, excluded from society, and miserable, but the demands he makes of his maker are for the particular form of society that would be found through a female companion. What he assumes will be beyond reproach is his demand for a mate, and it is this expectation that apparently makes him most human. "You must create a female for me," the creature demands, "with whom I can live in the interchange of those sympathies necessary for my being [...] I demand it of you as a right which you must not refuse" (156).[6] Victor at first does refuse, then acquiesces, then refuses again in a spectacular display of bodily violence produced especially for the creature himself as he tears to pieces the female companion he had previously promised to provide.[7] Throughout, the creature's loneliness induces sympathy in readers as well as in Victor himself. No male creature, it seems, should be without the option of a female counterpart, and the pain it causes him seems to at least momentarily excuse or explain any number of bad acts.

The creature's loneliness and isolation constitute the basis for his appeal both as they generate a sympathetic response to his profound sadness and as they make possible his triumphant self-determination by novel's end. As Frances Ferguson pithily put it, "If the monster longs for companionship, Victor Frankenstein does bequeath him one rare—and sublime—privilege: being alone means never having to say you're sorry."[8] Indeed, by novel's end there is no one left to whom the creature might apologize and he can disappear into darkness and distance without even having to leave anyone behind, as both Frankenstein and Walton have done. Vanishing into the space beyond the novel, the creature's final speech offers a rhetorical question that must shape the understanding of the novel that has preceded. "Was there no injustice in this," he asks, referring to the violence that has defined his short life, "Am I to be thought the only criminal, when all human kind sinned against me?" Readers of the novel can answer these questions only in the negative, and the creature's vanishing becomes a triumph in its signaled rejection of the world that has offered him nothing but injustice. Left to his own devices, the novel suggests, the creature can forge for himself the proper response to his blasted existence, and if Victor in going away to school had to "form [his] own friends," the creature will form his own justice and that justice can only be an improvement on the one the world has offered (73). What passes for justice in Shelley's *Frankenstein* after all is something of a disaster, as is made perfectly clear at the end of the 1818 first volume when Justine, the not-too-far-to-stretch allegorical representation of justice, dies in the miscarriage of justice that is her trial. Killed by the state, she has been framed by the creature, whose terrible loneliness has led him to destroy her. In the wake of her death and the travesty of justice that it reveals and embodies, the creature can both mourn his isolation and eventually obtain heroic status as the founder of a new form of self-determined justice superior to that available in extant human systems.

Celebrated—perhaps rightly enough—as a sublime emblem of suffering, the creature is also an embodiment of the most banal and everyday form of misogyny. Lashing out in rage at a female figure chosen almost at random, he sets into motion the mechanisms that will bring about her death. Once she is gone, the path is clear for his heroic triumph over the absence of justice through his own self-determined end. It is an old story: the sublime rejection of society, of women, and of predetermined systems in order to forge one's own way. What is surprising, perhaps, is that it is one that Frankenstein's creature completes even more perfectly than Victor Frankenstein himself. If the creature's self-sacrifice following the novel's end makes him something of a hero, or at least a martyr, his heroic self-determination depends in no small way on the death of Justine, whom he has, in most ways that matter, killed. His assertion of control over his own destiny becomes a comment on the injustice of the world that has rejected him, and that injustice has been rendered unavoidable through the fate of Justine, killed by the state and abandoned by the church. Her fate, however, was first determined by the creature himself as punishment for her imagined rejection of his attentions. What is striking is that sympathy for the creature, so often understood as allegorical sympathy for various marginalized and othered groups, risks crystallizing into the sympathy demanded by the man who can't get a date and therefore decides to destroy the world that he is convinced owes him one. That such a figure also may achieve heroic status in his triumph over the injustice that has produced his suffering seems all too fit.

Readers of *Frankenstein* know that the creature's fate at novel's end remains at least somewhat undetermined. That he might ultimately decide against his planned self-immolation and survive into a future has provided an initial plot point for a range of imaginative retellings of his story, from Dean Koontz's mystery/horror *Frankenstein* series (2004–2011) to Hal Hartley's whimsical film *No Such Thing* (2002) to Victor LaValle's trenchant and moving graphic novel *Destroyer* (2017). When the creature is "borne away by the waves, and lost in darkness and distance," he is lost as well to a reading audience, who are left to imagine where he has gone, and what, ultimately, he has made of himself. What we do know is that the creature has finally made his own fate and that whatever end he meets it is one that he has had to choose for himself. This combination of indeterminacy and self-determination constitutes the grounds for our sympathy with this mysteriously ensouled being, who must forge for himself a lonely path to righteousness reminiscent of other masculinist stories of individual heroism.

The creature's planned fate both derives from and seeks to preserve his singularity, an inescapable and absolute condition of being that has given him great pain. Denied the sympathy or fellow feeling that would come from knowing another creature like himself, he has sunk "into bitter and loathing despair," an absence of hope that stems from his having no peer or counterpart, and as a consequence no social world (219). His planned death is a strategy to end his pain; suicide promises escape from "the agonies which now consume" him and will provide, finally, rest (220). As such, the creature's imagined end is a private affair best completed away from the prying eyes of both the novel's frame narratives and the voyeuristic reader. The creature will die, as he has lived, alone, and in making for himself his own death he will find his first and only opportunity to choose a solitude that has been otherwise forced upon him throughout the few years of his existence.

The threat of the creature's reproduction partially explains Frankenstein's decision to leave him companionless. That the creature must remain singular necessitates that he must remain single, and Frankenstein destroys the work in progress that was to become the creature's mate once he has imagined that "the first results of those sympathies for which the daemon thirsted would be children" (174). Rather than being responsible for the "race of devils" he imagines such children to be, Frankenstein tears the female figure in progress to pieces. Taking to heart the threat that his own propagation poses, in imagining his final site of destruction the creature calls his planned death a "sacrifice" and suggests that it is necessary for both human safety and to prevent any other from suffering as he has. "I shall collect my funeral pile," he promises, "and consume to ashes this miserable frame, that its remains may afford no light to any curious and unhallowed wretch, who would create such another as I have been. I shall die" (220). Within the plot of the novel the creature must be destroyed to preserve human dominance; as a plot device, the creature must be erased to explain the fact of his continued mysterious existence, and his destruction ironically cements the notion of Victor's unmatchable genius.

If the plot of the novel requires the creature's self-destruction, so too does its logic, and specifically the logic that the novel develops around the idea of justice. Early in the novel, Justine Moritz, and justice with her, leaves the novel's narrative as a result of the creature's unappeasable desire: for love, for companionship, for a social world. By the end of the novel, though, all the creature has come to want is justice itself. When in his final speech the creature asks Walton, the novel's most externally facing narrator, to serve as the ultimate arbiter of the short life he has led, he focuses on this impossible desire:

> Was there no injustice in this? Am I to be thought the only criminal, when all human kind sinned against me? Why do you not hate Felix, who drove his friend from his door with contumely? Why do you not execrate the rustic, who sought to destroy the savior of his child? (219–20)

Failing to find justice in the world, the creature turns to a simpler goal, and his final question demonstrates his acquiescence to the terms that have come to attach to him: "Polluted by crimes, and torn by the bitterest remorse, where can I find rest but death?" (220). Undeniably responsible for the deaths of William Frankenstein, Henry Clerval, and Elizabeth Lavenza, the creature is legible, within certain parameters, as a murderer.[9] And the penalty for murder, despite Elizabeth Lavenza's extended exclamations near the end of the first volume, is death. However, even within the vigilante justice that Victor has attempted to mete out to his creation, there has been no way to kill this creature, and finally he takes on his own shoulders the burden of exacting the penalty that all, apparently, would agree was appropriate.

In his demand that his final interlocutor recognize that his life has been characterized by injustice, the creature stakes a claim on justice that requires a certain reckoning at the end of the novel. For when *Frankenstein* demands that we recognize injustice, it invites us to consider what justice might even be, or have been. If justice is, as Jacques Derrida writes, an "experience that we are not able to experience" (16), justice remains knowable only in its absence.[10] Differentiated from a law always grounded in violence, the possibility of justice depends on the fantasy of non-violent interpersonal relations. For Derrida, justice is always yet to come; for *Frankenstein*, it is always a past failure. When the creature promises at the end of the novel to destroy his body, he promises in effect to make his funeral pile the site of a form of justice knowable to himself in the act of its production. Exiled from and unrecognizable to the law, the creature will enact in his solitude a form of just conclusion.[11]

The creature laments his existence outside the social world, and the novel offers opportunity to lament his exclusion from the legal one. He is, after all, ultimately judged by laws that cannot protect or include him, and certainly he is right to complain at the end of his life that there was no justice in that. Regardless of definitional categories and their capacity to determine whether or not the creature—who has killed—is a murderer, the various systems in place to punish criminal acts cannot contend with him if they have no way to recognize his existence. While Victor repeatedly refuses to testify or admit to his own role in the deaths of his friends and family, when he finally attempts to do so the magistrate to whom he tells his tale cannot or will not act on it.[12] Although the magistrate, rather surprisingly, seems to believe Victor, he will not prosecute and pursue the creature within the parameters of the law; he retreats into disbelief, as, "when he was called upon to act officially in consequence, the whole tide of his incredulity returned" (201). Faced with what Sara Guyer calls the creature's "invisib[ility] before the law," first Victor and then his creation turn to other methods.[13] Victor returns to his plans of personal revenge. Revenge, though, is not justice, and the novel repeatedly indicates that Victor's quest to avenge the deaths of his family members is as self-involved and unabashedly egotistical as his initial act of creation.

One of the many truisms about this novel is that the creature mirrors his creator; his violence and obsession have not come from a vacuum but reflect Victor's own tendencies toward destruction and control. Like Victor, the creature seeks companionship and knowledge and attempts to cross the boundaries that he finds set before him. Like Victor as well, the creature is a dabbler in the scientific method and a conductor of experiments. While Victor tests the "ideal bounds" of life and death, however, his creation confirms the hypothesis suggested to him by his interactions with humanity: there is no justice in this human world (80). The material for his experiment, the matter through which he attains the confirmation of the thing he must have already known, is the body of Justine Moritz, a character whose very name suggests her relation to the justice the creature seeks. The remainder of this essay will consider what the creature (and the reader) learns and proves through the fate that he creates for her.

Justine Moritz enters the novel in a letter, as part of a "little story" told by Elizabeth to "please, and perhaps amuse" Victor (89). Imagining that Victor might not remember

Justine, Elizabeth provides her history. The daughter of a widow, Justine was the least favorite of her mother's four children; indeed, her mother so disliked her that Victor's mother brought her to live in the Frankenstein home where she was raised as a servant—though her status, Elizabeth insists, did not require "a sacrifice of the dignity of a human being," owing to what she describes as a kind of natural equity among social classes in their Genevan home. A respectable servant and respectful protégé, Justine was happy, pretty, kind, and "the most grateful little creature in the world" (91); indeed she nearly died tending to Victor's mother in the illness that took her life. When Justine's three siblings die in some other undisclosed illness, her mother calls her home, where she meets with inconsistent affection and frequent indifference. Eventually her own mother dies and she returns to the Frankenstein household, much to the delight of Elizabeth, and to Justine's own eventual detriment. The extent of the "story" that Elizabeth offers Victor is the fact of Justine's return, and the report that she is "clever and gentle, and extremely pretty," and that Elizabeth "love[s] her tenderly" (92). Later, when she is re-introduced as the villainous murderer of the young child William, she becomes the subject of a psychological mystery, as Victor's brother Ernest asks, "who would credit that Justine Moritz, who was so amiable, and fond of all the family, could all at once become so extremely wicked?" (102). Justine is, in short, a character made of the sketches offered by other people in the narrative, and those sketches present her as the good-natured recipient of all the blows life has to offer. Like Sade's Justine de Bertole, of whom Shelley may well have known, Justine Moritz provides a sign of the mockery her world makes of the justice suggested in her name through the legal structures in which it is imagined to be manifest, and the passivity with which she accepts the violence meted out to her by legal and ecclesiastical authority demonstrates the novel's subordination of justice to the institutions that ostensibly support it.[14] Even more disconcerting than the idea that institutions may render justice impossible is the reason Justine enters those institutions in the first place, as she is sentenced to her trial by a flippant act of revenge taken against, apparently, all womankind for their failure to smile sufficiently.

Most of the creature's homicidal acts are calculated, precise, and aimed at causing pain to Victor and damage to the Frankenstein family. The exception is his second, in which he brings about the death of Justine through his manipulation of social rules rather than his great bodily strength. His first murder follows an initial plan to kidnap. Struck by his loneliness and misery at having been driven away by the De Laceys and subsequently shot, he is "disturbed by the approach of a beautiful child" and imagines that he might generate in this child the companionship he seeks. "I could seize him," he imagines, "and educate him as my companion and friend" (154). While obviously a grievously poor ethical decision, the creature's intentions at this early moment are at least not homicidal, even if his planned "seizure" belies a violence of which he is perhaps as yet unaware.[15] It is only the child's invocation of his father, the Syndic Frankenstein, that induces the creature's homicidal act, which he initiates with a certain affectless calculus: "you belong then to my enemy [...] you shall be my first victim." Although his "heart swelled with exultation and hellish triumph" at his ability to inflict pain on the Frankenstein family, he describes himself as softened momentarily by the picture in the boy's locket, before being even more enraged by the realization that he is "for ever deprived of the delights that such beautiful creatures could bestow" (155). When Justine passes him just a few moments later, he does not know of her connection to the Frankenstein family but sees her as an embodiment of a womankind that he cannot possess for himself:

> Here, I thought, is one of those whose smiles are bestowed on all but me; she shall not escape: thanks to the lessons of Felix, and the sanguinary laws of man, I have learned how to work mischief. I approached her unperceived, and placed the portrait securely in one of the folds of her dress.[16] (155)

While the creature identifies his motive here as "mischief," he also continues the desire for revenge that governed the initial killing of William. Rather than aiming to avenge himself against the House of Frankenstein, though, here he attacks a broader version of humanity, embodied in women's smiles and represented by "sanguinary laws."

That the novel will end with a lament for a lack of justice should come as no surprise when justice itself, personified in the body of a servant girl whose life has been a series of injustices, has been killed off by none other than the justice system by the end of the novel's first volume. Bernard Duyfhuizen calls Justine's death the result of "monstrous forces operating within the fictional universe: the patriarchal institutions of the law and the church."[17] Incapable of hearing her defense, the law sentences her to a death the reader knows she does not deserve. Demanding her false confession, the church condemns her to a self-recrimination even more damning in its affront to modern virtues of authenticity and honesty. These two systems of law enact their power on the body and the feelings of the personified figure of justice, rendering her not only powerless but also self-contradictory and, eventually, dead. Daniel Stout argues that Shelley's novel offers "a prescient diagnosis of the curious contradictions that appear in a situation where a tragedy seems to have been authored by many hands."[18] William Frankenstein's death is the creature's fault, but also Victor's, and also, though more aggressively so in the 1831 text, Victor's father's. Even Elizabeth Lavenza at a certain point claims fault, announcing somewhat hysterically that she has "murdered my darling infant!" (96). The one person who seems not at all guilty of William's death is, of course, Justine Moritz, who dies for it. If as Stout discusses cogently, "What's frightening about this novel isn't so much the murderous creature as the asymmetry the creature lights up between a punishment that can only be meted out to one individual or another for a crime that has its source in everyone," then Justine's trial and sentence demonstrate the end result of such a failure of justice.[19] If the law is ultimately arbitrary, then just anyone will do when it comes time to assign blame. And if just anyone will do, then it might as well be the embodied figure of justice itself that bears the brunt of the "sanguinary law's" need for a culprit.

In this, as in so many things, it is remarkable that the creature learns to read as well as he does.[20] Attaining a level of literacy to rival at least an advanced and dutiful schoolboy, the creature learns from his Milton, his Plutarch, his Goethe, and his Volney what it means to be a (European) man in the (Western) world. Such lessons, as readers of these texts could attest, vary between broad strokes and minute details of subjective response. Rarely, though, do they dwell on what we might call the procedural. One might well wonder, then, how the creature understood so well what it was he was doing when he placed the locket in Justine's dress. "I have learned how to work mischief," he recalls himself thinking as he sees the face whose smile will be denied him, and "she shall not escape." It is Felix De Lacey, it seems, who has provided the lessons in the use of apparent evidence to produce the appearance of guilt as he narrated the events that led to his family's exile. Although the creature has not read his author's father's *Caleb Williams*, it is a lesson that could be learned there as well, for the particular form of mischief that the creature seems to have learned to work is the mechanism of a justice system tending toward anything but justice.

Justine's case rests on the virtues of apparent evidence. Victor, confident in Justine's innocence, approaches her trial with "no fear ... that any circumstantial evidence could be brought forward strong enough to convict her," although he acknowledges as the trial proceeds that indeed "[s]everal strange facts combined against her" (103). The facts are strange, and yet they are facts—pieces of apparently incontrovertible evidence proving Justine's presence in the locations pertinent to the crime and suggesting a mind inexplicably ill at ease in the wake of William's death. Her own defense rests upon what she calls "a plain and simple explanation of the facts," which she proceeds to offer without guile or theatrics (104), not imagining that, as Godwin writes, "nothing is more uncertain, more contradictory, more unsatisfactory than the evidence of facts."[21] The facts she can explain except for the presence of the locket, the accounting for which demands a narrative that she cannot imagine. She finds herself "checked," "left to conjecture concerning the probabilities by which it might have been placed in my pocket." She cannot conjure up a scenario in which another has placed it there, despite that being the most readily available explanation. As she insists, "I have no enemy on earth, and none surely would have been so wicked as to destroy me wantonly" (105). Failing to offer any alternative narrative to the one that the evidence presents, Justine all but accepts a story in which she has taken the locket for herself after killing her young charge.

Justine's conviction for the crime she did not commit occurs because of her inability to conceive herself the victim of a hatred she cannot imagine herself to have caused. Even Victor, who knows that his abandoned creation must have killed young William, has no ready explanation for how the portrait of his mother ended up in the pocket of Justine's clothes. It is there, of course, because the creature has placed it there, and while Victor readily imagines his creation capable of and even tending toward the murderous impulse that destroyed the life of the young boy-child William, he cannot or does not understand that the creature is also capable of a violent loathing of the women he imagines will reject him. He cannot imagine that his creation has already learned the misogynistic fury of an Elliot Rodger. The framing of Justine is indeed the only one of the creature's murderous acts that he commits entirely on his own behalf. Not seeming to know Justine's connection to the Frankenstein family, he destroys her because of the privation she embodies for him; he sees in her the site of his sexual denial. While he kills William Frankenstein, Henry Clerval, and Elizabeth Lavenza to cause pain to Victor, he frames Justine as retribution for the suffering he imagines the social world to inflict upon him in its denial of female companionship. If no woman will smile on him, then this one will die, and he will ensure that it is her social world that kills her.

The sexual nature of the creature's act of framing becomes even more apparent in Mary Shelley's revision of the novel. In both the 1818 and 1831 edition, the picture in William's locket spurs the creature on to rage even after an initial softening. The "delight" he finds in gazing on the eyes of the portrait turns to "rage" as he remembers that he is "for ever deprived of the delights that such beautiful creatures could bestow; and that she whose resemblance I contemplated would, in regarding me, have changed that air of divine benignity to one expressive of disgust and affright" (155). In narrating this moment he expects sympathy from Victor as he asks his creator, "Can you wonder that such thoughts transported me with rage?" (And indeed, the fact that Victor at first decides to make the creature's mate suggests that his call for sympathy is heard.) The creature then describes his turn away from William's body to find a place to hide. In 1818, it is at this moment that Justine happens by, an ill-fated woman about her own business. The creature sees her, resents her beauty on account of his assumption that her smiles are reserved for all but him. As punishment for the envy her beauty occasions in him, he plants the locket upon her person and sets into motion the mechanisms by which the Genevan system of justice will kill Justine, a woman who has committed no crime and yet whose name may mark her as destined for destruction. Not knowing, of course, that the woman he dooms to death bears a name that presents her allegorically as an ironic embodiment of justice, the creature sees her only as the embodiment of his own deprivation. In Shelley's revisions for the 1831 publication of her revised novel, the creature's interaction with Justine's unsuspecting person is more sinister. Still motivated by the same fury at a womankind whose imagined disdain spurs him to vengeance, the creature's actions are depicted as a decidedly more sexual threat. As in the earlier version, he turns to seek a hiding place. In 1831, he enters a barn he believes to be empty and there he finds a sleeping woman, whom he lingers over with the creeping malice of a voyeuristic intruder:

> A woman was sleeping on some straw; she was young: not indeed so beautiful as her whose portrait I held; but of an agreeable aspect, and blooming in the loveliness of youth and health. Here, I thought, is one of those whose joy-imparting smiles are bestowed on all but me. And then I bent over her, and whispered "Awake, fairest, thy lover is near—he who would give his life but to obtain one look of affection from thine eyes: my beloved, awake!"[22]

What does a reader imagine in this moment, given the opportunity to imagine the scene? The creature speaks in the ear of Justine, who sleeps and likely believes herself safe from harm, and alone. He promises her "his life" in exchange for a kind look. He demands an affection that he seems to believe is his due.

And then, of course, his feelings turn:

The sleeper stirred; a thrill of terror ran through me. Should she indeed awake, and see me, and curse me, and denounce the murderer? Thus would she assuredly act, if her darkened eyes opened, and she beheld me. The thought was madness; it stirred the fiend within me—not I, but she shall suffer: the murder I have committed because I am for ever robbed of all that she could give me, she shall atone. The crime had its source in her: be hers the punishment! Thanks to the lessons of Felix and the sanguinary laws of man, I had learned how to work mischief. I bent over her, and placed the portrait securely in one of the folds of her dress. She moved again, and I fled.[23]

Aware that to be caught in his voyeuristic gazing over the body of a sleeping girl would be tantamount to confession of all available crimes, the creature feels an appropriate "terror," a sense of urgency that demands he escape. What follows, though, as in 1818, is not only escape but the vindictive act of retribution that will lead to Justine's death. That retributive act even re-writes the cause of the creature's initial murderous impulse. Faced with the sleeping body of a woman he cannot possess, the creature re-imagines his killing of William not as part of the "eternal revenge" he has sworn toward Victor but instead as an act caused by the failure of women to smile at him. "The crime has its source in her," he insists, and so she should take the blame. Rather than (or at least in addition to) being an instance of what Stout calls the creature's "unhinged grammar," in this moment the creature achieves a certain clarity about the function that women can serve in the absence of their sufficient smiling. They do make excellent scapegoats.[24]

The procedural violence that the creature enacts upon Justine substitutes for a sexual violence that he only threatens. While in the 1818 edition of the novel, her appearance before him is coincidental, fleeting, in the 1831 edition he lingers over her body; he whispers in her ear. He blames her for the fear he imagines she would feel were she to awake and find him there, and so he dooms her for death. In his destruction of Justine, the creature shows the justice system that cannot make sense of him to be inoperable even without his interruption, as he demonstrates its failure to protect the entity that it seems designed to preserve: justice itself, embodied in a woman who cannot be kept safe from the entitlement of masculine desire. While Derrida may seek "to preserve the possibility of a justice" as "a law that not only exceeds or contradicts 'law,'" *Frankenstein* embodies justice in a woman's body in order to show its death at the hands of the law that operates in its name.[25] The creature has learned his desire from the books written to maintain the system that keeps her at its center, and the enactment of that desire throws into relief her constant danger. His demands for a companion are a structuring feature of the system represented in the books that he has read; that they cannot be met reveals the violence of the system itself in its dependence on a lack of reciprocity in which women's bodies are deemed protected only to the extent that they are available to desire.

Shelley's novel, so often identified as the story of scientific overreach or an allegory of bad parenting (or the apparently inevitable confluence of the two), is also and perhaps before all other things a story of accountability and responsibility. Whose responsibility is the creature's behavior and his insistence on his right to have his desires met? Who is to be held accountable for the acts he commits? Who kills William Frankenstein? Such questions reveal gaps between the contexts in which they might be answered. We might well blame Victor for the creature's bad behavior, but there is no way to prosecute him for it. There might be legal questions about Justine's guilt, but there is no way for the law to recognize the creature as murderer. Many are responsible for the potentially criminal and at least reprehensible actions of the walking corpse that Victor has animated, and the novel works to expand definitions of responsibility and accountability beyond that which the ultimately failed law can recognize.[26] It should come as no surprise that the most blatant failure of recognition the novel depicts follows one of the most egregious misappropriations of responsibility it represents. Justine is found irrevocably guilty for a crime she clearly did not commit, sentenced to her wrongful conviction initially not by the judge who will come to seal her fate but by the creature who determines her guilt for another crime against his person. She will not smile upon him. Because the creature finds himself "for ever robbed of all that she could give" him, "she shall atone," and her atonement will take the form of conviction for a crime that he himself committed. Where has he learned such entitlement? Whose responsibility is his sense of women's responsibility for his happiness? In this extended parable of shirked responsibility, where do we place the creature's insistence that his happiness depends upon a woman's smiling at him? And what have we done in spending decades finding ways to sympathize with this creature whose thwarted desire and unchosen celibacy he blames for the murderous rampage through which he aims to take vengeance upon his own creator? The creature is misunderstood; the creature is victimized. The creature is unfairly treated. The creature also blames his own bad acts on women's denial of his desires, and the one privilege granted to this being denied inclusion in human society is the opportunity to take everything out on the women who deny him the satisfaction he believes is his right. The creature reflects back to the society that rejects him its own utter failure to administer or imagine justice, and he does so as an embodiment of what David Sigler calls the "bloodlust of the state, into which all citizens are complicit."[27] That bloodlust though, that will to violence, does not come from nowhere. On the contrary, for the creature it comes from the simple realization that women will not give him the smiles that he feels he is owed. That realization has for too long been narrated as a story of understandably frustrated desire or of a privation that warrants empathetic tears. To see it instead as the entitlement that it is, and to ask how this creature has arrived at his assumption of it, may make all the difference in the world to the kinds of sympathy we allot in our reading of this novel.

The list of names of men who have inflicted harm upon the women who have rejected or refused them stretches well beyond the pages available here. Were we to wish to remember them, we could name the manifesto-writers and the mass killers in Toronto, in Tallahassee, in Santa Fe, Texas, and so many other places where men took out their fury at rejection by one on a group of others. A Tumblr started in 2014 called "When Women Refuse," for example, records instances of "violence inflicted on women who refuse sexual advances," cataloging news stories along with personal narratives to present a picture of what starts to appear to be a vast conspiracy against women's capacity to say no or to smile only at will. In this public airing of the pain, damage, and death wrought upon women and those they love in exchange for their having denied men the right to have their desires satisfied, a thread repeats. As Rebecca Solnit notes in her essay "All the Rage," "There is no shortage of examples," and the thousands of stories provide a simple fact: there are those who will kill the women who refuse them the smiles they think they deserve, and they believe themselves justified in doing so.[28] If the creature's "bloodlust" is that of the state and all of its citizens, it is a bloodlust that never separates its violence from the imperatives of heteronormative desire. When Justine imagines that she has "no enemy on earth" and that there are "none surely" "so wicked as to destroy [her] wantonly," she fails to account for the loathing that must accompany the insistence that she is responsible for men's desire not only for her but for any woman. She fails to acknowledge, or know, that another woman's failure to smile may in fact at any moment sentence her to death.

Notes

1   Gary O'Shea and Thea Jacobs, "Flakensteins: Snowflake Students Claim Frankenstein's Monster Was 'Misunderstood'—and Is in Fact a VICTIM," *The Sun*, March 5, 2018.
2   Chris Smyth, "Frankenstein's Monster? He Was Stitched Up, Say Millennials," *The Times*, March 5, 2018.
3   P. B. Shelley, "On Frankenstein," *Athenaeum* (November 10, 1832): 730. Included in Mary Shelley, *Frankenstein, or, the Modern Prometheus*, ed. D. L. Macdonald and Kathleen Scherf (Peterborough, Ontario: Broadview Press, 2012), 281–3.
4   Knight's *Quarterly Review* 3 (August 1824): 195–9.
5   David Barnett, "Just How Monstrous Is the Sun's 'Flakensteins' Story?" in *The Guardian*, March 7, 2018.
6   Mary Shelley, *Frankenstein, or, the Modern Prometheus*, ed. D. L. Macdonald and Kathleen Scherf (Peterborough, Ontario: Broadview Press, 2012). All references to the 1818 edition will be to this one and are cited parenthetically in the text.
7   Elsewhere I discuss this spectacle as central to the novel's vision of masculinity; see "Frankenstein, Dismembered Women, and What It Takes to Be a Man," *Litteraria Pragensia* 28, no. 56, "Frankenstein 200: A Literary Celebration" (December 2018): 34–46.
8   Frances Ferguson, *Solitude and the Sublime: The Romantic Aesthetics of Individuation* (New York: Routledge, 1992), 112.
9   Murder is the killing of one human being by another: an act defined by *Blackstone's Law* as occurring, "When a person, of sound memory and discretion, unlawfully killeth any reasonable creature in being and under the king's peace, with malice aforethought." William Blackstone, *Blackstone's Commentaries on the Laws of England*. Available online through The Avalon Project: Documents in Law, History and Diplomacy. Yale Law School. Book 4, chapter 14. §229 Frankenstein's creation remains well outside the status category of legal personhood, as *Blackstone's* affords no avenue toward considering the creature within the law: neither a naturally created person ("such as the God of nature formed us") nor an artificial one ("such as created and devised by human laws for the purposes of society and government"), Book I, chapter 1.

10   Jacques Derrida, "Force of Law: The 'Mystical Foundation of Authority'," in *Deconstruction and the Possibility of Justice*, ed. Drucilla Cornell, Michel Rosenfeld, and David Gray Carlson (New York: Routledge, 1992), 3–67, 16.

11   As Derrida writes elsewhere, "A just one is always more alone than any other," in "Justices," trans. Peggy Kamuf, *Critical Inquiry* 31, no. 3 (Spring 2005): 689–721, 702.

12   Gayatri Spivak describes Victor's attempt here as his effort to "try to tame the monster, to humanize him by bringing him within the circuit of the Law"; "Three Women's Texts and a Critique of Imperialism," *Critical Inquiry* 12, no. 1 (1985): 243–61, 258.

13   Sara Guyer, "Testimony and Trope in *Frankenstein*," *Studies in Romanticism* 45, no. 1 (2006): 77–115, 98. Guyer focuses on Victor's attempts to tell his story and the ways that his narrative "indicates a possibility of testimony (and ethics) that would not take the law as its model." In this as in so many things, the creature follows Victor's model, and his closing questions provide a form of testimony available only in unanswered and unanswerable questions. For further discussion of the necessity of the creature's erasure at the end of the novel, see Criscillia Benford, "'Listen to my tale': Multilevel Structure, Narrative Sense Making, and the Inassimilable in Mary Shelley's 'Frankenstein'" *Narrative* 18, no. 3 (2010): 324–46, in which she discusses the creature's ultimately alien and unassimilable status; and Deanna Koretsky, "'Unhallowed Arts': *Frankenstein* and the Poetics of Suicide," *European Romantic Review* 26, no. 2 (2015): 241–60, which argues that the creature's planned suicide constitutes the novel's central point about identity and identification.

14   For a discussion of Sadean echoes in Shelley's novel, see Will McMorran, "The Marquis de Sade in English, 1800–1850," *Modern Language Review* 112, no. 3 (2017): 549–66.

15   And also a form of love he might well have learned from *Paradise Lost*, in which Adam repeatedly "seizes" Eve's hand as a gesture of ostensible affection. See IV, 487 and IX, 1037.

16   It is indeed remarkable that it is in the creature's next paragraph that he requests a mate, as if having "learned how to work mischief" against a woman who denies him qualifies him for companionship.

17   Bernard Duyfhuizen, "Periphrastic Naming in Mary Shelley's 'Frankenstein'," *Studies in the Novel* 27, no. 4 (1995): 477–92, 489.

18   Daniel M. Stout, *Corporate Romanticism: Liberalism, Justice, and the Novel* (New York: Fordham University Press, 2017), 177.

19   Ibid., 185.

20   Walter Scott is likely the first to make this observation in his review for Blackwood's, in which he blusters, "The self-education of the monster, considering the slender opportunities of acquiring knowledge that he possessed, we have already noticed as improbable and overstrained," *Blackwood's Edinburgh Magazine* 2 (March 1818): 613–20. (Available online at *Romantic Circles*). For further discussion of the creature's self-learned literacy as a representation of women's education, see Alan Richardson, "From *Emile* to *Frankenstein*: The Education of Monsters," *European Romantic Review* 1, no. 2 (1991): 147–62. For an exploration of the creature's reading that finds fault not with his method but with his materials, see Maureen Noelle McLane's "Literate Species: Populations, 'Humanities,' and *Frankenstein*," *ELH* 63, no. 4 (1996): 959–88.

21 William Godwin, "Of History and Romance," in *Caleb Williams*, ed. Gary Handwerk and A. A. Markley (Peterborough, ON: Broadview, 2000), 453–68, 462. Godwin makes this comment about the writing of history, but his analogical model is the use of facts in "courts of justice, where truth is sometimes sifted with tenacious perseverance"; a reader of Godwin can underscore many times that *sometimes*.

22 The Project Gutenberg EBook of Frankenstein, by Mary W. Shelley [no pagination]. Chapter XVI. https://www.gutenberg.org/files/42324/42324-h/42324-h.htm.

23 Ibid.

24 Mary Jacobus makes a similar claim in her discussion of the creature's killing of Justine, on whom she claims "the monster wreaks his revenge on all women"; "Is There a Woman in This Text?" *New Literary History* 14, no. 1 (1982): 117–41, 133. In the same "monstrous logic" as the recent phenomenon of the so-called "incels," the creature threatens violence unless he is provided the mate that he has been taught to believe he deserves.

25 Derrida, "Force of Law," 6.

26 I say "potentially" criminal insofar as crimes must be committed by persons, and it is unclear and unlikely whether the creature could be one of these before the law.

27 Sigler describes the ways that Justine's case "encourages us to see Victor's creature, of whom she is unaware, as the embodiment of sovereign justice, instead of as a marginalized person victimized by a normative culture. The creature's bloodlust is the very bloodlust of the state, into which all citizens are complicit"; "'Doomed to Live': Reading Shelley's *Frankenstein* and 'The Immortal Immortal' with Derrida's Death Penalty Seminars," *Litteraria Pragensia* 28, no. 56, "Frankenstein 200: A Literary Celebration" (December 2018): 47–59, 59.

28 Rebecca Solnit, "All the Rage," in *Whose Story Is This?* (Chicago, IL: Haymarket Books, 2019), 106.

12

The Utopias of *Frankenstein*

Vivasvan Soni

An ugly, misshapen monster, crudely cobbled together from sundry misaligned parts, is animated with a spark of life by an overweeningly ambitious creator-scientist. This ill-conceived being staggers around wreaking havoc, rebels against its maker and is ultimately consumed by its own resentments. One easily hears in this Gothic tale a political allegory of the abominations of the modern constitutional state, founded on rational principles in a moment of revolutionary fervor. Hobbes already figures this state as a Leviathan, a biblical monster comprised countless atomized individuals who, animated by a social contract, cohere into the form of the sovereign.[1] Chris Baldick and David Collings have shown that, closer to Mary Shelley's historical moment, Edmund Burke's lurid Gothic imagination figures the revolutionary mob as monstrous and spectral, a veritable Frankenstein monster avant la lettre.[2] In the anti-Jacobin account of the Abbé Barruel, whom Percy Shelley had read avidly, this "disastrous monster Jacobin" even originates from a conspiracy of Illuminati in Ingolstadt![3] Paine, Godwin, and Wollstonecraft re-inflect Burke's image of monstrosity to their own political ends, aligning monsters with monarchy, the aristocratic court or even government itself.[4] Mary Shelley's creature, however, appears to share more with Burke and the anti-Jacobin novel of the 1790s than with her radical mentors.[5] Frankenstein's monster is marginal, oppressed, dispossessed, so that if his body is to be read as an allegory of a corporate body, it can only represent Burke's staggering revolutionary mob of the poor and disenfranchised, all those whom the revolution is supposed to liberate, but whom it only rouses to disoriented rage.[6] Shelley's *Frankenstein* seems to function as a cautionary tale, warning us not to wake the monstrous body of the slumbering people.[7] This reading, as Baldick shows, continues well into the nineteenth century, where the monster is used in political cartoons and rhetoric to figure dispossessed peoples, and the novel was "used by nervous liberal statesmen to delay reform" (60).[8] *Pace* Marilyn Butler, it remains easy to arrive at a Burkean reading of the novel even with the 1818 text.[9]

There is a puzzle here too easily glossed over by critics. Some accept the conservative reading of the novel at face value, citing Mary Shelley's growing disillusionment with radical causes, and her fraught relationships with Percy Shelley, William Godwin, and Mary Wollstonecraft. Others argue that this could not possibly be the political import of the novel, given her radical pedigree; the conservative reading of the novel as modern promethean hubris must have been put in place later.[10] But to understand the politics of the novel, we must be willing to linger in its paradox, and credit the conservative reading, in which the monster represents the vengeful and violent revolutionary mob, rather than assume hastily that this reading is mistaken. Only later, after carefully unpacking this Russian doll of a novel and mapping the interconnections among its several layers of embedded narrative, will we understand how the creature's troubling allegorization of the revolutionary crowd enables a critique of revolutionary politics "from the left," in the name of a utopianism which revolutionary fury has abandoned.

If this is *Frankenstein*'s strategy, the novel bears a greater formal resemblance to the literary text that is its avowed model than we have realized. *Paradise Lost* is not just window dressing; it does not merely provide the novel with its epigraph, the creature with his education, and the characters with their archetypes (Adam, Satan). Rather, it grapples with the same political problem as *Frankenstein*: the committed radical thinker confronting the experience of revolutionary disappointment. In order to reckon with the failures of revolution, Milton's epic scrambles political codes, and places the language of revolutionary republicanism in the mouth of Satan, the great tempter and the embodiment of evil. It would be easy, then, to read *Paradise Lost* as a condemnation of revolutionary aspiration in its entirety. Only the patient and careful reader, willing to wait until the Nimrod moment in Book 12, will discern the poem's commitment to freedom, an anti-monarchical politics and even revolution itself. Similarly, *Frankenstein* concedes the conservative critique of the revolutionary mob as violent and vengeful, but it offers a different diagnosis of *why* the mob acts this way than a traditional reactionary politics would. The problem is not an innate incapacity for self-governance, an inborn cruelty or a natural disorderliness; rather, the very experience of oppression, abuse, and injustice renders the creature violent and vengeful.[11] He begins life as a mild, benevolent being, yearning for communion with others. Tyranny turns the oppressed into a monster. Percy Shelley first grasped this reading in his review of the novel: "Treat a person ill, and he will become wicked."[12] Like *Paradise Lost*, *Frankenstein* offers the incautious reader a *mea culpa* from a seemingly reformed revolutionary, while in fact sympathetically searching out causes for the failure of revolution.

Even if this reading rescues the novel from the charge of reaction, its diagnosis of revolutionary failure appears to give little cause for political optimism. This bleak picture is confirmed when we look beyond the political symbolism of the creature to other moments in the text that allude to revolution. There are at least four, and each one is a meditation on revolutionary failure. First, *Paradise Lost*, the ur-text of revolutionary disappointment, is important in the creature's education and shapes his identity. Second, Victor's effusive reflections on his visit to the tomb of Hamden signal an unmistakable enthusiasm for the English revolution,[13] yet concludes on a note of revolutionary despair rather than inspiration: "For an instant I dared to shake off my chains ... but the iron had eaten into my flesh, and I sank again, trembling and hopeless, into my miserable self" (133–4).[14] Third, Victor himself is figured as a revolutionary, not a promising portent for radical hopes. His disruptive behavior, upon arriving in Ingolstadt, has all the hallmarks of a misguided insurrection against authority. As a man of science, Victor embodies the dialectic of enlightenment, unleashing revolutionary forces he hardly understands and cannot control.[15] Fourth, Walton's mutinous crew might be the least ambiguous figure of revolution in *Frankenstein* but they do not revolt in the name of some better social or political organization.[16] They simply want to return home. If Walton imagines the Arctic as a utopia of light at the beginning of the novel, then his forced departure from the frigid, inhospitable Arctic concedes that the Enlightenment's revolutionary aspirations are delusional. The novel's one "successful" revolution turns out to be another diagnosis of revolutionary failure.[17]

Is this all the novel has to say about politics, then, oscillating between a Burkean condemnation of the revolutionary crowd, a critique of the limited aspirations of actual revolutions and a sympathetic diagnosis of the way that the legacy of tyranny appears to derail revolution into a cycle of vengeance? Given these diagnoses, how can the novel be committed to a project of radical reform or even revolution, as recent commentators have suggested? Is there no sense in the text of the purpose for which revolution is undertaken, no vision of a better world for the sake of which the old one must be remade, no utopia to guide the revolutionary legislator? Elsewhere in Mary Shelley's literary constellation, a utopian vision is gestured toward if not clearly delineated: in Godwin's *Caleb Williams*, where the robber band functions as a flawed instantiation of an anarchist utopia; in Percy's *Prometheus Unbound*, which responds to Mary's bleak depiction of the modern Promethean problematic; in Mary's own *Valperga*, where Florence represents a republican, democratic politics of freedom, the alternative to Castruccio's tyrannical and Machiavellian machinations; and in her *Last Man*, where a post-monarchical England has glimmers of a dawning utopian politics before being destroyed by the plague.[18] In fact, if we attend to *Frankenstein* with these questions in mind, we discover that it offers us a series of utopian portraits, at least one for each narrator: Walton's Arctic utopia; the republican political world of Geneva with the utopian household in which Victor is raised; and, the utopian family of the De Laceys, which the creature so longingly observes as he comes to maturity, even though he remains forever shuttered from it.[19] Although scholars rarely align them in this way when discussing the novel's politics, there can be little doubt of their considered and systematic placement in the novel. What is the political vision underlying each of these utopias, and what is their narrative function within the novel?

This is the question my essay seeks to answer. I have argued that utopias embedded in Mandeville's *Fable of the Bees*, Fielding's *Joseph Andrews*, and Godwin's *Caleb Williams* serve to provide an immanent standard of judgment and guide the political readings of these texts.[20] Can *Frankenstein*'s utopias function this way? Their political visions diverge, leaving us with the problem of how to reconcile three different utopian schemes. Moreover, it is unclear whether the utopias offer viable political projects, or are simply flights of the imagination with little political value. The narrative situating of the utopias hints that, even if the utopias seem viable, they remain unavailable to the narrators, for reasons which are not easy to discern. The utopias of Victor and the creature are childhood utopias, functioning like the Eden of *Paradise Lost*. Instead of moving toward these utopias, the protagonists begin in them and leave as they mature. Walton does indeed move toward the Arctic for most of the novel, but the Arctic he finds is a far cry from the fantastic "region of beauty and delight" he imagines at the beginning (5). He is forced to turn around before reaching his destination, leaving the Arctic forever suspended in the realm of unactualized possibility. Even when *Frankenstein* gestures at utopian visions that might guide revolutionary politics, its narrative structure appears to portray these visions as inaccessible.

How, then, are we understand the formal role of these utopian vignettes in the novel, and what can we deduce about the novel's overall attitude toward utopian thought? In order to answer these questions, my essay compares the Genevan and De Lacey utopias, to show what political order each promises, and why each becomes inaccessible. I will argue that the novel's allegiances lie with the Genevan utopia. Nevertheless, all the novel's utopias are abandoned by the end, an apparently bleak prognosis for utopian thought. However, I show that the novel surprisingly makes the case that concrete utopian imagining (like the novel's Genevan experiment) must accompany political action. The novel offers a rigorous taxonomy of four modes of political motivation in which the utopian imagination is absent or dysfunctional: the negativity of critique, vengeance, Arendtian natality, the untethered flight of fancy. Each of these has catastrophic consequences, leaving the utopian lure of Geneva as the only viable political alternative. The case that utopian fictioning is essential to political action is bolstered if we consider anew one of the central questions of the novel: what brings the creature to life? If, ultimately, it is the creature's story, his narrative, his existence in language, that brings him to life, not a mere spark of electricity, then read as an allegory of the body politic, this suggests that it is only fictions, imaginings, and utopian aspirations that animate a political order. They constitute a necessary condition of our political agency.

Actual Utopias: Geneva and the De Laceys

The Genevan utopia of Victor's childhood is the most concretely delineated and realistic of *Frankenstein*'s utopias. It holds the greatest promise, both for a reading of the novel and as a political project. Its utopian character is evident from the first paragraph of Victor's narrative. Geneva is named a "republic," a charged word associated with a revolutionary politics. Victor's family plays an active role in the political life of this city where classical republicanism still thrives:[21] "My ancestors had been for many years counsellors and syndics; and my father had filled several public situations with honour and reputation. He was respected ... for his integrity and indefatigable attention to public business" (18). Genevan institutions of governance are close and familiar, accessible to ordinary citizens. Victor's father is a model of civic virtue and engagement, devoting his life to public service. In true republican fashion, he does not cling to power for its own sake. When he can no longer be of service to the polity, he willingly retires into domestic life to serve further there (18). Recall, too, that Geneva is not just any city in revolutionary iconography. Not only is it an example of recently existing republic (rare enough) and a failed revolution in 1782,[22] but it is also the home and political inspiration of Rousseau, guiding intellectual of the French Revolution. The Shelleys ardently read Rousseau in the summer of 1816 when *Frankenstein* was conceived in the environs of Geneva.[23] Rousseau's praise for republican Geneva in the preface to the radical *Discourse on Inequality* is relevant here, as is his utopian portrait of Geneva in the *Letter to D'Alembert*, as a second Sparta on the verge of being obliterated by the advent of modern commerce.[24]

The most compelling aspects of the utopian portrait of Geneva are to be found in the details of the protagonists' lives and education in the Frankenstein household. They are easy to miss, but reveal a consistent attention to the politics of domestic life so important to Rousseau, Godwin, Wollstonecraft, and other radicals.[25] Rousseau had made the case in *Emile* that in order to educate citizens for freedom, the very methods of pedagogy would have to become non-authoritarian, and this is reflected in the education Victor and Elizabeth receive, undoubtedly the most sustained utopian moment in the novel:

> Our studies were never forced; and by some means we always had an end placed in view, which excited us to ardour in the prosecution of them. It was by this method, and not by emulation, that we were urged to application. Elizabeth was not incited to apply herself to drawing, that her companions might not outstrip her; ... and so far from study being made odious to us through punishment, we loved application, and our amusements would have been the labors of other children. Perhaps we did not read so many books, or learn languages so quickly, as those who are disciplined according to the ordinary methods; but what we learned was impressed the more deeply on our memories. (21–2)

"Force," "discipline," and "punishment" are considered inappropriate in this education, as they would be in a political world of free, self-governing citizens. Students are instead incentivized by being taught to see the value and purposes of what they are learning ("an end placed in view"). In a market-oriented world that eschews orientation by ends, the attention to purposes and use is already a radical, even utopian commitment.[26] Moreover, corrosive competition is not permitted to serve as an incentive for activity in this community ("outstrip her"). The zeal that Victor and Elizabeth bring to their studies ("ardour") and the pleasure they take in them ("amusements") are palpable. We are witnessing here *the genesis of a political community*: the children's relation to their studies models their potential relationship to work. If work were configured in the way that education is in Victor's Genevan childhood, it would undoubtedly have a utopian cast: not forced or mandated, undertaken for tangible ends, and inspiring zeal and pleasure rather than seeming onerous.[27] Perhaps the most utopian feature of this domestic community is the absence of punishment, or a penal justice system, which is one of the most consistent features of the utopian tradition, and echoes the novel's own critique of institutions of justice in the Justine and Safie episodes. Nowhere is the *potential* violence of the law, its *potential* betrayal of freedom, more evident than in its ability to punish, and one of the first desiderata of utopias is often the abolishing of law itself. If the childhood education of Victor and Elizabeth foreshadows their future political lives, there can be no doubt that these lives would be utopian, in ways that hearken back directly to the tradition of utopian writing. The conclusion of the education chapter reiterates the utopian quality of the children's lives with a description of the salutary effects of their upbringing:

> Such was our domestic circle, from which care and pain seemed forever banished. ... Neither of us possessed the slightest pre-eminence over the other; the voice of command was never heard amongst us; but mutual affection engaged us all to comply with and obey the slightest desire of each other. (25–6)

Not only are care and pain excluded from this utopia, but the political structure of the community is egalitarian (no "pre-eminence") and anti-authoritarian (no "voice of command").[28] "Mutual affection" alone defines the structure of obligations that bind the community together, not the force of authority and law. This is as straightforward and concise a description of utopian life as one could find.[29]

The Fall from utopia is not attributed to any original sin or innate human incapacity to sustain an idyllic political system. Rather, the diagnosis is political. The Fall occurs only because tyranny and authoritarianism inadvertently contaminate Victor's education. When Victor discovers Cornelius Agrippa, his father, instead of taking the time to explain the deficiencies of Agrippa's science, dismisses it out of hand: "My dear Victor, do not waste your time upon this; it is sad trash" (22–3). For Victor, this attempt at an authoritative and peremptory dismissal, so contrary to a Rousseauvian pedagogical approach, spurs his rebellion:

> If, instead ... my father had taken the pains to explain to me, that the principles of Agrippa had been entirely exploded ... I should certainly have thrown Agrippa aside ... It is even possible, that my train of ideas would never have received the fatal impulse that led to my ruin. (23)

The casual and hardly noticeable tyranny of an otherwise benevolent father, not the rebellious freedom of the son, drives Victor from the Genevan utopia, the most promising and realistic one in the novel.[30]

It is tempting to compare Victor's Genevan domestic utopia and the creature's time with the De Laceys, but we must proceed carefully. Like Victor's Genevan family, the De Laceys seem to model a utopian community of mutual affection (107), although the creature can only participate in it surreptitiously. Perhaps the De Laceys even constitute an aesthetic utopia, given the repeated references to the old man's guitar playing (85, 92).[31] And like Victor, the creature receives a radical education during his "childhood,"[32] through Volney's *Ruins*, Goethe's *Werther*, Milton's *Paradise Lost*, and Plutarch's *Lives*, although it is an education that takes place in isolation. Felix acts on explicitly utopian ideals, with his critique of institutions like prisons (98), his refusal to accept Safie as a patriarchal trade (99) and his desire to perform noble deeds for their own sake rather than for any reward (98). Given these utopian aspects to the community of the De Laceys, it is no wonder that the creature takes pleasure in watching the family (86), and describes his own situation in utopian terms: "As yet I looked upon crime as a distant evil; benevolence and generosity were ever present before me, inciting within me a desire to become an actor in the busy scene where so many admirable qualities were called forth and displayed" (102–3). The utopian features of the De Lacey community stir in the creature a desire to become a political actor on the public stage, like Victor's father was in Geneva. But the creature's desire finds no outlet. When he attempts to join the community, he is beaten and driven off by Felix. The De Laceys then abandon their idyllic life, having awakened the creature fully to the magnitude of the injustice he endures. Why is the creature excluded from this community? Does the novel offer a diagnosis for the collapse of this utopia? Is there a political error lurking in this community as there was in Geneva?

In fact, the reasons for the failure of the De Lacey utopia are far more sinister and irremediable than those of Geneva. The "utopia" of the De Laceys is a utopia for some, not all; it is a utopia only if we ignore the invisible labor that sustains it, which the novel will not allow us to do. There is a name for this political order: aristocracy. It might sound far-fetched to read the De Lacey utopia as an allegory for aristocracy, since we only see a close-knit nuclear family, but if we pay attention to the clues, the evidence is overwhelming. We should begin by noting the obvious. Unlike the Frankensteins, who are Geneva republicans, the De Laceys appear to be a lesser noble family from Paris ("descended from a good family"; "Agatha had ranked with the ladies of highest distinction" [98]).³³ Unlike the egalitarian community of mutual respect in Geneva, we are told only that the young respect the old among the De Laceys, another hallmark of aristocracy, and that the family possesses "gentle manners" (87). The creature perceives the family to be beautiful while he recognizes his own ugliness (90), trading on the stereotype of aristocratic beauty being connected to nobility, lineage, and heredity (*to kalon*).

If this evidence seems circumstantial, the account of the creature's relations to the family leaves no room for equivocation. He thinks of the family as his "protectors," the myth that sustains aristocratic governance, even though he knows that they do nothing to protect him ("so I loved, in … self-deceit, to call them" [97]). He yearns to be treated with the same "protection and kindness" as the "poor that stopped at their door" (107). The relationship between the creature and the family is hierarchical: "I looked upon them as superior beings" (91). This is not just the creature's perception. His labor becomes the invisible and unacknowledged work ("invisible hand" [90, 91]) necessary to sustain this relatively privileged nobility, their own fall into poverty notwithstanding. The creature's relationship to work stands in stark contrast to the unalienated labor of the Genevan children.

Ultimately, what the creature desires is admission into the political community of the De Laceys on something like equal terms: recognition. He "required kindness and sympathy; but [he] did not believe [himself] utterly unworthy of it" (107). The creature wants to be a participant in politics rather than merely an object of benevolence (102). It is this demand that is intolerable to the aristocratic polity; when he sees the creature, the otherwise progressively minded Felix responds with all the ferocity of aristocratic reaction to revolutionary demands. In the end, then, the creature's story of his time with the De Laceys reveals an aristocratic "utopia" threatened by the revolutionary demands of the working poor; it is the story of the limits of aristocratic benevolence, and the viciousness of aristocratic reaction, much like the story of Falkland in Godwin's *Caleb Williams*.

"Unacknowledged Legislators": A Taxonomy of Motives for Revolutionary Action

It would be a mistake to conclude from the failure of the three utopias in the novel that the text itself is systematically anti-utopian.[34] Although all three utopias fail, they do so for different reasons. The Arctic utopia of Walton is fantastic and impractical, a mere flight of fancy not anchored in any actual political experience. The De Lacey utopia is only apparently one, because it refuses either to acknowledge the labor that makes it possible or to accord equal standing to the laboring classes. The Genevan utopia, however, is not internally or irremediably flawed; it only fails because of the inadvertent authoritarianism of the older Frankenstein. The novel's portrayal of this utopia could serve as a model for the sort of political imagining that is a requisite feature of any progressive politics. Indeed, there are a number of clues that the novel should not be read as a critique of utopian thought *tout court*. Rather, it calls for a more robust and concrete utopian imaginary, asserting that a revolution without a utopia to guide it is a futile and potentially catastrophic endeavor.

The first clue is found in the texts that the creature reads to educate himself at the De Laceys. These texts were politically exemplary for both Shelleys, and indispensable components of a political education. They were also, with the exception of *Paradise Lost*, connected in different ways to a Rousseauvian legacy. But what does the creature learn from each? The first text he encounters, as Felix reads and explains it to Safie, is Volney's *Ruins*. Volney provides the creature with the tools to critique actually existing institutions, the starting point for any utopian project:[35] "I heard of the division of property, of immense wealth and squalid poverty, of rank, descent, and noble blood" (95–6). The injustices of the current political order, Volney shows, are the reasons for wanting to imagine a different politics. *Werther* is the least overtly political of the texts the creature reads, and the lesson he claims to draw from it is not promising: "I learned from Werter's imaginations despondency and gloom" (104). But *Werther* is a key entry in the eighteenth-century sentimental tradition, and concerns the power of sympathy. Not only was the discourse of sensibility, by way of Rousseau, an essential feature of revolutionary political rhetoric; it is also a foundational component of both the Genevan and De Lacey utopias. Sympathy or "mutual affection" is the source of recognition, respect, and equality in both cases, and it is what the creature desires above all.[36] Sympathy, in the novel's terms, is the key condition of any utopian association; it is unacceptably denied to the creature, and sets him on his vengeful path.[37] Finally, *Paradise Lost* is not only a diagnosis of revolutionary failure and a meditation on revolutionary disappointment; it is also a promise of revolutionary possibility, a study of revolutionary indignation and aspiration, as Percy's rewriting in *Prometheus Unbound* makes clear. *Paradise Lost* suggests that the hope for political renewal is never misplaced.[38]

This leaves only Plutarch's *Lives* unexplained, the text which most inspires the creature, exciting him as it did the Rousseau of the *Confessions*. It is the most overtly political of the texts he reads, and the one for which he offers the most sustained analysis: "Plutarch taught me high thoughts; he elevated me above the wretched sphere of my own reflections ... this book developed new and mightier scenes of action. I read of men concerned in public affairs governing or massacring their species. I felt the greatest ardour for virtue rise within me, and abhorrence for vice" (104). Yet the *Lives* is the text least relevant to his situation. He has no access to a political life with others, and this is perhaps what he wants more than anything when he yearns for sympathy, describes his "desire to become an actor" (102), or imagines his own utopian life in South America (121). Every person he encounters makes this life impossible for him, by shutting him out of all human community, and even more, the possibility of community with his own kind. Precisely *because* Plutarch has no application in the creature's life, it stands out from this group of texts. It reveals a profound lacuna that structures the creature's existence: his exclusion from political life. However, it is not just any political life that Plutarch signifies, but a specifically utopian one. What he describes, particularly in the sections the creature singles out, are the most successful practical utopian thinkers of the ancient world: "I was of course led to admire peaceable law-givers, Numa, Solon, and Lycurgus, in preference to Romulus and Theseus" (104). The activity of giving laws to a people, particularly ones aimed at peace, is the work of the utopian imagination.[39] It is precisely this utopian imaginary that the creature can have no opportunity to exercise, because he remains so isolated despite his best efforts. One of the tragedies of the creature is that he remains forever a being without a city (*apolis*), in which alone he could exercise the full range of his capacities. A monstrosity indeed!

The novel makes a surprising argument, then, that it is necessary for utopian thought to accompany political action even in the face of the text's own failed utopias. But to rest the case for the novel's advocacy of utopian imaginings on the creature's enthusiastic reading of Plutarch is hardly sufficient. The novel's argument for utopian thought is substantially deepened if we consider what serves as an impetus for (political) action in each of the three narratives that comprise the novel (Walton, Victor, the creature). *Frankenstein* offers a taxonomy of modalities of action in which the utopian imagination is pointedly absent or dysfunctional, leaving only the Genevan utopia as a model exercise in utopian writing. By showing systematically the failure of modes of political or revolutionary action not grounded in what we might call "utopian realism," and offering the Genevan utopia as a viable alternative, the novel urges us to ground political action not in the merely destructive negativity of critique, the untethered flight of the imagination, the reactive cyclicity of vengeance, the obsessive pursuit of a single narrow purpose, or the freedom of new beginnings without ends (Arendt), but rather in a concrete and holistic vision of a different form of life actualized in tangible practices and described in rich psychological and political detail.

Although it is perfectly obvious why Walton's utopia fails, its failure also challenges my argument because an active utopian imagination is the reason for Walton's journey to the Arctic.[40] The fantastic place he fictions to himself provides the *motive* for him to equip a ship and undertake the arduous journey:

> Inspirited by this wind of promise, my day dreams become more fervent and vivid. I try in vain to be persuaded that the pole is the seat of frost and desolation; it ever presents itself to my imagination as the region of beauty and delight … we may be wafted to a land surpassing in wonders and in beauty every region hitherto discovered on the habitable globe. … What may not be expected in a country of eternal light? (5–6)

Although Walton never becomes a poet, his fevered imaginings are "romantic" (8, 9), and "poetic" in the broader sense that Percy Shelley later gives this word, in the *Defense of Poetry*. Walton's utopian fantasies about the Arctic ("favourite dream") are precisely what provide him with "steady purpose" (6), the impetus for his actions. Is this not exactly how the utopian imagination should work? And yet, are the consequences of his actions not disappointing and even dangerous? Walton's mission to the Arctic is indeed the direct result of his utopian speculations. The problem, in this case, does not lie with the way the imagination provides a motive for action; it works as it should, spurring Walton to action. The problem lies rather with the *content* of his imaginings, which are untethered from any relation to the actual Arctic.[41] Walton's imagination has become unhinged from the world it inhabits. He conceives the Arctic as a place of "eternal light," forgetting that for six months of the year, it is a place of darkness (6). The utopian imaginary ignores these facts at its peril. Unsurprisingly, Walton's ship finds itself trapped in a "seat of frost and desolation," and he is forced to return, "[his] purpose unfulfilled" (183). To be effective and not misguided, utopian thought has to be tempered by a hard-nosed realism; it has to work with what is given; otherwise, the visionary purpose it gives us will lead only to the Arctic and a "purpose unfulfilled." Or, to use the more precise language about the imagination that Coleridge offers us in the *Biographia*, Walton's utopian imaginings are the work of fancy and not the secondary imagination.[42] He cobbles together some shards of memory in haphazard fashion, without a *vital principle* to animate it. We will return to this vital principle in the essay's conclusion, when we consider the utopian import of Victor's animation of the creature.

The creature's case is also easily explained. When his desire to be part of a self-legislating political community is thwarted, first by the De Laceys and then by Victor, he turns to revenge, one of the most powerful but futile forms of political action, as Hannah Arendt describes it.[43] Revenge, according to Arendt, is purely mechanical and reactive; it responds to force with counterforce, and remains trapped in a cycle of violence. It cannot properly be called an action, because it is unfree, determined by the deed that preceded it. Only forgiveness, an imaginative act that liberates us from this enchaining legacy of the past, opens the space of free actions. No wonder Percy Shelley, in responding to Mary's "modern Prometheus," frames the problem of revolution in exactly this way in *Prometheus Unbound*. Percy's Prometheus is only liberated from his millennia-long bondage when he is able to "recall" his curse, in both senses of the word (remember and revoke), and forgive Jupiter. From that moment, an emancipatory revolution becomes possible. For the creature, this imaginative act of emancipation remains foreclosed. He becomes trapped in a reactive cycle of vengeance in which a utopian imagination has no place. If he experiences a measure of liberation at the end, as he heads off into the indefinite ("lost in darkness and distance" [191]), as Spivak suggests, it is only because Victor has died; but it is more likely that he will continue the cycle, and repay death with death, as he claims in despair that he will do (190).[44] Without other people to share it with, the creature can have no use for a utopian imagination; all that remains to him is a righteous but reactive indignation at the injustices he has suffered (190), a recipe for a revolution of the dispossessed certainly (189–90), but a revolution that is a turning in place, not an opening onto an alternative politics.

Thus, revenge (the creature) and ungrounded utopian fantasy (Walton) both fail as forms of political motivation. But what about Victor? What leads him to leave his utopian childhood in Geneva, and to act as he does? One reason is the inadvertent authoritarianism of the older Frankenstein. But there are other motives that drive Victor's actions. His desires, like those of Walton and the creature, are revolutionary without a plausible utopia, a vision of the good, to guide them. Indeed, he leaves the functioning utopia he inhabits, in order to find or accomplish something "better," the very madness of an excessive revolutionary desire that knows only how to find every utopia insufficient. Despite Victor's fascination with alchemy, he is a modern man of science and a figure of Enlightenment social critique much in the mold of Volney's *Ruins* before it arrives at the utopian council. He has no use for the imaginative world of fiction, which is relegated to Elizabeth, the figure of the utopian thinker in the novel killed by the modern Prometheans:[45] "I delighted in investigating the facts relative to the actual world; she busied herself in following the aërieal creations of the poets. The world was to me a secret, which I desired to discover; to her it was a vacancy, which she sought to people with imaginations of her own" (21).[46] In keeping with this characterization, Victor exhibits three modes of motivation that betray the utopian imagination and make it impossible for him to return to the Genevan utopia. The first is the leveling capacity of critique, which ever since Descartes has constituted the modern project of knowledge. Victor claims to distance himself from this position, which he attributes to modern scientific practitioners: "The ambition of the inquirer seemed to limit itself to the annihilation of those visions on which my interest in science was chiefly founded. I was required to exchange chimeras of boundless grandeur for realities of little worth" (29–30). However inaccurate this may be as a description of the scientific project—after all, Francis Bacon composed a utopia (*New Atlantis*) founded on the promise of scientific research—it is in keeping with the earlier portrayal of Victor as concerned with the actual rather than the imagined world, and with his needless departure from the Genevan utopia, which might be read as the act of a critical mind so restless, it cannot abide the imperfect utopia it inhabits.

The next two forms of motivation bring us to the heart of the novel, Victor's creation and subsequent bizarre abandonment of the creature. Victor offers lofty, even utopian reasons for why he would want to bring such a creature to life, having to do with "renew[ing] life where death had apparently devoted the body to corruption" (36). But since the creature remembers nothing, and begins life anew, these reasons are not plausible (36). In fact, Victor creates the monster simply because he can, as an act of the free play of the imagination without purpose or end ("the more fully I entered into the science, the more exclusively I pursued it for its own sake" [32]). The two forms of motivation Victor exhibits, then, are a desire for novelty, simply for its own sake, and the single-minded pursuit of an objective, without regard for the broader consequences of his actions. Each is a mode of acting without the utopian imagination. Victor himself describes the latter mode of motivation and its disastrous consequences lucidly:

> I was thus engaged, heart and soul, in *one pursuit*. ... I could not tear my thoughts from my employment, loathsome in itself, but which had taken an irresistible hold of my imagination. ... A human being in perfection ought ... never to allow passion or a transitory desire to disturb his tranquillity. I do not think the pursuit of knowledge is an exception to this rule. ... If this rule were always observed ... Greece had not been enslaved; Caesar would have spared his country; ... and the empires of Mexico and Peru had not been destroyed. (37–8, my emphasis)

In retrospect, Victor recognizes that his pursuit has been too narrow and single-minded ("one pursuit," the glory of a single scientific achievement), blinding him to the broader social consequences of his actions and destroying "the tranquillity of his domestic affections." Victor's concluding counterfactual history is an act of imagination, forethought, and responsibility, but it only occurs after the fact, and highlights how inattentive he is to these questions before he makes the creature. What will be his responsibilities to the new being he creates? How will it be received by others? How might this new creature behave, and are the risks worth taking? None of these ethical questions occur to Victor in his fervent desire to reanimate a corpse. He simply wants to make the creature because science has brought it within the realm of possibility. Only later does Victor begin to think about the consequences of populating the earth with a new race or species whose interactions with humans might be less than desirable, which causes him to destroy the mate (138–9). The obsessive pursuit of a single end, without attending to the consequences that end would have for the larger world we want to inhabit, is a form of motivation that abandons the holistic and totalizing utopian imagination, with dire consequences.

The desire for novelty and the single-minded pursuit of a narrow objective without regard for consequences are closely interrelated. Victor's bizarre response to his act of creation confirms this. For months, he has been occupied with nothing but the desire to bring the creature to life, but the moment he sees the creature's first movements, he abandons it and flees in horror. Victor brings something absolutely new into the world, a new beginning and origin, and then abandons the monstrous novelty to its own fate. How might Victor's action be interpreted in political terms? I have invoked Arendt's analysis of revenge as a failed mode of political action, trapped in unfreedom. The alternative she offers, the model of a free political action, goes by the name "natality."[47] It is the deed of a political agent who begins something new, without having the end in view, and abandons this action to its historical course without seeking to control or determine its outcome.[48] The essence of a properly political action, for Arendt, is to *give birth* to something new. To act with some utopian end in view, she thinks, would not only be to renounce one's freedom (because the end has determined the beginning), but to flirt with totalitarian management of the social order.[49] The act by which Victor makes the creature is very precisely a figure for this mode of action, allowing us to see the grim underside of Arendt's favored and anti-utopian mode of political agency. Viewed politically, Victor might have awakened the sleeping mass of people to action, but the results leave us wondering whether a legislative action guided by a vision of the political good (utopia) would not have been preferable to the raging monster Victor produces.[50] In fact, the novel allows us to see the deep affinities between the critical theorist, the Arendtian political agent, the Romantic idealist, and the vengeful revolutionary mob, in their shared abandonment of a utopian end to guide their political actions. The only alternative that remains is to let one's actions be guided by a concretely conceived and pragmatic utopian vision (a fiction) like the Genevan utopia within the novel itself.[51]

The Meaning of Life: Animated by Fiction, Not Physics

These modes of political action fail because they either overvalue the capacities of fiction and the imagination or refuse to grant them their due. The overvaluation of fiction and the imagination (Walton's case) is easy to understand. But why should we allow *any* scope to fiction and the imagination when it comes to political agency? Are we not risking the ravages of ideology and "fake news" when we do so? Are we not unmooring politics from the real, and ignoring the claims of the material world? The novel's response to these issues lies in the most fundamental question that *Frankenstein* asks, the one in which Mary Shelley's ghost story has its origin: namely, what gives something life, animation, or soul? What is the principle of life?[52] We know that this was a question the Shelleys, Byron, and Polidori were intrigued by, and Marilyn Butler and Richard Holmes have situated this question in the context of the vitalism debate between Abernethy and Lawrence taking place contemporaneously. *But how does the novel itself answer the question?* If the question had renewed purchase when *Frankenstein* was being written, it is because the science of the time was beginning to suggest a newly plausible materialist answer to this age-old conundrum: electricity or galvanism.[53] However, critics of the novel have been perplexed because its response appears to align it with the position that is both anti-materialist and politically conservative: Victor is the one committed to this answer, and what he produces is more monster than human.

But is this the only answer the novel has to offer? Are we to judge its response on Victor's assessment alone? Or should we ask a question that is rarely posed to the novel: when does the creature actually come to life for us? Victor believes that it is sufficient to add a spark of electricity to a jumbled aggregate of matter in order to animate the creature. And indeed, this is when the creature begins to *move*, and stumbles off into its autonomous material existence. But *it* remains a shadowy, ghostly presence in the novel, a mere moving corpse without a *soul* as it were, until Victor meets *him* on the Mer de Glace and hears his story. What actually brings the creature to life for us, animates him and gives him a soul independent of his body, are his story and the way that our imaginations interact that story.[54] His tale, not the amalgam of dead and reanimated body parts, constitutes the essence of who he is.[55] I mean nothing mysterious or mystical by this. It is the creature's existence in language that gathers him into a single thing, and gives him a distinct identity apart from the mismatched pieces of which he is composed; until then, he is simply a loosely and hideously connected set of body parts moving according to the laws of physics. The point may sound far-fetched but the novel subtly insists on it. The creature develops his own sense of identity through the fictions he reads, especially *Paradise Lost* (105). He views *Paradise Lost* as a "true history," calling attention to the ability of language to bring things into life, even those that have never existed. Indeed, the creature's existence for us has precisely the same status as Adam and Satan in *Paradise Lost*. He and they are fictions, and don't have life anywhere except through texts, as influential as these lives are. In *Frankenstein*, there is in fact no amalgam of body parts animated by a spark of electricity, only a story which gives life to an idea. The creature is in fact all soul or narrative and no body. This is not to diminish his existence, as so often happens when the fictionality of novelistic characters is noted. Rather, it is to marvel at the capacity of language to bring things to life, to animate and even ensoul them. Of course, for the creature to be able to read stories and tell his own, it is essential that he be able to use language.[56] This is why it is so important that he learn language in Mary Shelley's novel, unlike the plays and movies in which he is portrayed as mute and inarticulate.[57] It is in language above all that beings like us and the creature come to life.

The climactic scene of the creature's story, his attempt to join the De Lacey family and his brutal rejection from it, emphasizes this point. The creature desires sympathy, recognition, and belonging in a community. Significantly, he is able to find this sympathy when he tells his story to the blind old man because, for the old man, he exists only as his story. The moment Felix comes in, he drives the creature off without waiting to hear his narrative, horrified by his grotesque body.[58] To reduce the creature to his purely material bodily existence, then, a lifeless aggregate of parts mysteriously set in motion by electricity or some other technical trick, is to treat him like Felix or Victor does, to flee in horror from the monstrous specter of body parts that move as though they are alive rather than to listen to his story and sympathize with *him*, the beautiful soul that transcends the body through its linguistic ensoulment. This is perhaps the profoundest insight of the novel, and it is almost entirely lost when we translate the text into film or theater, where our horrified fascination with the creature's material existence must come to the fore, and forestall our ability to sympathize or even to recognize that a moving body is not a person.[59] This is why it is so important that Mary Shelley's *Frankenstein* takes the form of a novel, in which the body of the creature remains *largely* invisible to us as readers (but see 38–9). Invoking the title of the conference where this paper was originally presented ("The Body of Frankenstein"), we might say that to fixate on the body of Frankenstein's creature, as a subsequent tradition has done, is to miss the point of the novel entirely, indeed to fall into the most tempting trap it sets for us. I have invoked Coleridge's notion of "Fancy" as a lifeless aggregation of parts, and it is again relevant here. This is precisely what the body of the creature is. Coleridge contrasts this to the secondary imagination, which "dissolves, diffuses, dissipates, in order to re-create; or where this process is rendered impossible, yet still at all events it struggles to idealize and to unify. It is essentially *vital*, even as all objects (*as* objects) are essentially fixed and dead."[60] This description is infused with a mystical vitalism, but we need not resort to metaphysical or theological speculation to understand what Coleridge means. Indeed, *Frankenstein* is an extended illustration of the proposition. The creature only comes to life for us as a story ("re-create"), through the work of the secondary imagination; only in this way does the material aggregate of his body acquire a unity ("unify") and ideality ("idealize") that makes him an object for our sympathy.[61] Without the work of the secondary imagination, all that remains is the horror of the Frankenstein monster.

We appear to have strayed from the utopian politics of the novel, but it is not difficult to translate our insights about the creature coming to life through language and the imagination into the realm of the political. Hobbes's Leviathan may be taken as emblematic of the Frankenstein monster in the realm of the political, a disaggregated collection of individuals united only by a spark of fear for the sovereign. It stumbles around barely conscious, without knowing quite who it is or what vision of the good would give its life meaning. In order for this creature to come to life and acquire a soul, it must tell itself stories about who it is, and what is good and worth striving for. In short, what a modern materialist politics lacks are stories and a utopian imagination to guide it. Shelley's nineteenth-century interpreters had already grasped this lesson of the novel, but in a conservative idiom, which is precisely why the politics of the novel have always seemed so puzzling and so easily appropriated for conservative readings: "A state without religion is like a human body without a soul, or rather like an unnatural body of the species of the Frankenstein monster, without a pure and vivifying principle."[62] But the language of soul and spirit need not commit us to this conservative reading of the novel. It is precisely the alignment of materialism with a radical political project that the novel calls into question, an alignment that dominates modern political imaginaries. This is one reason the politics of the novel are so difficult to read. Where the novel questions materialism, we hear it questioning radical politics because the two are inseparable for us.[63] I hope I have shown, instead, that the novel's experimentation with modes of utopian thought and political motivation urges us to recognize that the soul of a polity, what brings it to life and animates it to aspirational action, is the stories it tells itself, the fictions it believes in (neither true nor false) and above all, the concrete utopian visions to which it commits itself. Without these, all that remains is a body that moves without purpose, merely re-acting to every immediate provocation, and without a conception of the good for which it is instituted. Even the most revolutionary action can only ever produce a Frankenstein monster, unless it has a utopia to guide it.

Notes

1   See the famous cover illustration of *Leviathan*. Hobbes also describes the state in terms similar to Victor's creature: "For by art is created that great LEVIATHAN called a COMMONWEALTH ... which is but an artificial man; though of greater stature and strength than the natural" (Thomas Hobbes, *Leviathan*, ed. J. C. A Gaskin (Oxford: Oxford University Press, 1996), 7). In *Frankenstein*, Victor says: "I resolved ... to make the being of a gigantic stature" (Mary Shelley, *Frankenstein; or, the Modern Prometheus: The 1818 Text*, ed. Marilyn Butler (Oxford: Oxford University Press, 1993), 35). All subsequent page references to this edition are cited parenthetically in the text.

2   Chris Baldick, *In Frankenstein's Shadow: Myth, Monstrosity, and Nineteenth-Century Writing* (Oxford: Clarendon Press, Oxford University Press, 1987), 17–20; David Collings, *Monstrous Society: Reciprocity, Discipline, and the Political Uncanny, c.1780-1848* (Lewisburg, TN: Bucknell University Press, 2009), 59–74, especially 70, 72. See also, Lee Sterrenburg, "Mary Shelley's Monster: Politics and Psyche in Frankenstein," in *The Endurance of Frankenstein: Essays on Mary Shelley's Novel*, ed. George Levine and U. C. Knoepflmacher (Berkeley, CA: University of California Press, 1979), 143, 152–66; Adriana Craciun, "*Frankenstein's* Politics," in *The Cambridge Companion to Frankenstein*, ed. Andrew Smith (Cambridge: Cambridge University Press, 2016), 86.

3   Baldick, *In Frankenstein's Shadow*, 19; Sterrenburg, "Mary Shelley's Monster," 155–6; Craciun, "*Frankenstein's* Politics," 86.

4   Baldick, *In Frankenstein's Shadow*, 18–25; Peter Dale Scott, "Vital Artifice: Mary, Percy, and the Psychopolitical Integrity of Frankensptein," in *Endurance of Frankenstein*, ed. Levine and Knoepflmacher, 201.

5   Sterrenburg, "Mary Shelley's Monster," 143, 148; Marilyn Butler, "Introduction," in Shelley, *Frankenstein*, l. Mellor offers perhaps the most sustained reading of the novel as a Burkean critique of Romantic prometheanism, the ideology of revolution and Godwinian/revolutionary abstraction. See Anne K. Mellor, *Mary Shelley: Her Life, Her Fiction, Her Monsters* (New York: Methuen, 1988), 80–6.

6   Collings, *Monstrous Society*, 16, 22; Baldick, *In Frankenstein's Shadow*, 54; Craciun, "*Frankenstein's* Politics," 88; Butler, "Introduction," xlv–xlvi.

7   Butler, "Introduction," l; Baldick, *In Frankenstein's Shadow*, 57, 61.

8   Baldick, *In Frankenstein's Shadow*, 60.

9   See Butler, "Introduction," xxxii.

10 Critics generally recognize the novel's ideological complexity and instability, and the puzzle posed by its political allegory. Sterrenburg acknowledges the conservative strains in the novel, but ultimately views the text as retreating from the political to the psychological and transcending ideology ("Mary Shelley's Monster," 143, 148, 157–60). Craciun finds a similar internalization of the political problematic, although

she still views Shelley as committed to a liberal project of reform (*"Frankenstein's Politics,"* 86, 95). Peter Dale Scott reads the novel as Mary Shelley's attempt to reconcile Percy's utopian idealism with his flawed personality ("Vital Artifice," 172–202), but he focuses on the psychological rather than the political dimensions of the struggle. Nevertheless, he makes the case for the ambivalent Shelleyan utopianism (Percy's) and feminist radicalism of the novel. Baldick argues that the conservative reading of the novel only comes later, tracing it to the first stage adaptations, particularly the 1823 play *Presumption* (*In Frankenstein's Shadow*, 4, 47, 55–62). Butler concurs with this assessment, making the case for the radicalism of the 1818 edition (xxxii). She attributes the retreat from the radical materialism of the first edition to the fate of Lawrence, the figure who prosecuted a materialist view of life against Abernethy in the vitalist debates (xlvii–xlviii, l–li). Betty T. Bennett confirms that Mary Shelley remains committed to a broadly reformist politics aligned with those of Godwin and Percy Shelley long after *Frankenstein*, in her novels *Valperga* (1823) and *Perkin Warbeck* (1830). See "The Political Philosophy of Mary Shelley's Historical Novels: *Valperga* and *Perkin Warbeck*," in *The Evidence of the Imagination: Studies of the Interactions between Life and Art in English Romantic Literature*, ed. Donald H. Reiman, Michael C. Jaye, and Betty T. Bennett (New York: New York University Press, 1978), 354–71. There are other political accounts of the novel not focused on the problem of revolution. For feminist readings, see Sandra M. Gilbert and Susan Gubar, *The Madwoman in the Attic: The Woman Writer and the Nineteenth-Century Literary Imagination*, 2nd ed. (New Haven, CT: Yale University Press, 2000), 213–47; Barbara Johnson "My Monster/My Self," *Diacritics* 12, no. 2 (1982): 2–10. For an analysis of the politics of the novel in relation to imperialism, see Gayatri Chakravorty Spivak, "*Frankenstein* and Devi's Pterodactyl," in *Empire and the Gothic: The Politics of Genre*, ed. Andrew Smith and William Hughes (New York: Palgrave, 2003), 56–68. Eileen Hunt Botting explores *Frankenstein*'s philosophical approach to the rights of children. See *Mary Shelley and the Rights of the Child: Political Philosophy in* Frankenstein (Philadelphia, PA: University of Pennsylvania Press, 2018).

11 Wollstonecraft offers the same diagnosis of how an oppressive upbringing can produce a tyrannical mentality, not a revulsion to authoritarianism. See Mary Wollstonecraft, *A Vindication of the Rights of Men; a Vindication of the Rights of Woman; an Historical and Moral View of the French Revolution* (Oxford: Oxford University Press, 1993), 75, 107, 111.

12 Cited in Baldick, *In Frankenstein's Shadow*, 57.

13 On the politics of this moment, see Craciun, "*Frankenstein*'s Politics," 89–90.

14 Victor's reflections recall the fascination political radicals have with the moment of revolutionary catastrophe, a fascination which seems to exceed the merely analytic or diagnostic. One might think not only of *Paradise Lost* and *Frankenstein*, but also of Godwin's *Mandeville* or Mary Shelley's *Valperga* or perhaps even Walter Benjamin's *Theses*.

15 On the scientific context in which Frankenstein was written, particularly the vitalism debate, see Butler, "Introduction"; Richard Holmes, *The Age of Wonder: How the Romantic Generation Discovered the Beauty and Terror of Science* (New York: Vintage, 2008), 305–36. Holmes points out that "in Victor Frankenstein … [Shelley] had created a composite figure who in many ways was typical of a whole generation of scientific men" (328). However, Victor's obsession with alchemy complicates the picture. Moran explains that alchemy in the early modern period was effectively

an artisanal practice not easily distinguished from laboratory experimentation. See Bruce T. Moran, *Distilling Knowledge: Alchemy, Chemistry, and the Scientific Revolution* (Cambridge, MA: Harvard University Press, 2005). On the radical, even utopian politics of early modern Paracelsianism, see Christian Thorne, *The Dialectic of Counter-Enlightenment* (Cambridge, MA: Harvard University Press, 2009), 213–17.

16   On ships as potentially democratic and even utopian spaces in the early modern period, see Peter Linebaugh and Marcus Rediker, *The Many-Headed Hydra: Sailors, Slaves, Commoners, and the Hidden History of the Revolutionary Atlantic* (Boston, MA: Beacon Press, 2000).

17   Arif Camoglu reminded me that Walton claims credit for this "revolution," undermining the agency of the sailors (*Frankenstein*, 184). In this, he resembles Milton's Satan, at the council of fallen angels. The comparison casts further doubt on the "success" of this revolution.

18   On the utopia of the robber band in *Caleb Wiliams*, see Vivasvan Soni, "Modernity and the Fate of Utopian Representation in Wordsworth's *Female Vagrant*," *European Romantic Review* 21, no. 3 (2010): 374–6. Elsewhere, I will take up the strangely negative utopia in Act III.iv of *Prometheus Unbound*. On the Godwinian politics of *Valperga*, see Bennett, "The Political Philosophy of Mary Shelley's Historical Novels," 357–63; Tilottama Rajan, "Introduction," in *Valperga*, ed. Mary Shelley, 7–42. For the concrete utopian moments in *The Last Man*, see Mary Shelley, *The Last Man*, ed. Anne McWhir (Peterborough, Ontario: Broadview, 1996), 82–3, 172.

19   We should add a fourth utopia, namely the life the creature imagines with his mate in South America. While this vision undoubtedly has utopian overtones—the creature promises to live peacefully, as a vegetarian, in an approximation of a Rousseauvian natural state (*Frankenstein*, 120–1)—its actual political content is minimal.

20   See Soni, "Modernity and the Fate of Utopian Representation"; Vivasvan Soni, "Judging, Inevitably: Aesthetic Judgment and Novelistic Form in Fielding's *Joseph Andrews*," *Modern Language Quarterly* 76, no. 2 (June 2015): 159–80; Vivasvan Soni, "Can Aesthetics Overcome Instrumental Reason? The Need for Judgment in Mandeville's *Fable of the Bees*," in *Mind, Body, Motion, Matter: Eighteenth-Century British and French Literary Perspectives*, ed. Alison Conway and Mary Helen McMurran (Toronto: University of Toronto Press, 2016), 254–78.

21   On the dominant political horizon of republicanism and civic humanism in the early modern period, see J. G. A. Pocock, *The Machiavellian Moment: Florentine Political Thought and the Atlantic Republican Tradition* (Princeton, NJ: Princeton University Press, 1975). On civic republicanism in historical Geneva, as it is inflected by Calvinism, see Helena Rosenblatt, *Rousseau and Geneva: From the First Discourse to the Social Contract, 1749–62* (Cambridge: Cambridge University Press, 1997), 10–29.

22   On the Genevan revolution, see Janet Polasky, *Revolutions without Borders: The Call to Liberty in the Atlantic World* (New Haven, CT: Yale University Press, 2015), 26–31.

23   See Richard Holmes, *Shelley: The Pursuit* (New York: EP Dutton, 1975), 326, 334. David Marshall argues for the influence of Rousseau's concept of sympathy and his *Essay on the Origins of Language* on *Frankenstein*. See *The Surprising Effects of Sympathy: Marivaux, Diderot, Rousseau, and Mary Shelley* (Chicago, IL: University of Chicago Press, 1988), 178–227. See also his account of Mary Shelley's relationship to Rousseau (228–33).

24 See Rosenblatt, *Rousseau and Geneva*. She argues that, in these texts, Rousseau's almost utopian portrait of Geneva is responding to the city's decline into oligarchy (159–63, 219–27). Rousseau sides with the bourgeois and artisan classes against the patriciate.

25 See Polasky, *Revolutions without Borders*, 172–93.

26 See Soni, "Can Aesthetics Overcome Instrumental Reason?"

27 For a version of this utopia writ large, see William Morris, *News from Nowhere*, ed. Stephen Arata (Peterborough, Ontario: Broadview, 2003).

28 For other utopian aspects of Geneva, see the discussion of why keeping servants in Geneva is not as hierarchical as in England (*Frankenstein*, 46), undoubtedly a troubling moment, and Victor's desire to "banish disease from the human frame" (23).

29 Critics have noticed the importance of the family and domestic affections as the figure for alternative social relations in Shelley. According to Mellor, Shelley is critical of "a Promethean, revolutionary ideology," and "grounded her alternative ideology on the metaphor of the peaceful, loving, bourgeois family" (*Mary Shelley*, 86). See especially her description of Shelley's brief experience with the Baxter household, which became the model for her utopian family (16). With growing revolutionary disillusionment in the 1790s, Butler argues that Godwin and Wollstonecraft re-situated their utopian hopes to the family, a move echoed by *Frankenstein* ("Introduction," xxxiii). Puzzlingly, though, these critics tend to view the De Laceys as more utopian and egalitarian, and the Frankensteins as more elitist and aristocratic, nearly the reverse of what I will be arguing. Thus, Craciun reads the De Laceys straightforwardly as a "utopian vision of an egalitarian society and unconventional family" ("*Frankenstein's* Politics," 94; see also Mellor, *Mary Shelley*, 49, 88; Butler, "Introduction," xxxiii). And Butler argues that "the Frankensteins are, though republicans, as much élitists as Godwin's Falkland, St. Leon and other narrator-protagonists" (xl; see also, xlv).

30 The connection between patriarchy and political authoritarianism is clearly marked in Rousseau's *Emile* and Volney's *Ruins*. See especially, Constantin François de Chasseboeuf, comte de Volney, *The Ruins: Or, a Survey of the Revolutions of Empires*, 3rd ed. (London: J. Johnson, 1796), 62.

31 Marshall links the old man's guitar playing to Rousseau's meditations on the origins of language (*Surprising Effects of Sympathy*, 185).

32 On the creature as child, see Botting, *Mary Shelley and the Rights of the Child*, 6–7; Holmes, *Age of Wonder*, 331–2.

33 Rosenblatt's *Rousseau and Geneva* shows that Rousseau's target was the French-influenced Genevan patriciate.

34 See Sterrenburg, "Mary Shelley's Monster," 143–8.

35 Although Volney's *Ruins* exemplifies the critical impulse of Enlightenment, it is not content with critique alone. There is a utopian dimension to this text, in the world council of legislators (132–5, 147–51).

36 On the complicated logic of sympathy in *Frankenstein*, see Marshall, *Surprising Effects of Sympathy*, 178–227.

37 Shelley records her own visceral aversion for the lower classes, seemingly incapable of the sympathy she demanded for the creature (Mellor, *Mary Shelley*, 25; Scott, "Vital Artifice," 180).

38 On the novel's complex rewriting of *Paradise Lost*, particularly its figuration of both Victor and the creature as Eve, see Gilbert and Gubar, "Horror's Twin," especially 232–5, 239–40, 246. They also offer an interpretation of the relevance of the other

texts the creature reads (238). See also Peter Brooks, "'Godlike Science/Unhallowed Arts': Language, Nature, and Monstrosity," in *Endurance of Frankenstein*, ed. Levine and Knoepflmacher, 210; Mellor, *Mary Shelley*, 49.

39 Sparta in particular has often served as a model for utopian thinkers, beginning with Plato. On "the institutors of laws and founders of civil society" as utopian thinkers, see Percy Shelley, "Defence of Poetry," 512 in Percy Shelley, *Shelley's Poetry and Prose*, ed. Donald H. Reiman and Neil Fraistat (New York: W. W. Norton, 2002)

40 On the utopian dimensions of the Arctic in contemporary discourse, see Craciun, "*Frankenstein*'s Politics," 90–3. On the imaginative importance of polar exploration in English culture of this period, see Francis Spufford, *I May Be Some Time: Ice and the English Imagination* (New York: Picador, 1997), 1–63, especially his reading of *Frankenstein* (58–63).

41 Spufford, *I May Be Some Time*, 58. Although it may seem impossible to imagine a concretely delineated polar utopia, it is not. See Kim Stanley Robinson, *Antarctica* (New York: Bantam, 1998).

42 See Samuel Taylor Coleridge, *Biographia Literaria; or, Biographical Sketches of My Literary Life and Opinions*, ed. James Engell and W. Jackson Bate (Princeton, NJ: Princeton University Press, 1983), 304–5.

43 See Hannah Arendt, *The Human Condition* (Chicago, IL: University of Chicago Press, 1958), 240–1.

44 Spivak, "*Frankenstein* and Devi's Pterodactyl," 61.

45 Elizabeth is also the one who sustains what remains of the utopia, when Victor leaves for Ingolstadt (*Frankenstein*, 27).

46 According to Mellor, this passage as well as that on the treatment of servants was interpolated by Percy Shelley (*Mary Shelley*, 64). See her full account of the revisions made by Percy (58–69, 219–24).

47 As feminist critics have pointed out, Frankenstein is among other things a novel about "anxieties [of] pregnancy, giving birth, and mothering," in a word natality (Mellor, *Mary Shelley*, 41). See also, Ellen Moers, "Female Gothic," in *Endurance of Frankenstein*, ed. Levine and Knoepflmacher, 77–87; Johnson, "My Monster/My Self."

48 See Arendt, *Human Condition*, 177–8, 184, 189–90.

49 Arendt critiques Plato's "substitution of making for acting" (*Human Condition*, 220–30). For her, acting to institute a utopia confuses properly political action with work.

50 On Victor as the "archetype of the irresponsible political leader," see Mellor, *Mary Shelley*, 70.

51 When this paper was pre-circulated, the consistent and recurrent criticism was that Geneva could not serve as the model I claimed. This criticism, I have been trying to show, is the position of the Victor-like critical theorist, for whose perfectionism no utopia will suffice. The flaws of the novel's Geneva must be acknowledged, and they are manifold. It is authoritarian (discussed above); it is patriarchal, at least until Victor leaves; it is exclusionary (the creature is shunned); its institutions of justice fail (with Justine). But, with the exception of the authoritarianism, none of these is internal to the utopia of Chapter 1, or a necessary consequence of it. *They are not failures of the utopia, but a failure to implement the utopia.* The novel offers no reasons, as far as I can tell, for the failure of implementation. Indeed, its experiment in utopian writing in Chapter 1 continues to offer political ideals worth striving to actualize: an

uncompromising egalitarianism, a non-authoritarian polity, unalienated labor, a non-competitive sociality.

52 See Butler, "Introduction," xxi on the conversations between Byron and Percy Shelley on "the nature of the principle of life," conversations "to which [Mary] was 'a devout but nearly silent listener.'" Holmes claims that the Romantics inherited this question about the materialist "vivifying principle" from Thelwall (*Age of Wonder*, 316).

53 On researches into the principle of life in the Romantic period, and attempts to animate human and animal corpses, see Holmes, *The Age of Wonder*, 305–36.

54 See Vivasvan Soni, "Believing in Ghosts, in Part: Judgment and Indecision in *Hamlet*," in *Shakespeare and Judgment*, ed. Kevin Curran (Edinburgh: Edinburgh University Press, 2016), 45–70.

55 For Arendt, the agent is disclosed both in deeds and in stories (*Human Condition*, 178). Only through action, and the stories we tell about it, does someone become a "who" and not a mere "what."

56 Brooks explains the importance of language learning to the creature's story, and argues that the problem of monstrosity is connected to the problem of language itself ("'Godlike Science/Unhallowed Arts,'" 205–20). However, he focuses on language's failure and its inability to signify, rather than its capacities for utopian animation (220).

57 On Mary Shelley's radicalism in giving the creature a voice, see Butler, "Introduction," l; Baldick, *In Frankenstein's Shadow*, 45, 58–60.

58 On the tension between sympathy produced through sight and sympathy produced through language, see Brooks, "'Godlike Science/Unhallowed Arts,'" 211; Marshall, *Surprising Effects of Sympathy*, 194–5, 214, 221–7.

59 On the concept of personhood, its impoverishment during the Enlightenment, and its recovery by Coleridge, see Thomas Pfau, *Minding the Modern: Human Agency, Intellectual Traditions, and Responsible Knowledge* (Notre Dame: University of Notre Dame Press, 2013).

60 Coleridge, *Biographia Literaria*, 304. For Coleridge's role in the vitalism debate, see Holmes, *The Age of Wonder*, 319–22.

61 In this context, see Thomas Pfau, "Romantic *Bildung* and the Persistence of Teleology," in *Brill's Companion to German Romantic Philosophy*, ed. Elizabeth Millán Brusslan and Judith Norman (Leiden: Brill, 2019), 143–72.

62 Cited in Baldick, *In Frankenstein's Shadow*, 60–1. See also, Butler, "Introduction," l. Hobbes describes sovereignty as the "artificial soul" of the Leviathan, "giving life and motion to the whole body" (*Leviathan*, 7).

63 Butler believes that the 1818 text is committed to Lawrence's materialism, although Mary tries to conceal it ("Introduction," xxiii). Holmes describes Abernethy's vitalist position, which seems at odds with the radicalism of the Godwin-Shelley-Byron circle, but which Mary's novel seems to flirt with (*Age of Wonder*, 309). I am suggesting that *Frankenstein* brilliantly combines a non-theological linguistic idealism with a radical politics.

13

Is That All There Is? No Regrets (after 1818)

Jacques Khalip

Remorse—is Memory—awake—
Her Parties all astir—
A Presence of Departed Acts
At window—and at Door—

Emily Dickinson[1]

Identifying remorse with sleepless vigilance, Dickinson evokes waking life as an inability to avoid regretting those "Departed Acts" we thought we forgot while our memory slept. Thwarted feelings often swirl around key scenes in Romantic literature, rife with "Departed Acts," and this chapter takes its prompt for exploring them from one familiar case study:

> It was on a dreary night of November that I beheld the accomplishment of my toils. With an anxiety that almost amounted to agony, I collected the instruments of life around me, that I might infuse a spark of being into the lifeless thing that lay at my feet …
>
> How can I describe my emotions at this catastrophe, or how delineate the wretch whom with such infinite pains and care I had endeavoured to form? (57)[2]

Dreary, indeed. I will more fully turn to this passage in a moment, but for now I want to ask the following: What if, all melodrama aside, nothing actually *happens* in *Frankenstein*'s notorious "creation" scene in chapter five? And what if, between the lines of the novel's familiar narrative of failed expectations, a narrative caught between anguished articulacy, self-doubt, and repentance, there was a more unspoken, unperturbed, and uncrossed recognition that, in spite of everything committed and remembered, everything involved in the work of thinking about, constructing, and then dealing with the creature, there was nothing to be regretted—about the work, about life, and about the creature itself? Imagine an alternative story where Victor Frankenstein's reaction would be just a shrug, a tonally understated acceptance of the creature and nothing to show for it but a silent nod. He would either continue working or not, leave satisfied, and perhaps remain happy. And the creature, too, would be in the world without rage. Characters might still thrive or die without incident; perhaps there would be less letter writing, less travel. In such a counterfactual, *Frankenstein* might be imagined to *not* stand at the window of its own acts and characters, anxiously watching and ruminating over things. Instead, it might try to get a good night's sleep. And what if we were to describe events in the novel with all the matter-of-factness of a phrase like "and that happened," a phrase simply put without further reflection—a constative in Anne-Lise François's sense of "a claim that hardly makes a claim"?³ Put another way: "And that happened" might hint at a way of having a minimized sense of a belief about things—a light faith or agnosticism about what did or did not happen—without worrying over the perceived success or failure of their consequences. Is that all there is? We might read such a claim as putting something into our heads but without force, a "reminder," as John McDowell writes, "that the idea of second nature is at our disposal is just that, a reminder—not a piece of news, not a report of a substantial achievement in philosophical theory. What we are reminded of should be something that we knew all along, but were intelligibly induced to forget under the stress of philosophical reflection."⁴ Unlike Dickinson's remorse that "stands awake" like a sentry forced to witness a drama into which it has been unwillingly conscripted, a reminder veers toward a mode of reconciliatory, mildly affirmative thinking "that causes anxiety to lapse, that opens our eyes to the obvious without insisting upon it."⁵

McDowell's reminder lies philosophically far afield from traditional philosophical and theoretical narratives of Romanticism, which often cast it as a site of crisis between mind and world. Take one classic example: in his book *In Quest of the Ordinary*, Stanley Cavell remarks that the "price" of what he calls Kant's "philosophical settlement"—that the bounds of human knowledge are limited—is that we are asked "to cede any claim to know the thing in itself, to grant that human knowledge is not of things as they are in themselves ... You don't—do you?—have to be a Romantic to feel sometimes about that settlement: Thanks for nothing."⁶ Cavell regrets the settlement because it seemingly denies us the right to have the epistemic flexibility to think beyond the given. He reads it as a finger-wagging proscription, an unsatisfying inheritance met with disappointment. But his version of regret also seems a bit too prideful: the fact that "You don't—do you?—have to *be a romantic*" means ultimately dismissing Romanticism *as* a problem, as if it were the very thing that we don't need to hold onto in order to challenge the settlement. I confess that I read the implications of Cavell's flippant remark a bit differently than what he seems to intend: what if the very little that Kant leaves to be desired is just that—a small settlement that literally *settles* or tidies the affairs of human knowing for us so that we don't have to worry about it any further? And even more, what *is* the structure of the act of thanking another for nothing at all? While it seems an empty "thank you" for an omitted gift, it is empty only if we assume that the point of the Kantian gift is that it is ours to exploit like a tool of thought. Romanticism is consistently skeptical about its own methods of competency about the world and competency about itself, and thus we might recast Kant's settlement as less a remembrance and more a reminder that skepticism *of* the world is, philosophically speaking, *no thing*, a disproportionately weighted form of knowing that is no more satisfying than complete ignorance of its gravity.⁷ Thanks here might be a way of showing no regret for things that, in spite of possibly being hurtful, do not parry and provoke a skeptical mind. Without regret, one might be inclined to graciously thank the very thing *as* nothing, rather than lament and destroy it as a sign of catastrophe. We would be quietly disabused of the thought that one has to do better in the future because one had supposedly done worse in the past. All we need reminding of is that we were doing just what we had to all along.

In *A Theory of Regret*, Brian Price describes regret as a politically generative mode of thinking and perceiving change even if past actions or events are no longer subject to review:

> Regret is more closely aligned with the impossible, insofar as regret leaves us in a state of attunement to what is not yet. Or else regret indicates the aspects that have not been featured thematically, even if they have appeared at the very same time as something linked, both thematically and independently, to other phenomena that do more than merely participate in the consistency of what is given.[8]

A virtue of Price's argument is that it conceives regret as form: thinking occurs by reading, apprehending, and reevaluating; one contemplates multiple possibilities in the face of past errors, but—and this is key for Price—regret isn't restorative: it never promises that something will redemptively come back a second time: "[Regret] trains us, in this way, against an expectation that what appears will always appear in the same way … In boasting that I have no regrets, I admit only that I am incapable of thinking."[9] Price's regret, however, veers toward Dickinsonian remorse in its call to stay attuned to what has "not been featured thematically" in the cinema of one's life, turning spectatorship into an unwelcomed attention to what might have been sooner left behind than recalled. Regret often becomes self-mortifying, tying the self to further incriminations—a point on which Coleridge, moreover, anticipates Dickinson in one of his lectures where he attempts to separate out regret from remorse:

> Where ever we are distinctly conscious, that our Will has had no share direct or indirect in the production of a given event or circumstance, that is painful and calamitous to ourselves or others, we feel *Regret* … we find no difficulty in distinguishing Regret from Remorse—and what regards our own selves, yet which is not voluntary, the same distinction, one would think out rationly to be made.[10]

But he goes on to state that

> in perhaps a majority of instances, however unconscious of Blame we may feel ourselves, yet a certain something more than Regret will mingle with the regret—a certain something will haunt and sadden the heart, which if not Remorse is however a phantom and Counterfeit of Remorse … that however independent the calamity may be of any [moral] fault as its proximate or immediate cause, it may nevertheless & often will be … yet a distant effect of something morally wrong in our past Actions.[11]

The "something more than Regret" isn't so much an excess or abject remainder as it is lingering ephemera, a "phantom or Counterfeit" of *something* between the range of regret and remorse that fails to find its own word. The striking out of "of ourselves" and then "own" are curious: they are like attempts to lessen the personal damage by externalizing it through words that write that damage but do not entirely deny it; by revising the text, Coleridge tries to get the argument right in order to further irradiate the idea, not so much to acquit himself fully (he doesn't) but to redo regret as the author's privilege rather than block.

Coleridge's reflections bring into relief for Romanticists a familiar critical movement of "melancholic regret and jubilant assay" that Alan Liu identified long ago as characteristic of Romanticism and certain strands of melancholically inflected new historicism that tarry with the absent causes behind texts: "Assay is haunted by regret, and regret finds itself open to assay—a sublime effort to imagine the perdurance of loss."[12] Here melancholy theoretically keeps the Romantic subject answerable to the needfulness of loss, to the overwhelming premium placed on privation as the modality through which, paradoxically, belief in the lostness *of* the lost object is preserved as a condition of skeptical perseverance. In a different vein, Joel Faflak has theorized Romanticism's "sublime effort" in terms of "failure," a perpetual (and valorized) breakdown of fantasies of progressive modernity. "I was never afraid of failure," wrote Keats in a letter to his publisher, "for I would sooner fail than not be among the greatest."[13] Keats's almost maudlin reflection absorbs what Faflak outlines as Romanticism's desire *for* thwarted desire, reconstituting itself through (and retaining a fidelity for) that thwarting. And insofar as desire is lack, Romanticism is, like Coleridgean regret, always excessive to itself—it is its own remainder.[14] In challenging any possession or "right" we have to that desire as sovereign subjects, we are already attesting to a challenge that is underwritten by the very Romanticism *of* failure.

In the following pages, I want to pursue another line of thought that imagines Romanticism offering other poetics and practices that deflect the needfulness of loss as a critical value. Living *without regret*, I argue, arises as a latent notion in texts that often seem to confirm the very opposite. Part of my methodological approach will be to improvise on the "thanks for nothing" as both a reminder and stylistic touch, as if to allow an indifference to regret to slowly gain familiarization as something one was awakened to as if in a mood in Thomas Pfau's strict sense: a "latent principle … [that] speaks … to the deep-structural situatedness of individuals within history as something never actually intelligible to them in fully coherent, timely, and definitive form."[15] Not to have regret is a complex kind of mood, then, insofar as it is situated by virtue of displacement in a negative relation to itself as mood—a *being-with* and a *being-without* regret that evokes non-eventful situatedness. I hope it will become apparent that my argument turns on how we understand the connection between regret and eventfulness, or how regretting what one did relates to what counts as an event in the first place. On the one hand, the differences are attributable to matters of scale and attention—to say that *something* is happening or happened is to endorse a perception of occurrence, change, materialization, as well as to insist that one could possibly regret things because our actions (or lack of them) are implicated in them. On the other hand, one might also regret the event that *doesn't* happen—after all, something not happening isn't just "nothing" per se. It could be precisely what was missed, misunderstood, or only came to be perceived later in its minimalia. Eventfulness is about implication, about being subject to it even if it isn't verifiable, and as the "void ... the 'not-known' of the situation," as Alain Badiou describes it, the event demands "fidelity" *in* the absence of any knowledge about it insofar as eventfulness here seems to provoke thinking—it evokes the problem of how to make "the decision to relate henceforth to the situation *from the perspective of its evental ... supplement.*"[16] But can one decide *not* to relate to the supplement, *not* to think that one needs to be interested in the uncertain status of an event? Regret can thus become a problem of weightings, of deciding on what is too much or too little to bear in a situation.

"Romanticism occurred," Marc Redfield remarks, "when, exactly, is forever uncertain, because romanticism altered our understanding of temporality."[17] Challenging periodization, Romanticism could have happened once, multiple times, or perhaps never. I take Redfield's insight as suggesting in another way that we read "Romanticism" in terms of contingency—it might be a "vain endeavor,"[18] without regretful metabolization and any further underlining. This would be a type of Romanticism that David L. Clark and I have referred to as minimal and minimizing, allergic to monumentality and expansiveness; it is also of a piece with what François has described as the recessive aesthetics and ethics of uncounted experience or William Galperin has analyzed as the missed opportunities of Romantic literature and culture.[19] Galperin reads the missed opportunity as a unit of the everyday, a category of analysis and experience in the eighteenth century that lends to a "history *without* memory. Such a history yields what is missed or indeed missing in the romantic stance to the world as typically understood in the way pure or actual perception returns in place of virtual perception."[20] Non-regrettable reading, I suggest, isn't so much recalcitrant and actual as it intimates aligning perception *with* an available conceptualization of what *did happen* while also remaining diffident to virtual possibilities since past experience is of little interest for further viewing—a "history *without* memory" that doesn't metabolize the difference that an event makes for further self-clarification. Jane Austen's *Persuasion* will help to illustrate my point: in an episode near the end of the novel that just precedes the concert scene (a novel that insists upon her supposedly exorbitant regret over breaking off an engagement to him several years earlier), Anne Elliot is breathlessly brought into close conversational proximity to Captain Wentworth, only to lose him for a moment as their social group walks into the concert room:

> The delightful emotions were a little subdued, when on stepping back from the group, to be joined again by Captain Wentworth, she saw that he was gone. She was just in time to see him turn into the concert room. He was gone—he had disappeared: she felt a moment's regret. But they should meet again. He would look for her–he would find her out long before the evening were over—and at present, perhaps, it was as well to be asunder. She was in need of a little interval for recollection.[21]

Between the phrases "she saw that he was gone" and "She was just in time to see him turn into the concert room," a microtemporal shift occurs that is as shallow as it is critically profound, as if between the reported statement that Wentworth had already gone *and* the narrative's qualification of Anne seeing him leave "just in time," a "moment's regret" arises. While that coincidence does to a degree sentimentally represent the two as ships in the night, it also makes their comings and goings with each other seem a kind of unfinished process that the novel prefers to keep going rather than halt, even if the characters themselves are unaware of it. Wentworth doesn't simply go, moreover: he disappears, which is to say his leave-taking is a kind of passing from sight that registers a fine difference for Anne. "She felt a moment's regret. But they should meet again. He would look for her—he would find her out long before the evening was over–and at present, perhaps, it was as well to be asunder." One could read the promissory power of these words—*they should, he would*—as less impactful than they seem, putting forth claims that do not so much evoke virtual vistas and happinesses as more mundanely state that *anything*, like *nothing*, might happen. And additionally, who speaks these lines? If, according to D. A. Miller, Anne's intelligence lies in precisely absorbing the slings and arrows of the narrator's deployment of free indirect discourse,[22] it is also the case that the mechanism of that much inflated literary device does not so much interpellate Anne into larger schemes as it suggests that some of these statements, although putatively ascribed to Anne or the narrator, work asymmetrically and are not necessarily intended to appear in this way. They seem *given* to be thought, or *thoughts given in parallel without every touching upon her.* Resembling her dynamic of distance from Wentworth, Anne stands "asunder" or in planar apartness from the commentary that frequently tries to look as if it is implanting itself into her reflections, the world of the novel, and our own readerly minds. Knowing here might evoke something more impersonally nonrelational and unintentional—neither for Anne nor for us, it takes place literally *beside* her in Eve Sedgwick's sense of the word: "*Beside* permits spacious agnosticism" about the narrative knowledge that we read next to Anne, but it is only lightly tangential to her world.[23] Anne doesn't work against this knowledge so much as side by side with it, her awareness of it opaquely inconclusive. She is without regret for something she could never have had access to, even if its stated content is supportively aspirational. In this sense, then, regret does last for a moment because, like Wentworth, knowing *what happened* disappears from Anne like a wiped-out regret: it might never have been "in mind" to begin with.

To perceive without regret in Anne's world would not entail a disregard for engagement or commitment to change. But it would question how change is read and to what ends and insights. In what follows, I want to begin with *Frankenstein* as a test case for exploring why and how thinking without regret becomes construed as an unsurmountable problem, a "thanks for nothing" that nevertheless leaves the door open for exploring distinctly Romantic dimensions of thought where irrecoverability is precisely welcomed for its nothingness. I will then turn to Keats's ballad "La Belle Dame Sans Merci," composed a year after *Frankenstein*, as a work that, contrary to surface readings of it, elaborates an aesthetics without regret: it is *made* by revising and annulling the regret that hovers over the poem but never quite takes hold of it. While

Frankenstein anxiously consumes the irreparability of loss with almost monolithic fixation, "La Belle Dame" seems unanswerable to the fantasized magnitude of that task both in its form and its content. As texts written in the post-Waterloo period of Britain that has often been characterized as a time of depression over the sense of the elimination of political reform *and* an era of economic prosperity and progress, we might think of Shelley and Keats as working alongside Austen's Anne Elliot to think through the question of whether regretting past experiences and actions might be a hollow reinforcement of various false plenitudes. To insist on the *superfluity* of regret might be a way to begin reading a Romantic commitment to being thankful for the nothingness we shouldn't be forced to accept.

Telling a Serious Story

It was on a dreary night of November that I beheld the accomplishment of my toils. With an anxiety that almost amounted to agony, I collected the instruments of life around me, that I might infuse a spark of being into the lifeless thing that lay at my feet. It was already one in the morning; the rain pattered dismally against the panes, and my candle was nearly burnt out, when, by the glimmer of the half-extinguished light, I saw the dull yellow eye of the creature open; it breathed hard, and a convulsive motion agitated its limbs.

How can I describe my emotions at this catastrophe, or how delineate the wretch whom with such infinite pains and care I had endeavoured to form? His limbs were in proportion, and I had selected his features as beautiful. Beautiful! Great God! His yellow skin scarcely covered the work of muscles and arteries beneath; his hair was of a lustrous black, and flowing; his teeth of a pearly whiteness; but these luxuriances only formed a more horrid contrast with his watery eyes, that seemed almost of the same colour as the dun-white sockets in which they were set, his shrivelled complexion and straight black lips.

The different accidents of life are not so changeable as the feelings of human nature. I had worked hard for nearly two years, for the sole purpose of infusing life into an inanimate body. For this I had deprived myself of rest and health. I had desired it with an ardour that far exceeded moderation; but now that I had finished, the beauty of the dream vanished, and breathless horror and disgust filled my heart. Unable to endure the aspect of the being I had created, I rushed out of the room and continued a long time traversing my bed-chamber, unable to compose my mind to sleep. At length lassitude succeeded to the tumult I had before endured, and I threw myself on the bed in my clothes, endeavouring to seek a few moments of forgetfulness. But it was in vain. (57)

I have quoted this scene at length in order to zero in on the commonplace observation that it is remarkably under-described, almost to the point of seeming unaccomplished—"one of the most tiresome clichés in the book," as Marshall Brown has witheringly glossed it, and not because of Shelley's greenness as an author but in spite of it: the clichédness of the text shores up the novel's formal imperfections as marks of its rechanneling of gothic literature into a child's tale.[24] To think of *Frankenstein* in this way hints that it operates via regression rather than maturation—always late to arrival like Walton's letters, which reach his sister well after events have transpired, the novel clunkily establishes itself on a series of disastrous misalignments. Its clichés amplify what Orrin Wang has theorized as an especially Romantic problem about how form does not "work" properly in many of the texts of the period: the palpable knowingness that makes a cliché *a cliché*—that one reads its inauthenticity for what it is, a kind of aesthetic mechanism of efficiency and repetition, "a functionless means insofar as its only function is to function" as a "device"—pushes narrative into meaninglessness and disarray and, in so doing, disarticulates it from the Romantic trope of the knowing subject.[25] If the passage *is* clichéd, then, it is implicitly regrettable *because* it works by showing itself as not working; it is as if Shelley wants to attend to the ways in which the practice of reading for "what is not yet featured thematically" is itself a cliché of the virtual insofar as it phenomenalizes regret as a historically ineffective and unbearably committed form of future discernment: one wants to read X *as* a symptom of a temporal difference that is profound, catastrophic, and life-altering in order to compensate for the possibility that no such catastrophe ever occurred. After all, it is worth remembering that whatever happens to Victor and the creature remains completely unknown to everyone else until the very end of the novel, but unlike the concert room scene in *Persuasion*, the eventlessness which is especially cathected in the description of the creature's creation in *Frankenstein* is presented as an outmoded device, an unremarkable kernel of nonmeaning that only turns up pressure for certain characters, but no one else.

Frankenstein's clichés thus evoke a distinct, historically anachronistic desistance from proficiency: "Beneath its placid, seemingly unruffled rapport with inherited rhetorical models," writes Pfau, "the cliché unmasks (allegorizes) an earlier period's excessive faith in linguistic mastery over the contingent world of intuition and perception."[26] Clichés mark a fault line between worlds or, even more, between the perception of the temporal and historical noncoincidence of different worlds to each other. In her later introduction to the novel, Shelley described her early writing, in contradistinction from the "refuge" and freedom of her dreams, as imitative—"doing as others had done" (5), but the cliché here is the very reflection on dreaming *as* refuge or shelter from contingency. It is for this reason that Victor's "emotions at [his] catastrophe" are cranked up to the level of high melodrama: his affect is generically assigned to what Linda Williams has described as cinematic "melodrama's pathos of the 'too late!'"—the failing push to preserve oneself from the contingent while also simultaneously embracing noncoincidence as the means through which to approach contingency in melancholic terms.[27] Indeed, as Anne Mellor has demonstrated, the novel's various literary allusions and citations place its action somewhere between 1791 and 1797,[28] as if to cast Romanticism as already late, turning Victor's regret into a historical symptom of Romanticism's obsolescence. And while the creature itself, as a messy assemblage of body parts, is aesthetically out-of-joint and out of sync, "the reconstruction of dead fragments from many bodies, the traces of many texts," in Fred Botting's summary,[29] I interpret *trace* here in Emmanuel Levinas's sense of "the movement that already carries away the signification it brought," turning the creature into less a host of multiple meanings than a figure for their dispersal.[30] It is a Rube Goldberg-like device whose function, while ostensibly to artificially simulate "the human," illuminates the way in which Victor's task is to compulsively exploit the *techné* that *is* the creature—the creature as an instance of what Mark Hansen describes as "technology beyond science," as it were, a "displaced figure" that is irreducible to principles of science and whose "transgression" is less an overleap than a weak exacerbation of the technology of *techné*, relentlessly using up every repeated, clichéd element of Romanticism to its exhaustively late finish.[31] Indeed, prior to his awakening, Victor describes the creature as "unfinished … but when those muscles and joints were rendered capable of motion, it became a thing such as even Dante could not have conceived" (58), not because it is too ontologically horrific to imagine, but because Victor sees it as an unfinished conception *made* to be regretted, a thought marked out as both too soon and already too late. Un-conserving and abandoned, Victor's thinking lets out what it shouldn't have conceived from the beginning.

The creature's regret thus becomes Victor's and vice versa, and as the former's regret marks an evacuation of human interiority, Victor becomes hollower and hollower in the novel in proportion to the amount of personal backstory he recounts, to the point where the creature on the last page addresses him as a zombie: "If thou wert yet alive" (223). Indeed, Victor's own educated life is presented in the novel as a series of clichéd propulsions to regret, "bound" by "slight ligaments … [of] prosperity and ruin" (41): his early enthusiasm for Cornelius Agrippa and alchemical writing is checked by his father who calls it "sad trash" (39), and Victor is soon to lose his youthful interest in favor of the hard science he learns at university: "by one of those caprices of the mind, which we are perhaps most subject to an early youth, I at once gave up my former occupations; set down natural history and all its progeny as a deformed and abortive creation; and entertained the greatest disdain for would-be science, which could never even step within the threshold of real knowledge" (41). Victor's narrative of *Bildung* here is predictably sobering in Wang's sense of that word—an attempt to ward off the enchantments of a Romanticism that is too often an object of regret, even if Victor continually falls off his wagon.[32]

I have been arguing thus far that *Frankenstein* narrates regret in its late fruition, a kind of jostling between thematic continuity and discontinuity within formal frames that are continually shown to be outmoded and ineffective.[33] And as acts of framing, this kind of regret is inevitably aesthetic and, in turn, also a regret *for* aesthetic work— something that also emerges sotto voce in the creation scene where beauty is just as soon rejected as it is avowed. No matter how many times I read the scene, I find it difficult not to stop and wonder why Victor's evocation of the beautiful is so quickly retracted. Between anxiety and agony, he tells us that the creature's limbs were selected "*as* beautiful," which is to say that they are raw material standing in for things that abstractly count for beauty. The *as* suggests comparison but also hesitancy: the limbs were chosen based on a judgment, a particular decision regarding what counts *as* beautiful because rather than make up beauty as he goes along, Victor has to repeat it—to do "as others had done." That is his first regret. One might think of Kant's reminder that aesthetic judgment is made without prior rule and should be freed of interest, a purposiveness without purpose. Such a judgment would not be subject to a predetermined rule at all but would also not be assignable to anything like subjective feeling either. The beautiful would give pleasure but not desire. In Victor's case, however, choosing the body parts evokes an instrumentalized beauty, a textual minutia that is worth comparing with the doubling exclamation of "beautiful" that follows it: "I had selected his features as beautiful. Beautiful!" I want to pause and dwell on what is imperceptibly elided here: in miniscule, this second *beautiful* seems irruptive, a point of exclamatory termination; it is an addition to a previous sentence but also something more—perhaps an aside, a gesture, a hopeful utterance, a self-incriminating moment of sarcasm, and a judgment. The word is additive but also revisionary: it tries to reclaim and own the beautiful in a different way from the first articulation, but the smallness of that difference also catalyzes seismic regret in the form of Victor's tantrum and immediate disownment of the creature and all his work. Could one regret the judgment of beauty *and* beauty itself? To exclaim "Beautiful!" is to announce a disinterested judgment in a thing, but it is as if in the absence of a rule and Victor's own failure (after Kant) to communicate the persuasiveness of that judgment, regret becomes the preferential mode through which to discern "what is not thematically featured," instead of allowing the judgment to just be made without any further demands or requests.

It isn't simply that Victor is a bad Kantian; rather, this small moment of saying "Beautiful!" does something quite different from what Shelley, in her description of how she wrote the novel, described as her initial failure to "*think of a story*," to turn around the "blank incapability of invention" (8). If the novel *is* the remedy to blankness, seeing the creature *as* beautiful means accepting another kind of blank invention, some *thing* that doesn't need to be proven by verification. In his book on Luchino Visconti, Alexander García Düttmann has described a version of this blankness as the making of a work of art as "a making of things in ignorance of what they are":

> For to the same extent that that the making of things in ignorance of what they are is a making, the production of an artwork, and not, say, a compulsive or unintentional movement, one may assert that this making is a kind of knowledge, a "practical knowledge" that does not rest on observation. When asked what he is doing when he does this or that, an artist replies: "I am making an artwork," not: "Well now, what *am* I actually doing, let's see, I've done this and that, so I must be making an artwork." If, then, his making is a making of things in ignorance of what they are, the making as making is not reflexively duplicated. Between the artist's making and every conceivable observation which cancels it as a making, as an intentional action, a gulf opens up, precisely because the making requires no additional observation, because no gulf may open up between it and the world if it is to validate itself as a making.[34]

Ignorance here evokes indifference to causality—one cannot know what one is making because there is no precedent to that intention, the latter term defined by Düttmann via Elizabeth Anscombe's formulation: "I *do* what *happens*. That is to say, when the description of what happens is the very thing which I should say I was doing, then there is no distinction between my doing and the thing's happening."[35] "I *do* what *happens*": Anscombe's point is that intention isn't aligned with conscious will or preconvention; whatever effects do occur and become part of what we are doing—whatever *happens*— contribute to a provisional vocabulary for taking seriously the indistinction between what *I do* and the *kinds of things* that arise out of what I do. Doing something in ignorance of things as they are sketches out an enclosure of subject and object through aesthetic work: "no gulf may open up between it and the world." Düttmann insists on the processual quality of art, irreducible to its objecthood: one doesn't know one is making art, even if the object one works with is typically an artwork, because the aesthetic marks out a different way of intending something.

Can we allow Victor's "Beautiful!" to be an ignorant judgment, i.e., a not-knowing within the aesthetic that does not give itself up to communicative knowledge? "Such making is a matter of practice, as it were, one which withdraws from any accounting or may be held to account only in retrospect."[36] The enclosure of the artist's work here might be a form of blithe "answer," as it were (to the degree that it is even interested), to the Kantian settlement, not by resolving it but by proceeding *in ignorance of it*. The more the artist relies on "preestablished conventions, rules, or models"—the more she tries to think of a story—the more her work "becomes something for which [she] must assume responsibility" as a work of knowledge and not art. And it is precisely because by *intending* it in this way, she is making it with regret. Düttmann brings out the precarity of this kind of labor, a precarity that haunts Victor's seriousness: "the more the seriousness of the undertaking grows, [the more] it touches on a border where it all seems not so important at all" and threatens to fall into unseriousness, "an abandonment and relinquishment of art, to a slackening of creative power out of indolence."[37] Unseriousness becomes a corrective to the serious here by "keeping it at a distance from dogmatism and rigorism, from a labored earnestness";[38] in this way, it makes it possible to try again next time, without suffocating regret. When the creature, after killing Victor's brother William, demands that he listen to him, it isn't simply for the sake of recognition, of a need to tell *his* story; rather, he says: "Yet I ask you not to spare me: listen to me; and then, if you can, and if you will, destroy the work of your hands" (101). The creature, as Victor's *serious* artwork, is also necessarily a regrettable and unserious instance of it; to destroy the work would be to test the border between seriousness and unseriousness, to consider how to begin again and perhaps differently, how to say "Beautiful!" multiple times without any anxiety or any rich claims. And perhaps, it would entail building another creature, a companion (144). But Victor cannot and will not imitate the work, not because he cannot will himself to create another one, but because he cannot *not ignore* the work, not suspend the knowledge of the work that compels him to imitate life much like the creature whose miseries revolve around studying and imitating others in the world, like the De Lacey family. Victor already knows all too well what he is doing; he isn't doing what happens but intends to do a prescribed thing—another commodified duplication. *Frankenstein* ultimately stages the tension that develops as a result of not quietly, non-regretfully smudging the border between fully committing to a work *and* entirely leaving it: "once again, I bid my hideous progeny go forth and prosper. I have an affection for it, for it was the offspring of happy days" (10).

Revising Regret

I now turn to my next example, Keats's "La Belle Dame Sans Merci," which tracks the other side of the coin—a poetics of expunged regret.

I.

O what can ail thee, knight-at-arms,
Alone and palely loitering?
The sedge is wither'd from the lake,
And no birds sing.

II.

Ah, what can ail thee, knight-at-arms,
So haggard and so woe-begone?
The squirrel's granary is full,
And the harvest's done.

III.

I see a lily on thy brow,
With anguish moist and fever dew;
And on thy cheek a fading rose
Fast withereth too.[39]

Stuart Hampshire has remarked that "[o]nly insofar as I have a belief, or some kind of idea, about the occasion and cause of the pleasure and displeasure that I feel can I experience, and be aware of, a complex intentional sentiment which is either regret, or shame, or embarrassment, or guilt about something, or which is boredom, or depression."[40] If regret, according to this account, is established by a belief in causality, then its other effect is to carve out an interiority suitable for holding that belief: I think therefore I regret. One must have a believer first in order for belief to exist. And like shame, embarrassment, guilt, boredom, or depression, regret becomes an affective shelter for the fragile, believing self. For Keats, however, the ballad is not only inconclusive about regret's efficacy—it is indifferent to believing in it. If Victor Frankenstein's despair invariably reemphasizes his commitment to the flawed seriousness of his projects even as their expiration date has arrived, Keats's own brand of aesthetic seriousness ignores any of the faults and recriminations of what he does because the blurred lines between what did or did not happen are less a "history" and more *made* experiences in Düttmann's sense of what the artist does—a laying of the ground for things that then cannot be made to yield any further information. As a Romantic instance of thinking without regret, I suggest that "La Belle Dame Sans Merci" is less about the fate—or weight—of knowledge, and more a reflection on the aesthetic task of working with an experience that one doesn't know anything about, which might be another way of saying that unlike trauma which evokes an event that comes belatedly and remains paradoxically available in its unintelligibility, Keatsian belatedness approaches something like a poetics of lateness without any prior time or earliness, a poetry without regret for a *before* because there was never any sense of a *before* to begin with.

For Stuart Curran, "La Belle Dame" creates an "impasse" by "juxtaposing the knight's duty to act against the uncertainties of his fantasy life. At its base the impasse is actually generic, between the ballad's recital of unelaborated event and the romance's emphasis on imaginative projection."[41] While critics have often pointed to the poem's compositional borrowings—its generic hybridity—as suggestive of its echo-chamber-like structure of question and answer,[42] I read the ballad as eroticizing the impasse between "recital" and "projection" as a space that allows for insignificance to reverberate.[43] Keats's cancellation of regret, moreover, doesn't produce an alternative, an access to "what is not yet featured thematically": if the poem's setting suggests a space that is seemingly done or finished—"The sedge is withered from the lake, / And no birds sing"; "The squirrel's granary is full, / And the harvest's done"—then we might read the loitering knight as ambiently folded into it, hanging around like a character at last call, queerly and comfortably fitted to his surroundings in an unworried relation: "And this is why I sojourn here, / Alone and palely loitering" (45–6). One might say that the knight is late because he loiters in the ballad's monadic, deflated space where exhaustion and apathy intimate an unwillingness to be forced to relate.[44]

That the poem's genre trouble anticipates this impasse of nonrelation is already hinted at in Leigh Hunt's comments on it when it was published in his journal *The Indicator* on May 10, 1820, ostensibly as a cleaned-up version of its more "Cockney" flavor when Keats wrote it out in a journal letter to George and Georgina Keats on either April 21 or April 28, 1819:

> Indeed, any lover, truly touched, or any body capable of being so, will feel them; because love itself resembles a visitation; and the kindest looks, which bring with them an inevitable portion of happiness because they seem happy themselves, haunt us with a spell-like power, which makes us shudder to guess at the sufferings of those who can be fascinated by unkind ones[45]

Laminating contemporary love onto archaic love, Hunt reads the poem as responding to anyone who feels, because love necessarily welcomes visitation, "an inevitable portion of happiness." These days, Hunt continues, "[L]ove in general has become either a grossness or a formality ... Instead of the worship of Love, we have the worship of Mammon ... Still our uneasiness keeps our knowledge going on" (339). It isn't clear if "our uneasiness" allows us to continue knowingly feeling or if it demystifies feeling altogether. Hunt's comments suggest a historic shift in love and love poetry, from feeling to capital (Mammon), but the comment also stresses that knowledge *makes a claim*, that it goes on in spite of the "visitations" that bodies should be involuntarily susceptible to under the thrall of love. This emphasis on knowing, I suggest, also filters the way in which the poem's Romantic "events" have been critically scripted into relationality: Theresa Kelley has noted that between the initial text of the ballad and its 1820 published version, Keats inverted the sequence of actions through which the knight/wight came to put the lady on the horse: in the journal letter (and the later 1848 transcribed version by Keats's friend Charles Brown and published by Monkton Milnes), he sets her on the "pacing steed" *after* making a "Garland for her head, / And bracelets too, and fragrant zone; / She look'd at me as she did love, / And made sweet moan" (17–20). "By putting the belle dame on the horse after she loves him, he implies that her enthrallment has led him to abandon chivalric responsibilities."[46] In my reading, the problem of parsing out the sequences here between revisions depends on the logic of uneasy knowledge that Hunt describes—one *should be* worried about love, worried that the encounter between the knight and the woman *should be* an interpretative necessity. The disinterested smudge I'm stressing, however, subtly revises these recursive pressures by bringing out the nuanced rhetoric of a poetic disinterestedness to the side of uneasy rumination, a state that doesn't just imbue the knight, but also (quite explicitly) the woman: as the titular character *sans merci*, she both deprives and is deprived, doesn't care and isn't cared for if we recall (after the *OED*) that *merci* evokes compassion, discretion, mercy, and thanks. *Without thank yous*, she is outside the governance of gratitude.[47]

To be sure, any consideration of the knight's lack of worry shouldn't cover over, as Karen Swann has argued, the degree to which the female character in the ballad is decidedly worried over, silenced, and sexually harassed *by* discourse in the service of masculine privilege.[48] But what I want to think about for a moment is how Keatsian conjecture renders an experience of non-regretfulness less as entitled disengagement and more as a *suspension* of the contours of that relation and its imagined consequences, as if the ballad, on the one hand, were fully poetic and then, on the other, it were not, something like an "experience without poetry"—a series of statements to be read as less than testimony, reporting, and referring.[49] In stanzas eight to twelve, for example, the frequency of *there* is posited with an almost machinic insistence evoking the slightness of a difference between something experiential and something materially inscribed: "And there she wept," "And there I shut her wild wild eyes," "And there she lulled me asleep," "And there I dream'd." Like the *there* in Shelley's "Mont Blanc" ("the power is there"), Keats's phrasing raises the question of referentiality as a condition one is never obligated to take on as a belief. While the *there* swirls in its "barren, formal, or *blank* rhetoricity,"[50] it also plays off other semantic echoes—"Pale warriors, death-pale were *they* all," "*They* cried," "hath *thee* in thrall," "I saw *their* starved lips in the gloam." Could the *there* do something other than just pointing or placing? Might it resemble the calming effect of "there, there," a poetic balm that reminds that there is no news to worry about, "that is all / Ye know on earth," as another ode famously says, "and all ye need to know,"[51] a Keatsian version of the Kantian settlement, to be sure, but one that *settles* by having the lines bear or endure the detritus of an experience that cancels itself out just as it coincides with their sumptuously deactivating momentum, warning the knight not of what happened, but of awakening into a world where heedlessness or recklessness are recursively pursued to prove their "false" starts—a world where consequence is always oppressively paramount.

In his notes for "La Belle Dame," Jack Stillinger draws attention to Joseph Addison's "the Pleasures of the Imagination" as one possible source for the poem's imagery, particularly the passage where Addison describes "what happens when the qualities of color, light, and shade are removed from our perception of nature":

> We are everywhere entertained with pleasing shows and apparitions, we discover imaginary glories in the heavens and in the earth, and see some of this visionary beauty poured out upon the whole creation; but what a rough unsightly sketch of nature should we be entertained with, did all her colouring disappear, and the several distinctions of light and shade vanish? In short, our souls are at present delightfully lost and bewildered in a pleasing delusion and we walk about like the enchanted hero of a romance who sees beautiful castles, woods, and meadows, and at the same time hears the warbling of birds and the purling of streams; but upon the finishing of some secret spell the fantastic scene breaks up, and the disconsolate knight finds himself on a barren heath or in a solitary desert.[52]

For Addison, delusion/illusion is aesthetic ideology: should all of the qualities of color, light, and shade disappear, nothing would remain. But demystification would not be the solution, and it is also the case that Addison smudges aesthetics with aestheticization or decoration, both of which suggest a commodified value-added to a perception. But a solitary desert is no less mediated; Addison's stronger point is that perception is a contingent faith, that we always want to see something more, something less, something richer or poorer, barren or full. Perception is unbearably regrettable because it is virtual; that is, to see *as if* things were different is not far from thinking they *ought to have been* different. Düttmann, citing Wittgenstein, describes the relation between seeing and seeing *as* in this way:

> Immediate perception, perception without thought, obliviousness to the 'as if' or semblance character of art, nonetheless pertains to the seeing of an artwork … whoever cannot naively let himself be overcome, overwhelmed, or overtaxed by the artwork … is incapable of taking art with due seriousness, since he remains forever imperious to the spell of semblance that is constitutive of it.[53]

For Keats, however, perceiving things *as if* means seeing without a thought *in* his poems, and not always as "poetry," which is to say: the idea that one could see a thought without being forced to have it or own it—"a piece of arras work," as De Quincey non-regrettably describes experiencing his past life, "not, as if recalled by an act of memory, but as if present and incarnated."[54]

Abiding by this poetics of no regrets, Keats even further deflates the distinctly Romantic memory Frances Ferguson has described as circumstantial—the "increasing pressure that Romanticism will come to put on the memory that can provide convincing evidence *that one hasn't acted*, that one hasn't yet seen things that would make one regret one's past for the consequences that have attended it."[55] Keats's shakeout of this form of memory is the effect of a commitment to stay diffident about regrettable judgments: for example, in his explanation for his rhyme of "sore" and "four" in stanza VIII of the early text—in part a response to criticisms of *Endymion*'s "Cockney" rhymes—Keats writes:

Why four kisses—you will say—why four because I wish to restrain the headlong impetuosity of my Muse—she would have fain said 'score' without hurting the rhyme—but we must temper the Imagination as the Critics say with Judgment. I was obliged to choose an even number that both eyes might have fair play: and to speak truly I think two a piece quite sufficient—Suppose I had said seven; there would have been three and a half a piece—a very awkward affair—and well gout out of on my side.[56]

Kelley says that Keats's explanations for changing the original rhyme of sore/four in the *Indicator* text "suggest that he gave up the sensuousness of the early draft as one too many provocations in a version that makes amorousness its theme" (352). And Andrew Bennett detects an "ironic pedantry" in Keats's remarks: "[O]nly a pedant would count syllables or kisses in the passion of enthrallment and abandonment, only a reader who applies inappropriate codes to a text that enthralls the imagination."[57] In both of these glosses, tempering *is* regrettably circumspect—Keats's revision becomes a kind of *apologia*, discarding something one had previously loved. I think, however, that Keats is being especially rigorous here in a much different way: he is *obliged* (in the etymological sense of being bound by oath) to the kisses even when he revises them, seeing them as interesting *because* they are not regrettable, whether or not they stay or have been omitted from the ballad. His response suggests equanimity: for all the Addisonian "imaginary glories in the heavens and in the earth" that could be deleted by the reality principle, Keats's kisses are not to be missed if the cinema projector suddenly dies. Indeed, nothing would change—a world would not collapse into a desert, and a poem would not be cried over.

By writing about the kisses, Keats keeps them in play by redistributing them in writing as things that just kiss, that can still relate albeit impersonally and don't need to stare us in the face, kissing the eyes *as words kiss us*, quenching seeing *and* reading.[58] Two for each eye, each kiss in the poem is carefully parsed, not for the sake of restraining "headlong impetuosity," but more as a *beat* in a line that requires attention. Keeping the beat of the kisses, like the "there, there," is a kind of quiet rhythm in the absence of seeing or feeling the kisses. The kisses are not for anyone at all: one could read the line as *kisses four/for*, their recipient never named or required. Keats's revisions do not merely replace one thing with another, or repress a thought or text that palimpsestically glitters in its erasure; rather, revision for Keats becomes an occasion to dwell on small details like kisses even after he has changed them in the manuscript, but doing so without any further artistic regrets.

Intimacy with what one has given up but not felt to have lost is a unique Keatsian mood that overtakes the revisions and the virtual lives of multiple versions of "La Belle Dame". As Keston Sutherland in another context writes: "the lines ... reemerge back into originality, not simply by being new or right, but by emerging from under the shadow of an overfamiliar or exhausted doubtfulness into the illumination of a new doubtfulness full of potential happiness. In their revision ... is heard the promise that for a while at least they can be owned more passionately than disowned."[59] Keats teaches this: That aesthetic seriousness about one's work can be expressed as love even when it is not known what one is doing; that one can love a thing confidently, fervently, even when one is ignorant of the fact that the thing we love has already been given up and has given us up, too; and that, unlike Victor Frankenstein, one could own it more passionately *for a time* before disowning it. Perhaps here lies Victor's largest regret: that he could not revise his life and love it in just the same way as *his* maker would come to love her own revisions: "I have an affection for it, for it was the offspring of happy days."

Notes

1   *The Poems of Emily Dickinson*, ed. R. W. Franklin (Cambridge: Harvard University Press, 2005), 347.

2   Mary Shelley, *Frankenstein* (Oxford: Oxford University Press, 1998). Page references to this edition are cited parenthetically in the text.

3   Anne-Lise François, "Unspeakable Weather, or The Rain Romantic Constatives Know," in *Phantom Sentences: Essays in Linguistics and Literature Presented to Ann Banfield*, ed. Robert S. Kawashima, Gilles Philippe, and Thelma Sowley (Zurich: Peter Lang, 2008), 148.

4   John McDowell, "Comments on Hans-Peter Krüger's Paper," *Philosophical Explorations* 1, no. 2 (1998): 122.

5   This is Oren Izenberg's comment on McDowell in his article, "Confiance Au Monde: Or, the Poetry of Ease," *nonsite* #4 (December 2011). https://nonsite.org/article/confiance-au-monde-or-the-poetry-of-ease.

6   Stanley Cavell, *In Quest of the Ordinary: Lines of Skepticism and Romanticism* (Chicago: University of Chicago Press, 1988), 31.

7   On this point, see Taylor Schey, "Skeptical Ignorance: Hume, Shelley, and the Mystery of 'Mont Blanc'," *Modern Language Quarterly* 79, no. 1 (March 2018): 53–80.

8   Brian Price, *A Theory of Regret* (Durham: Duke University Press, 2017), 77.

9   Ibid., 14, 9.

10 Samuel Taylor Coleridge, "1808 Lectures on Principles of Poetry," in *The Collected Works of Samuel Taylor Coleridge, Vol. 5*, ed. R. A. Foakes (Princeton: Princeton University Press, 1987), 63.

11 Ibid., 64.

12 Alan Liu, *Local Transcendence: Essays on Postmodern Historicism and the Database* (Chicago: University of Chicago Press, 2008), 165. Compare this with René Wellek's point that romanticism has been read as an "attempt, apparently doomed to failure and abandoned by our time, to identify subject and object, to reconcile man and nature, consciousness and unconsciousness by poetry which is 'the first and last of all knowledge'" (*Concepts of Criticism* [New Haven, CT: Yale University Press, 1963]), 221.

13 Quoted in *Johns Keats: Complete Poems*, ed. Jack Stillinger (Cambridge: Belknap Press, 1991), 432.

14 Joel Faflak, "Right to Romanticism," *European Romantic Review* 27, no. 3 (2016): 285–300.

15 Thomas Pfau, *Romantic Moods: Paranoia, Trauma, and Melancholy, 1790–1840* (Baltimore: Johns Hopkins University Press, 2005), 7.

16 Alain Badiou, *Ethics: An Understanding of Radical Evil*, trans. Peter Hallward (New York: Verso, 2001), 69, 41.

17   Marc Redfield, *The Politics of Aesthetics: Nationalism, Gender, Romanticism* (Stanford: Stanford University Press, 2003), 33–4.

18   Percy Bysshe Shelley, "Hymn to Intellectual Beauty," in *Shelley's Poetry and Prose*, ed. Donald H. Reiman and Neil Fraistat (New York: W. W. Norton, 2002), 94.

19   David L. Clark and Jacques Khalip, "Introduction: Too Much, Too Little: Of Brevity," in *Minimal Romanticism, Romantic Circles Praxis Series*, ed. David L. Clark and Jacques Khalip (May 2016). https://romantic-circles.org/praxis/brevity/praxis.2016. brevity.intro.html. Accessed May 1, 2020; Anne-Lise François, *Open Secrets: The Literature of Uncounted Experience* (Stanford: Stanford University Press, 2007); William Galperin, *The History of Missed Opportunities: British Romanticism and the Emergence of the Everyday* (Stanford: Stanford University Press, 2017).

20   Ibid., 34.

21   Jane Austen, *Persuasion* (New York: Penguin, 1998), 174.

22   D. A. Miller, *Jane Austen, or The Secret of Style* (Princeton: Princeton University Press, 2003), 70ff.

23   Eve Kosofsky Sedgwick, *Touching Feeling: Affect, Pedagogy, Performativity* (Durham: Duke University Press, 2003), 8.

24   Marshall Brown, *The Gothic Text* (Stanford: Stanford University Press, 2005), 186.

25   Orrin N. C. Wang, "Two Pipers and the Cliché of Romanticism," Unpublished ms. 17.

26   Pfau, *Romantic Moods*, 241.

27   Linda Williams, "Film Bodies: Gender, Genre, and Excess," *Film Quarterly* 44, no. 4 (Summer 1991): 2–13, 11. She describes melodrama as the "genre that seems to endlessly repeat our melancholic sense of the loss of origins" (10–11). For a reading of regret contra melancholy, see Price, *A Theory of Regret*, 10–12.

28   Anne K. Mellor, *Mary Shelley: Her Life, Her Fiction, Her Monsters* (New York: Routledge, 1989), 54–5. See also Brecht de Groote's "'Old Familiar Faces': Frankenstein, Anachronism, and Late Style," *Litteraria Pragensia: Studies in Literature and Culture* 28, no. 56 (2018): 71–8, where he reads Shelley as reinventing romantic lateness.

29   Fred Botting, *Making Monstrous: Frankenstein, Criticism, Theory* (Manchester: Manchester University Press, 1991), 22.

30   Emmanuel Levinas, "Enigma and Phenomena," in *Basic Philosophical Writings*, ed. Adriaan T. Peperzak, Simon Critchley, and Robert Bernasconi (Bloomington: Indiana University Press, 1996), 70.

31   Mark Hansen, "'Not Thus, after All, Would Life Be Given': 'Technesis', Technology and the Parody of Romantic Poetics in *Frankenstein*," *Studies in Romanticism* 36, no. 4 (Winter 1997): 575–609, 582.

32   I allude here to Wang's book *Romantic Sobriety: Sensation, Revolution, Commodification, History* (Baltimore: Johns Hopkins University Press, 2011).

33   Daniel Stout has perceptively remarked that Shelley's achievement lies in laying bare the unintelligibility of assigning individual failure to account for the infinite problems of agency and responsibility that *Frankenstein* registers in its multiplication of contexts. See *Corporate Romanticism: Liberalism, Justice, and the Novel* (New York: Fordham University Press, 2016), 171–86.

34   Alexander García Düttmann, *Visconti: Insights into Flesh and Blood*, trans. Robert Savage (Stanford: Stanford University Press, 2009), 8.

35   Elizabeth Anscombe, *Intention* (Cambridge: Harvard University Press, 2000), 52–3.

36 Düttmann, *Visconti*, 8.

37 Ibid., 3.

38 Ibid.

39 *Keats's Poetry and Prose*, ed. Jeffrey N. Cox (New York: W. W. Norton, 2009), 340. All further line numbers are cited parenthetically in the text.

40 Stuart Hampshire, *Freedom of Mind and Other Essays* (Princeton: Princeton University Press, 1971), 247.

41 Stuart Curran, *Poetic Form and British Romanticism* (New York: Oxford University Press, 1986), 182.

42 See Susan Wolfson, *The Questioning Presence: Wordsworth, Keats, and the Interrogative Mode in Romantic Poetry* (Ithaca: Cornell University Press, 1986), 274ff.

43 On the subject of impasse and space, see Rei Terada, "Looking at the Stars Forever," *Studies in Romanticism* 50, no. 2 (Summer 2011): 275–309.

44 Marjorie Levinson has called the ballad a work of "waiting … a state of permanent participiality, a *nun stans*" that contrasts with the kind of seemingly ideological "organic" productivity of Wordsworth. *Keats's Life of Allegory: The Origins of a Style* (New York: Blackwell, 1988), 87, 88. Compare this to Lauren Berlant's notion of an aesthetics of underperformativity or unfeeling, "Structures of Unfeeling: *Mysterious Skin*," *Journal of Politics, Culture, and Society* (September 2015): 191–213.

45 Quoted in Cox, 339.

46 Theresa M. Kelley, "Poetics and the Politics of Reception: Keats's 'La Belle Dame Sans Merci'," *ELH* 54, no. 2 (Summer 1987): 333–62, 337.

47 I want to thank Bill Keach for offering this brilliant formulation, and for his extended reading of the article.

48 Karen Swann, "Harassing the Muse," in *Romanticism and Feminism*, ed. Anne K. Mellor (Bloomington: Indiana University, 1988), 81–92.

49 Terada, "Looking at the Stars Forever," 301.

50 Deborah Elise White, *Romantic Returns: Superstition, Imagination, History* (Stanford: Stanford University Press, 2000), 111.

51 I refer, of course, to the "Ode on a Grecian Urn," *Keats's Poetry and Prose*, 462.

52 Quoted in *Johns Keats: Complete Poems*, ed. Jack Stillinger (Cambridge: Belknap Press, 1991), 464.

53 Düttmann, *Visconti*, 34.

54 Thomas De Quincey, *Confessions of an English Opium-Eater*, ed. Joel Faflak (Peterborough: Broadview Press, 2009), 96.

55 Frances Ferguson, "Romantic Memory," *Studies in Romanticism* 35, no. 4 (Winter 1996): 509–33, 528.

56 Quoted in Kelley, "Poetics," 351.

57 Andrew Bennett, *Keats, Narrative, and Audience: The Posthumous Life of Writing* (Cambridge: Cambridge University Press, 1994), 126–7.

58 Kelley writes (citing a letter Keats wrote to Fanny Brawne): "On July 1, 1819, he asks her to kiss the 'softest words' she writes in her next letter. A week later, replying to her reply, he writes: 'I kiss'd your writing over in the hope you had indulg'd me by leaving a trace of honey.'" "Poetics," 344–5.

59 Keston Sutherland, "Happiness in Writing," *World Picture* 3 (Summer 2009): 3.

14

Frankenstein in Practice (as Theory)

Sara Guyer

Holding ourselves together. Holding together

This is the challenge of everyday life in the time of crisis. Ourselves names both the individual self, in fragments and among others, in a shared time and project, in search of composure before a particular form of rage that, in the United States, but also in so many places—the UK, India, Brazil—has roiled everything since 2016. In it is also the possibility of relating to and with others, of assembly despite differences of strategy and interpretation. *Holding together* also is a name for figure, not as effacement or accomplishment, but as a downbeat, minimal way of getting by. It is a way of obtaining knowledge, voice, and position and a way of carrying on and through in a moment of shock and the risk of global disarray from which there is no easy or comfortable remove. Two examples, the exemplary moments of Romanticism, open up this way of thinking about figure as practice, as an intervention both practical and modest, as a method and means of getting by and one that does not replace critique or disparage it.

These examples are, first, Mary Shelley's *Frankenstein*, the focus of this collection and a novel that in every way reflects the challenge of holding together within crisis; and, second, the scene of *Frankenstein*'s composition and publication, Romanticism itself understood as a movement. In the novel, the challenge of figure, understood as holding together, appears in Victor's search for and loss of composure; the novel's divisions and unifications; and the creature's effort and failure to ameliorate his rage and disappointment. There are many sources and signs of this situation—from female authorship to new science to racist imperialism—but it is the *problem* of holding together, which is at once a problem of the individual self, of the creative work, of the family, and of the species, a problem of formation and making but also of living and surviving that I want to explore here. It is coincidentally poetic and critical, which means that it is a form of articulation with ethical, political, and aesthetic implications.

As much as *holding together* is a challenge that is thematized in *Frankenstein* and the formal condition of the novel's emergence, it is also a way of framing the aesthetic project from within which *Frankenstein* both can be said to emerge and that it creates: Romanticism. More specifically, it is Romanticism conceived as a *movement*, as a future-oriented project of creation that holds its members in common, that serves as my second example. Just as I will ask *how Frankenstein* and its characters hold it together so too will I consider what it means for Romanticism, for all of its differences of style, character, and situation to be figured as a movement. How is it held together? Holding ourselves together is another name for assembly. This is what Romanticism's categories and figures—allegory, movement, association, imagination, fragment, the sublime, the uncanny, comparison—seem to reflect as an aesthetic project. They also become a method for our time. Taken together are these signposts for another conception of figure, a minimal project of assembly? Composure as the ground of intervention? Holding together as a method?

These two examples are moments of literary invention where justification or explanation is lacking. They are sites of interpretation and speculation where the humanities flourish. I will conclude by arguing that we take these models of "assembly" or "assemblage" as a critical strategy. I want to suggest that we are still in need of a critical method that will allow us to hold ourselves—our texts, our differences— together, even without justification or understanding. This is not quite the allegorical imagination that Walter Benjamin describes; it does not hold the weak messianic potential so crucial to his studies. Nor is it comparison, or network theory, or global history. What is this critical practice—or practical criticism? Having first explored this question in terms of persons and their doubles and then in the relation of poetry and politics, I will conclude with an invitation to imagine institutional and critical forms that might model a response attentive to the questions the examples pose. It is a response that affirms the humanities. We might call it a new practice of figure.

Backgrounds

For a long time now, critics have sought to imagine forms of attachment and action that did not depend upon consciousness, power, identity, or belief, but that set out from irresolution or indeterminacy. They sought alternative possibilities of relation, relations that undid or even hollowed out the positive or empowered conceptions of relation with their residue of mastery and violence, in favor of tenuous, weak, contradictory modalities. Take, for example, the effort of Maurice Blanchot, which emerges as a vast project of resistance and hesitation, an ethical and political response to the violence of recognition and knowledge. Blanchot seeks to establish an experience oriented toward impossibility, not as a utopic or hopeful project, but one that occurs just this side of paralysis. He called this the neutral or neutered, a quasi-concept that others, namely Roland Barthes, also took up.[1]

Blanchot is attuned to the multiple forms of violence undertaken in the name of identity, particularly, but not exclusively in Europe, in the middle of the twentieth century. He is responding to the madness of belief that led to genocide, mass displacement, and slavery, but also to the frictionless movements of the status quo and the demands of just getting by; responses to the acceptance of bystanders, a term that has been central to Holocaust memorialization efforts, but has had insufficient traction outside of the Holocaust, say in terms of climate change, white supremacism, or immigration.

Relation without relation. Unavowable community. These are code words for a critical and ethical project of vigilance, patience, indirection. These projects—in the etymological sense of projection as throwing outward whether through a fiction of voice or a claim—are not rejections of the demands of the political or of action. Rather, they model forms of action and politics that could be understood as the precursors to what Michael Hardt and Antonio Negri have understood as contemporary "leaderless" movements—transitory, temporary, and, at their best, self-critical. Yet, what kinds of projects are they? Are they even projects at all insofar as their horizon and trajectory barely contain the sense of futurity that the concept of project holds?[2]

In this context, how do we develop thinking further or differently beyond the interventions of Blanchot and others who revealed forms of critical attention and patience? The radical neutrality developed as a critical stance in the face of Auschwitz, the politics of hesitation, the ethics of impossible responsibility, and the poetry of suspension all remain *beholden* to an experience of singularity and being alone, even with one another, and non-identity, even with oneself. The thought of the common and community, the experience of friendship, the face of the other and its priority (almost all of these are masculine or erotic, heterosexual encounters) are examples of how relations that resisted and recognized abusive hierarchies and aggressive exclusions might crucially need to be reimagined and reclaimed today. Is there a critical method or institutional form poised to inhabit this space, a space that Blanchot seductively called "the space of literature."[3] What, in other words, is the space of "holding ourselves together and apart."

In recent years, we have seen close reading, criticism, rhetorical reading, and deconstruction dismissed as reinforcing rather than resisting the problems of our time, including climate change and inequality. For example, when Caroline Levine recovers the "whole" in lieu of the fragment, she writes: "My final intervention is to offer a newly strategic solution to the power of unifying containers. If we imagine that our only option is to critique, shatter, or resist them, we reinforce the idea that bounded wholes are always and necessarily dangerous and successful, on their own terms, at organizing experience."[4] The challenge, here, is that the forms of resistance—critique, shattering, resistance—that Levine describes are not exterior to "bounded wholes," but already operating within them. The act or process is not the work of an aggressive, implicitly infantile agent separate from the object. Rather than identifying critique as merely the revalorization of its object, I would argue that the line of questioning we need might instead address *how* we can mobilize categories that shatter and resist and hold ourselves together within this fragmentation. How we can practice critique, rather than deny gaps or revalorize "wholes."

Foundational Romantic texts like the *Athenaeum Fragments* already have taught us that the relation between whole and fragment is not *produced* by critique, shattering, and resistance, but that the fragmentary mode is more originary, and that even a consideration of the originary reveals a site of division or incompletion. These are not gestures we simply choose and hence can avoid. The work of literature, art, community, or even politics—understood as whole or part—opens ways of reading incompletion or undoing. It reveals the absence of unity that is part of its project and that is part of the institutions of literature. As critics and readers, we have little to do with it. But there is much we *can* do with it. From here, let's turn to Shelley's novel.

Beholding *Frankenstein*

One of the things that we never learn about Victor Frankenstein's creature is how he is held together. What holds the monster together? We know that the problem of "holding oneself together" of remaining calm in the face of shock is largely Victor's problem. Composure seems to reveal Victor's uncanny strength, only to become the harbinger of his weakness. And, far from held together, we come to find Victor (and his doubles), strewn and fragmented across the novel, parceled out in Walton and the creature both.

In *Frankenstein, holding together* is both a persistent theme and an aesthetic project. *How are unrelated stories held together* is both a formal question, insofar as the novel is organized around three first-person narratives (plus the introductory narrative of its author—or her representative). *How persons—and species—are held together* is also an ethical or political question. The formal and the ethical converge when those persons are also the first-person subjects of these narratives. While it might seem a bit teasing to replace *Frankenstein in Theory* with *Frankenstein in Practice*, my aim here is to follow the novel itself in contemplating what is indistinguishably a theoretical and a practical problem, *holding together,* and one for which the example of *Frankenstein*— and, ultimately, the example of Romanticism, can prove to be especially illuminating: how do we hold ourselves together?

Frankenstein primarily approaches this challenge by mirroring or similarity. Three masculine figures are tethered to one another through resonances of character and experience. This occurs through a figural effect that produces both similarity—they are versions of the same—and difference—they are merely held together, and remain distinct. The relation of the three occurs *through* the novel as much as it is represented by it.

The novel, Mary Shelley's "hideous progeny," also is analogized to Victor's creature, but, how is the creature held together? How is it assembled? We know—more or less well enough—*what* is held together. That is described at various points, but we don't entirely know *how.* Not just how he is animated, or how he is brought to life—the secret that the novel holds in its folds and silences, but how do the bones and bits, teeth and eyes and lips, drawn from so many species, hold together? How does the creature hold together at the same time as Victor's, once composed, is falling apart: his "eye-balls were starting from their sockets" (55).[5] In the film, and the pop cultural images of the monster it has generated, we see the dowels, stiches, and scars reminding us that he *is* held together. But we also know the stiches don't actually do any holding, and the scars only imply some kind of growth: they line a face whose form, however ragged, is strange, yet intact. The novel promises us a different kind of approach, one that implies that adhesives, regrowth technologies, and magic itself might keep all the parts with their distinct lifetimes and forms held together so that they can operate as if one. One way we could figure out how the creature is held together would be to read *widely* in experimental science. Another would be to read *closely* to show how the novel achieves this work. To do so, is to seek out a model for thought and understanding

The *OED* provides two senses of *holding together*. First, the intransitive sense of a form or a whole *remaining* intact ("there was no hope that the ship would hold together") for which all of the modern examples are, like this last one, describing vessels on the verge of dissolution. The second, transitive, in which one unit *keeps* another together, hence Cowper, "The sacred band that holds mankind together" or Lyall "the roots also of trees ... holding the soil together."[6] The stiches appear to be transitive, but only refer to a separate object. The creature raises for us the question of autonomy and influence: does he hold himself together and is this shift from the transitive to the intransitive the moment in which holding together becomes a real question?

If the novel doesn't say anything at all about how the creature is held together, it does say quite a bit about Victor—about how Victor holds himself together, and about how he comes apart. Victor attributes his powers of self-control to an Enlightenment education. He explains that rationality as a condition of his powerful imagination: "Darkness had no effect on my fancy; and a churchyard was to me merely the receptacle of bodies deprived of life, which, from being the seat of beauty and strength, had become food for the worm" (51). And later, remembering his father, he recounts: "A human being in perfection ought always to preserve a calm and peaceful mind, and never to allow passion or a transitory desire to disturb his tranquility. I do not think that the pursuit of knowledge is an exception to this rule" (56).

Yet, as soon as he gets creative, Victor starts to lose it. He grows anxious, isolated, oppressed:

> I was oppressed by a slow fever, and I became nervous to a most painful degree; the fall of a leaf startled me, and I shunned my fellow creatures as if I had been guilty of a crime. Sometimes I grew alarmed at the wreck I perceived that I had become; the energy of my purpose alone sustained me: my labours would soon end, and I believed that exercise and amusement would then drive away incipient disease. (56)

He knows that he needs to hold himself together, at least for long enough to complete his "labor," but by the time his work is complete, he is "unable to endure," and most of the novel is an account of how Victor shuttles between falling apart and holding it together. We know that he is in a state of disarray, stumbling between gender identities, kinship roles, moralities, and ultimately life and death: all of the binaries he has helped to topple.

As I suggested earlier, some critics have tried to paint those intellectual and creative projects that read to the point of crisis as too negative, too destructive, too fragile, too critical, too infantile. Victor-like, they are sometimes held responsible for getting us into the situation we currently face.[7] Perhaps the most vivid of these examples, the one that struck closest to home, was Diana Taylor's column as president of the MLA, where insisting upon new forms of community, she offered a blasé dismissal of "the deconstruction of the administrative state." She writes: "Apparent followers of Paul de

Man, administration leaders aim to delink speech from meaning, lauding the virtues of education while placing the Department of Education in the hands of a person who has long attacked the public school system."[8] It is a strange way of holding together MLA's membership, even as the point of the column is to create a new "WE" dedicated to the future of education in the United States. Even the critics of deconstruction seem to have a hard time figuring out how to hold it together. And it makes sense. These are difficult and unsettling times. But can we see the difference between Steve Bannon's version of deconstruction and our own? Is this the outcome of deconstruction: an inability to hold things apart or is it the challenge of holding ourselves together?

With this in mind, we can look again at the moment that Victor realizes what he has done, when the monster—held together, how, we never learn—comes alive.

Recalling the restless and nightmare-filled first night, Victor reports to Walton,

> I thought I saw Elizabeth in the bloom of health, walking in the streets of Ingolstadt. Delighted and surprised, I embraced her; but as I imprinted the first kiss on her lips, they became livid with the hue of death; her features appeared to change, and I thought that I *held* the corpse of my dead mother in my arms; a shroud enveloped her form, and I saw the graveworms crawling in the folds of the flannel. (58, my emphasis)

Awoken by the yellow moon, Victor then continues:

> I *beheld* the wretch—the miserable monster whom I had created. He *held* up the curtain of the bed; and his eyes, if eyes they may be called, were fixed on me. His jaws opened, and he muttered some inarticulate sounds, while a grin wrinkled his cheeks. He might have spoken, but I did not hear; one hand was stretched out, seemingly to detain me, but I escaped and rush down the stairs. (58, my emphasis)

What's happening here? The lines between wakefulness and sleep, mother and sister, life and death, subject and object are torn asunder. Victor imagines holding and imprinting a healthy, upright Elizabeth only for her to transform into a corpse that needs to be held, as if prone, in Victor's arms, shrouded, and covered in flannel. Running throughout this passage is a problem of separation and confusion. But what we also encounter, here, is a drama of holding and beholding—seeing, exposure, propping what should—but cannot—hold itself upright.

Victor, trembling in his sleep, enclosed in his bed awakens when the moon "forces" itself through the shutters leading him to be-hold the creature. Yet this act of "beholding" is conditioned by a prior one, revealed only afterwards, of the creature holding open the curtain that brings him into view one of the very few times he is not veiled. And so long as Victor can't imagine that the creature he formed is now holding itself together (autonomous), without him, who knows how, Victor can hold, and be-held, but can't hold it together. Beholding, be-holding, is also a hybrid state of holding and being, read not just as etymologically linked to "*bi*"—or thoroughness (to fully or entirely grasp or observe), but more conventionally to *being*, be-holding, can also suggest the problem faced throughout the novel, the ontological problem of being in the world as a problem of holding—of holding together.

Holding and *holding together*, the novel seems to suggest, in this moment, are *not* one and the same. As Victor explains to Walton, the monster project "had taken an irresistible *hold* of my imagination" (55). In other words, Victor had fallen into the throes of an external force, a specter and an obsession had "taken hold" of him, and left him without power to deny it. But just as he falls prey to an obsessive idea and a form of masculine ambition, he frames his obsession as a form of victimization and submission. He is held by the creature—or perceives himself to be held by him—rather than holding himself together within the seduction. The projection of agency (onto the creature) and passivity (in his submission) shows both the enduring attachment and the transformation of an attachment into accusation and dispersal. Holding and beholding—being as holding, holding as being—and holding, being, and seeing— are precisely what the novel is negotiating at this moment. And it holds us, holds us—attentive to it—together and together with it. Before returning to this drama of holding together as a method, I want to turn to Romanticism to see how it emerges as a movement and aesthetic category in the challenge and unlikeliness of holding together, which, however conventional, is not entirely obvious.

The Romantic Movement

It is a bit strange that Romanticism is conceived as a movement. What holds it together? If we don't merely elide the question or dismiss it as error, can we find here a model of collective intervention that does not rely on unity? This is not merely a theoretical question, but one that recent editors of volumes of Romantic writing have had to address as a principle of collection.

In their introduction to the *Cambridge Companion to British Romantic Poetry*, James Chandler and Maureen McLane comment that "Unlike 'eighteenth-century,' the adjective 'Romantic' denotes not just a period, but a style, a *movement*, a way of thinking (an 'ideology' some have said), even a way of being in the world."[9] With nods to Arthur Symons (movement), and Jerome McGann (ideology), this account is both conventional and strange, marking the powerful ambiguity that arises when Romanticism is our subject. One reason for the strangeness is that movement suggests progress, interventionist politics, and communal activity, and, as Chandler and McLane remind us, the "Big 6" poets "came to see poetry as where the action was, even as they disagreed about what counted as poetry and what counted as action."[10] Recognizing the poets as belonging to a movement, in other words, is to see this "action," however contested in its shape and project, as its index.

Duncan Wu, introducing his Blackwell's anthology of *Romanticism*, notes how different the Romantics were from other schools, begging the question of what is meant by movement. While other schools had an actual program or manifesto, "The 'big six' male poets ... never met together, and if they had done, would probably have fallen out immediately."[11] Wu focuses not so much on the "movement" of Romanticism, not the connection between individuals or even the shared project, but another source of energy: "what really bound them together was the fact that they inhabited the same troubled world."[12]

In their anthology, Anne Mellor and Richard Matlak decide against reference to Romanticism altogether, noting the anachronism of the term and the fact that it is a nineteenth, even twentieth-century, invention, first used by Hippolyte Taine who refers to the "Romantic school" and then by William John Courthope who refers to the "Romantic movement" in the sixth volume of his 1895 history of English poetry. When Mellor and Matlak avoid Romanticism, they also avoid the implications of "movement" as a collective project, even one marked by differences and disagreements. Courthope, who points out "the spectacle of the general *movement* of Europe at large" (my emphasis), suggesting that movement suggests not so much a project, but a transformation, the becoming visible—even spectacular—of revolutions in politics, industry, and society, does not actually use the term "movement" to talk about the poetry and poets of the period.[13] Rather, he focuses the final volume of his massive study on individual poets and small clusters, like "the lake school" (Wordsworth, Coleridge, Southey). Even here, Courthope hesitates to claim too strong of a connection, affirming instead physical proximity, a shared space, not unlike Duncan Wu's shared time, when he writes:

> The three poets, whose close association with each other, and common residence in the Lake district, caused them to be classed in the public mind as a single group, could not be said to have acquired the title of 'school' from any close resemblance in their genius and artistic style; they were, in fact, distinguished by the most striking oppositions of character. Certain fundamental sympathies, however, drew them together, and, causing them to exercise a mutual influence on each other, justified the instinct of their critics in regarding them as literary allies.[14]

Soon after the publication of Courthope's volume, Arthur Symons published *The Romantic Movement in English Poetry*, which offers snapshot accounts of dozens of poets born before 1800. It is a deceptively strange project. On the one hand, all that holds these poets together is their birth year—and that they write poems. It is very much in the mode of Matlak and Mellor. Yet, Symons is anything but "anti-" or "un-"romantic. These poets are characterized as members of a movement with a more or less shared interest in the emancipation of verse. Symons devotes the Preface to a modest explication—even dismissal—of his title, and explains:

> In using the convenient word 'movement' I wish it to be understood that it is not meant in the usual historical sense, or with the <u>definiteness</u> with which we say, for example, the Tractarian or the Agrarian Movement. There a <u>definite</u> aim sets many minds working together, not in mere comradeship. No such thing ever happened in the creation of literature.[15]

So, Symons works under the heading of "movements" to show that literary movements differ from social or political ones. An aesthetic movement is not definite, neither oriented toward a single end nor reflecting anything other than an individual poet and their experience of poetry, even if that individual experience can be a resource for a set of relationships that are more than individual. In other words, Symons understands an aesthetic movement as grounded in a plurality of poetic experiences, rather than a set of worldly aspirations.

Taken together, we can see that there is not a common, critical account of Romanticism as a movement. Or, put another way, from the moment that Romanticism is described as a movement—it is represented as the acknowledgment of difference, accident, belatedness, even a certain misnomer and impossibility. It might be that the forms of relation evident between the poets are more like those manifest in the contemporary movement politics of what Michael Hardt and Antonio Negri call "plural ontologies" or the multitude—"a pluralism of subjectivities, multiple models of temporality, and a wide variety of modes of struggle, which emerge from different traditions and express different objectives."[16]

Hardt and Negri focus their efforts on a postcapitalist, radically interventionist effort at transforming institutions, leadership, and the sites of power. They see assembly—"the freedom to assemble and associate"—not only as a conventionally guaranteed right, but as a new index (or what they call a symptom) of contemporary movements, "the right to form new combinations and new productive assemblages."[17] This is what we have witnessed in Tunisia and Zucotti, but it is also what, in early 2020, we recognize in a new key, as in-person gatherings have been suspended or monitored and as new forms of assembly at a distance, new ways of holding ourselves together apart, become normal and essential.

We can re-read Symons's interest in two features of Romantic poetry, the imagination and emancipation, after Hardt and Negri. Symons writes: "What all these poets, so different in inspiration and tendency, united in was in an aim at the emancipation of the world and of the mind and of the vehicle of poetry from the bondage of fact, opinion, formality, and tradition; and when fact, opinion, formality, and tradition go out, imagination comes in."[18] Or as Symons says later: "The Romantic movement is an emancipation, and it cast off not only the bandages of eighteenth-century limitation, but all bonds that had tightened about it in the mere acceptance of tradition."[19] For Symons, the Romantic movement is freedom from orientation and restraint. It is a movement precisely because its members do not organize around a single aim, tradition, style, or idea; they merely enact the resistance to constraint in order to unleash an alternative freedom, a freedom that Symons calls *imagination*.

Even when Romanticism is understood as movement, rather than a period or epoch, it evokes the fulfillment of the conception of time. While Symons understands this notion of movement as a break with the past (tradition, inheritance) and orientation in the pure opening of the future, this opening is structured as a metalepsis. It is the condition of the very break that it seems to effect. It is in this sense that the aesthetic movement is at once achieved and stalled, and its relation to time at once a total break and mere re-alignment. Understood as emancipation through the imagination,

Romanticism is an aesthetic movement oriented that is at open-ended and still contained by the substitution that places an opening in the position of a goal.

In *Futures Past*, Reinhart Kosseleck points to the late-eighteenth century as the moment in which a new conception of time, oriented toward "movement thinking," began to emerge. As he explains, "a characteristic of the new epochal consciousness emergent in the late-eighteenth century was that one's own time was experienced not only as a beginning or an end, but also as a period of transition," which is to say, it assumed that the future will be different from the present.[20] For Kosseleck, as soon as Romanticism is conceived *as* Romanticism it is a movement. It is not simply a concept or ideology that the -*ism* indicates, but movement itself—futurity, difference, orientation. In other words, the instance of a break from one's own time is also what signifies belonging to a moment in time. Taken together, Symons and Kosseleck reveal how Romanticism can simultaneously be an historical and ahistorical project; how it can simultaneously break with and instantiate a moment; and how it can achieve this both as a collective, communal project and one that rejects identity, identification, and unity.

Holding—Ourselves—Together

From archive to novel to method. Is there a critical method that might take seriously the multiple forms of holding together? Beyond the work of national archives, disciplinary divisions, wars of theory and science, what is the mode of criticism that might help us hold together?

These questions are not new ones, but they show one way of casting the question of Romanticism. Rather than transcendentalism, natural supernaturalism, aesthetics and politics, or the triumphant lyric subject, Romanticism becomes the very question, of holding together. Rather than turn away from this question, allowing, for example, the precedent of certain syllabi, anthologies, or texts to account for our Romanticism— or critical theory, such as it is, might we not, instead, envision this "assembly" of authorships and texts otherwise and as a model for the demand of holding together. Romanticism reflects a common, for which the relation is often a minimal and virtually unjustified one, and, for that reason, one to which we might pay attention. It might look like *Frankenstein*'s creature, evoking all of the questions of creativity gone awry, of Enlightenment education, and of failed mourning. But that creature, too, is a form whose condition we cannot fully explain: it is a set of relations that also raises the question of holding together.

In many places, the disciplinary and institutional name for the analysis and teaching of literary work across difference is "comparative literature." Comparative literature is, among other things, a method designed to cut across national, linguistic, period, or genre lines. And while the actuality of its project has changed dramatically in the past thirty or so years, turning from linguistic singularities to theoretical constellations, comparison still assumes the similarity and formation of common categories across international and linguistic differences. Comparative literature has been especially valuable as a method that resists national character by resisting singularity, but at the same time, it can be used to reinforce national differences in order to register relations between them. But there are other possible relations, and ways of understanding relation. These are relations from which we can build institutions and projects that take us out of our archives without foregoing abstraction, figuration, or criticism and critique.[21]

My aim here has not been to produce yet another reading of *Frankenstein*, but rather to suggest, by way of this reading, that we cannot do the work we need to do—work on migration and displacement, on family separations, on climate change, on artificial intelligence, on inequality and racial violence (all of which we also can read in the novel)—without holding on to figuration. We cannot just abandon our figures as too clever or too minor or too compromising, as too distant from real bodies, real stories, real injuries. If there is any chance that we will do more than *behold* these conditions in horror and in shock, any chance that we can expose the conditions, see more than autonomous forms in terror, or insist upon speaking of what we cannot see, we need to read. We cannot just count. We cannot just describe. And we cannot just fall apart. Holding together is a problem and a power that holding and beholding cannot resolve. *Frankenstein* begs us to recognize the difference. It is a difference that we can call figure.

Romanticism's movement poetics and the creature's assembly reveal instances of holding together that also reanimate figural poetics. We can link them as examples of a new encounter with figure. One is expansive, holding together the many in their nonrelation. The other reveals a singularity whose autonomy is unconditioned. Both can be seen as dated, untimely, and fundamentally flawed. But what if we look at them otherwise and recognize in them models for reading and thinking across differences? These are models we don't quite have and models that we need.

The question that we face today is what other models of relation, of holding together—of assembly—can we imagine? What is a theory for the present? And how can we turn to a moment of fictional shock—the shock that produces and is produced by Mary Shelley's creature and creator—to gather ourselves anew? More than this, the *today* of this inquiry already has changed as a world pandemic has swept the globe, revealing at once our global entanglement, the porousness and power of national borders, and new forms of holding ourselves together at a distance. While this essay was conceived in another moment, the current moment, still unfolding, is the one that allows us to begin to read. Between late-2018 and now (with no sense of what the time of this piece's publication or of your reading will hold), the practice of bodies being together has come to be a site of risk. Social distancing has emerged as a form of separation that is also a statement of community. Unlike the nationalist efforts that erect border walls—useless and violent, both), this division between bodies has emerged as the most reliable measure against the spread of a virus without cure or vaccine. It also has renewed the effort to imagine multiple forms of holding ourselves together that are also forms of separation, not only as a project of theory or method—of difference, action, and recognition, but as a practical project of living together apart—or apart together. If this began as an exploration of how we might hold ourselves together in the sense of avoiding psychic collapse in times of shock, anxiety, disappointment, and radical disgust, and how we might hold on to figure a little bit longer, as a method and intervention, we now discover that this task, manifest through distance, also has become a name for survival: holding ourselves together—apart.

Notes

1   See Maurice Blanchot, *The Space of Literature*, trans. Ann Smock (Lincoln, NE: University of Nebraska Press, 1986), 259, 262; Maurice Blanchot, *The Infinite Conversation*, trans. Susan Hanson (Minneapolis: University of Minnesota Press, 1993), 298–313.
2   Blanchot, *Space of Literature*; See Michael Hardt and Antonio Negri, *Assembly* (Oxford: Oxford University Press, 2017), 8–14.
3   Blanchot, *The Space of Literature*.
4   Caroline Levine, *Forms: Whole, Rhythm, Hierarchy, Network* (Princeton: Princeton University Press, 2015), 29.
5   Mary Shelley, *Frankenstein: 1818 Text* (Oxford: Oxford University Press, 1993). Page references to this edition are cited parenthetically in the text.
6   *Oxford English Dictionary* online s.v. "to hold together." http//www.oed.com/. Accessed June 5, 2020.
7   See Rita Felski, *The Limits of Critique* (Chicago: University of Chicago Press, 2015); see Diana Taylor "Becoming We," originally published in the Summer 2017 *MLA Newsletter*, accessed online. https://president.mla.hcommons.org/category/columns-by-diana-taylor/. See Sara Guyer, "Critical Theory Represents the Power, Not the Corruption, of the Humanities," *Times Higher Education*, March 4, 2020. https://www.timeshighereducation.com/opinion/critical-theory-represents-power-not-corruption-humanities. Accessed June 5, 2020.
8   See Taylor, "Becoming We."
9   James Chandler and Maureen N. McLane, *The Cambridge Companion to British Romantic Poetry* (Cambridge: Cambridge University Press, 2008), 2.
10 Ibid.
11 Duncan Wu, *Romanticism: An Anthology*, 4th edn. (Oxford: Wiley-Blackwell, 2012), xxxi.
12 Ibid., xxxii.
13 Anne K. Mellor and Richard E. Matlak, *British Literature 1780–1830* (Fort Worth: Harcourt Brace, 1996); William Courthope, *A History of English Poetry*, vol. 6 (London: Macmillan, 1895–1910), 5.
14 Courthope, *A History of English Poetry*, 162.
15 Arthur Symons, *The Romantic Movement in English Poetry* (London: Archibald Constable and Company, 1909), n.p.
16 Hardt and Negri, *Assembly*, 68, 69.
17 Ibid., 293, 294.
18 Symons, *The Romantic Movement*, 18.
19 Ibid., 19.
20 Reinhart Kosseleck, *Futures Past: On the Semantics of Historical Time*, trans. Keith Tribe (New York: Columbia University Press, 2004), 240.
21 For discussion of the discipline see, among others, Gayatri Chakravarty Spivak, *Death of a Discipline* (New York: Columbia University Press, 2003).

Contributors

Andrew Burkett is Associate Professor of English at Union College. His research interests center on the intersections among science, technology, and imaginative literature in the Romantic era. He is the author of *Romantic Mediations: Media Theory and British Romanticism* (2016).

David L. Clark is Professor in the Department of English and Cultural Studies at McMaster University, where he is also Associate Member of the Department of Health, Aging, and Society and a member of the Council of Instructors in the Arts and Science program. He has published widely in British and German Romanticism and philosophy, as well as in contemporary Critical Theory and Critical Animal Studies.

Joel Faflak is Professor of English at Western University, where he was inaugural Director of the School for Advanced Studies in the Arts and Humanities (2012–17). His teaching and research interests are nineteenth-century literature, culture, and philosophy; psychoanalysis; contemporary theory; and leadership. He is author, co-author, editor, or co-editor of twelve books, including *Romantic Psychoanalysis* (2008), *Revelation and Knowledge* (2011), *Romanticism and the Emotions* (2014), *The Public Intellectual and the Culture of Hope* (2013), and *Blake: Modernity and Disaster* (2020). He is currently working on two books, one on Romantic psychiatry, the other on film musicals, both related to what he calls the psychopathology of happiness.

Erin M. Goss is Associate Professor of English at Clemson University. The author of *Revealing Bodies: Anatomy, Allegory, and the Grounds of Knowledge in the Long Eighteenth Century* (2013), she edited a collection of essays on *Jane Austen and Comedy* (2019) and has recent or forthcoming essays on *Frankenstein*, on eighteenth-century automata, and on Joanna Southcott and the project of feminist recovery. She is at work on a monograph currently titled "Complicity and Acts of Conscience: Mary Wollstonecraft to Mary Shelley," which focuses on women writers of the late-eighteenth and early-nineteenth centuries as they have been read in the twentieth- and early-twenty-first centuries.

Sara Guyer is Professor of English at the University of Wisconsin-Madison. She is the author of *Romanticism after Auschwitz* (2007) and *Reading with John Clare* (2015), as well as the editor with Brian McGrath of the book series *Lit Z*. She is the director of the World Humanities Report and President of the international Consortium of Humanities Centers and Institutes (CHCI).

Sonia Hofkosh is Associate Professor of English at Tufts University, where she teaches eighteenth- and nineteenth-century British literature and visual culture; feminist theory; and science fiction. She is the author of *Sexual Politics and the Romantic Author* and various essays on Romantic-era poetry, fiction, and early photography. She is also co-editor of *Romanticism, Race, and Imperial Culture* and editor of a recent *Romantic Circles Praxis* volume on Mary Wollstonecraft's legacy in contemporary feminisms. Her current book project addresses the dynamic relations between formulations of subjectivity and artefactual embodiment in Romantic writing and reading practices.

Jacques Khalip is Professor of English at Brown University. He is the author of *Last Things: Disastrous Form from Kant to Hujar* (2018) and *Anonymous Life: Romanticism and Dispossession* (2009). He is also the co-editor of *Constellations of a Contemporary Romanticism* (2016) and *Releasing the Image: From Literature to New Media* (2011).

Yoon Sun Lee is the author of *Nationalism and Irony: Burke, Scott and Carlyle* (2004), *Modern Minority: Asian American Literature and the Everyday* (2013), and numerous articles and essays on topics ranging from narrative theory, Lukács, Austen, and Edgeworth to the diasporic novel and Asian American literature. She is currently completing a book on plot, objectivity, and science in the realist novel. She teaches at Wellesley.

Patricia A. Matthew is Associate Professor of English at Montclair State University and writes about the history of the novel, British Romanticism, and British abolitionist literature and culture. She is currently writing a book on sugar, gender, and protest during Britain's abolitionist movement.

Samuel Otter is Professor of English at the University of California, Berkeley. He is the author of *Melville's Anatomies* (1999) and *Philadelphia Stories: America's Literature of Race and Freedom* (2010) and the co-editor of *Frederick Douglass and Herman Melville: Essays in Relation* (2008) and *Melville and Aesthetics* (2011). He currently is finishing a book titled *Melville's Forms*.

Richard C. Sha is Professor of Literature and Affiliate Professor of Philosophy at American University in Washington, DC, where he is also a member of its Center for Behavioral Neuroscience. His most recent book, *Imagination and Science in Romanticism* (2018), won the Jean-Pierre Barricelli Prize in that year. Previously, he published *Perverse Romanticism: Aesthetics and Sexuality in Britain, 1750–1850* (2008). In Spring 2020, he was a Fulbright Scholar at the University of Bologna, where he researched Galvani and Leopardi.

Vivasvan Soni is Associate Professor of English at Northwestern University. He is author of *Mourning Happiness: Narrative and the Politics of Modernity* (2010), which won the MLA's prize for a first book. He has written articles on the role of utopian representation in Wordsworth's *Female Vagrant*, Fielding's *Joseph Andrews*, and Mandeville's *Fable of the Bees*. He is currently completing a book manuscript on the "crisis of judgment" in the eighteenth century.

Rei Terada is Professor of Comparative Literature and a core faculty member of the PhD Program in Culture and Theory at UC Irvine. She is the author of *Feeling in Theory: Emotion after the "Death of the Subject"* (2001) and *Looking Away: Phenomenality and Dissatisfaction, Kant to Adorno* (2009). Articles related to her current project, *Open Relation—as Postracial Violence*, may be found in *Comparative Literature*, *English Romantic Review*, and *Radical Philosophy*.

Orrin N. C. Wang teaches English and Comparative Literature at the University of Maryland, College Park, and is Co-General Editor of *Romantic Circles*. His most recent book is *Techno-Magism: Media, Mediation, and the Cut of Romanticism*, in the *Lit Z Series* of Fordham University Press.

Chris Washington is Assistant Professor of English at Francis Marion University. The University of Toronto Press published his monograph, *Romantic Revelations: Visions of Post-Apocalyptic Hope and Life in the Anthropocene*, in September 2019. With Anne McCarthy, he is co-editor of the collection *Romanticism and Speculative Realism* (Bloomsbury, 2019). He has published essays in *Romantic Circles Praxis*, *The Keats-Shelley Journal*, *Essays in Romanticism*, *European Romantic Review*, *Romantic Circles Pedagogy Commons*, and *Literature Compass*. He is also the editor of the forthcoming volume of essays, "Teaching Romanticism in the Anthropocene," for *Romantic Circles Pedagogy Commons*. He is currently working on a monograph, "#OccupyRomanticism: Revolutionary Climate Protest from Then to Now" and, with Dr. Kate Singer, another book, "Intersex Intertexts."

Index

Printed in the USA
CPSIA information can be obtained
at www.ICGtesting.com
LVHW011037190424
777765LV00003B/36